ROCK
CONNEXIONS
THE COMPLETE ROAD MAP OF ROCK 'N' ROLL

ROCK
CONNE**X**IONS
THE COMPLETE ROAD MAP OF ROCK 'N' ROLL

BRUNO MACDONALD

FOREWORD BY **MICK ROCK**

MURDOCH BOOKS

A Quintessence Book

Published in 2010 by Murdoch Books Pty Limited

Murdoch Books Australia
Pier 8/9
23 Hickson Road
Millers Point, NSW 2000
Phone: +61 (0) 2 8220 2000
Fax: +61 (0) 2 8220 2558
www.murdochbooks.com.au

Copyright © 2010 Quintessence
Foreword copyright © 2010 Mick Rock

Every reasonable effort has been made to trace the owners of copyright materials in this book, but is some instances this has proven impossible. The author(s) and publisher will be glad to receive information leading to more complete acknowledgements in subsequent printings of the book and in the meantime extend their apologies for any omissions.

All rights reserved. No part of this publication may be reproduced, stored in a retrieval system or transmitted in any form or by any means, electronic, mechanical, photocopying, recording or otherwise, without the prior written permission of the publisher.

National Library of Australia Cataloguing-in-Publication data

Author: MacDonald, Bruno
Title: Rock connexions: the complete road map of rock 'n' roll / Bruno MacDonald
ISBN: 9781742661094 (pbk.)
Notes: Includes index/
Subjects: Rock music--History.
Rock groups--History.
Dewey Number: 781.66

This book was designed and produced by
Quintessence
226 City Road
London EC1V 2TT

QSS.RCON

Project Editor	Kelly Thompson
Editors	Becky Gee, Fiona Plowman
Designer	Dean Martin
Editorial Director	Jane Laing
Publisher	Tristan de Lancey

The moral right of the author has been asserted.

Color reproduction in Singapore by Chroma Graphics Pte Ltd.
Printed in China by Toppan Leefung Printing Ltd.

9 8 7 6 5 4 3 2 1

Contents

Foreword — 6

Introduction — 8

01 Who Put the Bomp in the Bomp Ba Bomp — 10

02 Turn On, Tune In, Drop Out — 34

03 Sex, Drugs & Rock 'n' Roll — 120

04 Big Hair & Big Hits — 188

05 Here We Are Now, Entertain Us — 236

Index — 282

Picture Credits — 288

Foreword by Mick Rock

If it weren't for Pink Floyd's 086▷ Syd Barrett I don't think I would have been a photographer. Syd was a friend of mine. His music and appearance were unforgettable and inspirational. Having first picked up a camera in a state of psychedelic inebriation, and indeed having explored the universe in a similar state with Syd one memorable night in the spring of 1969, in retrospect it makes cosmic sense that Syd would prove to be the subject of my first memorable photos taken that autumn.

My connection with David Bowie 134▷ in early 1972 (three months before the release of *Ziggy Stardust*) was fueled not only because he liked the early images I had taken of him but also because he was (and remains) a hard-core fan of Syd's and was hungry for any inside info. It also helped that I was an Iggy Pop 116▷ and Lou Reed admirer (only a small, select bunch in those distant days), and David had gotten to know them both in New York in the winter of 1971. Of course, in that fantastic breakout summer of 1972, David engineered the arrival of Lou Reed and The Stooges in glam-struck London just as his own unique star rocketed to the fore. And, as fate would have it, I lensed the covers for the now legendary albums *Transformer* and *Raw Power*, for which I received the princely sums of £100 and $200, respectively. Ah, those were the days . . . !

In 1972 and 1973, I produced and directed the seminal music videos for four Bowie/Ziggy tracks, "John, I'm Only Dancing," "The Jean Genie," "Space Oddity," and "Life on Mars?," all for minimal budgets; these were inducted in 2009 (along with later Bowie videos) into the permanent collection of New York's Museum of Modern Art. At the time they were made they were hardly aired at all, yet now they are regarded as significant art! It should be said that, in 2000, David, in his generosity, gave me the copyright of the visual for all four videos. A true gent!

The glam rockers were suddenly the hippest travelers in the universe. All the cute girls wanted a piece of the boys in make-up! So, when Roxy Music supported David at Lindsay Kemp-staged concerts at the Rainbow Theatre in London, in August 1972, I shot them for the first time. Post-Eno, I shot the band several more times between then and the summer of 1976, both in setup sessions and live performance.

Island Records 130▷ corralled me to shoot their *June 1, 1974* live album cover, which featured Lou Reed's erstwhile Velvet Underground 090▷ cohort, John Cale (whom I shot three or four more times in the Seventies), Nico (of whom I have a quirky and intimate session with Lou in 1975), Brian Eno 138▷, and Kevin Ayers (once of the Soft Machine and a subject of mine on later occasions).

And so to 1973 and a virtually unknown Queen 144▷, who approached me because of my work with Bowie and Reed. They wanted (or certainly Freddie wanted!) a piece of the "glam" image in a big way. And that's what they got through my lens, including the *Queen II* album cover (copied later for their "Bohemian Rhapsody" video), which would prove to be the most enduring image of their career. The shot was inspired by a photo of Marlene Dietrich on the set of Josef von Sternberg's 1932 movie, *Shanghai Express*. When I first showed the photo to Freddie, that fact seemed to excite him most. "I shall be Marlene," he beamed.

In the winter of 1975, Malcolm McLaren approached me. He had an unknown band called the Sex Pistols 166▷ and he asked if I would photograph their first London gig, at St. Martin's School of Art. He explained that he had no money, but could pay me in kinky underwear from his and Vivienne Westwood's King's Road shop, Sex. The underwear was made of rubber with holes in strategic places and was not at all comfortable. I wore it only once or twice, but I wish I'd kept it. It's probably worth a collector's mint today! I shot the Pistols a couple more times before my attention was dragged to the goings-on in New York and I began spending more and more time there, where I photographed all kinds of characters on the burgeoning punk scene, including the Ramones 158▷, the Dead Boys, Talking Heads (for all of whom I shot album covers), Patti Smith 164▷, and of course Blondie 172▷, the act that probably had the most image appeal for me because of the divine Ms. Harry. Many years later, when putting together *Picture This*—my 2004 book of Blondie pix—Debbie commented: "My immediate impression of Mick was that he was very tall, very handsome [!], and quite mad. It seemed he was using sleight of hand in our sessions. I thought if Mick were to be a drag queen, his name would be Miss Direction!"

The only time I shot Siouxsie and her Banshees was in New York around 1980. This connection came through a young lady who had done Bowie's personal P.R. in New York. A couple of the shots ended up on European 12-inch single covers, and late in the Nineties on a compilation album. I also did several sessions with one of my all-time fave rock ladies, Joan Jett, including the cover for her most successful album, *I Love Rock 'n' Roll*. A decade later I shot an album cover for Joan's former bandmate from The Runaways, Lita Ford. One of my biggest regrets is that I didn't get to shoot the entire Runaways ensemble in their short career.

In 1980, a very young Madonna (208▶) was brought to my studio on Madison Avenue, fresh out of Detroit, wearing a Detroit Tigers baseball T-shirt, and not yet launched on her musical career, although as I recall from our conversation that afternoon she did have aspirations. I did a bunch of test shots, including one in which she brazenly stuck her tongue out with no provocation from me. There's a rawness to her appearance and attitude that gives little indication of the pop powerhouse into which she would transform only a few years later. I completely forgot about these photos for twenty-five years or so, until they popped up out of my archive. Now the shot with the tongue is a standard in my exhibitions.

And in 1986, Mötley Crüe, who were in full "glam" mode at the time (smothered in make-up and wild costumes), flew me to L.A. for a promo session for their latest album, *Theatre of Pain*. It was a spectacular, chemical-fueled affair in which I did many exotic setups, including photos of them in a bubble bath that didn't surface until the new millennium and the emergence of their group autobiography, *The Dirt*, when the image served as an appropriate comment on the band's wild and wicked (and dirty!) ways.

In December 1996, I underwent heart bypass surgery. It was during my recovery that the rising interest of publishers, museums, and galleries in rock imagery and iconography brought my name to the eyes and minds of the nouveau rockers, rappers, and performers of the new millennium. As fate (again!) would have it, many of them are intrigued by the lives, music, and images of many of my early subjects: Syd, Bowie, Iggy, Lou, Queen, Blondie, Sex Pistols, the Ramones, Talking Heads, and so on. Coincidentally, I did new sessions with several of them, including Bowie, Lou, Iggy, Debbie Harry, and Mötley Crüe.

This new cycle brought me back to the present, and sessions with artists such as The Killers (280▶), the Yeah Yeah Yeahs, Kasabian, Foo Fighters, Daft Punk (268▶), Scissor Sisters, The Brian Jonestown Massacre, Nas, Maxwell, Snoop Dogg, and Ziggy Marley, right up to Daniel Merriweather, Alicia Keys, Lady Gaga, The Gossip, and Janelle Monae. New fusions abound: rock meets rap meets soul meets reggae and dance. It's an exciting time for music and I'm delighted to be part of it again. It's been a long, strange, and circuitous route, but I'm as sharp as ever and still hungry for the taste of new images.

As a photographer, I have been lucky enough to work with many of the greatest rock acts of our times. In this book you will discover thousands of links between these musicians and many others, as well as their labels, producers, studios, and gigs —the entire world of rock. Rock has a unique place in our collective history and indeed in my life. And to me and many others, Syd Barrett still lives on in the recesses of our imaginations. As I said at the start of this piece, no Syd, no Mick Rock photography.

Mick Rock

New York City, U.S.A.

FOREWORD

Introduction by Bruno MacDonald

A Beach Boy singing with Pink Floyd ... David Bowie talking Marianne Faithfull into wearing a backless nun's habit ... Little Richard sharing a bill with The Beatles ... Rock 'n' roll is rarely short of weird 'n' wonderful connections—and the following pages contain a treasure trove of them.

We've surveyed the best rock, pop, rap, and soul of the Fifties, Sixties, Seventies, Eighties, Nineties, and Noughties, to give you the lowdown on how the biggest stars hit the big-time, and how they have worked with each other, fought with each other, loved each other, and been inspired, incensed, and influenced by each other throughout the years.

Packed with inspirational photographs, sourced from worldwide archives to complement the connection-loaded text, this insightful book guides you through a wide selection of music's all-time greats (from Johnny Cash to Daft Punk, James Brown to the Sex Pistols, and Muse to Jay-Z), as well as legendary labels (from Sun to Def Jam), super producers (from Phil Spector to Rick Rubin), iconic clubs (from The Marquee to CBGB), and key festivals (from Woodstock to Lollapalooza), telling the fascinating inside story of each one.

We have arranged the acts in (more or less) the order in which they first found fame—an order that was, of course, subject to some judgment calls (we opted, for example, to place Aretha Franklin at the point where she began her world-beating run of hits and classics on the Atlantic label, rather than several years earlier when she recorded her fine but rather less celebrated material for Columbia).

In arranging the entries like this, within five evocatively named, chronological chapters, we hope to have provided you with a naturally unfolding story of the evolution of rock—from its roots in Fifties rock 'n' roll ("Who Put the Bomp in the Bomp Ba Bomp"), through the psychedelic Sixties ("Turn On, Tune In, Drop Out"), the wild, spandex-laden Seventies ("Sex, Drugs & Rock 'n' Roll"), and the eclectic Eighties ("Big Hair & Big Hits"), then on to the kaleidoscopic mish-mash of styles that has dominated the Nineties and the Noughties ("Here We Are Now, Entertain Us").

Inevitably, and despite fierce campaigning by a fan of The Strokes, we haven't had room to include everyone. But in panels that complement many of our main sections, you'll find a galaxy of stars, from Stevie Wonder to Sarah McLachlan, Sly Stone to The Smashing Pumpkins, and Limp Bizkit to Def Leppard. While we could (and indeed did) debate who could be left out of the spotlight, there can be little argument about who made it in. Do we really think Madonna and Duran Duran "rock"? Why, yes, we do! And, throughout the book, we've endeavored to include as many links between artists as we can. (Sadly, we couldn't squeeze in Elton John playing on the mighty Saxon's 1986 gem "Party 'til You Puke," so you can have that one for free, right here.)

In order that this information-packed book not be a by-the-numbers trek through well-trodden territory, we've written about different artists in different ways. Some huge acts, like Elvis and Led Zeppelin, have been treated to in-depth biographies. Others—including acts whose influence vastly outstrips their sales, like the Sex Pistols and The Velvet Underground—are given a varying treatment: an overview of their career, then a look at the artists who have followed in their rather large footsteps.

We've left out many of the seedier scandals, spells in rehab, and druggy demises—this book is for people who look at sleeve notes, not gossip columns. And you don't have to read the book cover to cover; just feel free to dip into it wherever and whenever you like—whether to enjoy a satisfying "I never knew *that* . . ." moment, be reminded of a song you haven't heard in years, or be inspired to listen to a long-forgotten album and sigh, "Oh yeah, it *is* great!" (We spent days just listening to Michael Jackson's *Off the Wall*, and the collected works of Metallica—sometimes, artists seem so famous and so familiar that you forget how great they *sound*.)

So turn up the speakers, or put on your headphones, and join us on a journey from Buddy Holly to the Rolling Stones, the Ramones to U2, and Motown to Muse. It isn't only rock 'n' roll . . . but we like it.

London, U.K.

How to use this book

Below are the types of pages used in this book to showcase great artists and bands, influential labels and producers, and key clubs and festivals. Below right is a symbol key to help you navigate your way through the insightful artist biographies, band stories, and musical legacies that these pages present, as well as to help you trace the many fascinating connections within the world of rock.

Artists & bands

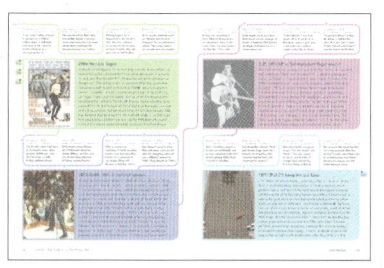

Labels & producers

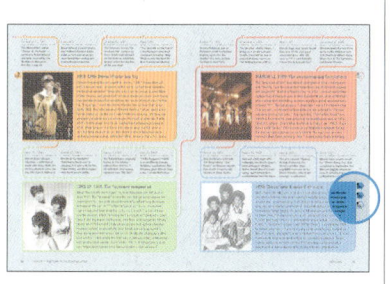

Clubs & festivals

Symbol key

◄062
208►
Page references are given in each act's introductory text for all other acts, labels, producers, clubs, and festivals that have entire pages dedicated to them.

1955+
1981+
Colored date boxes correspond to the colored sections of the biography timeline that follows.

A colored "play" button marks the beginning of an artist, label, or producer biography timeline.

A pink pick marks the start of each timeline that shows acts who have played at featured clubs or festivals, or who have been influenced by or are connected to the featured act.

1975
Influence
Colored and dated picks lead to panels about other acts related to the featured act.

❶
❷
❸
Circled numbers within panel text correspond to reference arrows next to the panel.

❶
170
❷
210
Colored arrows leading from panels provide page references for acts that have entire pages dedicated to them; outlined arrows provide page references for acts that have panels elsewhere dedicated to them.

Album covers on club and festival pages showcase seminal albums by acts that have played at the featured venue or event.

INTRODUCTION   9

Who Put the Bomp in the Bomp Ba Bomp

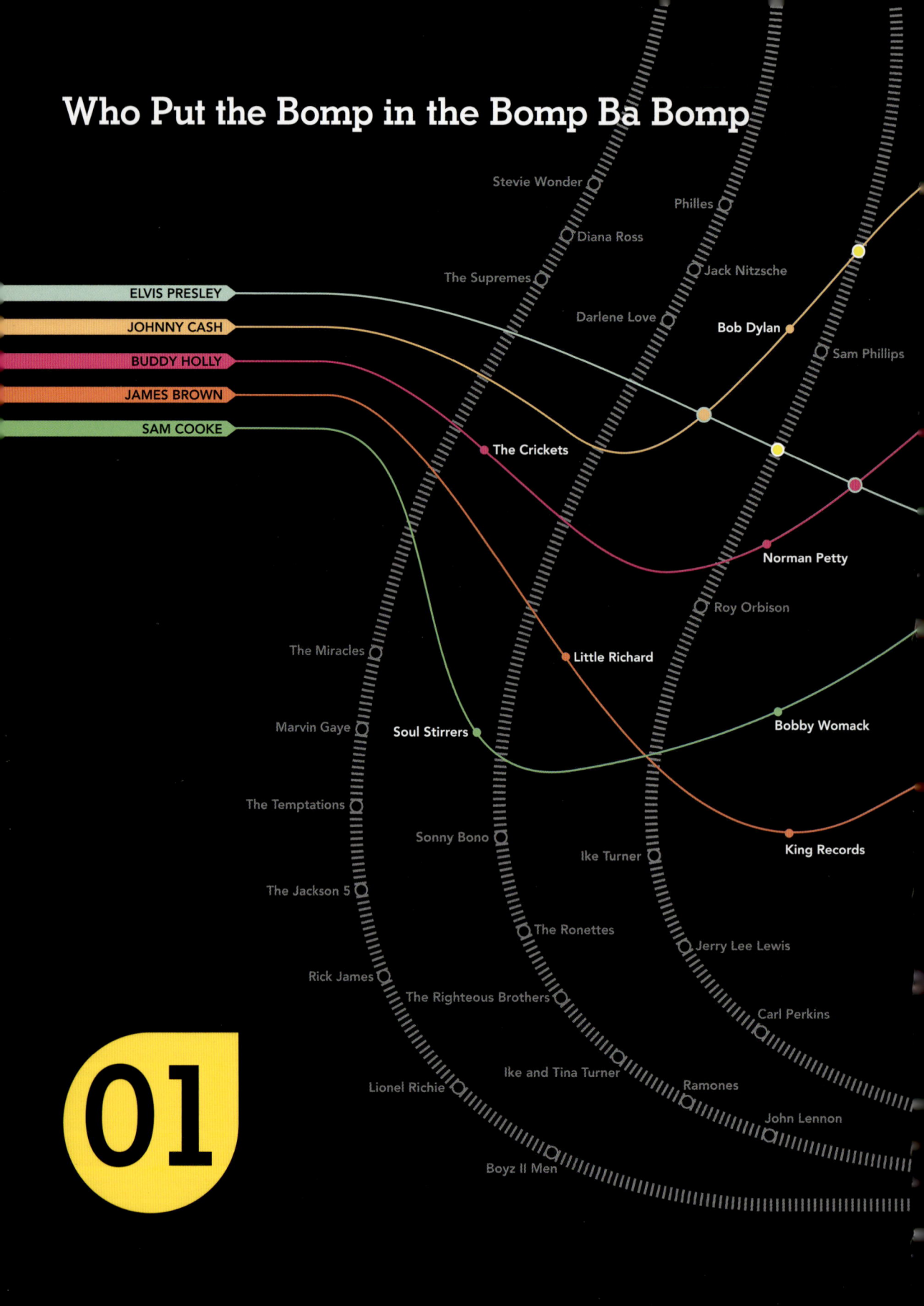

ELVIS PRESLEY
JOHNNY CASH
BUDDY HOLLY
JAMES BROWN
SAM COOKE

Stevie Wonder
Philles
Diana Ross
Jack Nitzsche
The Supremes
Darlene Love
Bob Dylan
Sam Phillips
The Crickets
Norman Petty
Roy Orbison
The Miracles
Little Richard
Marvin Gaye
Soul Stirrers
Bobby Womack
The Temptations
Sonny Bono
Ike Turner
King Records
The Jackson 5
The Ronettes
Jerry Lee Lewis
Rick James
The Righteous Brothers
Carl Perkins
Ike and Tina Turner
Ramones
Lionel Richie
John Lennon
Boyz II Men

01

Rick Rubin

Waylon Jennings

Willie Nelson

King Curtis

Kris Kristofferson

The Beatles

Jerry Lee Lewis

Luigi Creatore

Hugo Peretti

Carl Perkins

Public Enemy

The Famous Flames

Marvin Gaye

Bootsy Collins

Clyde Stubblefield

Smokey Robinson

SUN RECORDS

PHIL SPECTOR

MOTOWN

Elvis Presley 1935–77

When Public Enemy rapped "Elvis was a hero to most but he never meant shit to me" in 1989's "Fight the Power," the ensuing controversy confirmed that—over a decade after his passing—feelings for the Memphis Flash still ran deep.

He didn't invent rock 'n' roll, and Little Richard and Chuck Berry did much more to shape its form. (Indeed, Elvis would cover songs by both, including Richard's "Tutti Frutti," and Berry's "Too Much Monkey Business"—the latter also the inspiration for Bob Dylan's 062▷ "Subterranean Homesick Blues.") But Elvis' confidence, charisma, and humor—not to mention his knockout voice—combined to make him the first worldwide music star, and a role model for millions. "Elvis is like the Big Bang of rock 'n' roll," said Bono of U2 192▷. "It all came from there."

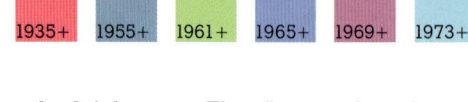

"If there hadn't been an Elvis," remembered John Lennon, "there wouldn't have been a Beatles 044▷." "All we ever wanted to be was Elvis Presley," confirmed Paul McCartney.

"He was a unique artist," enthused Mick Jagger. "An original in an area of imitators." His partner in The Rolling Stones 054▷, Keith Richards, agreed: "Before Elvis, everything was in black and white. Then came Elvis. Zoom, glorious Technicolor."

Even Little Richard concurred: "Elvis was God-given. There's no explanation. A messiah comes around every few thousand years, and Elvis was it this time." In fact, the star himself demurred at the term "the King," protesting that the only true King was Christ. Nonetheless, in the words of Madonna 208▷: "Elvis Presley? He's God."

WHO PUT THE BOMP IN THE BOMP BA BOMP

January 8, 1935

Elvis Aron Presley is born to parents Gladys Love and Vernon Elvis in East Tupelo, Mississippi. (He will later adopt the more common spelling "Aaron.")

October 3, 1945

Aged ten, an unaccompanied Elvis sings "Old Shep" at the Mississippi-Alabama Fair and Dairy Show's Children's Day talent show. He comes in fifth place.

July 4, 1954

Elvis auditions for Scotty Moore and Bill Black's band the Starlite Wranglers. Neither of them are impressed, but they give the boy another chance in Sam Phillips' studio.

JULY 5, 1954: The Big Bang

"I went to the [Sun❶] studio and they told me what they wanted me to sing and how they wanted me to sing it," Elvis recalled in 1956. "Well, I tried it their way, but it didn't work out so good. So while most of 'em were sitting around resting, a couple of us just started playing around with 'That's All Right,' a great beat number . . . It came off pretty good, and Mr. [Sam] Phillips—the man who owned the recording company—said I should go ahead and sing all the songs my own way, the way I knew best. We tried it, and everything went along a lot better." Two days later, Sam Phillips played "That's All Right" to Memphis DJ Dewey Phillips, who gave Elvis his first airtime on July 8. (At Dewey's insistence, Elvis' parents fetched him from the movies so that he could go in to the station to be interviewed.) "That's All Right," coupled with "Blue Moon of Kentucky," became the first of his five singles on Phillips' Sun label.

❶ 016

November 15, 1955

The RCA label agrees to buy the new star's contract from Sam Phillips for the then extraordinary sum of $35,000.

January 27, 1956

Having re-released all of Elvis' Sun singles in December, RCA issues his first single for them, "Heartbreak Hotel." It finally reaches No. 1 on April 28.

July 13, 1956

"Don't Be Cruel," backed with "Hound Dog," is released. By the end of the year, sales of the single will top four million, exceeding all expectations.

November 15, 1956

Elvis' first movie, *Love Me Tender*, opens in New York. He begins work on the next one, *Loving You*, just two months later.

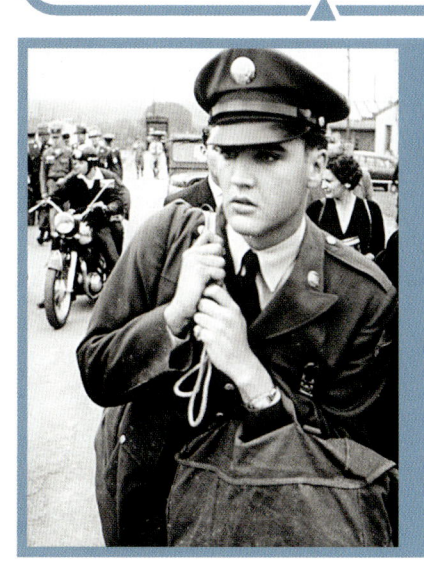

SEPTEMBER 22, 1958: G.I. Blues

Having been drafted earlier in the year, the King of Rock 'n' Roll left for maneuvers in Germany in September 1958. RCA continued to issue hit singles (such as "One Night") and LPs in his absence, and the star's new image as a patriotic soldier hardly hampered his reputation. He left Germany on March 2, 1960 (having met his future wife Priscilla there, six months previously), and was released from the army three days later. "He played some good stuff after the army," said John Lennon, years later, "but it was never quite the same . . . Elvis really died the day he joined the army. That's when they killed him, and the rest was a living death." But the star's first album of the new decade, *Elvis Is Back!*, proved Lennon's judgment was askew: it was the first of many brilliant recordings over the next decade, such as 1969's *From Elvis in Memphis* and an eerie 1966 version of Bob Dylan's❶ "Tomorrow Is a Long Time."

❶ 062

ELVIS PRESLEY   13

November 21, 1961

"Can't Help Falling in Love" is released as a million-selling single. It will later end most of his concerts and be adopted as a show-closer by U2.

December 17, 1961

The soundtrack to Elvis' *Blue Hawaii* film begins a twenty-week reign atop the U.S. mono album chart, making it his longest-running No. 1 album.

September 5, 1962

Filming begins for *It Happened at the World's Fair*. The star is kicked on-screen by eleven-year-old Kurt Russell, who will later star in 1979's *Elvis*.

May 26/27, 1963

Elvis records material such as "(You're the) Devil in Disguise" for an unfinished album. The songs appear on soundtracks and singles.

❶ 170
❷ 068
❸ 044

1964: *Viva Las Vegas*

History has not judged Elvis' movies kindly. *Love Me Tender* (1956) had proved that audiences would flock to a substandard movie if he was in it—and, after *Blue Hawaii* (1961), the beaches and bikinis formula was flogged with diminishing returns. However, his 1958 *King Creole* had been packed with musical gems such as Clash❶ man Joe Strummer's favorite, "Crawfish," and Elvis once again got it right in his 1964 *Viva Las Vegas*. Thanks largely to sizzling chemistry with Ann-Margret (who later played the mother in The Who's❷ *Tommy*), this became Elvis' most successful movie. But he never hit those heights on film again. In a clear omen, *Roustabout*, his final soundtrack to top the U.S. chart (in early 1965), was displaced after just a week by The Beatles❸. Sadly, a role that might have salvaged his celluloid reputation—in the 1976 Barbra Streisand movie *A Star is Born*—went instead to country star Kris Kristofferson.

August 27, 1965

The Beatles meet their hero at his Bel Air home. Elvis appears indifferent, and the Fab Four are left feeling underwhelmed.

June 1966

Elvis meets James Brown at a Hollywood show by Jackie Wilson, another soul star he has long admired. All three remain friends.

May 1, 1967

After a seven-year courtship, Priscilla Beaulieu, twenty-one, becomes Mrs. Presley at a ceremony in Las Vegas. (They will divorce in October 1973.)

February 1, 1968

Lisa Marie Presley is born. Elvis will name a private jet after his daughter, who will marry Michael Jackson in 1994. (They divorce in 1996.)

DECEMBER 1968: Comeback Special

No star has enjoyed such an iconic comeback as the one Elvis achieved. His record sales—though huge by modern standards—were in freefall by the late Sixties, and his movies excited little interest. But he was still a star, and his Comeback Special (sponsored by sewing machine company Singer) proved that he was more than worthy of all the adulation. On December 3, 1968, a year after the project had been first mooted as a Christmas special, Elvis delivered an hour of electrifying viewing. (He admitted to nerves at the filming: "I will go as far as to say I was petrified.") The show is best remembered for his sexy, swaggering performances in a black leather jumpsuit (left), notably the opening "Trouble." But there were also dramatized sequences for lesser-known songs such as "Little Egypt." One gem that wasn't aired remained in obscurity for more than three decades—"A Little Less Conversation."

14 WHO PUT THE BOMP IN THE BOMP BA BOMP

January 21, 1969
During the recording of *From Elvis to Memphis* (to be released in June of the same year), the star covers The Beatles' "Hey Jude."

March 10, 1969
Elvis begins work on a final Hollywood movie, *Change of Habit*. It features Phil Spector protégée Darlene Love in a small cameo role.

June 25, 1969
"In the Ghetto," the first single off of *From Elvis in Memphis*, earns a gold disc. It will sell over a million copies in the U.S.A. alone.

August 26, 1969
"Suspicious Minds" makes its debut. It will be the star's first U.S. No. 1 since 1962's "Good Luck Charm," and the last in his lifetime.

1969 ONWARD: The legendary Vegas season

Elvis had first played Las Vegas in April 1956. The reaction, he reported, had been frosty: "I was used to a bunch of . . . screaming teenagers, and in Las Vegas . . . they're all elderly folks." But, in the wake of his 1968 Comeback Special, he made a long-awaited return to the stage on July 31, 1969, at the International Hotel in Vegas. It was his first live show since early 1961 and attracted near-unanimous acclaim. Elvis admitted to being stricken with stagefright up until his 10:15 P.M. showtime, but, as he told the press the next day, he thought "What the heck, get with it, man, or you might be out of a job tomorrow." Despite extensive tours over the next seven years (albeit only in the U.S.A., owing to his manager's mysterious reluctance to travel), Elvis' fifteen seasons in Vegas, ending on December 12, 1976—with iconic costumes by Bill Belew—became his best-known performances.

January 14, 1973
Elvis' Honolulu concert is broadcast worldwide and is soon released as the U.S. chart-topping *Aloha from Hawaii via Satellite*.

May 11, 1974
Led Zeppelin's Robert Plant and Jimmy Page meet the King in Los Angeles, who remarks that he likes their "Stairway to Heaven."

February 5, 1976
Elvis records his last great songs: "For the Heart" and "Hurt." They are issued as the A- and B-sides of a single that will hit the U.S. top thirty in March.

August 16, 1977
The press is informed that the forty-two-year-old Elvis has died of "cardiac arrhythmia due to undetermined heartbeat." The precise causes are still hotly debated today.

THE LEGACY: Long live the King

Elvis' death had an immediate, galvanizing effect on his sales. *Moody Blue*, an indifferent album released just a month previously, shot to platinum status, and his work has continued to have gigantic success. Official statistics of the Recording Industry Association of America put his sales in the U.S.A. alone at more than one hundred and twenty million, and it was big news in 2006 when Kurt Cobain of Nirvana❶ displaced him from the top spot in the *Forbes* list of top-earning dead celebrities. But striking proof of his enduring appeal came when the funky but flop 1968 single "A Little Less Conversation"—from his forgotten film *Live a Little, Love a Little*—was used in the 2001 movie *Ocean's Eleven* and then remixed for an advertising campaign the next year, turning it into an international chart-topper. A further onslaught of successful reissues has certainly confirmed his title as the King of Rock 'n' Roll.

❶ 242

ELVIS PRESLEY

legendary label

Sun Records
1952–68

The early hits of the Sun Record Company read like a lexicon of rock 'n' roll itself: "Whole Lotta Shakin' Goin' On," "Blue Suede Shoes," "I Walk the Line," "That's All Right." Not until Motown 030▶ would another label make such a dramatic impact.

Sun was founded in 1952 by twenty-nine-year-old Sam Phillips. Unable to afford the fees to study law, he became an engineer, a DJ, then a producer. In 1950, he formed the Memphis Recording Service to cater for weddings and similar events. He then decided to focus on creating a music studio at 706 Union Avenue, in Memphis, Tennessee.

Phillips started off issuing singles by blues acts such as Little Junior Parker, but it was Jackie Brenton's "Rocket 88" (1951), featuring Ike Turner on piano, that gave the producer his first big hit when it topped the U.S. R&B chart (albeit on the Chess label, before he had set up Sun). In Phillips' words, it "really was the first rock 'n' roll record." Then, in the summer of 1953, eighteen-year-old Elvis Presley ◀012 entered the Sun studio, to cut an acetate for his mother, but in the process attracted the attention of Phillips and his assistant Marion Keisker. He cut a second in January 1954 and, in June, Keisker persuaded Phillips to summon "the boy with the sideburns" to record a new song. The most momentous story in rock 'n' roll had begun.

Roy Orbison was among others to make a splash for Sun. But its stars gradually decamped to major labels, its importance waned, and Phillips sold it in 1969. In the Eighties, he restored the studio, which has since been used by a host of contemporary acts.

1953+
1955+
1957+

March 1953
Rufus Thomas' "Bear Cat," an answer to Big Mama Thornton's 1952 "Hound Dog," is Sun's first pop hit.

July 1954
Elvis's first single, "That's All Right," is released with minor success. "Blue Moon of Kentucky" is the B-side.

January 1955
Elvis issues "Milkcow Blues Boogie," later covered by acts such as The Kinks and Aerosmith.

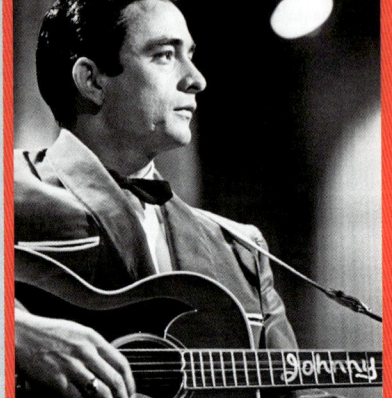

❶ 012
❷ 018

JUNE 1955: The man in black

If Elvis❶ represented the sunnier side of Sun, the label's grittier elements were embodied by Johnny Cash❷. Like Elvis, Cash's tenure on the label was fairly short, yet packed a real punch. His first single, credited to Johnny Cash and the Tennessee Two, was "Hey, Porter!" backed with "Cry! Cry! Cry!"—songs that still turn up on his "best of" albums five decades later. The classics kept coming: "I Walk the Line," "Get Rhythm" (originally written for Elvis), and "Folsom Prison Blues" in 1956; "Big River" and "Guess Things Happen that Way" in 1958. Having grown up not far from Elvis' birthplace—Tupelo, Mississippi—and being just three years older than him, Cash was raised on the same stock of songs as him—in Cash's own words, "everything from Bill Monroe to black gospel to the Chuck Wagon Gang." And from 1970, Elvis periodically introduced himself at concerts with "My name's Johnny Cash."

WHO PUT THE BOMP IN THE BOMP BA BOMP

July 1955

Elvis cuts "I Forgot to Remember to Forget"—his first No. 1 hit for Sun (albeit on the country chart rather than the pop chart).

December 1955

Sun releases its first million-selling smash: Carl Perkins' classic "Blue Suede Shoes." The song will be a hit again within three months, for Elvis.

May 1956

Roy Orbison and Teen Kings make their debut for Sun with the single "Ooby Dooby" and its flipside, the aptly titled "Go! Go! Go!"

November 1956

Sun unleashes the twenty-one-year-old Jerry Lee Lewis. His first record is "Crazy Arms," backed with "End of the Road."

DECEMBER 1956: The Million Dollar Quartet

Elvis' first EP, released in March 1953, had sold an unprecedented half a million copies. Among its highlights was a version of Carl Perkins' "Blue Suede Shoes." Perkins gave a hand to Jerry Lee Lewis, too, who played on his recording for the "Matchbox"/"Your True Love" single on December 4, 1956. During this session at Sun, Elvis❶ stopped by, and the musicians did an impromptu run through country, gospel, and rock 'n' roll numbers. (The King also impersonated Jackie Wilson, whose version of "Don't Be Cruel" was, he said, "much better than that record of mine.") Johnny Cash❷, who had been the first to arrive at the studio that day, also joined in briefly, and the one-off Million Dollar Quartet was born (left—Lewis, Perkins, Presley, and Cash; Sam Phillips wasted no time summoning a press photographer to capture the event.) The recordings, never intended for release, remained unissued for thirty years.

❶ 012

❷ 018

January 1957

Sun releases "Flyin' Saucers Rock & Roll," by Billy Riley and His Little Green Men. It will later be covered by guitarist Link Wray.

March 1957

Piano playing is changed forever when Jerry Lee Lewis releases the extraordinary "Whole Lotta Shakin' Going On."

September 1957

Phillips releases Billy Riley's "Red Hot" but puts more focus on a new single by the *pianist* on Riley's song —a certain Jerry Lee Lewis.

November 1957

Lewis' ludicrously explosive "Great Balls of Fire" is released, making him Sun's newest and highest-charting pop star.

1958: Goodness gracious, Mr. Lewis!

Jerry Lee Lewis❶ was the most dynamite act to hit rock 'n' roll since Little Richard❷. He initially balked at the "sacrilegious" lyrics of "Great Balls of Fire," but invested the tune with devilish intensity—not for nothing was he known as "The Killer." In 1958, he had further hits with "Breathless" and "High School Confidential," before embarking on a British tour, which was cancelled after just three shows when he was booed offstage due to the scandal surrounding his recent marriage to his teenage cousin. Known for his unpredictable temperament, Lewis more than once turned up at Elvis'❸ Graceland home, demanding to see the King, loaded gun in tow. Johnny Cash❹ commented wryly on this, "He didn't have an attitude about Elvis. He just had an attitude." More happily, in 1985, Jerry Lee joined Johnny Cash, Carl Perkins, and Roy Orbison at the Sun studio, to cut the *Class of '55* tribute album.

❶ 040

❷ 040

❸ 012

❹ 018

SUN RECORDS   17

Johnny Cash 1932–2003

1932+ 1983+

A contemporary of Elvis ◀012▶, collaborator with Bob Dylan ◀062▶, and inspiration to countless artists, notably Bruce Springsteen ◀150▶, Johnny Cash had impeccable rock 'n' roll connections.

He began as a gospel singer, but was advised by Sun Records ◀016▶ boss Sam Phillips to focus on country and western. Cash's interpretation of the form fueled a series of classic singles on Sun, the success of which led to him being snapped up by Columbia in 1958. The major label even let him issue a gospel album, *Hymns by Johnny Cash*.

The highlights of his Sixties output included the 1963 hit "Ring of Fire," and 1964's Bob Dylan cover, "It Ain't Me, Babe." The latter was a duet with singer-cum-comedienne June Carter, with whom he fell in love and subsequently married in March 1968.

In 1969, Cash duetted on "Girl from the North Country," on Dylan's *Nashville Skyline*. His success continued into the Seventies, thanks to relentless touring and TV's *The Johnny Cash Show*, but little was then heard of him until an unlikely renaissance in 1993 when U2 ◀192▶ invited him to contribute to their *Zooropa* album. The next year, producer Rick Rubin ◀226▶ issued *American Recordings*, featuring Cash's interpretation of songs by writers as diverse as metal maniac Glenn Danzig and boho iconoclast Tom Waits. Its success led to fascinating albums on which Cash tackled tunes by U2, Depeche Mode ◀196▶, Soundgarden, Tom Petty, Nick Cave ◀202▶, Beck, and Sting. As he said, "I don't dance, tell jokes, or wear my pants too tight like a lot of entertainers do, but I do know about one thousand songs."

WHO PUT THE BOMP IN THE BOMP BA BOMP

January 26, 1932

J. R. Cash, the son of a farmer, is born in Kingsland, Arkansas, one of seven children. He begins playing guitar and writing songs as a young boy.

December 1957

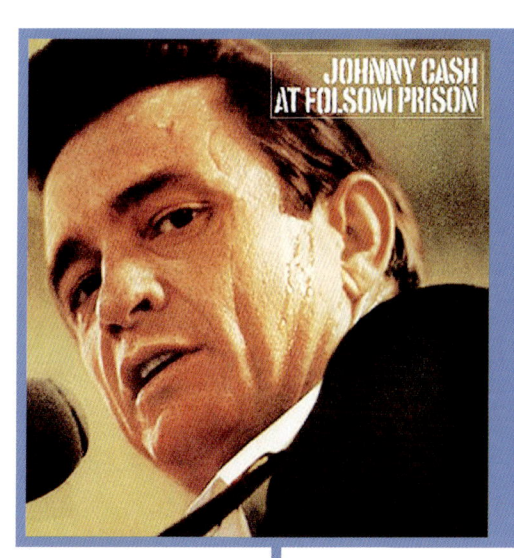

"Ballad of a Teenage Queen" and "Big River" are issued together as a single, one of Cash's classic couplings on the Sun label.

July 23, 1958

Cash records a first session for his new label, Columbia. This year, he will score hits with "What Do I Care" and *The Fabulous Johnny Cash*.

JANUARY 1960: Prison performances

Cash created an anthem for prisoners with 1955's "Folsom Prison Blues," with the legendary line, "I shot a man in Reno/just to watch him die." Then, on New Year's Day, 1960, he played the first of several Californian prison shows, at San Quentin (twenty-two-year-old inmate and future country star Merle Haggard was in the first row). Two key concerts—on January 13, 1968 and February 23, 1969—yielded the *At Folsom Prison* and *At San Quentin* albums, both of which have turned triple platinum. The latter illustrated three pillars of Cash's life: faith ("Peace in the Valley"), humor ("A Boy Named Sue"), and empathy ("San Quentin"). "He's speaking for the broken people," said James Hetfield of Metallica❶, "people who can't speak up or [who] no one wants to hear."

❶ 218

August 22, 1983

Cash issues *Johnny 99*, including "Johnny 99" and "Highway Patrolman" from Springsteen's Cash-inspired 1982 album, *Nebraska*.

February 24, 1986

"Highwayman," a 1985 single by Cash, Willie Nelson, Kris Kristofferson, and Waylon Jennings, wins a Grammy for best country song.

October 15, 1992

Cash and June Carter sing "It Ain't Me, Babe" at the Bob Dylan anniversary show at Madison Square Garden, in New York.

February 22, 2003

The music video for Cash's cover of Nine Inch Nail's "Hurt," by Mark Romanek —who also directed NIN's "Closer"—wins a Grammy.

SEPTEMBER 2003: "I Am Still Right Here"

Although June Carter Cash was captured visibly distressed at Cash's deteriorating condition in the "Hurt" video, she died before him, on May 14, 2003. Brokenhearted and in constant pain from a jaw injury, Cash died, at seventy-one, four months later, on September 12, in Nashville. 2002's *American IV: The Man Comes Around,* on which the gold-selling "Hurt" single appeared, promptly soared to platinum status. Interest in Cash peaked again with the 2005 release of *Walk the Line*, a biopic starring Reese Witherspoon alongside Joaquin Phoenix (left), whom Cash had picked for the role. Both were nominated for multiple awards, and Witherspoon won both an Academy Award and a Bafta. The movie, she said, "is about compassion in the long haul, not just the short solutions to problems."

JOHNNY CASH

Buddy Holly 1936–59

1936+ 1959+

Like Kurt Cobain, Buddy Holly paid his dues in minor league bands, enjoyed stratospheric success, and died within three years of his biggest hits, having changed the face of music forever.

Holly's group The Crickets was, as critic Dave Marsh observed, "The first modern rock band: self-contained for both playing and singing." The band had the basic two guitars-bass-drums lineup but they wrote their own songs. "Buddy was *the one*," said Keith Richards of The Rolling Stones ◁054▷. "Because he had glasses and looked like a bank clerk, you could say to yourself, 'Well, rock 'n' roll's not just for guys who look like Elvis ◁012▷.'"

These elements—combined with songs that, even now, sound much less dated than those of Holly's contemporaries—proved a key influence on The Beatles ◁044▷, among many others. Indeed, the Fab Four made one of the few covers that does justice to a Holly original, with "Words of Love" on 1964's *Beatles for Sale*. (Blind Faith also took a good stab at "Well All Right" on their self-titled 1969 album.)

Holly's popularity had begun to level off toward the end of his life, but there were signs of his work developing in fascinating directions. In contrast to the string-laden loveliness of "It Doesn't Matter Anymore"—the last single of his lifetime—he was working with R&B star King Curtis and country singer Waylon Jennings. He was also a fine lyricist, and had learned a trick or two from his producer and frequent co-writer, Norman Petty.

As it is, classics such as "That'll Be the Day" and "Think It Over" form an unimpeachable legacy.

September 7, 1936

Charles Hardin Holley is born in Lubbock, Texas. "Buddy" was a nickname, while "Holly" was a misprint on a record label, which the star adopted.

February 13, 1955

Half of country duo Buddy & Bob, Holly appears at a Lubbock show where Elvis headlines. Inspired, he swaps country for rock 'n' roll and later forms The Crickets.

January 23, 1959

Minus his band The Crickets, from whom he had parted company in 1958, Holly embarks on the "Winter Dance Party" tour that will be his last, in Milwaukee, Wisconsin.

FEBRUARY 3, 1959: The day the music died

❶ 208

"I hope your plane crashes," quipped Waylon Jennings to Buddy Holly, having swapped his seat on a charter flight for a place on their tour bus. Sadly, the aircraft—en route from Clear Lake to Moorhead—did just that, crashing in a blinding snowstorm, minutes after takeoff (left). All aboard were killed, including Holly's fellow rock 'n' rollers The Big Bopper (Jiles Perry Richardson, Jr., aged twenty-nine) and Ritchie Valens (Richard Steven Valenzuela, aged seventeen). Singer Dion DiMucci had declined to pay thirty-six dollars for the plane ticket and so lived to enjoy later hits such as "Runaround Sue" and "The Wanderer" (1961). The tragic accident is commemorated as "the day the music died" in Don McLean's 1971 classic "American Pie"—later covered by Madonna❶.

April 24, 1959

Released a month before his death, "It Doesn't Matter Anymore" gives Holly his first posthumous No. 1 on the U.K. singles chart.

July 1, 1976

Paul McCartney purchases the rights to Holly's songs. The ex-Beatle will celebrate the late star's fortieth birthday with "Buddy Holly Week" in the U.K.

May 18, 1978

The Buddy Holly Story movie, starring Gary Busey, opens in Holly's home state, Texas. Busey's performance earns him an Academy Award nomination.

October 12, 1989

Buddy—The Buddy Holly Story opens in London. It becomes one of the city's longest-running musicals, soon transferring overseas.

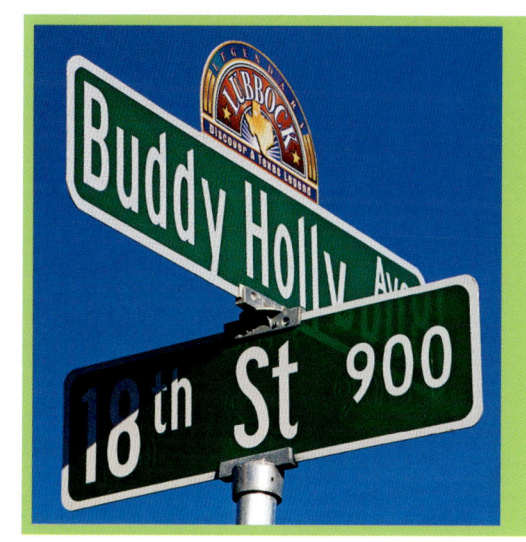

THE LEGACY: Rave on

❶ 050
❷ 054
❸ 172

Buddy Holly's legacy was evident soon after his death. The Regents' 1961 single "Barbara Ann"—later covered by The Beach Boys❶—refers to Peggy Sue, the heroine of Holly's 1957 hit. His sequel, "Peggy Sue Got Married," was used as the title of a 1986 movie. Other celluloid connections include the 1987 Ritchie Valens biopic *La Bamba*, in which Holly is played by Marshall Crenshaw. Memorable covers of Holly's work range from The Rolling Stones'❷ "Not Fade Away" to Blondie's❸ "I'm Gonna Love You Too." Weezer's hit "Buddy Holly" is notable both for its title and the Holly-esque spectacles of leader Rivers Cuomo. Holly has also had a street named after him in his hometown (left) and was inducted into the Rock and Roll Hall of Fame at its first dinner in 1986.

BUDDY HOLLY

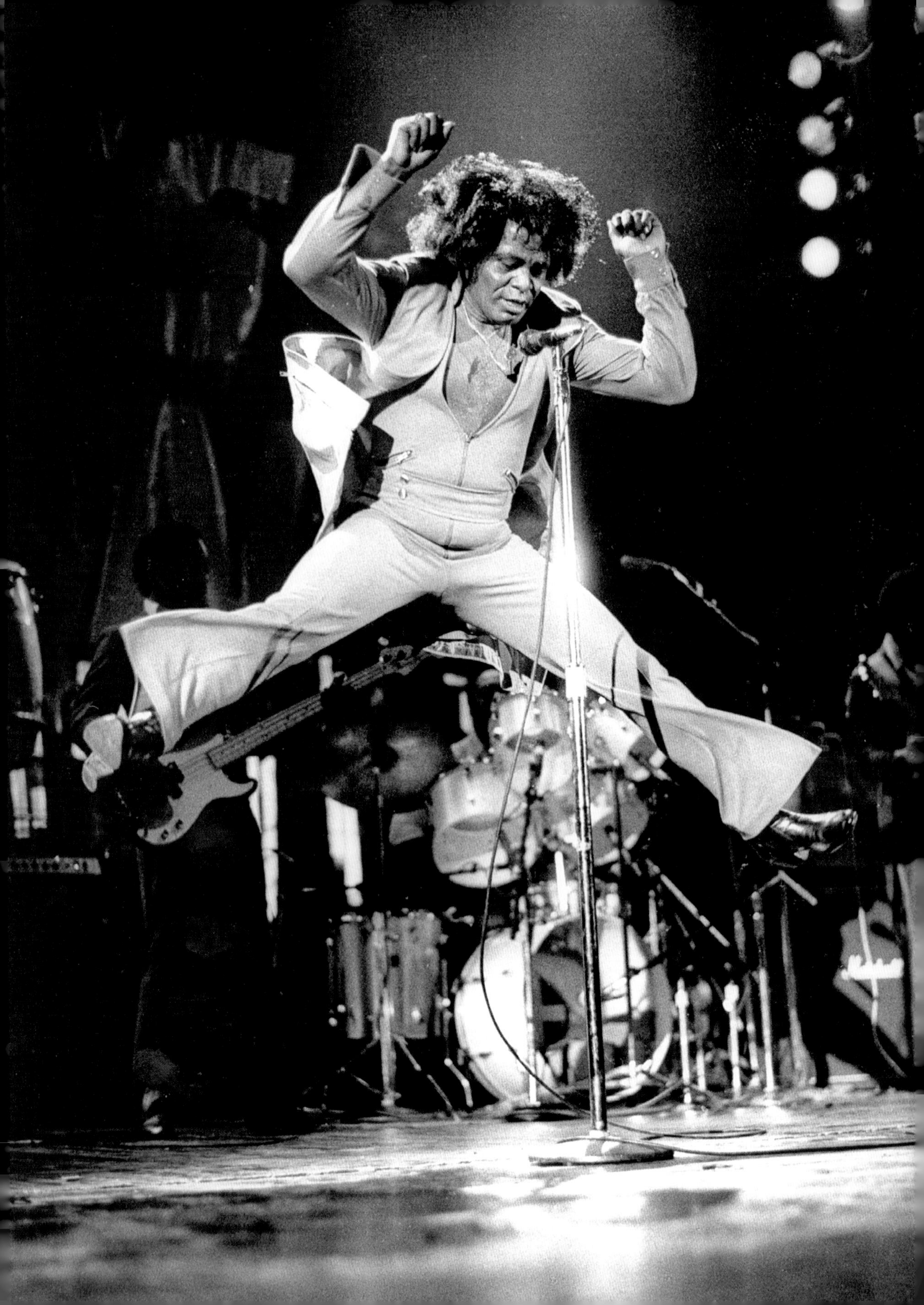

James Brown
1933–2006

As accurate as it is, the title "Godfather of Soul" is almost inadequate for James Brown. He was indeed responsible for some of the finest and most innovative soul music of all time. But he also inspired countless other major acts including The Beatles 044▷, The Rolling Stones 054▷, Michael Jackson 122▷, and Prince 174▷; helped create funk; stamped a musical template for hip-hop; and became an inspiration and icon for black America. (When race riots erupted in his hometown of Augusta, Georgia, in 1970, Brown returned to help quell the troubles.)

> "He was a work of art. He was as valuable and as rare as any Rembrandt or Picasso."
> —Aretha Franklin

An equally pivotal figure in Brown's own career was Little Richard, for whom Brown's band The Famous Flames opened. "He couldn't believe it [our performance]," Brown told the BBC. "And he went and told his manager, so in a way he discovered us."

Brown's chart legacy is slightly distorted by his songs showing up on the R&B rather than pop list, but his tally of fifty top ten smashes eclipses both The Beatles and Elvis ◁012. The first of these was 1956's "Please, Please, Please" (dismissed by his future record label boss Syd Nathan, of King Records, as a "piece of shit"). Then "Try Me," in 1958, gave him his first R&B No. 1 and a debut on the pop chart.

The first key year, however, was 1962. Brown's wonderful remake of Jimmy Forrest's "Night Train" proved that he could give dance band and jazz pieces a funky twist; and that he didn't have to have a very vocal presence for his records to sound unmistakably "James Brown." Ultimately, his grunts, screams, asides, and instructions to his well-drilled bands would become as distinctive as any of his soaring or rasping vocal performances.

The same year, 1962, saw the release of *Live at the Apollo*, the sensational album with which he smashed into the U.S. mainstream (see below).

Thereafter, Brown was unstoppable. In 1964, he was the star attraction of *The T.A.M.I. Show*, a two-hour showcase of the finest names in pop and R&B, from The Beach Boys 050▷ to Chuck Berry. "We had to follow James Brown," marveled Keith Richards, "the tightest machine in the world!" (Director Steve Binder, who also helmed Elvis' *'68 Comeback Special*, concurred, making Brown the climax of the film). Super producer Rick Rubin 226▷ recalled once visiting Prince's office and finding Brown's *T.A.M.I.* routine showing on an endless loop. "That may be," Rubin wrote in *Rolling Stone*, "the single greatest rock 'n' roll performance ever captured on film."

Later work inspired musical revolutions from funk to hip-hop. Equally important was his unapologetic pride, evidenced by the 1968 smash "Say It Loud—I'm Black and I'm Proud." "It's how boxers walk into the ring . . ." observed Mick Jagger. "James Brown did the same thing."

The star, as his road manager Alan Leeds noted, "was not going to be wrong. He would say two plus two equals three. You'd say it was four and he'd say, 'Mr. Leeds, that is a white man's illusion.'"

The electrifying *Live at the Apollo* (1962) reached No. 2 in the U.S.A. Its success blazed a trail for future live LPs such as 1971's *Revolution of the Mind*, also recorded at the Harlem venue.

In the Jungle Groove (1986) was a collection of some of Brown's funkiest material from 1969 to 1971. It became a "one-stop shop" for hip-hop samples for at least the next decade.

The rise and fall of Sly Stone

"There's a cat, a prime example of a performer not working at full-tilt pitch," James Brown told *NME* of Sly Stone. "Lord knows he had it made . . . But, see, I was checkin' his act from the start. Cos when I was doin' 'Brand New Bag' and 'I Feel Good,' and also cos I was getting a little political and heavy, he and his band just up and stole my groove and watered it down. Just check out the riff on 'Everyday People.'" While James invented funk, Sly & The Family Stone ❶—who exploded in 1967—added a riot of flavors to the Godfather's formula. Within four years, Sly's vision darkened: the veiled social commentary of hits such as "Hot Fun in the Summertime" evolved into full-blown cynicism on *There's a Riot Goin' On*. As Sly succumbed to narcotic excess, George Clinton took over the funk scene; meanwhile, Brown soldiered on. Between them, they created the holy trinity of all things funkified.

James Brown

1965
Brown scores two R&B chart-toppers that become classics: "I Got You (I Feel Good)" and "Papa's Got a Brand New Bag." The former is Brown's biggest pop hit.

1967 Influence

November 1969
Brown records *Gettin' Down to It* with the Dee Felice Trio. The next year, he records *Soul on Top* with the Louie Bellson Orchestra, including a retake of "Papa's Got a Brand New Bag."

May 1967
Funk in its purest form is born with the recording of the astounding "Cold Sweat." On its release in July, the single is another R&B No. 1 and goes top ten on the pop chart.

1968
Brown buys a Tennessee radio station, performs for U.S. troops in Vietnam, and scores another smash with August's anthemic "Say It Loud—I'm Black and I'm Proud."

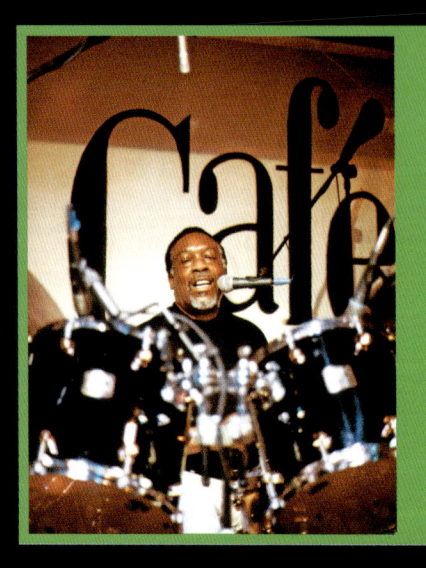

Connection 1970

The Funky Drummer takes center stage

Despite making hit records for more than a decade, James Brown was still breaking new ground as the Seventies dawned. Among his first singles of the decade was "Funky Drummer (parts 1 and 2)," in March 1970, of which the most remarkable aspects were Brown's organ playing and the irresistible drums of Clyde Stubblefield (left). Indeed toward the end of the track, the evidently impressed Brown remarks, "The name of this tune is 'The Funky Drummer,'" as if Stubblefield's work had inspired a brainwave. When the track was included in unedited form on 1986's *In the Jungle Groove*, producers seized on an eight-bar break featuring Stubblefield alone. "Funky Drummer" promptly became one of the most sampled records of all time, with documented examples totaling well over one hundred—from Public Enemy's "Bring the Noise" to George Michael's "Waiting for That Day," and Alyson Williams' "Sleeptalk."

WHO PUT THE BOMP IN THE BOMP BA BOMP

Aah . . . the name is Bootsy, baby!

"My brother Catfish [a.k.a. guitarist Phelps Collins] and I had met James a couple of times on the street," bassist William "Bootsy" Collins told *Mojo*, "but we were just kids to him." Then, in 1970, eighteen-year-old Bootsy was hauled aboard by Brown—as part of the group to become known as The J.B.'s—when most of Brown's own band had quit after a pay dispute. The J.B.'s debuted with the amazing "Get Up (I Feel Like Being a) Sex Machine." And so began an astonishing career for Bootsy. On graduating to George Clinton's P-Funk empire (whose influence rivaled that of Brown), he proved pivotal to Parliament❶ gems such as "Up for the Down Stroke" and "Flashlight." His extra-curricular adventures yielded more much sampled tracks, such as "I'd Rather Be with You" by Bootsy's Rubber Band and "More Bounce to the Ounce" by Zapp. He's also the cosmic dude who raps in Dee-Lite's "Groove Is in the Heart"!

❶ 143

1970 Connection

September 1974
Brown headlines Zaire 74, intended to be part of the build-up to "the rumble in the jungle," the legendary boxing match between Muhammad Ali and George Foreman.

November 2002
Brown co-stars with Clive Owen and Marilyn Manson in the short film *Beat the Devil*, in which he negotiates with the Devil (Gary Oldman) to turn back the hands of time.

December 10, 2003
At the prestigious Kennedy Center Honors ceremony, U.S. Secretary of State Colin Powell describes Brown as the "Secretary of Soul and Foreign Minister of Funk."

March 28, 1973
Led Zeppelin release *Houses of the Holy*, featuring the Brown pastiche "The Crunge." "A complete imitation," admits Robert Plant, ". . . especially with the bass and drums."

Influence 1986

June 24, 2003
"Nobody has influenced me more than this man right here," says Michael Jackson, giving Brown a lifetime achievement award for Black Entertainment Television.

December 25, 2006
The Godfather of Soul dies of congestive heart failure. "James Brown's family and friends," says President Bush, "are in our thoughts and prayers this Christmas."

Public Enemy on the J.B. train

"The first big record in hip-hop that used a Brown sample was Eric B. and Rakim's 'Eric B. Is President,'" recalled Rick Rubin❶. "That opened the floodgates." Rubin's protégés Public Enemy were among the acts who made James Brown the most sampled artist in music. Notable examples included the brassy shriek in 1987's "Rebel Without a Pause" (from 1970's "The Grunt"), the searing squeak in 1988's "Don't Believe the Hype" (from 1971's "Escape-ism"), and their 1991 re-tooling of his 1962 classic "Night Train." "I have a lot of musical heroes," Public Enemy mainman Chuck D told *Mojo*, "but I think James Brown is at the top of the list. Absolutely the funkiest man on Earth. 'Say It Loud—I'm Black and I'm Proud' was a record that really convinced me to say I was black instead of a negro . . . James said you can say it loud; that being black is a great thing instead of something you have to apologize for."

❶ 226

Sam Cooke 1931–64

History has not been kind to Sam Cooke. While Ray Charles and Little Richard are (rightly) recognized for their pioneering roles in R&B and rock 'n' roll, Cooke is often overlooked. Yet he contributed greatly to pop's evolution—helping to blaze a trail for soul stars such as Marvin Gaye 036▶, influencing Otis Redding, discovering talents such as Billy Preston and Bobby Womack, and inspiring stars such as Smokey Robinson, Rod Stewart, and Van Morrison. He also ran a publishing company, management firm, and record label—remarkable achievements given the racial bias of the times.

When he replaced R. H. Harris as lead singer of the Soul Stirrers in 1950, Cooke had big shoes to fill: the Harris-led incarnation were an influence on the likes of Aretha Franklin 084▶ and The Temptations. But Cooke made the role his own—and, as Joe McEwan wrote for *Rolling Stone*, "he never sang songs that were more erotic or buoyant than the love songs he sang about his Lord." The effect of his voice on gospel audiences—aided by his good looks—pointed to his future as a pop star; although he released his first secular 45, "Lovable," as Dale Cook, so as not to offend his original following.

Yet once he crossed over the hits just kept coming. Many have become standards: "Wonderful World," "Twistin' the Night Away," "Cupid," "Chain Gang," "Having a Party." His songs have been sung by stars from John Lennon to Bruce Springsteen 150▶, and, as Keith Richards acknowledged, when rating his own band's place in rock 'n' roll hierarchy, "I'd rather have Sam Cooke than The Rolling Stones 054▶!"

January 22, 1931

Samuel Cook (later Cooke) is born in Clarksdale, Mississippi. He is raised in Chicago, where his father, the Rev. Charles Cook, is a minister.

December 1, 1950

Cooke—just nineteen years old—replaces R. H. Harris as lead singer of the Soul Stirrers. He will remain with them for six years.

December 2, 1957

"You Send Me," the first of twenty-four pop hits that Cooke will score in his lifetime, replaces Elvis' "Jailhouse Rock" at the top of the U.S. chart.

JANUARY 1964: "A Change Is Gonna Come"

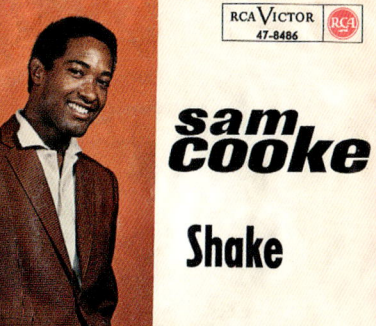

Inspired by Bob Dylan's ❶ 1963 "Blowin' in the Wind"—which he covered—Sam Cooke created immortal social commentary of his own in the form of the early protest song "A Change Is Gonna Come." Produced by his regular collaborators, Hugo Peretti and Luigi Creatore—who had already etched themselves into history by co-writing Elvis' ❷ "Can't Help Falling in Love"—and released as the flipside of the carefree "Shake," "A Change Is Gonna Come" only became a hit after Cooke's death. Even shorn of a verse about being refused admission to a movie theater, it evoked the spirit of Martin Luther King, Jr. and the Civil Rights movement. Fittingly, its title was quoted by Barack Obama when, forty-five years after its release, he became the U.S.A.'s first black president.

❶ 062
❷ 012

March 12, 1964

Cooke produces "I Need a Lot of Love" by Johnnie Taylor, who had replaced him in the Soul Stirrers when he went solo.

July 9, 1964

The Cajun-flavored "Good Times" is released. Written by Cooke, the song reaches No. 11 in the chart as had its predecessor—"Good News."

September 16, 1964

"Cousin of Mine," backed with "That's Where It's At"—the last 45 of Cooke's lifetime—is released. It gives him another top forty hit on the pop chart.

November 16, 1964

Cooke cuts "Shake" during one of his final sessions, in Los Angeles. The musicians include a guitarist destined for fame: Bobby Womack.

DECEMBER 11, 1964: Death of a legend

The elegance of Sam Cooke's image as a star was utterly at odds with the brutality of his death. In Los Angeles, the star—though married to his high school sweetheart—checked into a motel with twenty-two-year-old Elisa Boyer (testifying, left). She claimed that Cooke "began to rip my clothes off," and that she fled when he went to the bathroom. Enraged, the singer—drunk and partially clad—charged into the office of motel manager Bertha Franklin in search of her. In the ensuing scuffle, Franklin fired shots from her pistol, the last of which penetrated Cooke's lungs and heart. She finished the job by breaking a stick over his head. With no witnesses, there was speculation about motives. Smokey Robinson ❶ and Muhammad Ali were among the mourners at Cooke's funeral.

❶ 031

SAM COOKE

super producer

Phil Spector
1939–present

From The Beatles 046▶ to Bruce Springsteen 150▶ and The Righteous Brothers to the Ramones 158▶, Phil Spector had an incalculable impact on music.

Few producers have created such an identifiable sound—one that knocked Brian Wilson sideways when he heard The Ronettes' "Be My Baby," and so inspired Springsteen that he created "Born to Run" as a sonic homage. As Spector once told U.K. newspaper the *Daily Telegraph*, "I knew that Mozart was more important than his operas; that Beethoven was more important than whoever was playing or conducting his music. That's what I wanted to be."

His rock 'n' roll associations began in high school, when he played in Sleepwalkers with other future stars Sandy "Let There Be Drums" Nelson, Bruce Johnston—later to join The Beach Boys 050▶—and Kim Fowley (Svengali for The Runaways). At eighteen, he scored a chart-topper with The Teddy Bears' "To Know Him Is to Love Him"—the words on his father's tombstone—then began to build his legendary Wall of Sound. "Little symphonies for the kids," he called his groundbreaking singles.

After a string-laden mix of The Beatles' swan song *Let It Be* that infuriated McCartney, Spector helmed albums by Lennon (*John Lennon/Plastic Ono Band*, *Imagine*, *Some Time in New York City*, and *Rock 'n' Roll*) and Harrison (*All Things Must Pass* and *Concert for Bangla Desh*) in the Seventies. His last major credits graced *Death of a Ladies Man* by Leonard Cohen 106▶ and *End of the Century* by the Ramones, yet his sound is still the yardstick for all ambitious pop productions.

1939+
1964+
1970+

December 26, 1939
Harvey Phillip Spector is born in New York City. His father kills himself when Spector is nine.

August 1958
The Teddy Bears' "To Know Him Is to Love Him"—written and produced by Spector—is released.

December 1960
"Spanish Harlem"—co-written by Spector, and sung by Ben E. King—is released.

1961–63: Building the Wall of Sound

Having relocated to Los Angeles, Spector assembled a crack core team, including arranger Jack Nitzsche, former Duane Eddy backing singer Darlene Love, and percussionist Sonny Bono (whose future wife, Cher, sang uncredited on several Spector hits). Early smashes on his Philles label included The Crystals' "He's a Rebel" and "Da Doo Ron Ron." The success accelerated in 1963 with the advent of a trio led by Veronica "Ronnie" Bennett (left, with Spector, whom she married in April 1968). This trio, called the Ronettes, duly debuted with the astounding "Be My Baby." The producer's other triumph that year, the album *A Christmas Gift for You (from Phil Spector)*, flopped in the wake of President Kennedy's assassination in November, but has proved a perennial favorite ever since.

28   WHO PUT THE BOMP IN THE BOMP BA BOMP

February 4, 1964

With Gene Pitney, Spector sits in on a Rolling Stones session. He contributes to a handful of songs destined for their debut LP.

February 6, 1965

The Righteous Brothers' soon-to-be classic "You've Lost That Lovin' Feelin'"—which Spector produced and co-wrote—tops the U.S. chart.

August 28, 1965

The Righteous Brothers release "Hung on You." It will rapidly be eclipsed by its B-side: a version of "Unchained Melody."

November 29, 1965

Spector produces *The Big T.N.T. Show*, showcasing mostly new stars (including The Lovin' Spoonful, who he tries in vain to sign to Philles).

JUNE 1966: "River Deep, Mountain High"

❶ 044
❷ 054
❸ 030

Having met The Beatles❶ and The Rolling Stones❷, it initially seemed that Phil Spector would step up to the British Invasion in the U.S.A. But he lost the battle after, contrarily, one of his greatest productions: 1966's "River Deep—Mountain High," performed by Ike and Tina Turner (left), a duo he had met while producing the documentary *The Big T.N.T. Show*. Featuring future stars Glen Campbell on guitar and Leon Russell on keyboards, the song was rightly acclaimed in Europe, but a flop at home. Wounded, Spector wrapped up the Philles label and began to focus on a career in film. The label's final single was "A Love Like Yours (Don't Come Knockin' Every Day)"—written by former Motown❸ whizzes Holland-Dozier-Holland and performed by Ike and Tina.

January 27, 1970

Spector produces "Instant Karma!" for John Lennon, who suggests giving Spector tapes of the abandoned 1969 LP, *Get Back*.

May 8, 1970

The resulting album, *Let It Be*, is released. McCartney hates it; three decades later he will issue *Let It Be . . . Naked*, stripped of Spector's sound.

February 1974

After filing papers in 1972, Phil Spector is granted a divorce from "Ronnie" Bennett. The marriage will be dissected in her 1991 book, *Be My Baby*.

May 1975

Dion DiMucci's *Born to Be with You* is released on its producer's new label, Phil Spector International. Neither album nor label prove to be successful.

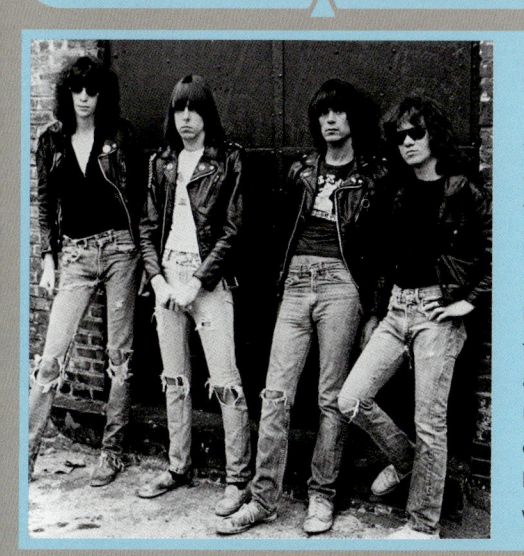

JANUARY 1980: The Ramones connection

❶ 158
❷ 142

"This is ten times more powerful than we've ever been in the studio," Joey Ramone enthused to *Trouser Press* about working with Phil Spector, "like you're getting blown up!" The union between the producer and the punk pioneers began with his mixing of two tracks for their movie *Rock 'n' Roll High School* (1979). "We're pals," Joey explained, "and have thought about getting together for some time." From there they progressed to *End of the Century* (1980), featuring a cover of The Ronettes' "Baby, I Love You," which gave the Ramones❶ their only top ten hit. Other tracks include one of the band's finest numbers: "Do You Remember Rock 'n' Roll Radio?" (later covered by Kiss❷). Spector, Joey reported, was "a little temperamental," but "a gas to work with."

PHIL SPECTOR   29

legendary label

Motown
1959–present

1959+ 1961+ 1964+ 1965+ 1970+

Long before Iggy Pop 116▶, Madonna 208▶, and The White Stripes 272▶ put Michigan on the musical map, Berry Gordy turned its largest city, Detroit, into the center of the pop universe. Gordy first hit the top ten as co-writer of Jackie Wilson's 1958 "Lonely Teardrops," the success of which he used as a springboard for the Tamla and Motown labels (and their subsidiaries).

Motown's polished, poppy R&B proved both popular and highly inspirational. The Beatles 044▶ covered Smokey Robinson's "You Really Got a Hold on Me," and The Rolling Stones 054▶ had a go at Barrett Strong's "Money." ("We thought we were the only people who knew that tune," said Mick Jagger, "and when we went to the North of England, we found everyone had done it. It was really funny.")

Motown stamped its mark on the Sixties with Smokey, Marvin Gaye 036▶, Stevie Wonder, the Four Tops, The Supremes, and The Temptations. With Marvin and Stevie blazing a trail in the Seventies, the label became almost as well known for classic albums as for perennial singles (though there were plenty of the latter, thanks to emerging superstars, such as Diana Ross and The Jackson 5).

Rick James and Lionel Richie flew the flag in the Eighties, with hits such as "Super Freak" and "Say You, Say Me." The Nineties saw the company's most spectacular sales, thanks to Boyz II Men, and renewed credibility in the form of Erykah Badu.

Although Motown has now been swallowed by the Universal group, it retains a huge presence, due to mega-sellers such as Akon and Colbie Caillat.

January 1959

Berry Gordy founds the Tamla Record Company, which debuts with a single by Marv Johnson. Tamla becomes Motown in 1960.

November 7, 1959

Smokey Robinson marries his Miracles bandmate Claudette Rogers. To honor the label, they name their children Berry and Tamla.

January 1960

Motown moves into its first headquarters on West Grand Boulevard, Detroit. A sign outside reads "Hitsville USA."

JANUARY 16, 1961: Motown scores its first No. 1

Motown's first R&B chart-topper—"Shop Around" by The Miracles—was co-written by label boss, Berry Gordy, and his right-hand man, William "Smokey" Robinson. Robinson (left) proved to be one of pop's finest writers. As well as classics such as "The Tracks of My Tears" and "Tears of a Clown," he penned gems such as Mary Wells' "My Guy," Marvin Gaye's❶ "Ain't That Peculiar," The Temptations'❷ "My Girl," and the Four Tops' "Still Water (Love)." Despite being much younger than Gordy, Robinson—barely in his twenties—was made vice-president of Motown before 1961 was out. "He's been offered all kinds of deals to leave," Gordy told the *Sunday Times* in 1970. "He's been offered a million dollars cash." But he stayed with the company for more than three decades, during which his songs were covered countless times and he influenced artists from Pete Townshend of The Who❸ to D'Angelo.

❶ 036
❷ 033
❸ 068

MOTOWN 31

December 11, 1961
....
The Marvelettes' debut "Please Mr. Postman"—written by Brian Holland and later covered by The Beatles—is Motown's first No. 1 pop hit.

June 1962
....
Brian Holland, Lamont Dozier, and Holland's brother Eddie unite to form one of music's most formidable writing and production partnerships.

October 20, 1962
....
The Contours' rowdy "Do You Love Me" (written by Berry Gordy and released on the Motown subsidiary Gordy) enters the top five of the pop chart.

April 1963
....
"You Beat Me to the Punch"—by Motown's then most consistent hitmaker, Mary Wells—earns the label its first Grammy nomination.

1963: Little Stevie Wonder hits big

Despite featuring Marvin Gaye❶ on drums, "Little" Stevie Wonder's early releases made no impact on the charts. He had been signed to the Motown subsidiary Tamla after a tip from his cousin, Ronnie White of The Miracles, and proved a knockout at the label's shows. Berry Gordy duly decided to issue live recordings: the results of which were his first hit, "Fingertips," and *Little Stevie Wonder: The 12 Year Old Genius* (both 1963). The latter became Motown's first No. 1 album and the first live recording to top the chart—and made Wonder, then thirteen, the youngest person to reach the pinnacle. He struck another No. 1 with 1974's *Fulfillingness' First Finale*, but his finest achievement came in 1976, when *Songs in the Key of Life* entered atop the U.S. chart—only the third album to do so. This classic is one of Motown's most enduring success stories, selling ten million copies in the U.S.A. alone.

April 15, 1964
....
Marvin Gaye releases *Together*, a collection of duets with Mary Wells. It's his first album to enter the Top 200 chart in *Billboard*.

August 22, 1964
....
Martha & the Vandellas' "Dancing in the Street" is released. It is later a hit for Van Halen (1982), and Mick Jagger with David Bowie (1985).

March 6, 1965
....
The Temptations—originally known as The Primes—achieve their first No. 1 hit with their now-famous, signature tune "My Girl."

May 22, 1965
....
"I'll Be Doggone," which is co-written by Smokey Robinson and features The Miracles, gives Marvin Gaye a No. 1 on the R&B chart.

JUNE 12, 1965: The Supremes conquer all

When "Back in My Arms Again" topped *Billboard*'s Hot 100 chart in June 1965, The Supremes became the only U.S. group to release five consecutive No. 1s—quite an achievement for an act long dismissed in-house at Motown as "The No-Hit Supremes." Seven more chart-toppers bagged them most No. 1s by a U.S. band. The last of these was the ironically titled "Someday We'll Be Together," credited to Diana Ross & The Supremes but featuring only Ross, with songwriter Johnny Bristol. Mary Wilson and Cindy Birdsong (who had replaced founder Florence Ballard) continued with Jean Terrell, but were upstaged by Ross. Long groomed for solo stardom by Gordy, she ultimately added six more No. 1s to her tally (the last being a platinum-selling collaboration with another Motown star, Lionel Richie: 1981's "Endless Love"). Ross also helped launch pop's most famous brothers—the Jackson 5.

WHO PUT THE BOMP IN THE BOMP BA BOMP

August 15, 1965

Brenda Holloway, one of Motown's most overlooked singers, opens for The Beatles' U.S. tour, at Shea Stadium in New York.

November 1, 1965

The Miracles' classic album *Going to a Go-Go* is issued. Its title track will be one of several Motown covers by The Rolling Stones (1982).

April 1967

Marvin Gaye and Tammi Terrell form one of the era's most successful duos, with hits such as "If I Could Build My Whole World Around You."

December 14, 1968

Motown holds the top three spots on the *Billboard* Hot 100, thanks to Marvin Gaye, Diana Ross & The Supremes, and Stevie Wonder.

MARCH 12, 1969: The award-winning Temptations

❶ 031

The "Emperors of Soul" had started scoring hits in 1962, peaking early with "My Girl." But the songs that made them one of Motown's classiest acts began with "Ain't Too Proud to Beg" in 1966. This track marked the replacement of their producer Smokey Robinson❶ with Norman Whitfield, who married their astonishing vocals to equally stupendous productions. In March 1969, The Temptations' "Cloud Nine" earned the label its first Grammy and, as Motown's official history notes, ushered in "the new sound of 'psychedelic soul.'" Appropriately, "Psychedelic Shack" was their first Seventies hit, paving the way for blockbusters such as 1971's "Ball of Confusion (That's What the World Is Today)" and 1972's "Papa Was a Rollin' Stone." All were written by Whitfield and Barrett Strong, the duo who gave Motown an early hit with "Money" and who also penned Edwin Starr's storming "War," issued on the Gordy subsidiary.

March 14, 1970

Rare Earth have a hit with The Temptations' "Get Ready" on Motown imprint Rare Earth, home to cult favorite R. Dean Taylor.

March 16, 1970

Two and a half years after collapsing into Marvin Gaye's arms onstage in Virginia, Tammi Terrell dies of a brain tumor, aged twenty-four—a devastating blow for Gaye.

June 3, 1970

The effervescent "Signed, Sealed, Delivered, I'm Yours"—another huge pop/R&B crossover hit by Stevie Wonder (who is just twenty)—is unleashed.

July 6, 1970

Marvin Gaye records vocals for "What's Going On." It is completed in September, but Motown initially refuses to issue it, viewing it as too political to be a hit.

1970: The Jackson 5 make their mark

❶ 036
❷ 122
❸ 122

With Marvin Gaye❶, The Temptations (see above), and Stevie Wonder (see above left) focusing on increasingly weighty songs, Motown's pop success was reinvigorated by five brothers from Gary, Indiana: Jackie, Tito, Jermaine, Marlon, and Michael Jackson❷. Although first tipped to Motown by Gladys Knight, The Jackson 5❸ were presented as protégés of Diana Ross. They made a spectacular debut with the irresistible "I Want You Back," which—combined with three further chart-toppers ("ABC," "The Love You Save," and "I'll Be There")—helped make 1970 Motown's best year to date. As a group, they never hit such heights on the label again, although "Dancing Machine" was a smash in 1974, two years before they decamped to Epic to became The Jacksons. Randy Jackson replaced Jermaine, whose 1973 marriage to Berry Gordy's daughter doubtless influenced his decision to stick with Motown.

MOTOWN 33

Turn On, Tune In, Drop Out

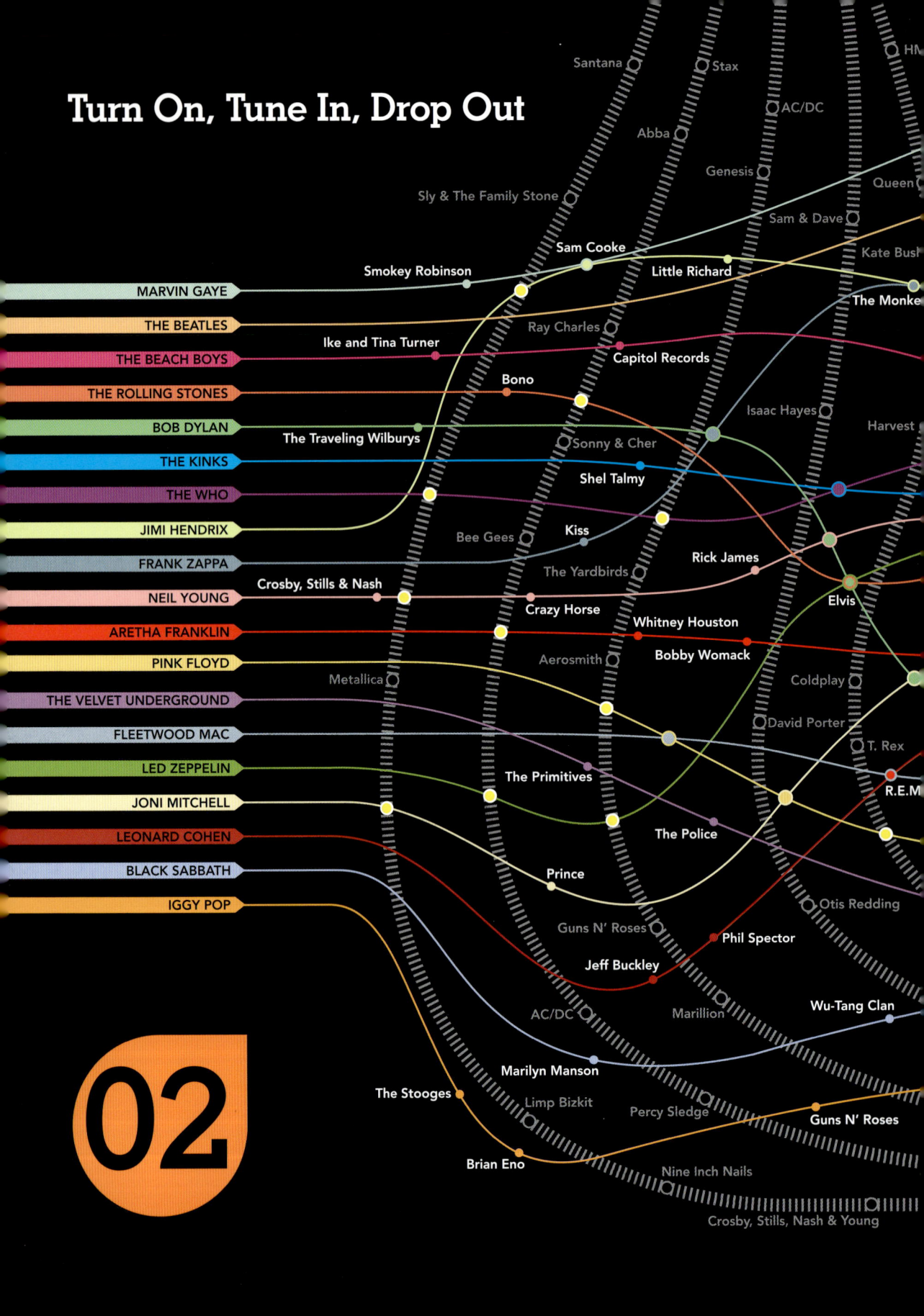

02

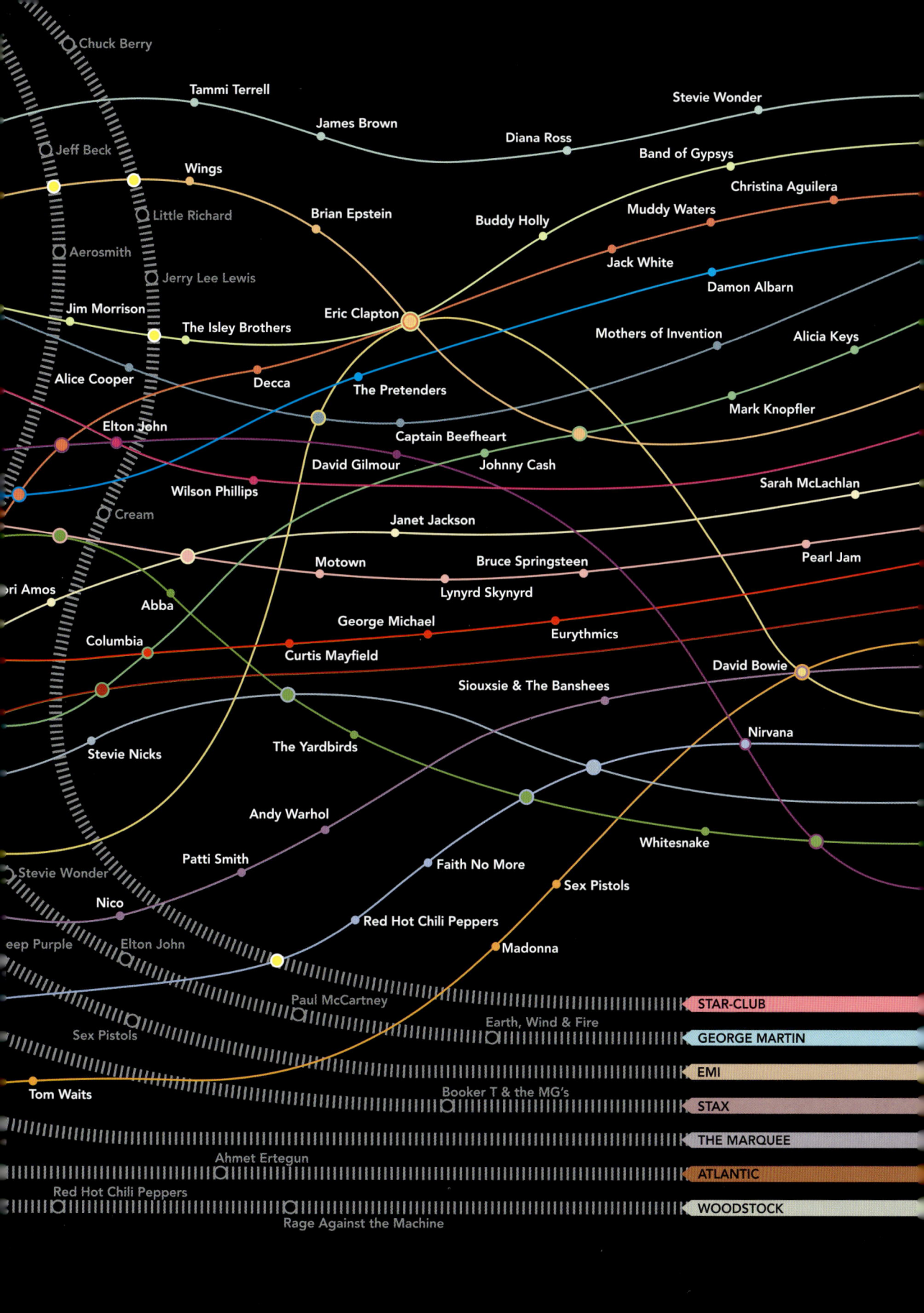

Chuck Berry
Tammi Terrell
Stevie Wonder
James Brown
Diana Ross
Band of Gypsys
Jeff Beck
Wings
Christina Aguilera
Little Richard
Muddy Waters
Brian Epstein
Buddy Holly
Aerosmith
Jack White
Jerry Lee Lewis
Damon Albarn
Eric Clapton
Jim Morrison
Mothers of Invention
Alicia Keys
The Isley Brothers
Alice Cooper
Decca
Mark Knopfler
The Pretenders
Elton John
Captain Beefheart
David Gilmour
Johnny Cash
Sarah McLachlan
Wilson Phillips
Cream
Janet Jackson
Pearl Jam
Motown
Bruce Springsteen
Lynyrd Skynyrd
Tori Amos
Abba
George Michael
Columbia
Curtis Mayfield
Eurythmics
David Bowie
Siouxsie & The Banshees
Stevie Nicks
The Yardbirds
Nirvana
Andy Warhol
Whitesnake
Patti Smith
Faith No More
Stevie Wonder
Sex Pistols
Nico
Red Hot Chili Peppers
Deep Purple
Elton John
Madonna
Paul McCartney
STAR-CLUB
Earth, Wind & Fire
GEORGE MARTIN
Sex Pistols
EMI
Booker T & the MG's
Tom Waits
STAX
THE MARQUEE
Ahmet Ertegun
ATLANTIC
Red Hot Chili Peppers
WOODSTOCK
Rage Against the Machine

Marvin Gaye 1939–84

1939+ 1972+

Rock history's select band of drummers-turned-successful front men includes Phil Collins of Genesis, Chris Cornell of Soundgarden, and Steven Tyler of Aerosmith ◁154▷. Marvin Gaye also did rather well after drumming on Motown ◁030▷ classics such as Stevie Wonder's "Fingertips," Martha & the Vandellas' "Dancing in the Street," The Miracles' "Shop Around," and The Marvelettes' "Please Mr. Postman." After some minor successes and flops, he hit big with 1963's "Pride and Joy," and was rarely off the charts for the next six years.

He duly starred with James Brown ◁022▷ and The Rolling Stones ◁054▷ in the 1964 musical showcase *The T.A.M.I. Show*. "The hippest one on the whole T.A.M.I. Show was Marvin Gaye," enthused Rolling Stones drummer Charlie Watts, ". . . a lovely guy."

An impressive run of classics peaked with the 1968 gem "I Heard It Through the Grapevine" (see above right). But Gaye was then sent into a tailspin by the death of his singing partner Tammi Terrell in 1970. In addition, he had severe financial problems, his marriage to Anna Gordy was proving difficult, and he felt pressure to deliver more and more hits.

The result of this personal turmoil was one of music's most remarkable reinventions: from three-minute love songs to the lush suite of social commentary that comprised 1971's *What's Going On*. Later albums on which he played his sex symbol image to the hilt—notably 1973's *Let's Get It On* and 1976's *I Want You*—proved equally potent. Yet the *thoughtful* songwriter image of *What's Going On* was the one that lingered.

April 2, 1939

Marvin Gay is born. The "e" later added to the end of his surname is a tribute to Sam Cooke. Initially signed to Motown subsidiary Anna, Gaye will graduate to Tamla in 1960.

December 1962

Gaye issues his first pop top forty hit "Hitch Hike," the riff of which, as Lou Reed admits, will be recycled on The Velvet Underground's "There She Goes Again."

January 1965

"I'll Be Doggone"—the first of Gaye's twelve R&B No. 1s—is released. It is produced and co-written by Gaye's friend and fellow Motowner Smokey Robinson.

DECEMBER 14, 1968: Grapevine triumph

Marvin Gaye (left, with Motown's ❶ Barney Ales) finally topped the U.S. chart in 1968 with "I Heard It Through the Grapevine." Displacing The Supremes' "Love Child," it stayed at No. 1 for seven weeks. This success might have come sooner had the label not withheld its release for a version by Gladys Knight. Gaye's rendering—superbly produced by Norman Whitfield—has since inspired covers by acts from Creedence Clearwater Revival to the Kaiser Chiefs. One of the most successful was by the fictional group The California Raisins (voiced by Buddy Miles, drummer in Jimi Hendrix's ❷ Band of Gypsys). This 1986 version, created on behalf of the California Raisin Advisory Board, spawned TV specials, albums, and even a cartoon series for the singing raisins! The fruity group's success also enabled their label, Priority, to bankroll gangsta rap pioneers N.W.A.'s ❸ classic album, *Straight Outta Compton*.

❶ 030
❷ 072
❸ 256

November 21, 1972

"Trouble Man," the title track of a soundtrack by Gaye, is issued as a single, the lyrics aptly evoking Gaye's troubles at the time.

October 26, 1973

Diana & Marvin is released. Much of it was recorded in separate studios as Gaye refused to stop smoking dope while he and Ross worked.

December 15, 1978

Here, My Dear is released. The double album dissects the end of his marriage to Anna Gordy—to whom Gaye is required to give half of the LP's royalties.

December 30, 1982

Midnight Love, featuring the hit "Sexual Healing," goes gold in the U.S.A. Gaye's all-time best-seller will later turn triple platinum.

APRIL 1, 1984: Death of a troubled man

Long plagued by depression and drug use, Gaye hit rock bottom when his house was repossessed—obliging him to move back to his parents' home. The star's relationship with his father had long been fraught (the additional "e" in his surname had helped to distance him from Marvin, Sr.). On April 1, 1984, mounting tensions in the house culminated in a fight between the two, which ended when Marvin, Sr. shot his son with a gun that the star had given him for Christmas. (It has been speculated that Gaye provoked his father, as a roundabout route to suicide.) Three days later, 10,000 mourners gathered to view Gaye's body at Forest Lawn Memorial Park in Los Angeles (left). His father received five years' probation for killing his son, and died in a nursing home, aged eighty-four, in October 1998. When asked whether he had loved his son, Marvin, Sr. responded, "Let's say that I didn't dislike him."

MARVIN GAYE 37

iconic club

Star-Club
1962–69

From Bo Diddley to Black Sabbath ⓘ108▶, there was certainly no shortage of legends and soon-to-be legends who played at the Star-Club in Hamburg, Germany. However, no one did more for its reputation than The Beatles ⓘ044▶. "A man with a beard cut off said—'Will you go to Germany and play mighty rock for the peasants for money?'" wrote John Lennon. "And we said we would play mighty anything for money."

Manfred Weissleder—formerly an electrician in the Reeperbahn red light district—opened the club, on Grosse Freiheit 39, with the "Rock and Twist Parade" on April 13, 1962. The bill featured The Bachelors, Tex Roberg & The Graduates, Roy Young, and the four Liverpudlian scruffs—at that time consisting of John Lennon, Paul McCartney, George Harrison, and Pete Best. The not-yet Fab Four were the opening act.

With bitter irony, the group were informed, on their arrival at Hamburg airport, of the death of former bassist Stuart Sutcliffe. (The bearer of this sad news, Sutcliffe's German girlfriend Astrid Kirchherr, is often credited, erroneously, in her view, with giving the group their famous "moptop" hairdos.) Better news came for the band in May of the same year, when they learned that EMI ⓘ048▶ had requested an audition from them.

The Beatles' residency at the Star-Club continued through May 1962, when they were joined by Tony Sheridan and Gerry & The Pacemakers. "Hamburg bordered on the best of Beatles times," recalled Harrison. "We didn't have any luxury, we didn't have any bathrooms or clothes, we were grubby, we couldn't afford anything . . . but, on the other hand, we weren't yet famous, so we didn't have to contend with the bullshit that comes with fame."

Jerry Lee Lewis
"Live" at the Star-Club, Hamburg
(1965)
Philips

Black Sabbath
Black Sabbath
(1970)
Vertigo

The Beatles
Live! at the Star-Club in Hamburg, Germany; 1962
(1977)
Lingasong

Manfred Weissleder, determined that the club's attractions would live up to its name, booked big stars, including Ray Charles, The Everly Brothers, Gene Vincent, Little Richard, Jerry Lee Lewis, and Bo Diddley. Meanwhile, The Beatles returned to the club in November 1962, by which stage Ringo Starr—formerly with fellow Hamburg veterans Rory Storme & The Hurricanes—had replaced Pete Best on drums. During this stint, the Fab Four got the chance to share a bill with their idol, Little Richard.

On the final night of the engagement—during which The Beatles scored their first hit at home, "Love Me Do"—the club's stage manager recorded most of the acts. These tapes were later released, without the group's consent, as the 1977 album *Live! at the Star-Club in Hamburg, Germany; 1962*. The music confirmed that the group had more energy than expertise; nonetheless, other British "beat" groups, including The Searchers and The Swingin' Blue Jeans, followed their lead of using the club as a training ground and stepping stone.

By the end of the Sixties, rock 'n' roll had shifted from clubs to arenas. Many smaller venues, unable to afford the fees that the acts now commanded, turned into discos, or closed. The Star-Club shut its doors on December 31, 1969, after a show by Spencer Davis Group alumni Eddie Hardin and Peter York. The venue then became Salambo, a live sex club, which was destroyed by fire in February 1983, rebuilt, then razed three years later to make way for a shopping complex. There was one final, ironic legacy. Early Nineties British band Starclub—named after the club—would be totally unknown, had drummer Alan White not graduated to the all-conquering Oasis 260▶: an act who founded much of their career on ideas looted from . . . The Beatles!

Little Richard November 1962

Richard Wayne Penniman was one of the founding fathers of rock 'n' roll, thanks to pyrotechnic hits like 1955's "Tutti-Frutti" and 1957's "Lucille." Having abandoned rock 'n' roll for evangelism for over four years, he began a comeback tour in 1962. When he shared a bill with The Beatles❶ at the Star-Club in November, his band included Billy Preston, later to play with both the Fab Four and The Rolling Stones❷.

Jerry Lee Lewis April 1964

Having switched from the Sun❶ label to Smash, Lewis first cut "Pen and Paper," which returned him to the U.S. country chart in 1964. Then, on April 5, he cut "*Live*" *at the Star-Club, Hamburg*. "Not an album," enthused *Rolling Stone*, "it's a crime scene: Jerry Lee Lewis❷ slaughters his rivals in a thirteen-song set that feels like one long convulsion." It includes Elvis'❸ "Hound Dog" and Ray Charles' "What'd I Say."

Star-Club
1962–69

Chuck Berry June 1964

This root of the rock 'n' roll tree played the club in 1964. Berry's singles that year included three of his all-time greats: "Promised Land," "You Never Can Tell," and "No Particular Place to Go." "His lyrics are absolutely brilliant," enthused Keith Richards. "Succint, original, witty, so cutting and filthy." In November, Berry issued *St. Louis to Liverpool*, its title referring to his influence on U.K. acts.

Gene Vincent July and August 1964

The Virginia-born rock 'n' roller, best known for the 1956 hit "Be-Bop-A-Lula," played the club in 1964. (In May that year, in London, he had recorded "Long Tall Sally" and "Good Golly, Miss Molly," first cut by another Star-Club player, Little Richard.) Having survived the 1960 car crash that killed Eddie Cochran, Vincent regularly toured in Europe. He died in October 1971 from a ruptured stomach ulcer.

TURN ON, TUNE IN, DROP OUT

Cream February 25, 1967

Guitarist Eric Clapton❶, drummer Ginger Baker, and bassist Jack Bruce were a pioneering power trio and supergroup. They made an unofficial debut at a club in Manchester, England, in July 1966—two days before a more high-profile unveiling at a festival in Windsor. After playing the Star-Club in 1967, they topped the bill at a festival in England's Lincolnshire in May, with fans of theirs: Hendrix❷ and Pink Floyd❸.

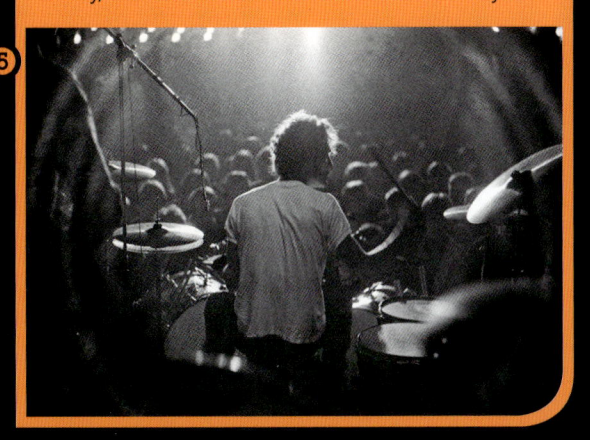

Jimi Hendrix March 1967

When The Jimi Hendrix❶ Experience—featuring drummer Mitch Mitchell and bassist Noel Redding—played the Star-Club, audiences enjoyed some of their best-known hits, including "Foxy Lady," "Hey Joe," "Stone Free," and "Purple Haze." At later shows elsewhere, Hendrix would cover the club's best known alumni, The Beatles❷ (including "Day Tripper" and "Sgt. Pepper's Lonely Hearts Club Band").

Black Sabbath August 1969

These heavy metal pioneers, then still known as Earth (an improvement on their previous name, The Polka Tulk Blues Band) played a seven-night stint at the Star-Club. Their support act was Junior's Eyes, whose alumni include Rick Wakeman, and whose name would provide the title for a song on Sabbath's❶ last album with singer Ozzy Osbourne (a devoted fan of The Beatles❷), 1978's *Never Say Die!*

Yes August 20, 1969

In September 1968, prog rock gods Yes❶ had replaced Sly & The Family Stone❷ at London club Blaises. Their success secured them gigs at London's legendary Marquee❸, then they played the Star-Club in August 1969. Their lineup—which became nuttily complex in later years—was founders Jon Anderson (vocals) and Chris Squire (bass), with drummer Bill Bruford, keyboardist Tony Kaye, and guitarist Peter Banks.

STAR-CLUB 41

George Martin

super producer

1926–present

1926+   1976+

Although George Martin's discography ranges from UFO to Ultravox, Jeff Beck to Celine Dion, and Peter Sellers to Earth, Wind & Fire, his legacy is inextricably entwined with The Beatles ⓞ₄₄▸. However, as he told *Mojo*, "I wasn't at all impressed by their music. I thought they were crap."

Having joined EMI ⓞ₄₈▸ in 1950, Martin was given responsibility for its Parlophone imprint. He honed his production techniques on comedy records by the likes of Peter Ustinov, and Spike Milligan and Peter Sellers of The Goons. "I was getting very involved on the floor," Martin told the BBC, "instead of just being in the control room saying, 'Yes, that's nice,' or, 'You're singing a bit flat.'"

Impressed more by The Beatles' charisma than by their music, he signed them in 1962. "They were," he recalled, "doing 'Roll Over Beethoven' and 'Over the Rainbow'—a weird collection of songs—and their own material was 'The One After 909,' 'P. S. I Love You,' nothing great. The best song I could find was 'Love Me Do.' I didn't think it was a hit, but we put it out. They had one other thing: their attempt at writing a Roy Orbison-style song, called 'Please Please Me.' It was a horrible dirge."

Once Martin had worked his magic, the band's potential was realized. He produced all their albums, as well as later releases such as the 2006 remix set, *Love*. This made him a natural choice to produce the best-selling single of all time, "Candle in the Wind 1997" by Elton John ⓝ₁₂₆▸. In the words of Joe Perry of Aerosmith ⓝ₁₅₄▸—whose 1978 cover of "Come Together" he helmed—"The guy's a genius."

42   TURN ON, TUNE IN, DROP OUT

January 3, 1926
George Martin is born in London, England. By the age of forty, he will help change the face of pop forever by producing The Beatles' classic *Revolver*.

October 1972
Martin reunites briefly with Paul McCartney to produce Wings' title track for the 1973 Bond movie *Live and Let Die*, which is later covered by Guns N' Roses.

April 17, 1974
Martin starts work on *Holiday* by America, for whom he will helm seven albums (including remixing half of their "best of"); making them the act he works most with after The Beatles.

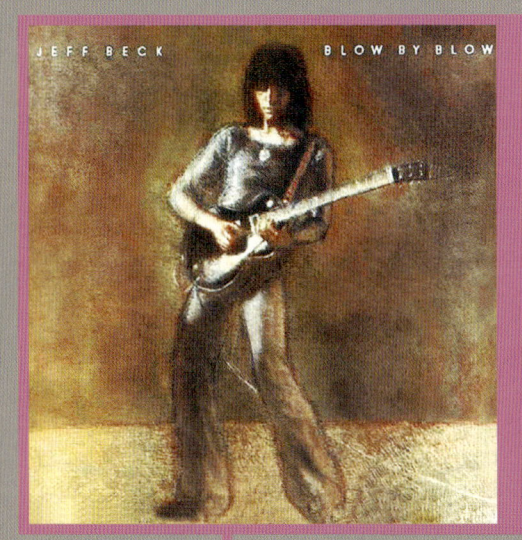

MARCH 1975: Jeff Beck's *Blow by Blow*

❶ 032
❷ 044

"I was advised by someone pretty high in the record industry at that time," remarked George Martin, "who said, 'Don't touch Jeff Beck, because he's a loser.'" The unlikely pairing of the unpredictable guitar hero and the dependable producer defied the skeptics: *Blow by Blow* gave Beck his first gold album in the U.S.A., despite its seemingly uncommercial, instrumental jazz fusion. It included covers of two songs by Stevie Wonder❶ (who originally wrote "Superstition" for Beck), as well as "She's a Woman" by The Beatles❷. "The only raised eyebrows I got from Jeff," Martin told the BBC, "was when I suggested putting strings on a couple of tracks ['Diamond Dust' and 'Scatterbrain']." The partnership continued for the 1976 classic *Wired*, this time with platinum-selling results.

1976
Release of American Flyer's debut LP, featuring The Velvet Underground's Doug Yule. Martin calls it "the biggest bomb I'd made."

May 5, 1977
The Beatles at the Hollywood Bowl—mixed, and with liner notes, by Martin—goes gold in the U.S.A. within one day of its release. It will promptly gain platinum status, too.

July 24, 1978
The *Sgt. Pepper's Lonely Hearts Club Band* movie is released to critical disdain. The George Martin-produced soundtrack includes gems by Aerosmith and Earth, Wind & Fire.

October 24, 1980
All Shook Up by the Beatles-inspired group Cheap Trick is released. "Charming people to work with," says Martin. "Great fun, and good musicians."

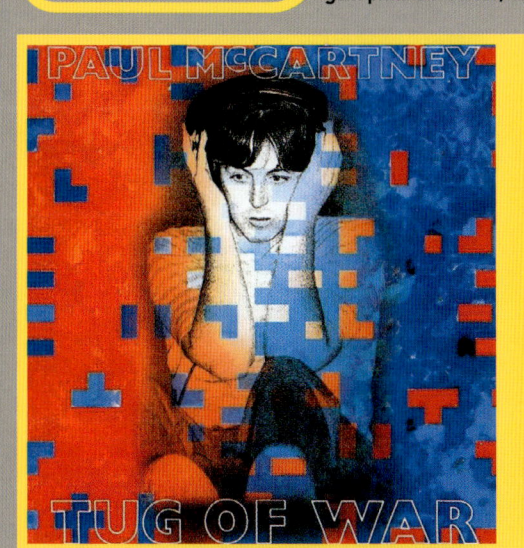

APRIL 1982: McCartney's *Tug of War*

❶ 032

The reunion of Martin and Paul McCartney for their first full-length project since The Beatles' *Abbey Road* was a smash. It featured Ringo Starr, rock 'n' roll legend Carl Perkins, jazz virtuoso Stanley Clarke, and—on two songs, including the chart-topping "Ebony and Ivory"—Stevie Wonder❶. The result was McCartney's first U.S. No. 1 since 1976's *Wings Over America*. Yet triumph was tainted by tragedy: during its recording, John Lennon was murdered. "I rang Paul that morning when I heard the news," Martin told *Billboard*'s Craig Rosen, "and said, 'I don't suppose you want to come in today,' and he said, 'I must come in today; we must work as usual' . . . We chatted most of the day, but at least he got out of his home. It was a tremendous shock for him."

GEORGE MARTIN

The Beatles 1960–present

1940+ 1964+ 1967+ 1973+ 1984+

For such a commercially mindboggling, musical and cultural phenomenon, history's greatest group sure had a bad name. "Why Beatles?" John Lennon wrote in 1960. "Ugh, Beatles, how did the name arrive? So we will tell you. It came in a vision—a man appeared on a flaming pie and said unto them, 'From this day you are Beatles with an *a*.'"

The name was actually inspired by the backing band of Buddy Holly ◀020. "I was looking for a name like The Crickets that meant two things," Lennon told *Merseybeat* magazine. "From Crickets I went to Beatles . . . when you said it, people thought of crawly things; when you read it, it was beat music."

The Fab Four's influence is incalculable. Their songs have been covered by many of the major acts in this book—from "Hey Jude" by Elvis Presley ◀012 to "Helter Skelter" by U2 192▶; from "Something" by James Brown ◀022 to "In My Life" by Johnny Cash ◀018; and from "Day Tripper" by Jimi Hendrix 072▶ to "Across the Universe" by David Bowie 134▶.

The Liverpudlian band's success gave a stay of execution to the EMI 048▶ subsidiary label Parlophone, later the home of Radiohead 264▶, Gorillaz 274▶, and Coldplay 276▶. Their publishing rights were purchased by Michael Jackson 122▶. In 2004, Danger Mouse mashed their so-called "White Album" with *The Black Album* by Jay-Z 266▶ to create one of the Internet's biggest bootlegs: *The Grey Album*. John Lennon's solo classic "Imagine" has been covered by Madonna 208▶, while Oasis 260▶ paid homage to it on "Don't Look Back in Anger." In the words of The Rolling Stones 054▶ Mick Jagger, "Everything to do with The Beatles was sort of gold and glittery."

1940
Richard Starkey (July 7) and John Winston Lennon (October 9) are born in Liverpool. The former will become Ringo Starr, and the latter John Ono Lennon.

June 18, 1942
James Paul McCartney is born in Liverpool. In 1957, he will join Lennon's The Quarrymen, who, with drummer Pete Best and bassist Stuart Sutcliffe, will evolve into The Beatles.

February 24, 1943
George Harrison is born in Liverpool; he will join The Quarrymen in 1958. After names such as Johnny & the Moondogs, the band settle on "The Beatles" in 1960.

❶ 038
❷ 048
❸ 054
❹ 012

1963: Beatlemania begins

The Beatles had honed their act in German venues such as the Star-Club❶ and at home in Liverpool's Cavern Club. By the time they were signed to EMI❷ in 1962 (after rejections from other labels), McCartney had replaced Stuart Sutcliffe as bassist. Pete Best failed to meet producer George Martin's standards and was replaced by Ringo Starr. Their 1962 debut, "Love Me Do," made the U.K. top twenty and paved the way for a chart takeover in 1963. Their fortunes were sealed with key appearances on the U.K.'s *Sunday Night at the London Palladium* in October 1963 (see fans outside the venue, left) and, in early 1964, on America's *The Ed Sullivan Show*. The latter triggered the U.S. "British Invasion"—whose other leading lights, The Rolling Stones❸, had a hit ("I Wanna Be Your Man") penned by Lennon and McCartney. In February 1964, Elvis❹ said: "If these young people can come over here and do well . . . more power to them."

TURN ON, TUNE IN, DROP OUT

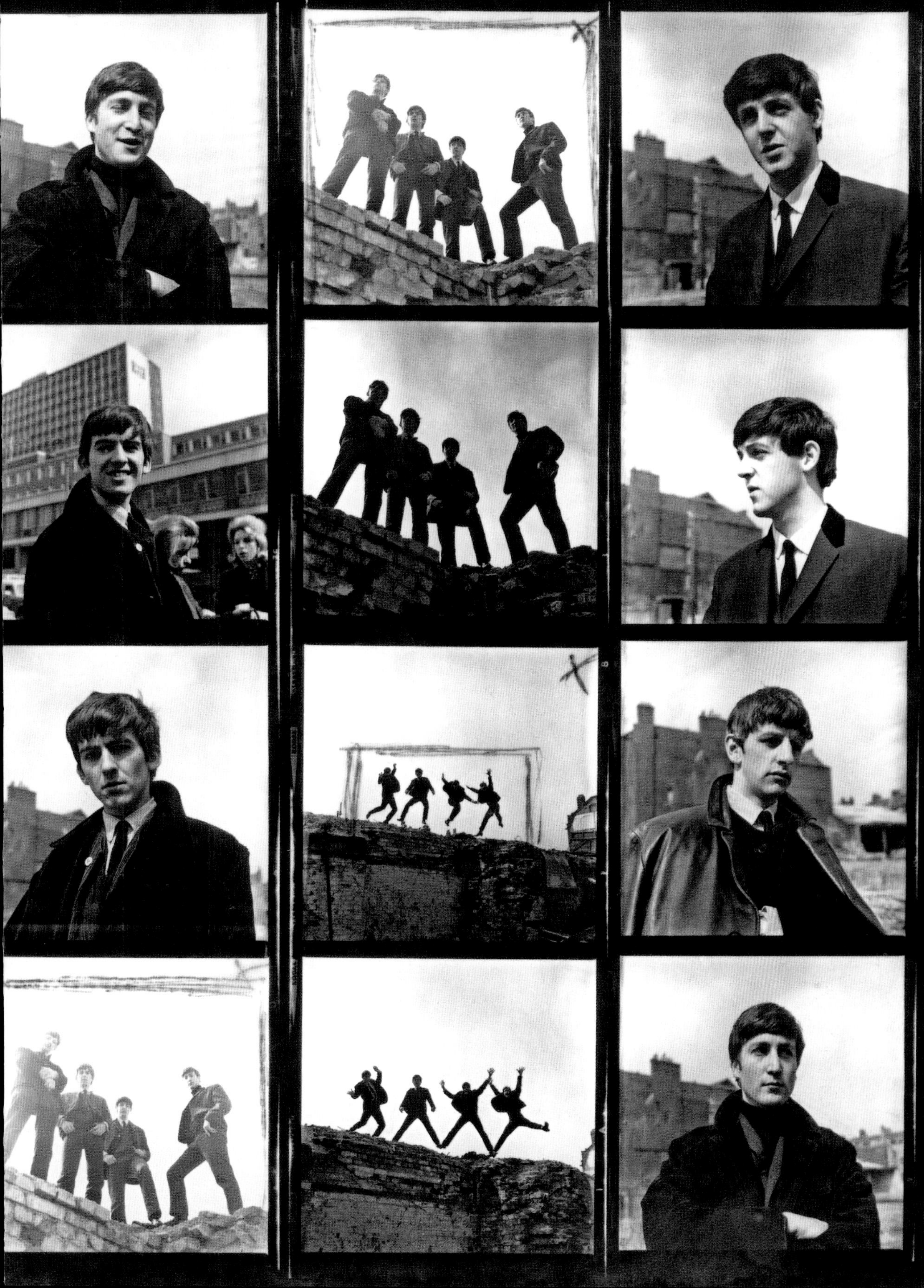

July 6, 1964

A Hard Day's Night, the band's first movie, opens in the U.K. (A young Phil Collins is among the extras.) It will be followed by *Help!*, just over a year later.

August 28, 1964

The Beatles meet Bob Dylan in New York. He introduces them to marijuana but a more obvious influence is on their increasingly poetic lyrics.

October 16, 1965

At Buckingham Palace, the band receive MBEs (Members of the Most Excellent Order of the British Empire), awarded by Her Majesty The Queen.

January 8, 1966

Rubber Soul becomes the band's fourth U.S. No. 1 album in under a year, following *Help!*, *Beatles VI*, and *Beatles '65*.

MARCH 4, 1966: "We're more popular than Jesus."

With the above inadvertently inflammatory remark in London's *Evening Standard*, Lennon incurred international wrath. When the interview ran in the U.S.A. on July 31, such fury erupted that he was obliged to call a press conference to apologize. With unfortunate timing, the band had recently released their latest U.S. No. 1, *"Yesterday" . . . and Today*, in a blood-spattered sleeve, depicting them dismembering plastic dolls. The hysteria barely dented their success: they knocked themselves off the top of the U.S. chart with *Revolver*. The album's first and last tracks alone ("Taxman" and "Tomorrow Never Knows") secured its classic status. On August 29, they played their final live concert (bar a 1969 performance on the rooftop of their London office) in San Francisco. Free to spend more time in the studio, they crafted 1967's sonic steps forward *Sgt. Pepper's Lonely Hearts Club Band* and "Strawberry Fields Forever."

June 1, 1967

Sgt. Pepper's Lonely Hearts Club Band displaces The Monkees' *Headquarters* at the top of the U.S. chart and stays there for the next fifteen weeks.

June 25, 1967

On TV's first worldwide live broadcast, *Our World*, The Beatles perform the newly composed "All You Need is Love," featuring Mick Jagger.

August 27, 1967

The band's visionary manager Brian Epstein is found dead of a drug overdose. A London concert by Jimi Hendrix is cancelled as a mark of respect.

July 17, 1968

The *Yellow Submarine* film opens in the U.K. The band contributes four great new songs, and, impressed with the animation, appear in a brief, live-action coda.

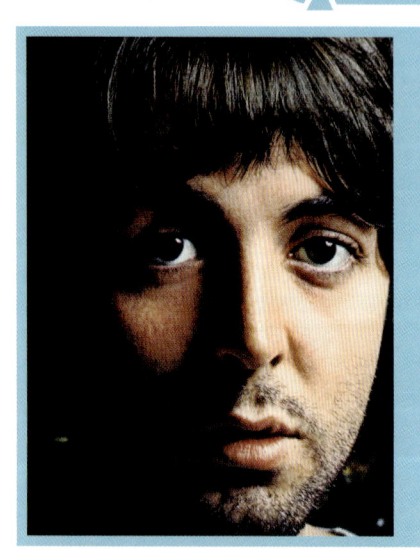

NOVEMBER 22, 1968: "While My Guitar Gently Weeps"

For fans, even *Sgt. Pepper* was eclipsed by 1968's *The Beatles*, a.k.a. "The White Album." (In 2001, *The Beatles* was certified for sales of nineteen million in the U.S.A., making it their official best-seller.) But, as McCartney remarked, "That was *the* big tension album." Lennon was more interested in his new partner, Yoko Ono; Harrison was frustrated at his songs being overlooked; Starr was fed up with his bandmates' mystical indulgences. On April 10, 1970, McCartney announced that he was leaving. Before *Let It Be* limped out in May, he and Starr had issued their own albums. Harrison and Lennon weighed in at year's-end with *All Things Must Pass* and *John Lennon/Plastic Ono Band*. The following year brought Lennon's *Imagine*, featuring Harrison on "How Do You Sleep?," a dig at McCartney. For the remainder of the 1970s, however, McCartney enjoyed the highest profile, with his group, Wings.

TURN ON, TUNE IN, DROP OUT

May 26, 1973

The Beatles / 1967–70 hits U.S. No. 1. It will be replaced by McCartney's *Red Rose Speedway*—which will, in turn, be toppled by Harrison's *Living in the Material World*.

November 28, 1974

John Lennon joins Elton John at Madison Square Garden, New York, to perform three songs, including "I Saw Her Standing There." It will be his last live performance.

January 9, 1975

Four years after McCartney had started legal proceedings, The Beatles' partnership is legally dissolved. Wings begins work on *Venus and Mars*, another No. 1.

September 20, 1975

David Bowie's "Fame," co-written by Lennon, tops the U.S. chart. After a final session in June 1976, for an album by Starr, Lennon will retire for four years.

1980: "Hello Goodbye"

The Eighties began badly when McCartney was jailed in Tokyo, after marijuana was found in his luggage. It was, he explained, "too good to flush down the toilet." There was happier news when his "Coming Up"—"a good piece of work," said Lennon—topped the U.S. chart in June of the same year. In August, Lennon finally resumed recording in New York, and, on December 8, sat in on Ono's session for her "Walking on Thin Ice." Returning home, he was fatally shot by the delusional Mark David Chapman, for whom he had signed an autograph earlier that evening. McCartney paid tribute with "Here Today" on 1982's *Tug of War*; Harrison with "All Those Years Ago" (featuring McCartney and Starr) on 1981's *Somewhere in England*. The tragedy was exacerbated by the revelation that, in November, Lennon had referred to plans for a Beatles reunion show, to be filmed for a long-mooted documentary.

December 25, 1984

Thomas the Tank Engine & Friends, narrated by Starr, debuts on U.S. TV. Starr will return to the stage in 1989 (as will McCartney).

January 16, 1988

Harrison's "Got My Mind Set on You" hits the U.S. No. 1 spot. He and producer Jeff Lynne will form supergroup The Traveling Wilburys.

June 30, 1990

Despite a bill featuring Pink Floyd, Robert Plant, and Jimmy Page among others, McCartney's set is the highlight of a charity concert at Knebworth, England.

December 1–17, 1991

Harrison tours Japan with Eric Clapton, who had played on *The Beatles*. The pair had stayed pals, despite Clapton's relationship with Harrison's former wife, Pattie Boyd.

DECEMBER 4, 1995: The Fab Four fly again

Envisaged as an archival curio, 1994's *Live at the BBC* album had turned multi-platinum. This set the scene for the mid-Nineties *Anthology* series, which was launched with 1995's "Free as a Bird"—a 1977 demo by Lennon, finished by Harrison, McCartney, Starr, and ELO's Jeff Lynne, making it the first "new" Beatles single since 1970. This resurgence of interest in the band added more multi-platinum awards to their tally. In November 1999, they were confirmed as the best-selling act of the century, having sold more than 100 million albums in the U.S.A. alone. Then, in 2000, the hits set *1* became one of pop's all-time best-sellers. Sadly, triumph was tainted by tragedy: Harrison, having survived a 1999 stabbing, succumbed to cancer on November 29, 2001. But Beatles business continued apace: *Love*, a 2006 remix project led by George Martin❶ and his son Giles, was another platinum-selling smash.

THE BEATLES 47

legendary label

EMI
1931–present

The Beatles ◀044, Pink Floyd 086▶, David Bowie 134▶, Queen 144▶, Iron Maiden 190▶, Duran Duran 200▶, Radiohead 264▶, Gorillaz 274▶, and Coldplay 276▶ are among acts who have made EMI one of music's most successful companies.

The EMI label itself was established in 1972, and scored an early hit with "Metal Guru" for T. Rex 128▶. Previously, the company had put its acts on subsidiaries, such as Columbia (Pink Floyd's first home), Parlophone (the Fab Four's alma mater), Harvest (see below), and HMV. The latter—long used as a classical label—was revived for pop purposes when the company signed Morrissey, the former front man of The Smiths 212▶.

EMI's immense success has, inevitably, entailed controversies along the way. After Coldplay's 2005 global best-seller *X&Y*, lead vocalist Chris Martin was horrified to learn that the company's share values partially rested on his band's shoulders. "When people are saying, 'The success of the new Coldplay album is vital to EMI's future,' you just want to curl up and die," he told the U.K.'s *Daily Telegraph*.

In 2004, Radiohead acrimoniously left the label, which promptly issued a "best of" album without the band's consent, while Paul McCartney decamped after four decades, accusing EMI of being "boring."

Notoriously, EMI signed the Sex Pistols 166▶ in 1976, only to drop them after one single, "Anarchy in the U.K." The Pistols responded with the vitriolic "EMI" on *Never Mind the Bollocks*, issued by Virgin. So when EMI bought Virgin, it landed in the novel position of reissuing a song that criticized itself.

1958+

August 9, 1958
British pop icon Cliff Richard signs to the Columbia imprint. Remarkably, his debut "Move It" will score U.K. hits well into the next millennium.

1970+

July 1, 1967
EMI's U.S. label Capitol begins seventeen weeks atop the album chart, with *Sgt. Pepper* and Bobbie Gentry's *Ode to Billie Joe*.

1973+

August 26, 1968
The stirring "Hey Jude" is one of the first four singles issued on The Beatles' label, Apple. (British releases follow four days after U.S. ones.)

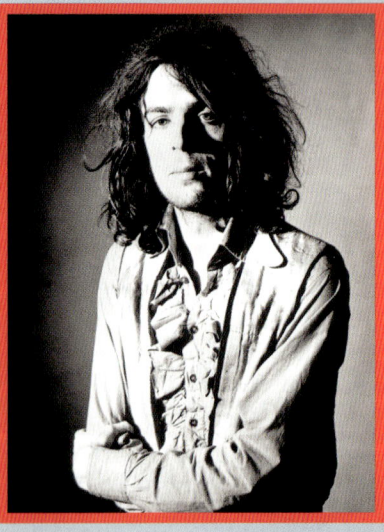

---

❶ 086

1969 ONWARD: Harvest Records

For a niche label founded to showcase the theoretically uncommercial progressive rock genre, Harvest enjoyed spectacular success. Many of its acts were cult favorites—hippy troubadour Kevin Ayers, Pink Floyd's ❶ frazzled founder Syd Barrett (left), Soft Machine (who backed Barrett on *The Madcap Laughs*), Bill Nelson's musical mavericks Be-Bop Deluxe, and post-punk pioneers Wire. The label became a force in hard rock, too, when Deep Purple (see above right) and the Scorpions abandoned prog and riffed their way to the top. But even these mega-sellers were eclipsed by Pink Floyd. Originally on EMI's Columbia imprint, they moved to Harvest for 1969's *More*, and remained on it through 1983's *The Final Cut* (whose political themes contrasted with the label's hippy origins). Abandoned in the mid-Eighties, Harvest was revived for rockers The Beyond in 1991, and is now used for occasional archival releases.

June 13, 1970

Paul McCartney's *McCartney* is knocked off the top of the U.S. chart by The Beatles' *Let It Be*, which has already hit No. 1 in the U.K.

October 24, 1970

Pink Floyd score their first U.K. No. 1 with *Atom Heart Mother*, despite EMI's grim reaction to its cover: a cow, with no band name or title.

October 30, 1971

In a year that began with George Harrison's *All Things Must Pass* at the top of the U.S. chart, John Lennon's *Imagine* now hits the spot.

March 30, 1972

EMI Electrola GmbH is formed in Germany when two smaller labels merge. Kraftwerk will debut on EMI with their fifth album, 1975's *Radio-Activity*.

APRIL 22, 1972: Deep Purple tops the album chart

❶ 076
❷ 108

In their early years, British rock band Deep Purple had made inroads in the U.S.A. but had not troubled chart compilers at home. The tide started to turn with 1970's *In Rock*, which marshaled their quasi-classical leanings into monsters such as "Speed King" and "Child in Time"; and 1971's *Fireball* earned Purple a first U.K. No. 1. But their immortality was sealed by 1972's *Machine Head*, which topped the U.K. album chart. The song from this that really etched the group into legend was "Smoke on the Water," which married a lyric about a fire-ravaged Frank Zappa❶ show to one of rock's most memorable riffs. In 1983, Purple singer Ian Gillan—replaced by future Whitesnake star David Coverdale in 1973—joined fellow founding fathers of metal Black Sabbath❷ (and performed "Smoke on the Water" with them). Founding Purple member Ritchie Blackmore (left) had, meanwhile, formed Rainbow in 1975.

1973

Despite scoring a first U.S. No. 1 with *Dark Side of the Moon*, Pink Floyd quit EMI's U.S. label Capitol for the non-EMI Columbia.

March 5, 1976

EMI reissues The Beatles' U.K. singles. They all hit the chart, while "Yesterday" (not previously issued as a U.K. single) reaches No. 8.

October 8, 1976

The Sex Pistols sign to EMI, only to be dropped after swearing on live TV. The band will immortalize the label as "stupid fools who stand in line," in their song "EMI."

1977

The Rolling Stones sign to EMI. The band will leave in the Eighties, only to return when EMI buys Virgin, to whom they have signed.

MARCH 11, 1978: Kate Bush hits the big time

❶ 086

Just a few months after shooting to fame and fortune with *Dark Side of the Moon* in March 1973, David Gilmour of Pink Floyd❶ oversaw a session by the fifteen-year-old daughter of a friend of a friend. Three years and much work later, she was signed to EMI, who funded further demos and sent her on tour. On March 11, 1978, this hard work finally paid off: "Wuthering Heights" topped the U.K. chart, and the public was introduced to the eccentric genius of Kate Bush (left). Her fame peaked in 1980, when her third album, *Never for Ever*, became the first by a British female artist to top the U.K. chart (which it entered at No. 1). Gilmour also appeared on two of Bush's later (and increasingly infrequent) albums, singing on 1982's *The Dreaming* and playing on 1989's *The Sensual World*. She also sampled a helicopter sound effect from Floyd's *The Wall* for "Waking the Witch," on 1985's sensational *Hounds of Love*.

EMI   49

The Beach Boys 1961–present

1961+ 1968+

Identifying major artists who actually *sound* like The Beach Boys is tricky. They have, however, proved highly influential for nearly five decades.

"I love The Beatles," said Elton John ❰126❱, "but I don't think they influenced me as a songwriter. The Beach Boys' sound and their way of writing and their melodies were a much bigger influence on me." Much of the credit for this wide-ranging effect is due to resident genius, Brian Wilson. Initially content to turn out surf pop, such as "Fun, Fun, Fun" and "I Get Around" with cousin and co-writer Mike Love, Wilson was spurred to more ambitious work by The Ronettes' Phil Spector ❰028❱-produced "Be My Baby," and The Beatles' ❰044❱ *Rubber Soul*.

This sonic evolution culminated in 1966 with *Pet Sounds* (see above right) and the astonishing No. 1, "Good Vibrations." The latter's recording, according to Todd Rundgren ❰140❱ (who covered it in 1976), cost a then unprecedented $75,000. But the public preferred the boys' poppier hits, leaving great albums such as *Friends* (1968), *Sunflower* (1969), and *Love You* (1977) in the shadow of their earlier work.

The distinctive element throughout their history is the band's harmony vocals. Pink Floyd ❰086❱ had hoped to utilize their sunny sound on *The Wall* (1979), but The Beach Boys, other than Bruce Johnston, balked at Floyd's lyrics. (In the end, the recording featured Johnston with a group of soundalikes.) Echoes of the real band's glorious harmonies and ambitious production can be detected in many classics since—from Fleetwood Mac's ❰094❱ *Tusk* to Animal Collective's *Merriweather Post Pavilion*.

December 8, 1961
The Beach Boys debut with "Surfin'," which will scrape into Billboard's Hot 100 two months later. On December 31, they are signed to Capitol Records.

July 16, 1962
The group gets their first paying gig, at the Ritchie Valens Memorial Dance in Long Beach, headlined by Ike and Tina Turner.

April 1965
Bruce Johnston replaces future solo star Glen Campbell, who had himself filled in for Brian Wilson in The Beach Boys' touring incarnation.

1966: *Pet Sounds*

❶ 090
❷ 134
❸ 078

Like The Velvet Underground's❶ *The Velvet Underground & Nico*, The Beach Boys' most enduring classic, *Pet Sounds* (released on May 16, 1966), initially made more of an impact on musicians than on record-buyers—it took more than twenty years to be certified platinum in the U.S.A. Yet its songs have been covered by artists as varied and successful as David Bowie❷ ("God Only Knows"), Aimee Mann ("I Just Wasn't Made for These Times"), Linda Ronstadt ("Don't Talk—Put Your Head on My Shoulder"), the Pixies' Frank Black ("Hang On to Your Ego," the forerunner of "I Know There's an Answer"), and Neil Young❸. Young closed 1972's *Journey Through the Past* with "Let's Go Away for a While," and mentioned "Caroline, No" in 1976's "Long May You Run." The album also helped inspire *Sgt. Pepper's Lonely Hearts Club Band*. "No one is educated musically 'til they've heard *Pet Sounds*," enthused Paul McCartney.

November 22, 1968
The Beatles' "White Album" is released, featuring "Back in the U.S.S.R." McCartney later says, "I wrote that as a kind of Beach Boys parody."

October 1972
"I Get Around" enters the U.S. chart. It will hit No. 1 on Independence Day, before being displaced by The Beach Boys' rivals, The Four Seasons.

July 12, 1974
"California Girls" is issued. It will become one of their most enduring songs, and be covered by Van Halen singer David Lee Roth.

August 14, 1974
Hits set *Endless Summer* far outsells the band's albums of originals like 1970's *Sunflower* and 1971's *Surf's Up*.

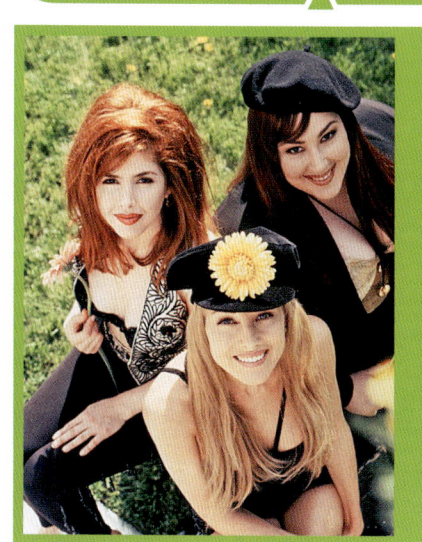

1990: Wilson Phillips' debut

❶ 122

Carnie and Wendy Wilson, daughters of The Beach Boys' Brian, had an unorthodox upbringing. Alice Cooper first met one of them around 1971: "He's holding the kid by the leg, going, 'This is my baby!' I'm going, 'Wow, this guy's gone, man!'" Chynna Phillips, daughter of heroin addict John of The Mamas and the Papas, fared even worse. But musical inspiration was rife, and the three childhood friends went on to form Wilson Phillips. Thanks to three U.S. chart-toppers—including "Hold On"—their self-titled debut album, released on June 9, 1990, sold five million copies within a year in the U.S.A. alone. (Credit is also owed to producer Glen Ballard, who honed his hit-making skills with Michael Jackson❶ and, later, Alanis Morissette.) The female trio split after 1992's *Shadows and Light* but reunited for 2004's *California*. Meanwhile, the sisters teamed with their father for 1997's *The Wilsons*.

THE BEACH BOYS

legendary label

Stax
1961–76

Motown ◁030 may be better known, but Stax produced a plethora of riches. Founded as Satellite Records by Jim Stewart and Estelle Axton in the late Fifties before becoming Stax in 1961, this Memphis label gave the world such classics as Jean Knight's "Mr. Big Stuff," the Staple Singers' "Respect Yourself," and Sam & Dave's "Soul Man."

Its principal artists were black, but many of its musicians were white, which was remarkable amid the turmoil of the Civil Rights era, in which it took a white singer—Elvis ◁012, another Memphis resident—to popularize a black creation. "We were," recalled Stax singer William Bell, "an upstart company that had the audacity to be integrated."

Thanks to stars such as Otis Redding, Stax scored hit after hit. Indeed, Redding's death in 1967 could have put an end to its success. But the label rebuilt itself by launching an icon to rival Redding—Isaac Hayes, who they promoted from songwriter to superstar. The company even spawned its own film: 1973's *Wattstax*, a record of a star-studded L.A. show on August 20, 1972, interspersed with footage of the once riot-torn L.A. district, Watts.

Stax succumbed to bankruptcy in 1975, but its legacy lives on, from The Rolling Stones' 054▷ early take on Rufus Thomas' "Walking the Dog," via David Bowie's 134▷ bash at Eddie Floyd's "Knock on Wood," to The Black Crowes' version of Redding's "Hard to Handle." Meanwhile, Booker T. & The MG's backed Bob Dylan 062▷ for his thirtieth anniversary concert at Madison Square Garden in 1992 and toured with Neil Young 078▷ the following year.

1957+
1967+
1968+

1957
Fred Byler & The Tunetts' "Blue Roses" is the first single on Satellite, the label that will evolve into Stax.

August 1, 1960
A handshake seals the deal that gives the legendary Atlantic record label the distribution rights to Stax.

1962
The first single to be issued with an actual Stax label is Barbara Stephens' jazz-inflected "The Life I Live."

---

❶ 082

JUNE 1966: Sam & Dave storm to the top

After several regionally released singles, Sam Moore and Dave Prater (left) had been snapped up by the Atlantic label❶—who loaned them to Stax. There, they were teamed with writing and production team Isaac Hayes (see right) and David Porter. "You Don't Know Like I Know" gave them a first chart entry in 1965, but the real breakthrough came the next year, with the sexually charged "Hold On! I'm Comin'"—which hit No. 1 on the R&B chart, on June 18. The duo's profile rose further with 1967's "Soul Man" and 1968's "I Thank You." Their popularity waned in the late Sixties and they split in 1970, only to periodically reform throughout the decade. After a terminal split in 1981, Dave Prater took to touring with an entirely different Sam; a partnership that lasted until Prater's death in 1988. The original Sam & Dave, however, influenced many acts, including Dan Aykroyd and John Belushi's *The Blues Brothers*.

April 7, 1967
The rapturously received Stax-Volt Revue tour of Europe—featuring Otis Redding, Sam & Dave, Eddie Floyd, Arthur Conley, and others—is filmed in Norway.

June 1, 1967
The signature instrumental of Stax band Booker T. & the MG's—"Green Onions," first released in 1962—gains a gold record in the U.S.A.

August 1967
Albert King's *Born Under a Bad Sign* album is released. Its title track will become a much imitated and quoted blues standard.

November 22, 1967
Sam & Dave's "Soul Man" is certified gold in the U.S.A. Sam Moore will release a new version of it, with Lou Reed, in 1986, for the movie of the same name.

DECEMBER 1967: The end of "Mr. Pitiful"

Otis Redding had scored more than twenty hits in just five years. These included versions of The Rolling Stones'❶ "(I Can't Get No) Satisfaction" and Sam Cooke's❷ "Shake," plus the original "Respect," later the anthem of Aretha Franklin❸. Yet most impressive were the songs that are forever associated with Redding alone: the roof-raising ballads "That's How Strong My Love Is" and "Try a Little Tenderness," and the wry "Tramp" (with Rufus Thomas' daughter, Carla) and "Mr. Pitiful." Redding had become a favorite of both black soul and white rock audiences—the latter snared by a set at the Monterey Pop Festival in June 1967. But, on December 10 of the same year, he was killed in a Wisconsin plane crash, aged just twenty-six. "(Sittin' on) The Dock of the Bay" promptly became the first of ten posthumous hits. Singers from Christina Aguilera to Whitesnake's David Coverdale have since hailed him as an inspiration.

❶ 054
❷ 026
❸ 084

March 11, 1968
Four months after his death, Otis Redding scores a U.S. gold award for "(Sittin' on) The Dock of the Bay." In the U.K. it rose to No. 3.

August 30, 1968
The Byrds cover William Bell's 1961 signature tune, "You Don't Miss Your Water" on their classic *Sweetheart of the Rodeo* album.

November 22, 1970
Shortly after Jimi Hendrix's death, an album featuring both his and Redding's sets at the 1967 Monterey Pop Festival turns gold in the U.S.A.

April 1972
Cult favorites Big Star issue their debut, *#1 Record*, on the Stax-distributed Ardent Records—the label's ill-fated venture into rock.

APRIL 1972: Isaac Hayes wins an Oscar®

In the early Sixties, Stax label president Jim Stewart offered Tennessee boy Isaac Hayes a job as a keyboard player. "My first session was for Otis Redding," he told *Mojo* magazine. "Talk about being scared." Hayes honed his songwriting with co-Stax man David Porter, before being thrust into the solo spotlight after Redding's death. His 1969 *Hot Buttered Soul* proved iconic. "I was given the freedom to exercise my creativity with no boundaries," he recalled. "It outsold everything at the label that spring." Further extraordinary albums followed, notably 1971's *Black Moses*. But it was for another 1971 release that Hayes would long be celebrated: the irresistible theme from the movie *Shaft*, which made its composer the first African-American to win the Academy Award for film music, in 1972. Hayes was later immortalized as Chef, a character in TV's *South Park*, before suffering a fatal stroke on August 10, 2008.

STAX 53

The Rolling Stones
1962–present

1941+ 1967+ 1971+ 1981+ 1991+

Asked who his favorite group was in 1965, Elvis Presley ◁012▷ cited The Rolling Stones—an enviable endorsement from the King of Rock 'n' Roll, who had inspired the Stones themselves.

They in turn, of course, would inspire countless other artists. "To say I worshipped the Stones . . ." said Steven Tyler of Aerosmith ◁154▷, "would be a gross understatement. Everybody told me that I looked . . . like Mick Jagger with my big lips, and Keith Richards . . . *was* the music I used to love."

At the heart of that music was R&B, from the wry rock 'n' roll of Chuck Berry to the gritty grind of Muddy Waters—indeed, the latter's "Rollin' Stone" inspired the band's name. "The music came across the airwaves," recalled Richards, "and suddenly it felt as if the world was actually changing."

When the filthy five followed the Fab Four ◁044▷ to the U.S.A., they had a similarly seismic effect. "Five lusty images gave me my first glob of gooie in my virgin panties," wrote Patti Smith ◁164▷ in 1973.

Ironically, the Stones helped introduce U.S. fans to the American blues sound that had first inspired them. As Iggy Pop ◁116▷ remarked, "I learned more about music from looking at the writers' credits on Rolling Stones albums than anything else."

"The Stones were really what made me wake up," recalled Pete Townshend of The Who ◁068▷. "At The Beatles' shows, there were lots of screaming girls. The Stones, I think, were the first to have a screaming boy. The sheer force of the Stones on stage, and that perfectly balanced audience—a thousand girls and me—kind of singled them out."

54 TURN ON, TUNE IN, DROP OUT

June 2, 1941	1943	June 1, 1947
Charles Watts is born in London, England. He will later play in Alexis Korner's Blues Incorporated with "Elmo Lewis," a.k.a. Brian Jones (born February 28, 1942).	**Michael Jagger (July 26) and Keith Richards (December 18) are born in Kent, England. The latter will use "Richard" from 1963, at his manager's suggestion.**	**Ronald Wood is born in Middlesex, England. His brother, Art, will sing with Blues Incorporated and later form The Artwoods.**

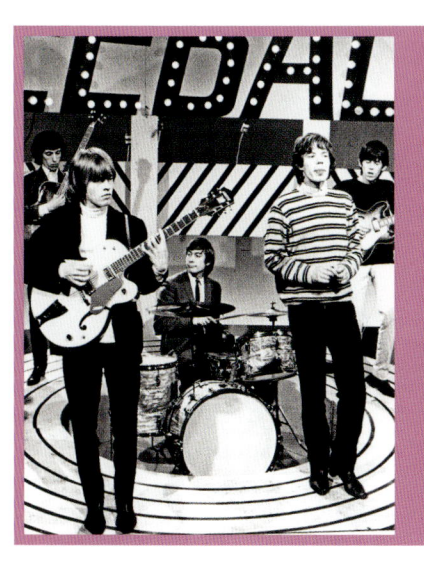

1962: The rise of "England's Newest Hit Makers"

On July 12, 1962, The Rolling Stones gave a first show at The Marquee❶, London, with Jagger and Richards joined by Brian Jones, Dick Taylor, Ian Stewart, and either Tony Chapman (later of The Herd) or Mick Avory (later of The Kinks❷) on drums. By the time the band signed to Decca in May 1963, Taylor (who later formed The Pretty Things) had been replaced by bassist Bill Wyman, pianist Ian Stewart had become the rarely seen "sixth Stone," and Watts was the drummer. The band's global conquest began with a cover of Buddy Holly's❸ "Not Fade Away" and peaked in 1965–66 with the transatlantic No. 1s "(I Can't Get No) Satisfaction," "Get Off of My Cloud," and "Paint It Black." However, a "bad boy" image made them law enforcement targets, and Jagger, Jones, and Richards were all busted for possession of drugs in 1967. "Up until then," Richards remarked, "it had been showbiz." Not any more . . .

❶ 058
❷ 066
❸ 020

THE ROLLING STONES   55

December 6, 1967

Their Satanic Majesties Request goes gold in the U.S.A. An attempt at their own *Sgt. Pepper*, this album's "2,000 Man" will be covered by Kiss in 1979.

June 19, 1968

A startling return to rock 'n' roll, "Jumpin' Jack Flash" tops the U.K. chart. Aretha Franklin (produced by Keith Richards) will cover the song in 1986.

December 6, 1968

Beggars Banquet, featuring "Sympathy for the Devil," is released after a wrangle with Decca over its original cover, a picture of a graffiti-covered bathroom wall.

December 11–12, 1968

The Who, John Lennon, and Eric Clapton are on the bill of *The Rolling Stones Rock and Roll Circus*, a proposed (but shelved) TV special.

❶ 075
❷ 094

1969: *Let It Bleed*

The Stones were forced to fire guitarist Brian Jones in 1969, as his drug habits had come to outweigh his musical versatility. His replacement was Mick Taylor, formerly of John Mayall's Bluesbreakers (the alma mater of Eric Clapton❶ and Fleetwood Mac's❷ Peter Green). Then, on July 2, of the same year, Jones was found dead in his swimming pool. A Stones show in London's Hyde Park (left) just three days later—their first full concert in two years—became a memorial to him. The tour that followed marked the advent of arena rock, but ended in tragedy when a fan was fatally stabbed, on December 6, by a Hell's Angel at California's Altamont Speedway. "People wanted to say that Altamont was the end of an era," sniffed Jagger. "People like that are fashion writers." The Stones' just-released album (the rear cover featuring a figurine of Brian Jones face down in a cake) was, with grim irony, titled *Let It Bleed*.

May 29, 1971

The Stones top the U.S. album and singles charts, with "Brown Sugar" and *Sticky Fingers* (with a sleeve designed by Andy Warhol).

May 12, 1972

Exile on Main St. is released. Its title refers to the band's tax exile in France. Lennon was a guest at their "farewell to England" party in 1971.

July 26, 1974

"It's Only Rock 'n' Roll (But I Like It)" is released, featuring Kenney Jones and Ron Wood on drums (both of The Faces; and Kenney later of The Who).

December 23, 1974

Richards guests at a Faces show in London. Wood's bandmates, including Rod Stewart, see the writing on the wall, and split in 1975.

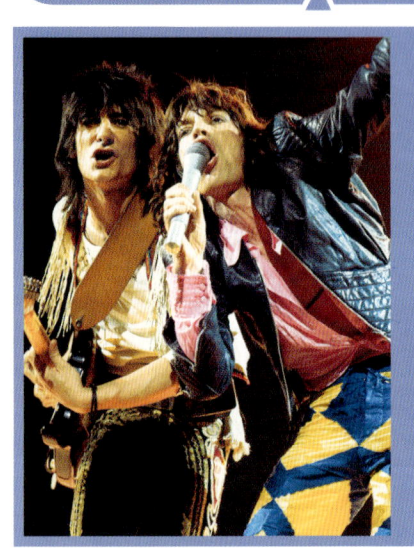

MAY 15, 1976: America turns *Black and Blue*

Ron Wood was drafted in when Mick Taylor jumped ship in November 1974, although he would have to wait until 1976 for confirmation. ("He's got his badge and his membership card," said Jagger.) That year also brought the underrated *Black and Blue*, the Stones' fifth consecutive U.S. No. 1 album. (In tax exile, plagued by hangers-on, and drowning in drugs, the Stones had nonetheless eked out 1973's *Goats Head Soup* and the following year's *It's Only Rock 'n' Roll*.) While Richards (who had reverted to his original surname—with an s) faced one drug bust after another, the band issued the scrappy *Love You Live*, then regrouped for *Some Girls* (1978), their best-received effort since *Exile*. The album even generated sufficient goodwill to boost its hopeless successor, *Emotional Rescue* (1980), to the top of the chart. Much better was 1981's No. 1 *Tattoo You*, which spawned "Start Me Up" and a huge stadium tour.

July 3, 1981

Bill Wyman releases his "(Si Si) Je Suis un Rock Star." "Keith acts like it doesn't exist . . ." says Wyman, but "Mick is very interested."

April 22, 1982

New guitar hero Stevie Ray Vaughan auditions for the band's record label. He will be snapped up by Jagger's old rival, David Bowie, for 1983's *Let's Dance*.

January 4, 1984

Despite being the Stones' first studio album since 1969 not to top the U.S. chart, and the video of its title track being banned, *Undercover* goes platinum.

September 20, 1985

Wood and Richards record "Silver and Gold" with U2 front man Bono for "Little" Steven Van Zandt's anti-apartheid *Sun City* project.

DECEMBER 12, 1985: Death of "sixth Stone"

Jagger, disenchanted with his druggy, boozy band, refused to tour to support *Dirty Work* (1986). They scraped a final hit with a cover of Bob & Earl's "Harlem Shuffle," but *Dirty Work*'s "One Hit (to the Body)" was their least successful British single, despite featuring Zeppelin's ❶ Jimmy Page. The band's disintegration had been sealed by the death of "sixth Stone" Ian Stewart, the down-to-earth pianist (left, with Brian Jones in 1966) who had long held them together. After a tribute show in London (featuring Jeff Beck❷, Eric Clapton❸, and The Who's❹ Pete Townshend), the band fell apart. While Richards issued *Talk Is Cheap* in 1988, Jagger toured Japan, his band featuring Joe Satriani (ex-guitar tutor for Steve Vai and Metallica's❺ Kirk Hammett). But, in 1989, they reunited for *Steel Wheels* and a record-breaking tour—setting a pattern of enjoyable albums, eclipsed by fantastic shows, that endures to this day.

❶ 098
❷ 043
❸ 075
❹ 068
❺ 218

April 8, 1991

Drummer Watts releases the Charlie Watts Quintet's debut album, *From One Charlie*, a tribute to jazz legend Charlie Parker.

January 15, 1992

At the Rock and Roll Hall of Fame ceremony in New York, Richards shares a stage with Jeff Beck, Neil Young, Johnny Cash, Jimmy Page, and John Fogerty.

October 20, 1992

Richards' *Main Offender* is released a few weeks after Wood's *Slide on This* and just months before Jagger's *Wandering Spirit* (the latter featuring Lenny Kravitz).

January 6, 1993

Wyman quits. ("It was a huge surprise when he actually said, 'I'm going to leave the group' . . ." Richards remarks. "That's a kind of *Spinal Tap* line.") He is replaced by Darryl Jones.

1994–PRESENT: You got me rocking

Putting not-so-hot solo albums behind them, the Stones enjoyed their best sales in years with *Voodoo Lounge* (1994). They duly spiced up the obligatory post-tour live album, *Stripped* (1995), with rare tracks and a cover of Bob Dylan's❶ "Like a Rolling Stone." The next decade saw well-received albums—*Bridges to Babylon* (1997), the hits set *Forty Licks* (2002), and *A Bigger Bang* (2005)—and spectacular tours, on which the band played a mixture of stadium, arena, and club dates (the latter featuring more interesting setlists). Director Martin Scorsese fulfilled a personal ambition when he filmed the Stones, the results forming 2008's *Shine a Light*, featuring Jack White of The White Stripes❷ and Christina Aguilera. "We've been doing this music thing for two years now," Jagger is shown saying in an archive clip, "and we never thought we would last this long, but I can see us doing it for maybe another year."

❶ 062
❷ 272

THE ROLLING STONES 57

iconic club

The Marquee
1958–present

Four plucky hopefuls played the U.K.'s foremost rock venue, The Marquee club, in 1966. "They played a forty-five-minute set . . ." recalled club secretary John Gee, "and the leader came to me afterward and said, 'Well, what do you think?' I said, 'I thought it was bloody awful and it's not Marquee material. I'm sorry, but there's nothing I can do for you.' Well, Decca Records turned down The Beatles ◀044—I turned down The Pink Floyd 086▶."

This lapse can be overlooked, as The Marquee, in central London, England, has an otherwise impeccable record. It has hosted artists from John Lee Hooker and Jimi Hendrix 072▶ to David Bowie 134▶ and Bauhaus, and from The Rolling Stones ◀054 and The Yardbirds to AC/DC 182▶ and the Sex Pistols 166▶.

The club began with jazz nights in 1957, before officially opening on April 19, 1958, at 165 Oxford Street. Despite an early show by blues giant Muddy Waters, it initially remained focused on jazz. "London clubs," complained Mick Jagger, "had this aesthetic that you could only play *this* kind of music with *this* kind of lineup in *this* kind of way." "Some of those musicians—who shall remain nameless and who are probably dead anyway—really resisted . . ." concurred Keith Richards. "They'd say, 'Take this fucking rock 'n' roll shit out of here, my son.'"

However, in 1962, The Marquee began hosting R&B nights. "Within about a month . . ." recalled soon-to-be Rolling Stones drummer Charlie Watts, "[founder] Harold Pendleton had 950 people packed in there. He wasn't allowed to admit any more. I think it was because people liked the players, and you could dance to the music."

By 1964, jazz had given way to rock and R&B. Fittingly, one of the acts on the final bill before the club moved, in March 1964, to 90 Wardour Street

The Yardbirds
Five Live Yardbirds
(1964)
Columbia

The Who
My Generation
(1965)
Brunswick

AC/DC
High Voltage
(1976)
Atlantic

(the address with which it is most associated) was a band that launched no fewer than three guitar heroes: The Yardbirds. At that point, their guitarist was Eric Clapton, with whom the band recorded their debut album, *Five Live Yardbirds*, at the club on March 13, only days after it had opened. But Clapton quit the next year to be replaced by Jeff Beck—who, a year later, was joined by Jimmy Page.

Meanwhile, The Marquee welcomed The Who 068▶, and, in September 1965, Davy Jones & The Lower Third. Mid-month, Jones—who sometimes slept in an old ambulance outside the venue—changed his stage name to the more distinctive David Bowie.

Cream, Pink Floyd, and Yes' forerunners The Syn maintained The Marquee's record for talent-spotting in 1966, which also saw a one-off show by Simon & Garfunkel. Then, in January 1967, Jimi Hendrix smashed attendance records at the club.

The final years of the decade saw one legend-to-be after another grace the Marquee stage: Jethro Tull, Fleetwood Mac 094▶, Joe Cocker, Free, Black Sabbath 108▶, Deep Purple, Yes, and—in 1968—The New Yardbirds, soon to become Led Zeppelin 098▶.

This continued into the Seventies, with the likes of Genesis, Elton John 126▶, and Supertramp. And the volume was raised in 1976 by the Sex Pistols and AC/DC. By the end of the decade, The Police, The Jam, Dire Straits, and Iron Maiden 190▶ had all played.

The Eighties saw metal acts and prog rockers dominate the club, notably Marillion (who sang "I'm a Marquee veteran" on "Incommunicado" in 1987). The club also became known for surprise shows by big acts, such as Kiss and Metallica 218▶.

The Marquee closed in 1992 but resurfaced a decade later, at various venues. It remains *the* British launch pad for superstars in waiting.

The Who November 1964

With the slogan "Maximum R&B," The Who❶ began a Marquee residency on November 24, 1964, recalled by Roger Waters of Pink Floyd❷ as "the loudest thing I'd ever heard." "Our shows at The Marquee were scary, cultish events . . ." Pete Townshend commented. "What we were doing was slightly different to what the Stones❸ were doing… We were working old blues songs into expositions of repressed emotion."

The Yardbirds March 1965

Having failed to get Jimmy Page to give up lucrative session work to replace Eric Clapton❶, The Yardbirds played their first show at The Marquee with Jeff Beck❷ in March 1965. When Page was eventually persuaded to join them a year later, the version of the band featuring both him *and* Beck debuted at the club on June 21. Page also went on to play the club with The New Yardbirds❸.

The Marquee 1962–69

David Bowie October 1965

Having first played at The Marquee as an unknown in 1965, Bowie❶ returned in October 1973, to film the U.S. TV special *The 1980 Floor Show,* also featuring British rockers The Troggs, the Spanish vocal group Carmen, and Marianne Faithfull. For a cover of Sonny & Cher's hit "I Got You, Babe," Bowie recalled, "I dressed Marianne in a nun's habit with the back cut out, and I dressed as the Angel of Death [above]."

Pink Floyd March 1966

The Floyd❶ first played The Marquee in March 1966. "We were not really Marquee material . . ." drummer Nick Mason admitted. "We would have been doing what can only be described as 'early Pink Floyd,' which is abstract rhythm and blues . . . rather nasty operations on Chuck Berry❷ material." They also played there in 1967, to an audience including Phil Collins, who recalled, "I didn't think much of the music."

TURN ON, TUNE IN, DROP OUT

098 ❶ 072 ❷

Genesis February 1970

Two years and one album into their career, Genesis supported Keef Hartley at The Marquee on February 4, 1970. They then headlined there on May 24, but guitarist Anthony Phillips called it "a terrible gig." Drummer Phil Collins' association with The Marquee stretched back to the Sixties: "I swept the floor there on many occasions, put the chairs out. Queued for the first gigs by Zeppelin❶, Hendrix❷ . . ."

❶ 182

AC/DC May 1976

These Scottish-Australian headbangers hit The Marquee on May 11, 1976, supporting Back Street Crawler. The latter had featured former Free guitarist Paul Kossoff, until his death in March. AC/DC❶ ended up playing the club fourteen times that year to promote their first international album, *High Voltage*. Their sets included the very appropriate "It's a Long Way to the Top (If You Wanna Rock 'n' Roll)."

Guns N' Roses June 1987

Guns N' Roses❶—or, as *Kerrang!* called them, Lines N' Noses—played three shows at the club in June 1987. "Those Marquee shows were loud and hell-bent," recalled Slash❷. "We did AC/DC's❸ 'Whole Lotta Rosie' and Aerosmith's❹ 'Mama Kin' . . . One of those nights was also the first time that we ever played [Bob Dylan's❺] 'Knockin' on Heaven's Door,' which we put together at soundcheck on a whim."

❶ 228 ❷ 118 ❸ 182 ❹ 154 ❺ 062

Aerosmith August 1990

Having just co-headlined the U.K.'s Monsters of Rock festival, Aerosmith❶ played The Marquee on August 20, 1990. With special guest Jimmy Page—"The man who set us on the path!" announced singer Steven Tyler—they played classics by The Yardbirds (see above left), "Red House" by Hendrix❷, and Zeppelin's❸ "Immigrant Song." In true British style, a fuse blew just as Page was about to play a solo.

❶ 154 ❷ 072 ❸ 098

THE MARQUEE 61

Bob Dylan 1941–present

1941+ 1967+ 1974+ 1980+ 1997+

Amid the mass-marketed fame of modern times, the enigmatic Bob Dylan is still as fascinating as he was when songs such as "Mr. Tambourine Man" first jingle-jangled into the hearts of fans. "He means more to me than anybody living in music or art," declared U2's 192 Bono, one of many disciples.

His songs have been sung by stars who became legends before him, such as Elvis 012 and Johnny Cash 018 ("Tomorrow Is a Long Time" and "It Ain't Me, Babe"), as well as by his contemporaries, such as The Rolling Stones 054, Jimi Hendrix 072, and Neil Young 078 ("Like a Rolling Stone," "All Along the Watchtower," and "Just Like Tom Thumb's Blues").

Even artists who seem to exist far from his world have had a go, including Sam Cooke 026 ("Blowin' in the Wind"), the Ramones 158 ("My Back Pages"), Guns N' Roses 228 ("Knockin' on Heaven's Door"), Pearl Jam 248 ("Masters of War"), Rage Against the Machine 254 ("Maggie's Farm"), and The White Stripes 272 ("One More Cup of Coffee"). He is even a favorite of stars who are hardly slouches at songwriting themselves. "I admire Dylan's work tremendously," said Leonard Cohen 106.

"If I were to list fifty songs I wish I had written," remarked Roger Waters of Pink Floyd 086, "very few of them would not be by Dylan or Lennon."

"I've admired Bob Dylan since I was fifteen . . ." said singer-songwriter Patti Smith 164. "When I talk to him, I still feel sort of like a schoolgirl."

As for the much-vaunted enigma, a remark by Bono spoke volumes: when he was reeling from the band's newfound superstardom in 1987, he said Dylan "looked at me, in a very still way, and said, 'Imagine going through this on your own.'"

May 24, 1941
Robert Zimmerman is born in Duluth, Minnesota. He will later adopt the name Bob Dylan (inspired by poet Dylan Thomas) and will claim to be an orphan.

October 26, 1961
Dylan is signed to Columbia by John Hammond, who will later sign Bruce Springsteen. In November, he will record his self-titled debut album.

March 19, 1962
Bob Dylan is issued to little fanfare. The artist dismisses it and premieres "Blowin' in the Wind" and "A Hard Rain's a-Gonna Fall."

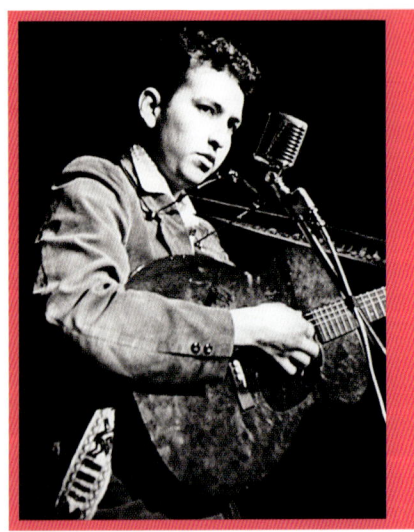

1963: "A Hard Rain's a-Gonna Fall"

The Freewheelin' Bob Dylan became his first success, thanks in part to Peter, Paul & Mary's hit cover of "Blowin' in the Wind" the same year. But when he followed it up with *The Times They Are a-Changin'*, Dylan earned the "voice of a generation" tag that would burden him for years. On the self-explanatory *Another Side of Bob Dylan*, he bid adieu to folk ("It Ain't Me, Babe") and his girlfriend Suze Rotolo ("Ballad in Plain D"), and subsequently became as well-known for writing about relationships as for commenting on society. To the horror of folk purists, he became a bona-fide rock star with 1965's *Bringing It All Back Home* and *Highway 61 Revisited*, and their hits "Subterranean Homesick Blues" and "Like a Rolling Stone." Overnight, the lyrics of John Lennon and Mick Jagger became identifiably Dylan-influenced. The star unleashed his first gold album, 1966's *Blonde on Blonde*, then ducked out of the limelight.

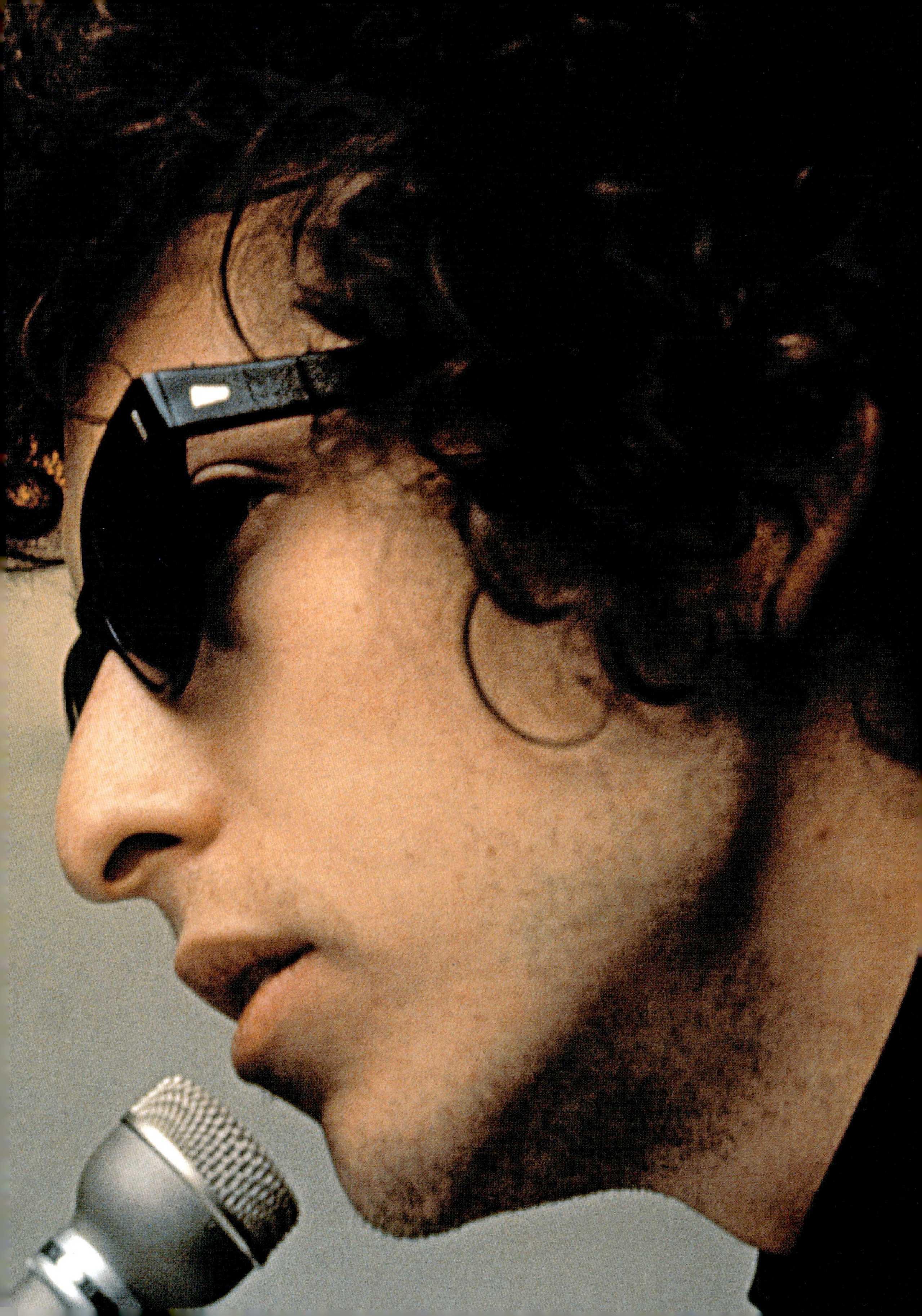

May 17, 1967

Don't Look Back premieres in San Francisco. Documentary-maker D. A. Pennebaker's look at Dylan, on tour in the U.K. in 1965, will become a yardstick for rock movies.

January 28, 1968

After Woody Guthrie's death on October 3, 1967, Dylan appears at a New York tribute show with The Band, Odetta, Judy Collins, Pete Seeger, and Arlo Guthrie.

February 1969

Dylan cuts *Nashville Skyline*, joined on two sessions by Johnny Cash. The album, released in April, will give him another hit: "Lay Lady Lay."

December 9, 1969

Jakob Luke Dylan is born to Bob and Sara. He will later follow in his father's footsteps, as front man of rock band The Wallflowers.

1970: "I Threw It All Away"

After a motorcycle accident that removed Dylan from the fame treadmill at the end of the Sixties, the new decade began promisingly. *Self Portrait* and *New Morning*, both released in 1970, completed a six-year run of transatlantic top ten albums. Living in Woodstock with his wife Sara, Dylan zealously guarded his privacy and seemed to be putting rock 'n' roll behind him: his only high-profile appearance was on August 1, 1971, at George Harrison's Concert for Bangladesh in New York, playing with Harrison (left), Leon Russell, and Ringo Starr. But neither his impenetrable book, *Tarantula*, nor—bar "Knockin' on Heaven's Door"—a soundtrack to Sam Peckinpah's 1973 Western *Pat Garrett & Billy the Kid* did much for his reputation. Then, when he temporarily jumped ship from Columbia to Asylum, his old label exacted their revenge with *Dylan*, a set of outtakes (mostly from *Self Portrait*).

February 16, 1974

Planet Waves, with The Band, gives Dylan his first U.S. No. 1. His first tour of the decade—a spectacular sell-out—will yield the live album *Before the Flood*.

March 1, 1975

Back on the Columbia label, Dylan earns another No. 1 with the fantastic *Blood on the Tracks*—largely inspired by the decline of his marriage.

June 1975

Dylan visits Rubin Carter in jail for the first time. The boxer, falsely convicted for murder, is the subject of one of his best-loved songs, "Hurricane."

November 13, 1975

Two weeks after the Rolling Thunder Revue begins, Joni Mitchell joins the tour in Connecticut, remaining until December. Dylan wears Kiss-inspired make-up.

1976: The rise and fall

By the close of 1976, Dylan seemed to be on another career high. The Rolling Thunder Revue tour had seen the return of Sixties compadres Roger McGuinn of The Byrds, who turned his "Mr. Tambourine Man" into a transatlantic chart-topper in 1965, and ex-girlfriend Joan Baez. That year's *Desire* scored the star his first platinum disc and completed a trio of superb U.S. No. 1 albums. But, as his divorce took its toll, a decline set in. Dylan's woes were compounded by the death of Elvis ❶, one of his heroes, on August 16, 1977. "I went over my whole life," he recalled. "I went over my whole childhood. I didn't talk to anyone for a week." Meanwhile, *Street Legal* (1978) was sandwiched by two equally unremarkable live albums. To much astonishment, he converted to Christianity and scored a million-seller with *Slow Train Coming* (1979)—the last highlight before the worst decade of his career.

64 TURN ON, TUNE IN, DROP OUT

February 11–15, 1980

Saved is recorded at Muscle Shoals Sound (as was *Slow Train Coming*), an Alabama studio famed for R&B records by the likes of Aretha Franklin.

August 10, 1981

Shot of Love is released. It will fail to make the U.S. top thirty but finds a champion in Bono: "I love that album . . . You're in a room hearing him sing."

April–May 1983

Produced by Mark Knopfler, Dylan cuts twenty-five takes of the brilliant "Blind Willie McTell," but will, bafflingly, omit it from *Infidels*.

July 13, 1985

Soon after the release of *Empire Burlesque*, Dylan expresses well-meaning but misplaced support for U.S. farmers at Live Aid.

1988: A Traveling Wilbury on a Never Ending Tour

The Eighties proved disappointing for Dylan. He toured with Tom Petty & The Heartbreakers, who often had to guess what they were supposed to play, and also with the Grateful Dead (hence 1989's *Dylan and the Dead*). Meanwhile, customers had steered clear of *Knocked Out Loaded* (1986) and *Down in the Groove* (1988). But a stint with Petty, Jeff Lynne, Roy Orbison, and George Harrison in The Traveling Wilburys (left) restored public affection. Evolving from sessions for Harrison's *Cloud Nine*, the Wilburys convened in April 1988, in Dylan's garage. He then began his Never Ending Tour in June (with a California show at which Neil Young❶ guested), subsequently pausing only to issue *Oh Mercy* (1989), *Under the Red Sky* (1990), *Good as I Been to You* (1992), *World Gone Wrong* (1993), and *Unplugged* (1995). And, in 1991, he collected a Lifetime Achievement award at the Grammys.

❶
078

September 27, 1997

At the World Eucharistic Congress in Bologna, Italy, Dylan sings three songs for an audience that included the Pope.

June 2, 1998

The Grammy-winning *Time Out of Mind* (1997)—his first set of new material in seven years—earns a platinum disc, Dylan's first since 1979.

September 11, 2001

On the worst day possible as New York is attacked, *Love and Theft* is issued. Despite its unfortunate release date, the album is generally well-received.

April 2004

Nearly four decades after he quipped that he would be tempted to sell out for "ladies' undergarments," Dylan appears in a commercial for Victoria's Secret lingerie.

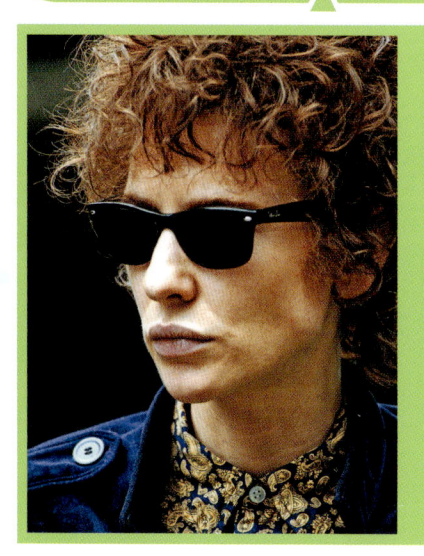

2006–PRESENT: "It's All Good"

Both Dylan's *Modern Times* (2006) and *Together Through Life* (2009) topped the U.S. charts, proving that his work was once again worth buying. 2006 also saw the launch of his *Theme Time Radio Hour* satellite show, a beguiling blend of eclectic music and droll spoken word. Plus this year brought the *Rolling Stone* interview that featured his now-famous endorsement of Alicia Keys, whom he namechecked in *Modern Times*' "Thunder on the Mountain": "There's *nothing* about that girl I don't like." (Keys considered responding in a song of her own, but concluded that "'Dylan' is not very easily rhymeable.") In 2007, Todd Haynes' film *I'm Not There* saw stars such as Cate Blanchett (left) in vignettes based on Dylan's life and work. With affection for the legend at its highest in three decades, even his baffling charity album, *Christmas in the Heart* (2009), received polite reviews. In Bob we trust.

BOB DYLAN

The Kinks 1963–96

1944+ 1970+

While The Beatles ◁044▷, The Rolling Stones ◁054▷, and The Who ◁068▷ stormed the U.S.A., The Kinks—their "British Invasion" contemporaries—scored a smaller niche but were equally well-loved.

Their first transatlantic smashes—1964's "You Really Got Me" and "All Day and All of the Night"—were proto-metal powerhouses. They could have blueprinted a successful career (as evidenced by 1966's *The Kinks Kontroversy*), but the group—or, specifically, singer-songwriter Ray Davies—instead pursued a peculiarly English path of deadpan observation in the songs' lyrics, making the group hugely influential at home and cult favorites abroad. "I was influenced more by The Kinks than any other group," remarked Pete Townshend. (The Who duly hooked up with The Kinks' producer, Shel Talmy.)

A series of singles secured a niche for the band: "Dedicated Follower of Fashion," "Sunny Afternoon," "Waterloo Sunset," and "Dead End Street" were exquisite vignettes of English life, and an evident influence on future Britpop bands such as Blur.

The Kinks might even have pioneered "the concept album" had their label not vetoed plans to link the songs on *Face to Face* (conceived a year before *Sgt. Pepper*). The band did, however, create some masterpieces, such as *The Kinks Are The Village Green Preservation Society*; and they even returned to the U.S. top forty with four Seventies albums, notably 1979's *Low Budget.* As Davies told British newspaper *The Times*, "We'd make records like *Village Green*, knowing that it might be a flop—but it was a cause. We all believed in it."

TURN ON, TUNE IN, DROP OUT

June 21, 1944

Raymond Douglas Davies is born in London, England. His younger brother, Dave—who will later form a band called The Ravens—is born in February 1947.

January 1964

With Ray having joined Dave and bassist Pete Quaife's band The Ravens, the newly christened Kinks recruit ex-Rolling Stones drummer Mick Avory.

March 1964

The Kinks embark on their first tour, with headliners The Dave Clark Five, who will also prove influential on the hard rock genre.

AUGUST 1964: "You Really Got Me" hits it big

"I heard 'You Really Got Me,'" Pete Townshend admitted to *NME*, "and instantly knew that The Kinks had filled the hole we wanted to fill." Townshend promptly ripped it off to create The Who's❶ "I Can't Explain," but other acts found it easier to simply cover the song. (Mott the Hoople cut it after catching sight of The Kinks at a studio.) Artists from Iggy Pop❷ to Robert Palmer have since recorded it—few as successfully as Van Halen❸, who scored a first U.S. hit with it in 1978. Oddly, controversy has long reigned about who played on the original. "I played with The Kinks several times," Deep Purple's❹ Jon Lord told *Modern Keyboard*. "I even played the piano on 'You Really Got Me.' I was paid five pounds for it. The guitar solo was played by Led Zep's❺ Jimmy Page, but The Kinks have denied it." As Ray Davies remarked, *whoever* played on it, "There's determination and guts in that record."

❶ 068
❷ 116
❸ 156
❹ 049
❺ 098

June 12, 1970

"Lola" is released after a reference to "Coca-Cola" is changed to "Cherry Cola" to appease the anti-advertising BBC.

June 1973

Ray Davies announces onstage at London's White City that he is "sick of the whole thing" and will be "quitting." (He doesn't.)

February 25, 1977

Newly signed to Arista, The Kinks begin a triumphant comeback with *Low Budget*. It gives them a U.S. album chart peak and will go gold.

January 27, 1982

Give the People What They Want earns the band a fourth and final U.S. gold disc thanks to "Destroyer" and "Better Things."

OCTOBER 2009: The Kinks go "metal"

Ray Davies guested at Metallica's❶ induction into the Rock and Roll Hall of Fame on October 30, 2009 (left), singing "You Really Got Me" and "All Day and All of the Night"—evidence of The Kinks' influence on a huge variety of artists. Their songs have been covered by Green Day❷ ("Tired of Waiting"), Steve Vai ("Celluloid Heroes"), The Jam ("David Watts"), Kirsty MacColl ("Days"), David Bowie❸ ("Waterloo Sunset"), and many others. Particularly notable are "Stop Your Sobbing" and "I Go to Sleep" by The Pretenders, whose singer Chrissie Hynde had a relationship (and a daughter) with Ray Davies. She also later performed "I Go to Sleep" with Blur's❹ Damon Albarn (another Davies disciple), shortly after Albarn performed "Waterloo Sunset" with Davies himself. Davies has also mooted a collection of the band's classics, reworked by Bruce Springsteen❺, The Killers❻, and others.

❶ 218
❷ 258
❸ 134
❹ 275
❺ 150
❻ 280

THE KINKS 67

The Who
1964–present

1944+ 1966+ 1970+ 1975+ 1985+

Popular legend has it that the members of The Who always hated each other. The tensions are said to have started when guitarist Pete Townshend took over the band that singer Roger Daltrey had started. Bassist John Entwistle and drummer Keith Moon, meanwhile, were so fed up within two years of the band forming that they discussed leaving. The latter even considered jumping ship to The Jimi Hendrix Experience 072▶ or The Moody Blues. "I had to say no," he reported of the offer from Hendrix, "because that was a good week with The Who."

Yet this disharmony and angst fueled a host of classic songs—which, for all their masterpieces such as *Tommy* and *Quadrophenia,* is where the band's strength lies. "I Can't Explain"—some claim with guitar by future Led Zeppelin 098▶ maestro Jimmy Page—set out their stall: choppy riffs and snarling nihilism, anchored by rock-hard rhythms.

The Who's influence has spanned the musical generations. The bass-drums-guitar-angst formula was upheld by Nirvana 244▶, whose front man Kurt Cobain referred to *Nevermind*'s "Drain You" as their very own "Won't Get Fooled Again." Pearl Jam 248▶ have often covered Who classics such as "Love Reign O'er Me." And *American Idiot* by Green Day 258▶ owes an obvious debt to *Quadrophenia*.

The Who even earned respect from those whose material they covered. "I like what they did with my song," said singer and pianist Mose Allison, who wrote "Young Man Blues" (featured on the band's barnstorming 1970 album, *Live at Leeds*). "They made an anthem out of it, for young men."

TURN ON, TUNE IN, DROP OUT

1944	May 19, 1945	August 23, 1946
In London, Roger Harry Daltrey is born on March 1 and John Alec Entwistle on October 9. Daltrey later forms The Detours with John Entwistle, Colin Dawson, and Doug Sandom.	Peter Dennis Blandford Townshend is born in London. Entwistle will recruit Townshend to The Detours, who become The Who in February 1964.	Keith John Moon is born in Middlesex, England. He will join The Who in April 1964, having boasted that he was better than Doug Sandom.

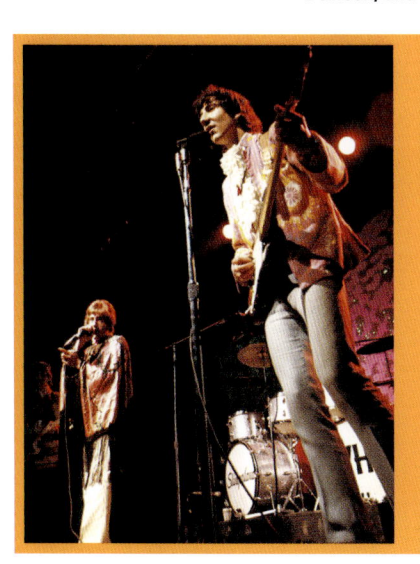

1964: The start of the *Amazing Journey*

After a flop single as The High Numbers, Daltrey, Entwistle, Moon, and Townshend reverted to the name The Who in late 1964. A residency at The Marquee❶, London, secured a fanatical following, who helped their debut single "I Can't Explain" become a hit in 1965. After firing, then re-hiring, Daltrey in fall of the same year (the first of many band disputes), The Who etched themselves into legend with "My Generation"—source of the immortal lyric, "Hope I die before I get old." "We *did* mean it," Townshend insisted to *Melody Maker*. "We were hoping to screw the older generation, screw the rockers [enemies of The Who's fans, the Mods], screw The Beatles❷, screw the record buyers, and screw ourselves. We've been most successful on that last account . . . We wanted to die in plane crashes or get torn to pieces by a crowd of screaming girls. It all began to change when Paul [McCartney] sang 'When I'm Sixty-Four.'"

❶ 058
❷ 044

THE WHO 69

March 4, 1966

"Substitute" is released. Its title was inspired by Smokey Robinson's use of the word "substitute" in The Miracles' 1965 hit "The Tracks of My Tears."

May 1966

Moon and Entwistle conceive the name Led Zeppelin. Their driver, Richard Cole, takes the idea to Jimmy Page, and Led Zep later becomes a reality.

September 18, 1967

"I Can See for Miles"—one of the songs on which Moon's explosive drumming is best showcased—is released. It will be a transatlantic top ten hit.

November 20, 1968

In Liverpool, at the close of a British tour, Small Faces drummer Kenney Jones joins Moon for The Who's encore, "Magic Bus."

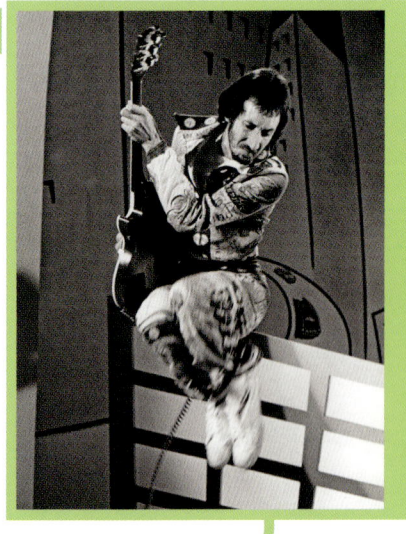

❶ 112

1969: "That deaf, dumb and blind boy . . ."

Townshend had long toyed with "mini rock operas"—notably 1966's "A Quick One (While He's Away)," and 1967's excellent *The Who Sell Out*, which boasted the conceptual conceit of sounding like a pirate radio station broadcast. One of its songs, "Rael," was extracted from a piece that Townshend intended to be played by a full orchestra: "Musically it is interesting because it contains a theme which I later used in *Tommy*." *Tommy*—issued in May 1969, and trailed by the hit "Pinball Wizard"—was a fully-fledged concept album about a "deaf, dumb and blind boy" that would ultimately overshadow The Who's career. At first, however, as Daltrey told *Q*, "*Tommy* was not a particularly big success . . . It was only after us flogging it on the road for three years, doing [the 1969 festival] Woodstock❶ and things like that, that it got back in the charts. Then it stayed there for a year and took on a life of its own."

February 14, 1970

Live at Leeds is recorded. In its original form, it boasts three covers and, unlike future live releases, nothing from *Tommy*.

December 20, 1970

The Who perform *Tommy* in full for the final time (until 1989), at The Roundhouse in London. They dedicate it to their support act, Elton John.

September 18, 1971

Who's Next becomes their only No. 1. It includes "Won't Get Fooled Again," recording for which took place at Mick Jagger's country estate.

December 9, 1972

Rod Stewart, Peter Sellers, Ringo Starr, Maggie Bell, Steve Winwood, and The Who appear in a London stage version of *Tommy*.

❶ 086
❷ 166
❸ 275

1973: *Quadrophenia* and the beginning of the end

As the band's tenth anniversary loomed, Townshend was determined to "encapsulate everything The Who had ever done with a big sort of flourish." The result was *Quadrophenia*—a production as troublesome as *Tommy* (the movie of which drove Townshend to a 1974 breakdown). After mixing *Quadrophenia*, Townshend and Daltrey had a fistfight. Onstage, Moon resented wearing headphones to stay in time with malfunctioning backing tapes, and Townshend interrupted when Daltrey tried to explain the piece's concept. *Quadrophenia* was revived for a 1996 performance in London, featuring Pink Floyd's❶ David Gilmour, and for a subsequent tour starring Billy Idol. But the greatest version was Franc Roddam's 1979 movie, which featured a cameo by Sting (left) and—after distributors blocked plans to enlist the Sex Pistols'❷ Johnny Rotten for the lead—made a star of Phil Daniels (later to grace Blur's❸ "Parklife").

TURN ON, TUNE IN, DROP OUT

March 1975
Ken Russell's movie *Tommy* premieres. Roger Daltrey stars, with cameos by Elton John, Tina Turner, Eric Clapton, and Keith Moon.

May 31, 1976
A 120-decibel show at a British stadium earns The Who the Guinness World Record for "the loudest pop group."

May 25, 1978
Moon plays his last show with The Who at U.K.'s Shepperton Studios, filmed for the excellent documentary *The Kids Are Alright*.

September 7, 1978
Moon dies of an accidental overdose, in Harry Nilsson's London flat, where Cass Elliott of The Mamas and the Papas died in 1974.

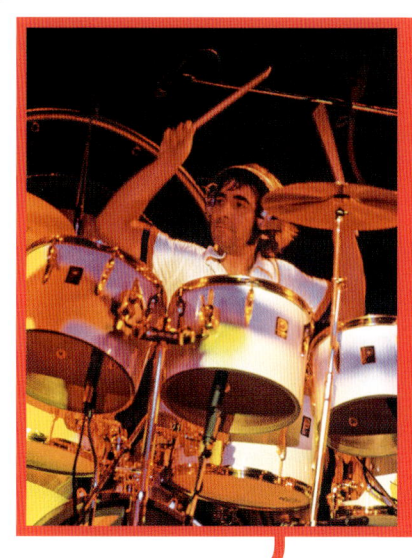

1979: Short-lived renaissance

The band's final albums with Moon—*The Who by Numbers* (1975) and *Who Are You* (1978)—had been bitter and tired. The group had stopped touring and were replaced as rock's bad boys by the Sex Pistols❶, an encounter with whom inspired *Who Are You*'s title track. The arrival of new drummer Kenney Jones in 1979 prompted a brief rebirth, including being featured on the cover of *Time*, but the death of eleven fans at a Cincinatti show proved a fateful omen. Townshend was sick of having to channel his songs through the band's "war machine," and, as Jones observed, kept his best material for his solo albums (though 1981's *Face Dances* went platinum thanks to "You Better You Bet"). After a final tour in 1982—including two Shea Stadium shows supported by The Clash❷— The Who called it a day. Bar brief reunions—such as for Live Aid (1985)❸ and the Brit Awards (1988)—the members then focused on solo work.

❶ 166
❷ 170
❸ 214

November 1–2, 1985
Pink Floyd's David Gilmour joins Townshend in London for two shows. Highlights of the fun sets are issued as *Deep End Live!*

June 21, 1989
With Simon Phillips on drums, The Who reform for a spectacular tour. In New York, L.A., and London, they perform *Tommy* in full, with guests such as Billy Idol.

March 1993
A stage version of *Tommy*, with musical direction by Townshend, opens on Broadway. It will transfer to London three years later, starring Kim Wilde.

February 23–24, 1994
Alice Cooper, Eddie Vedder, Lou Reed, Townshend, and Entwistle are among guests at shows that Daltrey stages at New York's Carnegie Hall to celebrate his fiftieth birthday.

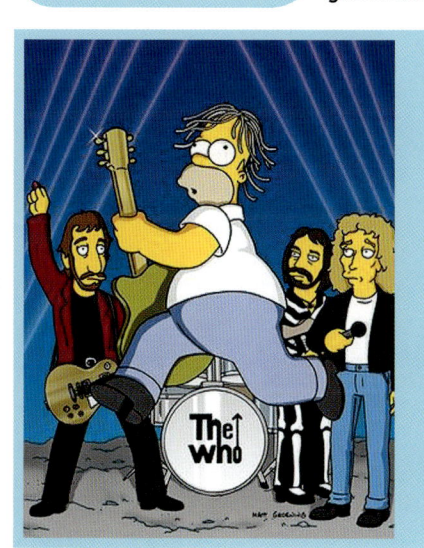

OCTOBER 2001: The Concert for New York City

"A band that loves New York, and a band loved by New York!" With a roared introduction from actor John Cusack, The Who stormed into the performance of their lives at the post-9/11 Concert for New York City, at Madison Square Garden, on October 20, 2001. Their four-song set (with Ringo Starr's son Zak on drums) eclipsed every other act on the bill, including Mick Jagger, David Bowie❶, and Paul McCartney. "They were real *men*," marveled Bono of U2❷. That power was also harnessed to wall-smashing effect on a 2000 episode of *The Simpsons* (left); songs of theirs have also been adopted by all three shows in TV's *CSI* franchise. Sadly, Entwistle died in Las Vegas on June 27, 2002. "I just hope," said Daltrey, "that God has got his earplugs ready." He and Townshend forged ahead with 2006's *Endless Wire*, and The Who played the half-time show at the 2010 Super Bowl—another highlight of a seemingly endless story.

❶ 134
❷ 192

THE WHO

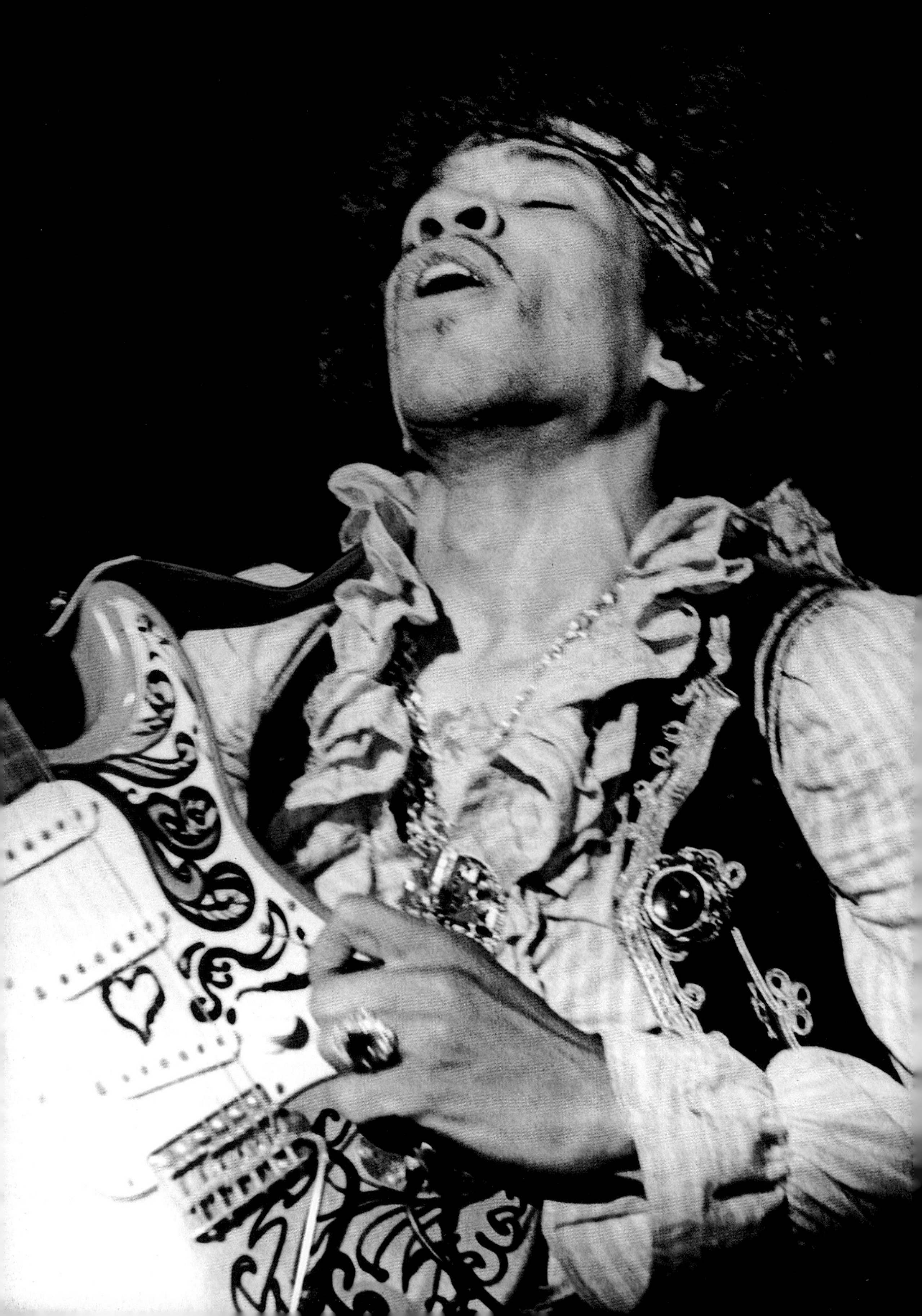

Jimi Hendrix
1942–70

July 1967: the summer of love. The Doors' "Light My Fire" was climbing to No. 1, *Sgt. Pepper* ruled the world. Meanwhile, the hottest guitarist of the era was on tour with . . . The Monkees. "Hendrix would be up there belting out 'Foxy Lady,'" recalled drummer Micky Dolenz, "and the kids would be screaming for The Monkees. It was kinda strange!"

"Kinda strange" indeed. Unable to read or write music, Hendrix still revolutionized rock in just four years of fame. As Deep Purple's Ritchie Blackmore observed, "Even the way he *walked* was amazing."

> "He was going to burn out very, very quickly. He was so insecure and shy. Really sweet." —Pete Townshend

Johnny Allen Hendrix was born on November 27, 1942, in Seattle, and later renamed James Marshall by his father. With influences ranging from Howlin' Wolf to Buddy Holly ◀020▶, he had his first guitar by the summer of 1958, and joined his first band, The Velvetones. The following year, now armed with an electric, he joined with The Rocking Kings.

Hendrix served in the U.S. Army, then played with stars including The Isley Brothers, Sam Cooke ◀026▶, and Little Richard. With his own Jimmy James and the Blue Flames, he was spotted by The Animals' Chas Chandler, who moved him to the U.K., rechristened him Jimi, and introduced him to British drummer Mitch Mitchell and bassist Noel Redding. As The Jimi Hendrix Experience, the trio laid waste to the clubs of London.

"I was sick when I saw him . . ." recalled guitar god Jeff Beck. "Everybody was . . . Everybody you talked to was saying, 'Have you heard Jimi Hendrix?'"

"He did things which were magical," agreed Pete Townshend of The Who ◀068▶. "You felt pain in his presence and in the presence of that music . . . What was also painful was to meet him afterwards and realize he didn't know what he was doing. He had no idea of his greatness . . . Really nice guy."

The 1966 hit "Hey Joe" paved the way for *Are You Experienced*, the first in an extraordinary sequence of albums, including 1968's *Axis: Bold as Love* and *Electric Ladyland*, and 1970's *Band of Gypsys*. A lyric from the song "Are You Experienced" served as a de facto slogan (hence its ubiquity on T-shirts): "Not necessarily stoned, but beautiful . . ."

An incendiary set at 1967's Monterey festival made Hendrix a hero in the U.S.A., too. Another festival appearance, at Woodstock ▶112◀, featured his iconic mangling of "The Star-Spangled Banner."

A new incarnation of the Experience, with Mitch Mitchell and Billy Cox, began work on *First Rays of the New Rising Sun*. But work was interrupted by touring and then halted by Hendrix's death in 1970. His legacy, however, has never faded. Legions have tried to follow in his footsteps but few have matched his innovations. Even Prince ▶174◀, whose sound owed more to Carlos Santana, was inspired. "You're talking about a guy who played 'The Star-Spangled Banner,'" he said, "but in a way that showed exactly what it was about. He played it on Dick Cavett's TV show and [when] Cavett said it was 'unorthodox,' Hendrix said, 'Well, it's beautiful to me.'"

Are You Experienced (1967) was ludicrously excellent (especially for a debut): stuffed to the gills with classics such as "Fire" and "Foxy Lady." "Purple Haze" was added to later reissues.

Amid Hendrix's bewilderingly vast, posthumous discography, *Radio One* (1986) stands out for its concise cuts (including The Beatles' "Day Tripper"), clear production, and good humor.

Hendrix testifies with The Isleys

Jimi Hendrix featured on three Isley Brothers singles, including 1964's "Testify"—whose shout-outs to soul heroes included another of the guitarist's employers, Little Richard ❶. Neither on "Testify," the same year's "The Last Girl," 1965's "Move Over and Let Me Dance," nor on their B-sides, was there any evidence of Hendrix's rulebook-shredding playing (even after the songs were remixed to showcase the guitar once he had become famous). But The Isleys (left) carried quite enough star power on their own, having written the pop standard "Shout," and turned "Twist and Shout" into a hit before it was covered by The Beatles ❷. In the Seventies, with another remarkable guitarist in their ranks—their younger brother Ernie—they took their rock-soul fusion (nothing like Hendrix's, but equally excellent) into the charts, with hits such as "That Lady," "Summer Breeze," "Harvest for the World," and the furious "Fight the Power."

Jimi Hendrix

Connection: 1964

December 16, 1966
The Jimi Hendrix Experience debut on record (on the Polydor label) with "Hey Joe." Previously recorded by The Byrds and The Leaves, it will become a top ten U.K. hit.

November 14, 1967
Pink Floyd, The Move, and The Nice are among the support acts as Hendrix tours the U.K. Future Hawkwind member and Motörhead mainman Lemmy is among the roadies.

Connection: 1966

June 18, 1967
Hendrix's triumphant set at California's Monterey festival includes covers of Bob Dylan's "Like a Rolling Stone" and The Troggs' "Wild Thing." For the latter, he sets his guitar alight.

December 1, 1967
Axis: Bold as Love is released in the U.K. Among its classic songs is the lovely "Little Wing," subsequently covered by guitarists from Eric Clapton to Metallica's Kirk Hammett.

Hendrix catches the eye of an Animal

The Animals' Chas Chandler (far left) spotted Hendrix at a July 1966 show at New York's Cafe Wha (owned by Van Halen ❶ front man David Lee Roth's uncle). Chandler returned in September to persuade Hendrix to relocate to London and form a new band—with famous results. Chandler himself was no stranger to fame, having topped transatlantic charts in 1964 with his band's "House of the Rising Sun." This song had paved the way for Animals classics such as "Don't Let Me Be Misunderstood" and "We Gotta Get Out of This Place," but Chandler was dismayed to find that fame did not necessarily entail fortune. Aiming to improve on his haul of $3,000, two guitars, and an apartment, he went into management and production; first with Hendrix, later with Slade. The Animals' singer, Eric Burdon, also enjoyed an immensely successful association with a black act: he discovered, then fronted, War.

TURN ON, TUNE IN, DROP OUT

Jimi H and Jim M

The late Sixties produced no shortage of iconic rock stars. On March 7, 1968, two of them—Hendrix and Doors front man Jim Morrison—were at New York club The Scene (with guitarist Johnny Winter and drummer Buddy Miles). A jam ensued, featuring songs such as Cream's ❶ "Sunshine of Your Love," The Beatles' ❷ "Tomorrow Never Knows," and the Doors singer's "Morrison's Lament." Neither star's reputation was enhanced by the 1980 release of the jam as *Woke Up This Morning, and Found Myself Dead!* Fortunately, both had amassed more than enough material for a worthier legacy; Morrison with classic albums, as well as hits such as "Light My Fire." Sadly, he and Hendrix have something else in common: they died less than a year apart, both twenty-seven (as did singer Janis Joplin, the month after Hendrix). When Nirvana's ❸ Kurt Cobain died at the same age, his mother said that he had joined "that stupid club."

❶ 041
❷ 044
❸ 242

1968 Connection

November 16, 1968
With *Are You Experienced* still in the U.S. top ten after sixty weeks on the chart, the new *Electric Ladyland* hits No. 1, despite a controversial cover that Hendrix himself detests.

August 18, 1969
Hendrix and his band Gypsy Sun and Rainbows close the Woodstock festival on the Monday morning after the main weekend event. Around 180,000 fans stay to see him.

August 31, 1970
In the early hours, Hendrix closes Britain's Isle of Wight festival. His on-site sound is mixed by Pink Floyd's David Gilmour, who went along as a fan and got roped in to help.

March 19, 1968
Are You Experienced earns a first gold disc in the U.S.A. It will sell over four million copies in Hendrix's homeland alone, becoming the best-seller of his original albums.

Connection 1969

December 31, 1969
With Army-era pal Billy Cox and Electric Flag drummer Buddy Miles, Hendrix launches his post-Experience group, Band of Gypsys, who will release a self-titled live album.

September 18, 1970
An intoxicated Hendrix dies in London. "Voodoo Chile" will quickly top the U.K. chart; the first in a flood of posthumous releases. "New" material is still being released in 2010.

Clapton—the Cream of the crop

On her TV show *Happening with Lulu*, on January 4, 1969, the Scottish singer Lulu blithely introduced Hendrix playing "Hey Joe." The guitarist responded with a tumultuous introduction to a ramshackle rendition of his hit, then called a halt after three minutes. "We'd like to stop playing this rubbish," he drawled, "and dedicate a song to the Cream ❶, regardless of what kind of group they might be in. We'd like to dedicate it to Eric Clapton, Ginger Baker, and Jack Bruce." With that, his band launched into "Sunshine of Your Love," by Cream, who had recently split up. This slice of mischief sealed the link between Clapton and Hendrix (left; the latter had reportedly agreed to accompany Chas Chandler to London on the condition that he was introduced to the former Yardbird ❷). The admiration proved two-way. "He had this enormous gift and a fantastic technique . . ." recalled Clapton, "yet he didn't seem aware of it."

❶ 041
❷ 060

Frank Zappa 1940–93

1940+ 1969+

From Alice Cooper to Aerosmith ◀154▶, from Steve Vai to *The Simpsons*, and from Deep Purple to The Monkees, Frank Vincent Zappa has had a far-reaching impact on rock and pop culture.

The Baltimore-born maestro's 1966 debut *Freak Out* influenced The Beatles ◀044▶, yet 1968's *We're Only in It for the Money* skewered *Sgt. Pepper*. (John Lennon, clearly not offended, jammed with Zappa in 1971.) One of *Money*'s songs featured on The Monkees' TV show, as did Zappa himself (he also appeared in their 1968 movie, *Head*).

His catalog of nearly one hundred albums zooms from rock and doo-wop to classical and jazz. The safest with which to start is his top-seller, 1974's *Apostrophe (')*, although the 1982 hit "Valley Girl"—featuring his daughter Moon Unit—is also fantastic.

Many stars passed through Zappa's bands, such as Warren Cuccurullo of Duran Duran ◀200▶ and Terry Bozzio, whose résumé includes Korn. Most famous was "stunt guitarist" Steve Vai (who graduated to Public Image Ltd., David Lee Roth, Whitesnake, and a solo career). Zappa, too, was a fine guitarist—check out "Watermelon in Easter Hay" on *Joe's Garage*.

Zappa lyrics were used by Aerosmith (in "Girl Keeps Comin' Apart") and Spinal Tap (in "Big Bottom"), and he is namechecked in Deep Purple's "Smoke on the Water," the tale of a fire at a 1971 show. The star, said Purple's Ritchie Blackmore, announced: "'There is absolutely no need to panic.' Then he threw his guitar away and raced off the stage!"

"Frank Zappa," said *Simpsons* creator and long-time admirer Matt Groening, "was my Elvis ◀012▶."

TURN ON, TUNE IN, DROP OUT

December 21, 1940

Frank Vincent Zappa is born in Baltimore, Maryland. He will move to California nine years later—an environment that will shape much of his work.

June 30, 1964

Zappa joins, and promptly takes over, California band The Muthers (shortly to be renamed, less suggestively, the Mothers of Invention).

June 26, 1967

Absolutely Free **is Zappa's acerbic contribution to the so-called Summer of Love. It includes the classic "Brown Shoes Don't Make It."**

JUNE 16, 1969: *Trout Mask Replica* released

❶ 156

❷ 107

Seeking to showcase music's more outré artists, Zappa and his manager established the labels Bizarre (in 1968) and Straight (in 1969). Neither was a commercial success, but both proved a breeding ground for many a maverick talent. Alice Cooper❶ was an early signing, his intention of "driving a stake through the heart of the Love Generation" doubtless finding favor with Zappa himself. Other stars in the stable included Wild Man Fischer, as well as Tim Buckley, who wrote "Song to the Siren" and fathered Jeff Buckley❷. But the most remarkable was Zappa's old school friend Don Van Vliet, a.k.a. Captain Beefheart. His 1969 album *Trout Mask Replica*, produced by Zappa, is one of rock's most divisive works, regarded as either an avant-garde masterpiece or utterly unlistenable.

October 25, 1969

Zappa joins Pink Floyd onstage at a festival in Belgium. He plays on a twenty-minute version of "Interstellar Overdrive."

December 22, 1982

Bob Dylan asks Zappa to produce his next album. The job will go to Mark Knopfler, but Zappa is later thanked on Dylan's *Knocked Out Loaded*.

March 14, 1986

Zappa appears in a rare acting role in TV cop show *Miami Vice*. The episode's music includes Chris Isaak, Sly & Robbie, X, and INXS.

February 2, 1988

Led Zeppelin's "Stairway to Heaven" features on the setlist of Zappa's final tour. He will also cover The Allman Brothers' "Whipping Post."

DECEMBER 4, 1993: "Trouble every day"

❶ 142

Zappa's plans to run for president were put on hold when he was diagnosed with prostate cancer in 1990. During years of treatment, he received "a sweet letter" from Tipper Gore—Al Gore's wife and head of the Parents' Music Resource Center, with whom he had locked horns in congressional hearings about music censorship in 1985. At the debut performance of his classical *The Yellow Shark*, in 1992, he said, "I have no intention of checking out within the foreseeable future." The end came more than a year later, and he was buried near Roy Orbison. In the next decade, Gene Simmons of Kiss❶ was given access to his unreleased material and built "Black Tongue" around Zappa's guitar. The maestro's wife Gail and children Dweezil, Moon Unit, and Ahmet sang on the 2004 song.

FRANK ZAPPA   77

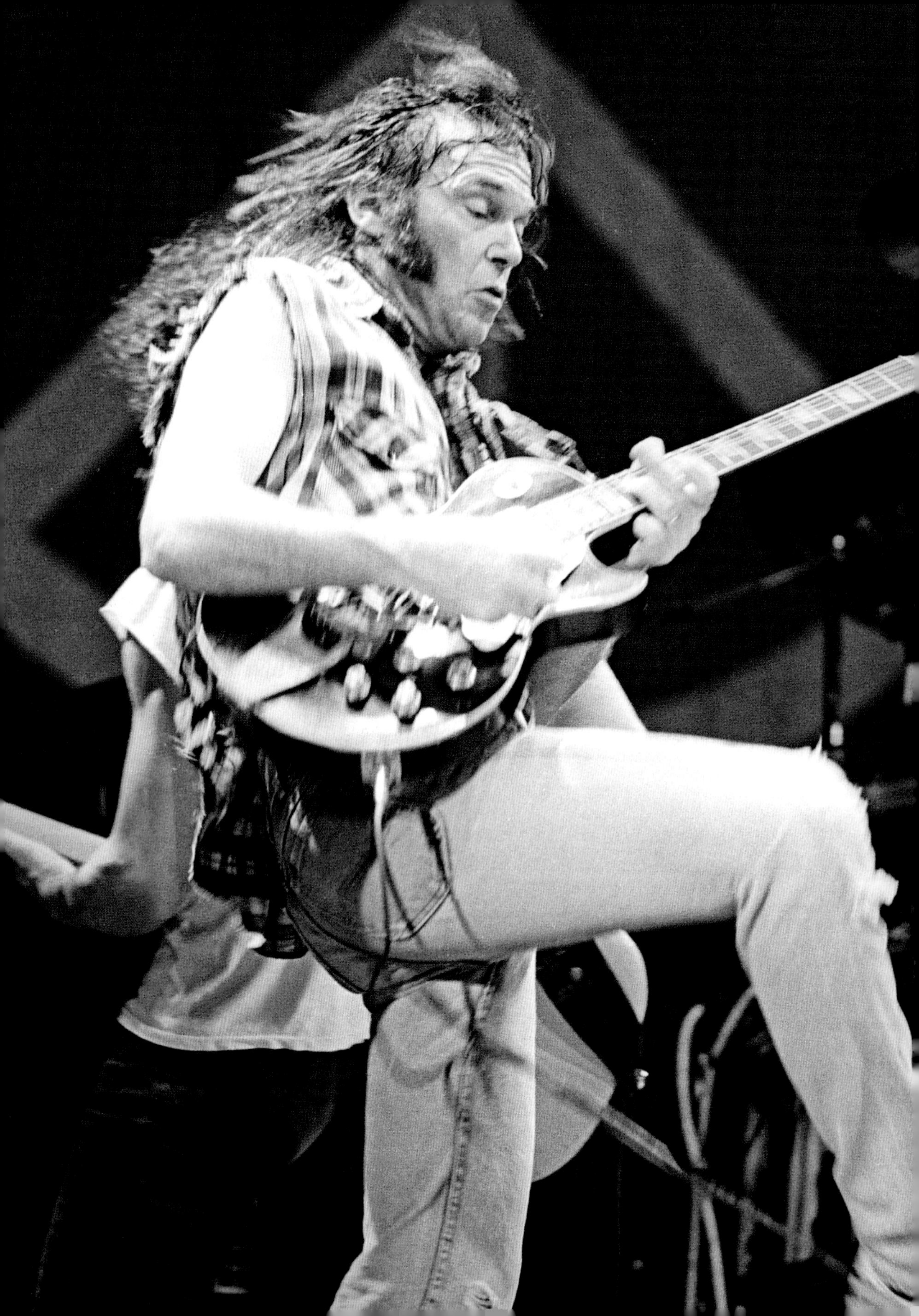

Neil Young
1945–present

Long before Kurt Cobain of Nirvana (242) quoted "My My, Hey Hey" in his suicide note, Neil Young had stamped his authority on rock 'n' roll.

"In 1965," recalled Joni Mitchell (102), "I was up in Canada, and there was a friend of mine [Young] up there who had just left a rock 'n' roll band in Winnipeg, Manitoba . . . to become a folk singer à la Bob Dylan, who was his hero at that time. And, at the same time, there were breaks in his life and he was going into new and exciting directions." Young had graduated through playing Ventures-style instrumentals, Duane Eddy covers, and Beatles/Shadows hybrids. He dallied with folk, then joined future funk star Rick James' band.

After relocating to California, he formed Buffalo Springfield with Stephen Stills. When that band fell apart, his solo career kicked into gear with 1969's *Everybody Knows This Is Nowhere*. In the ensuing classics—with Crosby, Stills & Nash, and his own Crazy Horse—Young proved a gifted successor to Bob Dylan. But when 1972's *Harvest* and its hit "Heart of Gold" drove him into the mainstream, he passed the country rock baton to the Eagles (132) and headed into the darkness. Young's albums from 1972 to 1975—*Time Fades Away, On the Beach*, and *Tonight's the Night*—were ragged and nihilistic enough to mark him as a forefather of punk even before he namechecked the Sex Pistols' (166) Johnny Rotten on 1979's *Rust Never Sleeps*.

In the Eighties, his startling leaps from rockabilly to country to electronic rock yielded at least one classic—1982's *Trans*—and put him in the unique position of being sued by his record company for making music that was "unrepresentative."

"He's made whole albums that aren't great," said Flea of the Red Hot Chili Peppers (232), "and, instead of going back to a formula that he knows works, he would rather represent where he is at the time . . ."

The *Rust Never Sleeps*-esque *Freedom* (1989) rescued his career, and helpfully coincided with a tribute album featuring Pixies (224), Nick Cave (202), and other upstarts. With 1990's *Ragged Glory*, he secured a place as a godfather of grunge. "I don't know if you could name anybody better who came out of rock and roll," admired Randy Newman.

Ensuing years have seen a high output: some great (1993's *Unplugged*, 2003's *Greendale*), some interesting (1994's *Sleeps with Angels*), and some patchy (2002's *Are You Passionate?*). All are marked by his guitar playing (from soothing to searing), poetic lyrics, yearning vocals, and fierce disinterest in giving his fans what they want (hence 2006's criticism of U.S. foreign policy, *Living with War*).

> *"There's youthful redemption in everything he does— a joyfulness about being an independent thinker in America."* —David Bowie

"The guy just inhabits the damn music," Bonnie Raitt marveled. "When some twelve-year-old kid sees that, he's going to remember and one day he's going to play like Neil Young, not like some wuss."

Young's live albums range from beautiful (1993's *Unplugged*) to barnstorming (1991's *Weld*). *Live Rust* (1979) is both—and serves as an introduction to his Sixties and Seventies work.

Greendale (2003) was a return to form after several albums that did little more than recycle old ideas (albeit to pleasant effect). Its quirky concept is engaging and its songs are gorgeous.

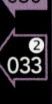

Mr. Young meets the future Mr. "Super Freak"

One of rock's nuttier connections was forged in 1966, when Neil Young joined the Mynah Birds. Their leader was James Ambrose Johnson, Jr., later better known as funk star Rick James (left). "He was a little bit touchy, dominating," Young recalled, "but a good guy." The Mynah Birds became "the only white band at Motown❶," thanks in no small part to James' uncle, Melvin Franklin, being a member of The Temptations❷. But the band fell apart when James was busted for deserting the U.S. Navy. Young and bassist Bruce Palmer packed up a hearse, drove to California, and formed Buffalo Springfield. Meanwhile, James developed a brand of "punk funk" that made him a superstar with 1981's *Street Songs*. His songs, including "Super Freak" and the Mary Jane Girls' "All Night Long," were huge hits that have been endlessly sampled ever since. Sadly, James' defiantly rock 'n' roll habits took his life in August 2004.

Neil Young

November 12, 1945
Neil Percival Kenneth Robert Ragland Young is born in Toronto, Ontario. He will later mention Ontario in 1970's beautiful Crosby, Stills, Nash & Young classic, "Helpless."

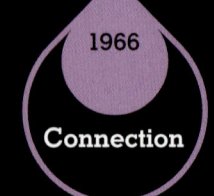

1966 Connection

November 12, 1968
Young's self-titled debut LP is released. "The Old Laughing Lady" features Merry Clayton, who will later sing on Lynyrd Skynyrd's song "Sweet Home Alabama" (see above right).

July 23, 1963
Young records with The Squires, his fifth band after The Classics, The Stardusters, The Esquires, and The Jades. He will also play with The High Flying Birds and 4 To Go.

December 5, 1966
Buffalo Springfield's self-titled debut LP is released. It will be reissued in March 1967 with the hit "For What It's Worth," written by Young's bandmate Stephen Stills, added.

Connection 1969

Crosby, Stills, Nash, and . . .

The Byrds' David Crosby, Buffalo Springfield's Stephen Stills (left, with Young), and The Hollies' Graham Nash were an immediate hit when they united in 1969. To flesh out their sound on tour, they hired Young (and, at Rick James' recommendation, Motown❶ bassist Greg Wells). Crosby, Stills, Nash & Young graced two key 1969 events: the Stones'❷ blood-soaked Altamont and the iconic Woodstock❸. (Joni Mitchell's❹ song about this event was a hit for CSN&Y.) The band had an eventful evolution: between their U.S. No. 1s—1970's *Déjà Vu* and 1971's *4 Way Street*—they split, only to reform in varying combinations (and with frequent acrimony) over the ensuing decades. They made it as far as the studio for 1988's *American Dream* and 1999's *Looking Forward*—although their heartbreaking harmonies and enviable musicianship are best experienced on their rare appearances as a quartet onstage.

80 TURN ON, TUNE IN, DROP OUT

Lynyrd Skynyrd's "Sweet Home Alabama"

❶ 044

"Like The Beatles❶," said Lynyrd Skynyrd's Gary Rossington (left), "Neil Young was another guy who helped us get started writing real songs." One of the most popular of those songs was 1974's "Sweet Home Alabama." Mentioning "Mr. Young," it responded to generalizations in tracks on 1972's *Harvest*—"Southern Man" and "Alabama." "We thought Neil was shooting all the ducks in order to kill one or two," said Ronnie Van Zant. But the song led the members of Lynyrd Skynyrd to be branded as redneck conservatives. Nonetheless, Young thought "Sweet Home Alabama" was a great song. "I've actually performed it live a couple of times," he said. He duly wrote "Powderfinger" for Skynyrd, but a 1977 plane crash tore the band apart before they got a chance to cut the song. However, on the cover of their final pre-crash album, *Street Survivors*, Van Zant is wearing a Neil Young *Tonight's the Night* T-shirt.

March 11, 1972

Harvest tops the U.S. chart, thanks to the hit "Heart of Gold," with backing vocals by Linda Ronstadt and James Taylor. Both the album and single will quickly go gold.

1974 Influence

March 22, 1985

Bruce Springsteen joins Young onstage in Sydney (the latter's former guitarist, Nils Lofgren, was in Bruce's E Street Band). They perform a long version of "Down by the River."

January 13, 1995

At a Rock and Roll Hall of Fame ceremony, Young jams with Led Zeppelin on "When the Levee Breaks." The night will inspire "Downtown" on Young's album *Mirror Ball*.

May 1974

Young's odd movie *Journey Through the Past* is released. It features Crosby, Stills and Nash, with whom he will start a tour in July. (Bob Dylan attends a Minneapolis show.)

November 25, 1976

Young guests at The Band's star-studded final show. A rock of cocaine in Young's nose will be edited out For Martin Scorsese's film of the event, *The Last Waltz*.

Connection 1992

March 15, 1999

Young inducts Paul McCartney —"one of the greatest songwriters ever"—into the Rock and Roll Hall of Fame. The ex-Beatle duly declares, "I love Neil!"

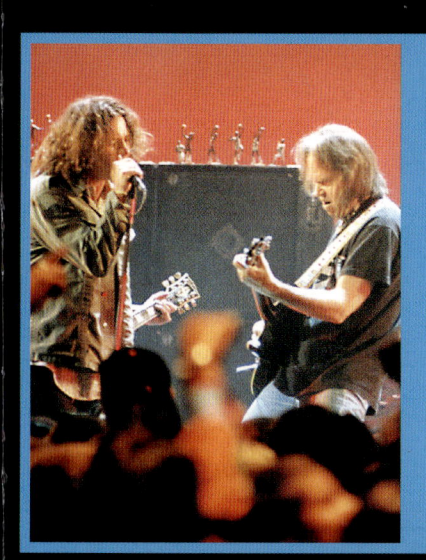

Pearl Jam keep *Rockin' in the Free World*

❶ 248
❷ 062
❸ 150
❹ 218
❺ 050

Shortly after Pearl Jam❶ and newly crowned "godfather of grunge" Neil Young played a Bob Dylan❷ tribute in New York in 1992, the former were invited to Young's annual Bridge School Benefit. These charity events, organized by Young and his wife Pegi, have attracted acts from Bruce Springsteen❸ to Metallica❹ and Bob Dylan to The Beach Boys'❺ Brian Wilson. But Pearl Jam enjoyed the most fruitful link with Young. They jammed on his "Rockin' in the Free World" at a 1993 MTV awards show (left), and Eddie Vedder inducted Young into the Rock and Roll Hall of Fame. This association blossomed into 1995's collaborative album *Mirror Ball*, and the band (minus Vedder) backed Young on tour. The two acts have often worked together since then—and, as Young fansite thrasherswheat.org notes, Pearl Jam's 1996 song "Off He Goes" sounds like a tribute to their mentor, whose "thoughts are too big for his size."

NEIL YOUNG 81

legendary label

Atlantic
1947–present

A $10,000 loan from Ahmet Ertegun's dentist kick-started one of music's best-loved labels. "We started Atlantic," said Ertegun, son of a Turkish diplomat, "simply because we wanted to sign a few artists whose music we liked, and make the kind of records that we would want to buy."

The label, initially associated with R&B, scored a first major hit in 1949 with Stick McGhee's "Drinkin' Wine Spo-Dee-O-Dee." Ray Charles proved a star signing—his hits such as "What'd I Say" turned the label into a major player. Ertegun even bid for Elvis ◀012, but "he was a little too expensive for us."

A distribution deal with the Stax ◀052 label added further gems to its catalog. Its soul credentials were sealed when Ertegen took Aretha Franklin 084▶ from obscurity on Columbia to legend on Atlantic.

The label proved adept at moving with the times. "We recorded a group called Cream," Ertegun told Schwann Spectrum, "then I got the Bee Gees, and then Led Zeppelin 098▶. Then we signed up Buffalo Springfield . . . Suddenly, we're in the new music—in the new white rock and roll syndrome."

The breadth of the label's subsequent success can be measured by its multi-platinum albums—from Yes' *Fragile* to Tori Amos' *Little Earthquakes*, Stevie Nicks' *Bella Donna* to Stone Temple Pilots' *Core*, and INXS' *Kick* to Jewel's *Pieces of You*.

Perhaps the greatest testimony to Atlantic came when Led Zeppelin reunited for a tribute show to Ertegun, who died in 2006. "Ahmet Ertegun was a major foundation of solidarity and accord," said Robert Plant. "For us, he *was* Atlantic Records."

1950+
1972+
1977+

December 1950
Ruth Brown's "Teardrops from My Eyes" begins an eleven-week stint at the top of the U.S. R&B chart.

August 1965
Sonny & Cher, graduates of the Phil Spector stable, give Atlantic a transatlantic No. 1 with "I Got You Babe."

July 15, 1966
Percy Sledge's self-penned, chart-topping ballad "When a Man Loves a Woman" earns the label its first of many U.S. gold discs.

❶ 054

APRIL 1, 1971: Rolling Stones Records gets rolling

The Rolling Stones'❶ rotting relationship with the Decca label culminated in the band responding to demands for a single by cutting "Cocksucker Blues." "They are very welcome to put that out," said Mick Jagger, "but somehow they've declined to do so." When the band's Decca contract expired, Jagger talked to Atlantic about establishing their own label. "They wanted to be on a funky, independent label," Ertegun (left, with Jagger) recalled. "Mick knew our catalog very well—it was some of the music he grew up with, and he was a fan. On the other hand, they were an enormous group who needed a major distribution network. We had a bit of both." The association proved profitable, as the Stones scored fifteen gold and platinum albums—from 1971's *Sticky Fingers* to 1986's *Dirty Work*—and two, big-selling singles, 1973's "Angie" and 1978's "Miss You." "I was flattered," said Ertegun, "and thrilled."

TURN ON, TUNE IN, DROP OUT

April 15, 1972

Roberta Flack's version of Ewan MacColl's "The First Time Ever I Saw Your Face" tops the *Billboard* chart and will become the year's most successful single.

April 17, 1972

Pictures at an Exhibition, by supergroup Emerson, Lake & Palmer (from King Crimson, Atomic Rooster, and The Nice), goes gold in the U.S.A.

April 12, 1973

Three years after signing to Atlantic, R&B revivalists The J. Geils Band release the album that will be their first top ten hit, *Bloodshot*.

January 1975

Eight hundred cases of beer are shipped to Atlantic's New York office to toast their latest signing: Alice Cooper. He will hit big with *Welcome to My Nightmare*.

APRIL 9, 1977: Abba's "Dancing Queen" soars

❶ 098

Mind-bogglingly big in most countries, Swedish superstars Abba were initially a minor concern in the U.S.A. After a top ten smash with 1974's "Waterloo," their profile waned, although 1975's *Greatest Hits* went gold. No one, however, could resist "Dancing Queen"—one of the Seventies' most stupendous singles—and the U.S.A. was one of eleven countries in which it topped the chart (in April 1977). The band scored more hits on Atlantic: the 1978 single "Take a Chance on Me," and, from 1976 to 1980, the albums *Arrival*, *The Album*, *Voulez-Vous*, *Greatest Hits Vol. 2*, and *Super Trouper*. Abba forged another Atlantic connection when—in a bid to put their newly opened Polar Studios on the map—they persuaded Led Zeppelin❶ to record 1979's *In Through the Out Door* there. The experience was not entirely happy: bassist John Paul Jones complained that it was "continually night time in Stockholm."

August 13, 1977

With Rick Wakeman back in the fold, Yes score a second U.K. No. 1, after *Tales from Topographic Oceans* (1973), with *Going for the One*.

May 31, 1978

Thanks to the hit "Follow You Follow Me," Genesis score a first U.S. gold album with . . . *And Then There Were Three* . . .

December 9, 1978

Having already sold more than a million copies, Chic's disco anthem, the later much sampled "Le Freak," tops the U.S. chart for the first of three times.

April 10, 1980

Atlantic collects more gold awards for two big sellers: Bette Midler (the soundtrack *The Rose*) and the Spinners (the single "Workin' My Way Back to You").

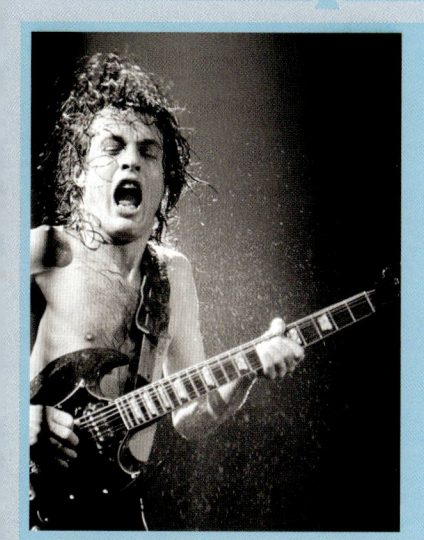

DECEMBER 26, 1981: AC/DC *About to Rock* . . .

❶ 182

❷ 098

There's nothing quiet about AC/DC's❶ music. Yet, with little fanfare, they became one of the world's most successful bands. Signed to Atlantic in 1976, their fortunes rose with 1976's *High Voltage* and U.S. top three hit *Dirty Deeds Done Dirt Cheap*, 1977's *Let There Be Rock*, 1978's *Powerage* (one of Keith Richards' favorites), and 1979's *Highway to Hell*. The latter was their last with singer Bon Scott, who died in 1980. Within months (and now with Scott's replacement Brian Johnson), *Back in Black* scored them another hit, and, with the demise of Led Zeppelin❷, they became the world's biggest hard rock band. *For Those About to Rock (We Salute You)* was their first U.S. No. 1, in December 1981, and sold over four million in the U.S.A. alone. Yet even that was eclipsed by *Back in Black*, which—with more then twenty-two million U.S. sales—is among rock's top five, all-time biggest sellers (just behind *Led Zeppelin IV*).

ATLANTIC

Aretha Franklin 1942–present

Whitney Houston's godmother is the all-time Queen of Soul. Immortal hits such as "Respect," "I Never Loved a Man (The Way I Love You)," and "Chain of Fools" have made her the most successful woman in the history of the *Billboard* charts (and the fifth most successful overall).

Despite being signed by John Hammond—who snared Dylan ◁062 and Bruce Springsteen 150▷—she was never a big success on the Columbia label. "I don't think Columbia let her play the piano much . . ." Jerry Wexler, the man who gave Franklin a home on Atlantic ◁082, told *Rolling Stone*. "When a singer plays an instrument, you should let them play it on the record, even if the singer is not a virtuoso . . . In Aretha's case, there was no compromise in quality. She was a brilliant pianist."

That piano was integral to hits such as "Bridge Over Troubled Water," "Think," and "Do Right Woman—Do Right Man," but it is for her voice that Franklin is renowned. "When she opens up," remarked Tom Jones, "this volume comes out . . . Pop singers don't often have that projection. Aretha Franklin is the only one that made me go, 'Jesus!'"

She even impressed Atlantic's biggest star, Otis Redding, who wrote her best-known hit, "Respect." "Otis came up to my office right before 'Respect' was released . . ." recalled Wexler. "He said, 'She done took my song.' He said it benignly and ruefully. He knew the identity of the song was already slipping away from him to her." As British singer-songwriter Paul Weller said, "Once you've heard Aretha Franklin . . . you judge everything by that standard."

March 25, 1942

Aretha Louise Franklin is born in Memphis. She will release *The Gospel Sound of Aretha Franklin* on a local label at fourteen, then sign to Columbia at eighteen.

November 20, 1961

An old Al Jolson number, "Rock-a-Bye Your Baby with a Dixie Melody," gives Franklin her sole hit on the Columbia label. She will sign to Atlantic in 1966.

June 3, 1967

Having already gone gold, Franklin's Grammy-winning reinvention of "Respect" tops the U.S. charts. It will also go top ten in the U.K.

JUNE 13, 1967: A first gold album for the queen

Franklin was one of the first soul stars to conceive albums as a whole, rather than singles plus filler. Her 1967 Atlantic debut, *I Never Loved a Man the Way I Love You*, was a prime example—opening with the storming "Respect" and closing with Sam Cooke's ❶ "A Change Is Gonna Come." Released in March, it peaked at No. 2 during seventy-nine weeks on the U.S. chart, and was followed by three further classics: the same year's *Aretha Arrives* and 1968's *Lady Soul* and *Aretha Now*. This outpouring of creativity was assisted by Franklin's sister Carolyn (her backing singer and a gifted writer), and session men such as Bobby Womack. "One day," recalled Womack, "Jerry Wexler whispered in my ear, 'Would you be opposed to us trying out this guy Eric Clapton ❷?' I laughed out loud when he walked in with his guitar in a pillowcase. But his playing blew me out. I really believed that a white boy had soul."

❶ 026
❷ 075

1971

Hits such as "Spanish Harlem" and the funky "Rock Steady" keep Franklin's success going into the new decade.

February 20, 1974

"Until You Come Back to Me"—first recorded (but long unreleased) by Stevie Wonder—goes gold. It is her last big pop hit until 1982.

May 1976

Sparkle, produced by Curtis Mayfield, will prove a big-selling return to form. Two of its songs will be covered on En Vogue's 1992 classic *Funky Divas*.

July 6, 1985

Franklin's renaissance—which began with 1982's, Luther Vandross-helmed *Jump to It*—pays off as "Freeway of Love" hits the pop chart top ten.

APRIL 18, 1987: Twenty years at the top

Two decades after "Respect" topped the U.S. chart, Franklin returned to No. 1 with George Michael on "I Knew You Were Waiting (for Me)." It was the peak of a period that confirmed her pre-eminence, and came just months after she was inducted into the Rock and Roll Hall of Fame by Keith Richards (with whom she covered "Jumpin' Jack Flash" for the 1986 movie of the same name). Franklin's other triumphs included the 1988 gospel album *One Lord, One Faith, One Baptism*, and the 1985 Eurythmics collaboration, "Sisters Are Doin' It for Themselves." "It was conceived as a duet, but originally for Tina Turner ❶ . . ." said Annie Lennox. When Turner declined, "The song was put to Aretha, and she loved it . . . It was really an interesting encounter because we come from such different backgrounds . . . but it was beautiful. She sings as only Aretha can, and she put so much into the song. It was inspiring."

❶ 029

ARETHA FRANKLIN

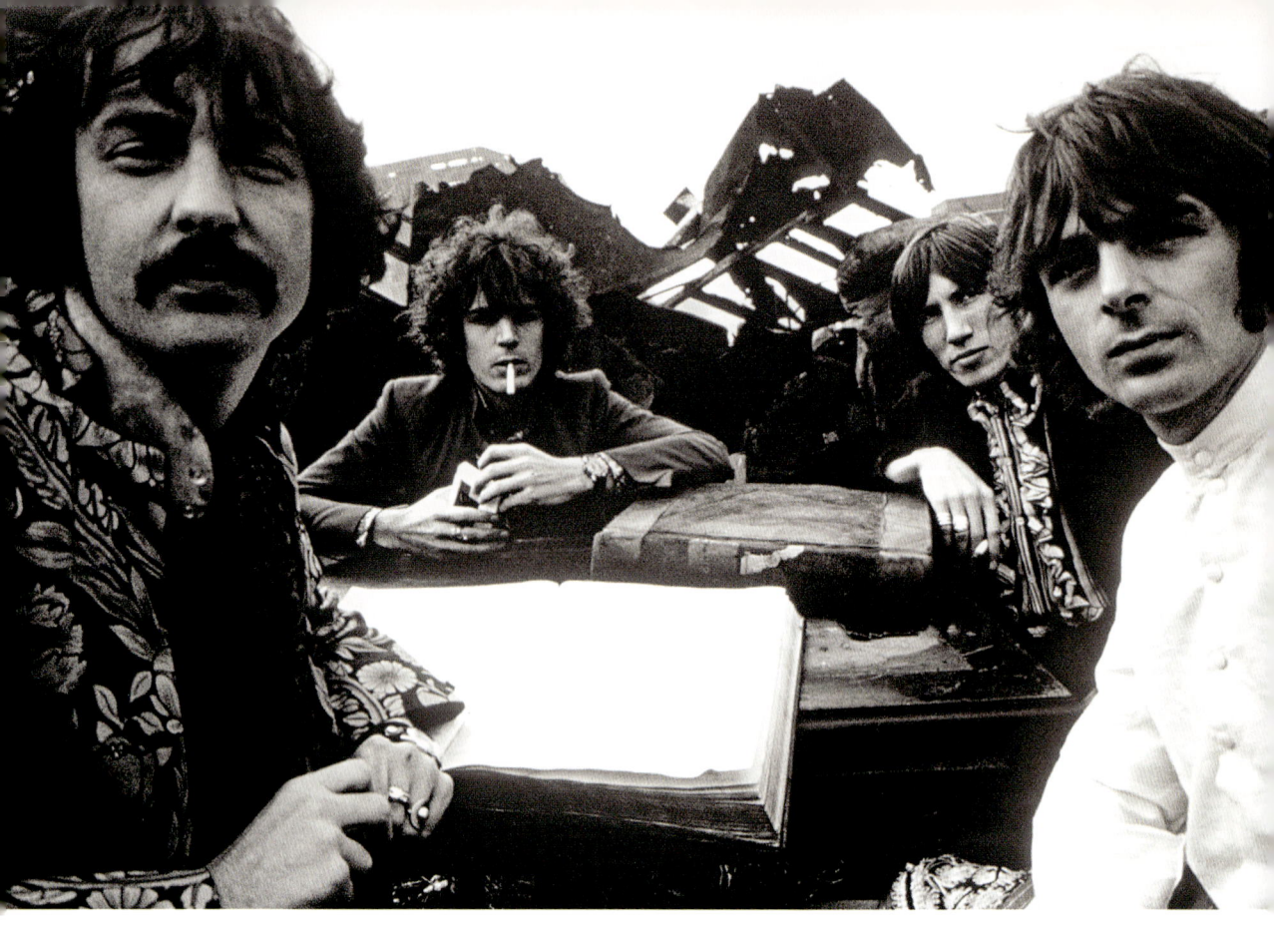

Pink Floyd 1964–2005

| 1943+ | 1967+ | 1970+ | 1974+ | 1981+ | 1992+ |

Pink Floyd could once stroll unrecognized through their own audiences, boasted at least two members who were barely above bar band levels of musical competence, and had only two big international hits (1973's "Money" and 1979's "Another Brick in the Wall Part II"). However, they have been staggeringly successful and influential.

They made two of the biggest-selling albums in history—*Dark Side of the Moon,* a favorite of Brian Wilson of The Beach Boys ◁050▷, and *The Wall*—which have, respectively, sold more than fifteen and twenty-three million albums in the U.S.A. alone.

The poppy psychedelia of the band's formative era influenced acts from Marc Bolan ◁128▷ to Blur, and the solo material of early leading light, Syd Barrett, counts R.E.M. ◁204▷ among its aficionados.

Radiohead ◁264▷—regularly cited as "the new Pink Floyd"—have flouted commercial constraints in distinctly Floydian fashion (lyrical misanthropy, few hits, idiosyncratic art rock, and massive sales). And the Floyd have influenced stadium spectacles by The Stones ◁054▷ (whose riffs David Gilmour spent a year teaching to Barrett). "The show, just musically, leaves me cold," said Mick Jagger. "But when they add the whole spectacle, it's great."

Even John Lydon—whose "I hate Pink Floyd" T-shirt is a key component of the legend of the Sex Pistols ◁166▷ (and who rechristened his friend and bandmate Simon Richie "Sid Vicious" in honor of Syd Barrett)—eventually admitted to *The Quietus:* "You'd have to be daft as a brush to say you didn't like Pink Floyd. They've done great stuff."

1943

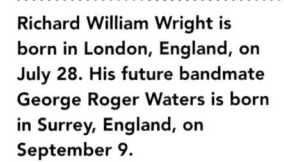

Richard William Wright is born in London, England, on July 28. His future bandmate George Roger Waters is born in Surrey, England, on September 9.

January 27, 1944

Nicholas Berkeley Mason is born in Birmingham, England. The drummer will eventually be the only person to appear on every Pink Floyd album.

1946

Roger Keith "Syd" Barrett (January 6) and David Jon Gilmour (March 6) are born in Cambridge, England. The pair become good friends.

❶ 068
❷ 075
❸ 048
❹ 044

DECEMBER 23, 1966: The UFO takes off

The house band of British psychedelia, the Floyd became synonymous with London's leading underground club, UFO, which they first played in December 1966. "Syd Barrett was an influence . . ." The Who's❶ Pete Townshend recalled. "Syd influenced Eric [Clapton]❷ as well. We went to see the Floyd at the UFO club a couple of times . . . One of the most frightening bands I'd ever seen, and it wasn't just because everybody was doing LSD." Signed to EMI❸ in 1967, Pink Floyd picked "Arnold Layne"—one of the few concise songs in their repertoire—as a single. Hyped into the charts by their management, the song hit the U.K. top twenty. The band then recorded their debut album, *The Piper at the Gates of Dawn*. "The Beatles❹ were making *Sgt. Pepper* in the other studio [at Abbey Road]," Waters recalled. "Ringo, Paul, and George came into our studios and we all stood rooted to the spot, excited."

November 4, 1967

A U.K. top ten act, the Floyd begin their first U.S. tour. "An amazing disaster," said Waters. "Syd by this time was completely off his head."

January 12, 1968

Having failed to recruit Jeff Beck, the Floyd play their first gig with Gilmour. Fed up with Barrett's druggy eccentricities, they will soon sack him.

July 13, 1968

A Saucerful of Secrets—which features both Barrett and Gilmour—hits the U.K. chart. Its title track is a key step on the band's path to elaborately planned epics.

July 20, 1969

At a London TV studio, the Floyd provide a live soundtrack to the BBC's coverage of NASA's *Apollo* moon landings.

NOVEMBER 1969: *Ummagumma*

From spacey jams to sonic silliness, 1969's half-live, half-studio, double set *Ummagumma* was a signpost to the Floyd's future. It demonstrated that Waters was the only one who could write decent lyrics, that Mason ought not be allowed in the studio alone, and that Gilmour and Wright could transform mundane ideas into magical music. The album spent twenty-one weeks on the U.K. chart and was their first to crash the U.S. top 100. This blazed a trail for 1970's *Atom Heart Mother* to top the British chart and narrowly miss the U.S. top fifty—success that was out of all proportion to its monstrous, quasi-classical contents. "If," cracked Waters over a decade later, "somebody said to me now, 'Right, here's a million pounds—go out and play 'Atom Heart Mother,'" I'd say, 'You must be joking. I'm not playing that rubbish.'" Gilmour concurred: "'Atom Heart Mother' strikes me as absolute crap."

PINK FLOYD

February 7, 1970

Barrett makes his solo debut, *The Madcap Laughs*. Co-produced by Gilmour and Waters, it also features backing by members of the band The Soft Machine.

November 20, 1971

Meddle features "Echoes"—a small step from The Beatles' "Across the Universe," but a giant leap toward the *Dark Side of the Moon*.

January 20, 1972

In Brighton, England, *Dark Side of the Moon* receives its premiere—a performance that falls apart amid what Waters describes as "severe technical horror."

June 3, 1972

Obscured by Clouds is released. It is their second soundtrack for movie director Barbet Schroeder, following 1969's *More*.

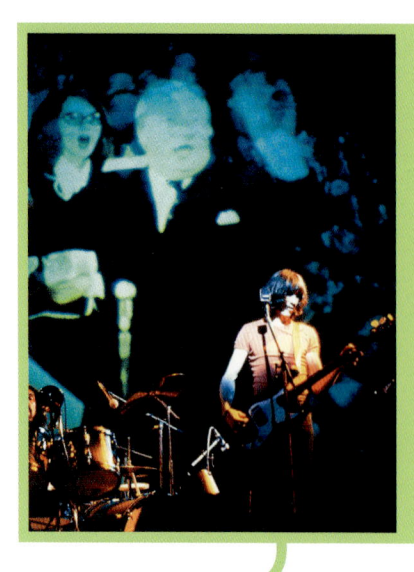

MARCH 1973: *Dark Side of the Moon*

At a meeting in Nick Mason's kitchen in late 1971, Waters proposed a concept album of sorts, based on what Gilmour called "the pressures that drive a young chap mad"—from money to mortality. From these humble origins sprang *Dark Side of the Moon*—which, buoyed by the hit "Money," vaulted to the top of the U.S. chart and turned the Floyd into reluctant superstars. A timeless joy, *Dark Side* never stopped selling and has enjoyed full-length stage revivals courtesy of Phish, The Flaming Lips, and, in 1994, the Floyd themselves. In the short term, however, its success left the band with no idea how to follow it up. Eventually, they hit on the idea of creating music using household objects. "We spent something like four weeks in the studio on it," recalled engineer Alan Parsons (later to front The Alan Parsons Project), "and came away with no more than one and a half minutes of music."

June 1974

"Gotta Be Crazy," "Raving and Drooling," and "Shine On You Crazy Diamond" receive their premiere on a French tour.

June 1975

Barrett turns up at Abbey Road while the band are mixing a tribute to him, "Shine On You Crazy Diamond." His verdict: "Sounds a bit old."

July 5, 1975

Captain Beefheart and Steve Miller are among the support acts at the U.K.'s Knebworth festival. The Floyd headline with one of their worst sets.

September 1975

Wish You Were Here is the first Floyd album to top both the U.K. and U.S. charts. It will ultimately sell more than six million copies Stateside.

❶ 122

❷ 132

JULY 6, 1977: Pig Floyd build *The Wall*

Chiming oddly with punk, 1977's roaring *Animals* boasted new versions of their three-year-old "Gotta Be Crazy" and "Raving and Drooling" (now titled "Dogs" and "Sheep" respectively). The album—famed for its artwork of a pig hovering over London's Battersea Power Station—occasioned a stadium tour that Waters (left) hated. By the end, in Montreal on July 6, he found himself spitting at an over-excited fan. This was the final catalyst for a concept with which he had been toying since an equally unhappy U.S. tour in 1975: *The Wall*. Ironically, given that this 1979 album expressed Waters' alienation from fans, it became their greatest commercial success. Propelled by the No. 1 "Another Brick in the Wall Part II," it spent fifteen weeks atop the *Billboard* chart and ranks behind only Michael Jackson's❶ *Thriller* and the Eagles'❷ *Their Greatest Hits* in the best-selling albums in U.S. sales history.

June 17, 1981
The Waters-Gilmour-Mason-Wright lineup plays its last show for twenty-four years. Wright has in fact been fired, and is on *The Wall* tour as a session player.

May 23, 1982
Alan Parker's *Pink Floyd The Wall* premieres at the Cannes Film Festival. Bob Geldof, its star, can't stand Pink Floyd, as he tells Waters and Gilmour.

April 2, 1983
The Final Cut enters at the top of the U.K. chart. Conceived as the soundtrack to *The Wall* movie, it evolves into Waters' Floydian swan song.

May 8, 1984
Waters releases *The Pros and Cons of Hitch Hiking*. A pretty dire song cycle, it is redeemed by Eric Clapton's impressive guitar playing.

DECEMBER 1985: Troubled Waters

❶ 048

❷ 102

Long at odds with his bandmates, Waters announced at the end of 1985 to the Floyd's record labels (EMI❶ in the U.K., Columbia in the U.S.A.) that he was leaving. To his fury, Gilmour and Mason elected to continue as Pink Floyd, and recruited Wright to make them stronger "legally and musically." The subsequent war overshadowed their 1987 albums *Radio K.A.O.S.* (Waters) and *A Momentary Lapse of Reason* (Floyd). Ultimately, the brand name won (just as it had done in 1968 when Barrett's departure left the band without its chief songwriter). Waters' audiences dwindled while the Floyd sold out stadiums (hence 1988's live *Delicate Sound of Thunder*). Waters, however, had a trick up his sleeve. In 1990, he staged *The Wall* in Berlin (left), to an audience of more than a quarter of a million. The show featured Joni Mitchell❷, The Scorpions, Sinéad O'Connor, Van Morrison, Bryan Adams, and The Band.

September 7, 1992
Jeff Beck guests on Waters' *Amused to Death*, his biggest solo success. Sections by Flea of the Red Hot Chili Peppers are cut.

April 1994
The Division Bell (titled by author Douglas Adams) is the first Floyd album to top both the U.K. and U.S. charts in its first week.

January 16, 1996
Floyd are inducted into the Rock and Roll Hall of Fame by Smashing Pumpkin Billy Corgan. (They will join the U.K. "hall" in 2005, with Pete Townshend inducting.)

November 5, 2001
Echoes, a nicely sequenced "best of" is released. It is the finest of Floyd's compilations, although the 1992 set *Shine On* had the best working title: *The Big Bong Theory*.

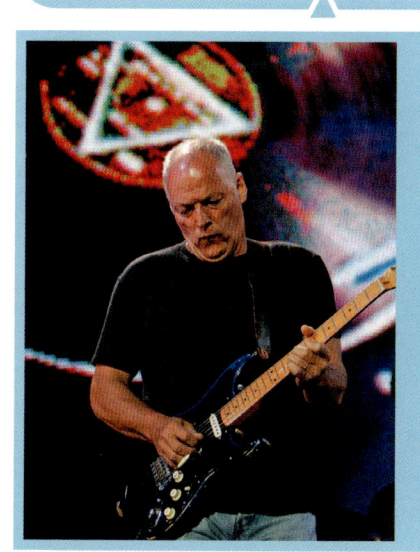

JULY 8, 2005: Shine on you crazy diamonds

❶ 216

❷ 134

In a turn of events that made the front page of British newspapers, Pink Floyd reunited with Waters for Live Aid's sequel, Live8❶. Waters hailed this "small window of opportunity to play together for one last time" as "a terrific experience." He even seemed open to a longer-term venture, though that was rejected by Gilmour (left), whose *On an Island* (2006) was the highest charting solo effort by any Floyd member. The two parties duly performed separately at a tribute show for Barrett, who died of cancer on July 7, 2006. Wright also played with Gilmour (most notably at a May 2006 show in London where David Bowie❷ sang the Floyd's first hit, "Arnold Layne"), while Mason drummed for Waters. Lingering hopes of a reunion were dashed by Wright's death from cancer on September 15, 2008—but the Floyd name has long proved that it can outlive the departure of even the most valuable individual.

PINK FLOYD 89

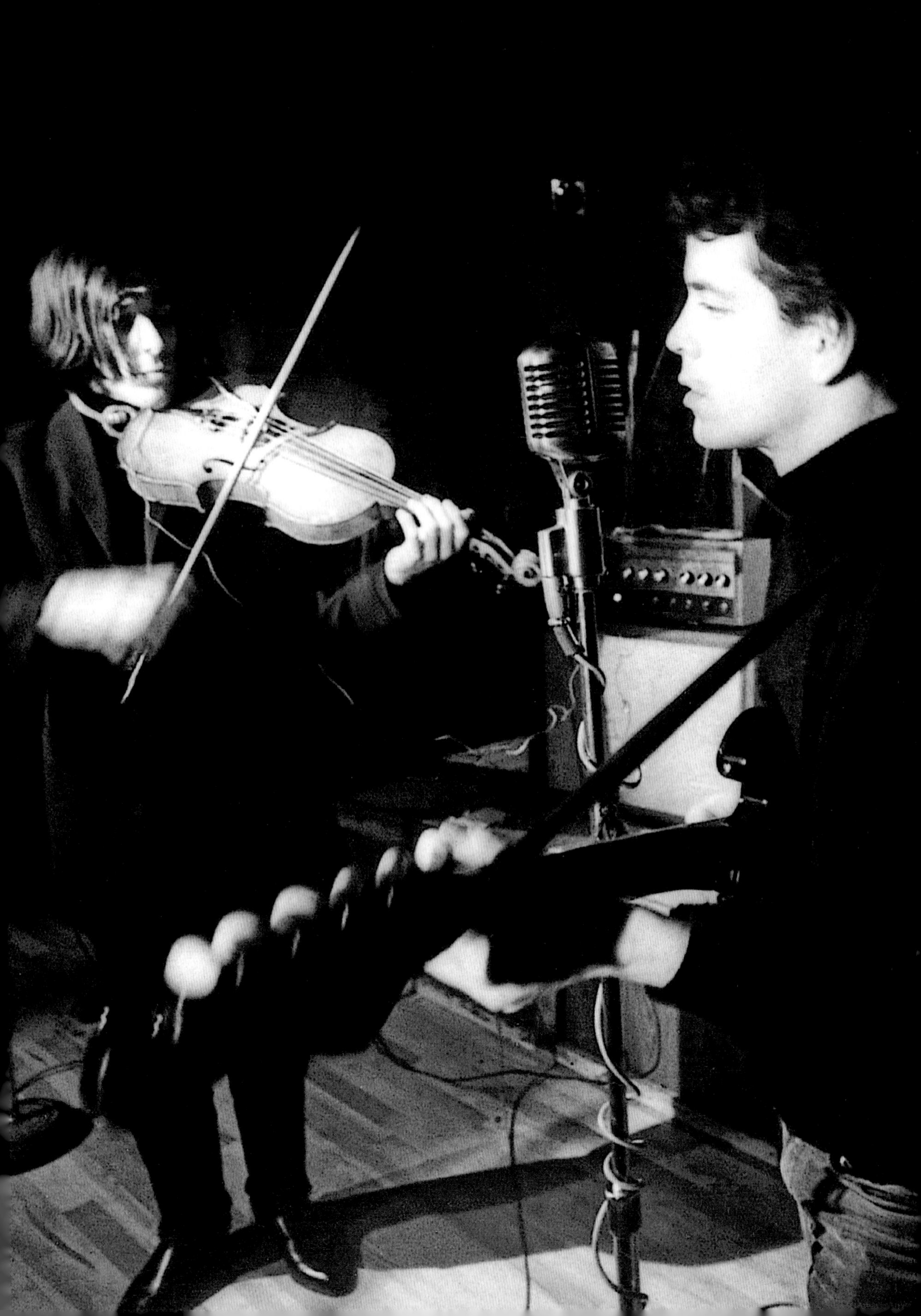

The Velvet Underground
1965–73

Brian Eno 138▶ famously observed that hardly anyone bought The Velvet Underground's first album, but everyone who did so went on to form a band. Indeed, that legendary 1967 debut album peaked at No. 171. (Remarkably, the group's other three U.S. charting albums performed even worse.)

Their most obvious successors are indie acts—The Strokes, Spacemen 3, Sonic Youth, Yo La Tengo, and The Jesus and Mary Chain. But their influence can be heard in songs by major acts as diverse as U2 192▶ ("Exit," "One") and Prince 174▶ ("The Cross").

> "I must have been the first person in the world to cover a Velvet Underground song."
> —David Bowie

Velvets songs have been covered by David Bowie 134▶ ("I'm Waiting for the Man"), Joy Division 184▶ ("Sister Ray"), Martin Gore of Depeche Mode 196▶ ("Candy Says"), Duran Duran 200▶ ("Femme Fatale"), Nick Cave 202▶ ("All Tomorrow's Parties"), R.E.M. 204▶ ("After Hours," among others), Nirvana 242▶ ("Here She Comes Now"), and others from Tori Amos ("New Age") to Jane's Addiction ("Rock & Roll").

Much of the attraction for acts at the outset of the Velvets' career was their seemingly easy-to-play sound. Their songs were simple yet ambitious, like those of a garage band with delusions of grandeur —which was, effectively, exactly what they were.

They emerged from The Primitives, featuring guitarist Sterling Morrison, multi-instrumentalist John Cale (who brought viola, keyboards, and bass to the new band), and singer/guitarist Lou Reed. The latter—a fan of doo-wop and R&B—had been a staff writer for Pickwick Records: a role he rapidly outgrew with songs such as "Heroin" (memorably described by Ryan Adams as "the sound of Bob Dylan getting his ass kicked behind a gas station").

The Velvets were adopted by Pop Art mastermind Andy Warhol, who—to the band's displeasure—installed model Nico (born Christa Päffgen) on vocals. With androgynous drummer Maureen Tucker replacing Angus MacLise, they became the house band for Warhol's multimedia events, known as the *Exploding Plastic Inevitable*. The association with Warhol and Nico lasted for only one album but this one record altered the course of rock, with extraordinary songs such as "Venus in Furs," as well as more simple tracks such as "Femme Fatale," which were rendered startling by Nico and Reed's deadpan variants on pop singing.

Ego-fueled musical differences led to a series of Velvet lineup changes: Reed replaced Cale with bassist Doug Yule, then quit the band himself. Morrison and Tucker left in 1971, leaving Yule to preside over the final Velvets album, *Squeeze* (which, weirdly, was made with Deep Purple's drummer, Ian Paice). Yet the albums in those years yielded a treasure trove of material, including "Sister Ray" and the title track from 1968's *White Light/White Heat*, "Candy Says" and "Pale Blue Eyes" from 1969's *The Velvet Underground*, and "Sweet Jane" and "Rock & Roll" from 1970's *Loaded* (the latter two being the band's first songs to make it onto U.S. radio).

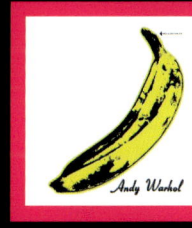

There is astonishing breadth on *The Velvet Underground & Nico* (1967); compare Reed and Cale's lovely opener "Sunday Morning" to the brutal, group-composed closer "European Son."

1969 Velvet Underground Live with Lou Reed (1974) is a handy summation of their career and definitely a more rewarding listen than the reformed band's 1993 effort, *Live MCMXCIII*.

- 116
- 163
- 164
- 138
- 168

John Cale—the Welshman who weaved wonders

Lou Reed (below) is the best known ex-Velvet, but Cale (left) has had an intriguing career. The year after his final gigs with the band (in September 1968), he began his new life by producing Nico (below right) and The Stooges❶. The Seventies found him guesting on Nick Drake's *Bryter Later*, collaborating with Terry Riley, and producing demos by The Police❷. Most significant were his helming of Patti Smith's❸ *Horses* (1975; "an immutable force meeting an immovable object," said Cale), and his solo classics such as 1973's *Paris 1919* (with Lowell George of Little Feat) and 1974's *Fear*. Cale's Eighties were even more eclectic: he produced the soundtrack to John Hughes' *Sixteen Candles* and the first album by U.K. cult band Happy Mondays (whose narcotic temptations he warded off by eating heaps of oranges). The Nineties saw him work with Reed and Eno❹ and producing Siouxsie & The Banshees❺; and his solo career is still flourishing today.

The Velvet Underground

July 12, 1965

"Venus in Furs," "Heroin," and "I'm Waiting for the Man" are among the songs recorded at Cale's Manhattan apartment by himself, Reed, and Morrison for the Velvets' first demo.

March 12, 1967

The Velvet Underground & Nico is released. Its famous but commercially unhelpful cover omits the band's name and the LP's title, but boasts rock's best-known banana.

1969 Connection

1970 Connection

August 23, 1970

Reed's final appearance with The Velvet Underground is taped by an enterprising fan. The awful, bootleg-quality results are issued as 1972's *Live at Max's Kansas City*.

September 1970

Loaded, Reed's final Velvet LP, is issued. It includes "New Age," "Rock and Roll," and "Sweet Jane," later covered by Tori Amos, Jane's Addiction, and The Cowboy Junkies.

- 192
- 280
- 218

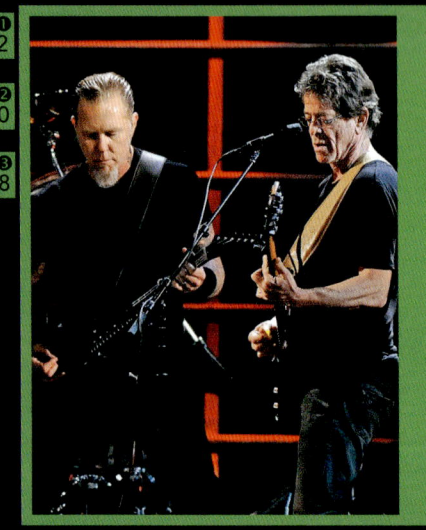

Lou Reed—the glam rock icon and grumpy art rocker

Having flounced from the Velvets in 1970, Reed made a doomed bid to return to his old calling as a staff songwriter. More sensibly, he began a solo career that peaked early with 1972's *Transformer* (source of "Walk on the Wild Side") and 1973's grueling *Berlin*. Subsequent work ranged from rocking (*Rock 'n' Roll Animal*) to wretched (*Metal Machine Music*). By the mid-Eighties, he seemed destined for cult status. But 1989's *New York* proved his best album yet, and since then his work has, on the whole, been worth hearing. Along the way, he has intersected in weird ways with the mainstream: hip-hop group A Tribe Called Quest sampled "Walk on the Wild Side" on their "Can I Kick It"; his "Perfect Day" was used in *Trainspotting* as well as being covered by a starry cast for a charity single; he guested with U2❶ and The Killers❷; and, in 2009, he made an appearance with Metallica❸ (left) at a Rock and Roll Hall of Fame show.

David Bowie—an enthusiastic fan

Bowie❶ was struck by the Velvets before most people in the U.K. had even heard of them and waged a one-man campaign to raise their profile. He covered "I'm Waiting for the Man" and "White Light/White Heat," and paid homage to them on the Velvet soundalike "Queen Bitch." He later helmed Reed's *Transformer* and played Warhol in the 1996 film *Basquiat*. But an apparent first meeting with his Velvet heroes in 1971 was rather inauspicious. "I got to the gig early," he told *Esquire*, "and positioned myself at the front by the lip of the stage. The performance was great." Afterward, Bowie eagerly asked one of the band if he could speak to Lou Reed and spent ten minutes discussing songwriting with the man who appeared—"a teenage ambition achieved." The next day, he told his U.S. tour guide about the meeting, only to learn that Reed had left the band some months beforehand, so he must have been talking to Doug Yule.

❶ 134

1971 Influence

Dec 3, 1989 / June 15, 1990
Playing the Warhol homage *Songs for Drella*, Reed and Cale are joined by Tucker in New York ("Pale Blue Eyes"), then by Tucker and Morrison in France ("Heroin").

June 1, 1993
Reed, Cale, Morrison, and Tucker begin a European tour that will include five shows with U2. "Stadiums suck to play in," Tucker will observe. "Really, it wasn't fun at all."

August 30, 1995
A month before the release of the acclaimed retrospective box set *Peel Slowly and See*, Sterling Morrison dies of non-Hodgkin's lymphoma in Poughkeepsie, New York.

Connection up to 1988

December 5, 1992
A week after rehearsing with Tucker, Reed and Morrison guest at a Cale show in New York, playing "Style It Takes" (from *Songs for Drella*) and Cale's "Forever Changed."

November 18–19, 1994
At The Andy Warhol Museum in Pittsburgh, Cale, Morrison, and Tucker (having fallen out with Reed) perform music to accompany Warhol's 1963 silent movies *Eat* and *Kiss*.

January 17, 1996
Patti Smith inducts the Velvets into the Rock and Roll Hall of Fame. Reed, Cale, and Tucker perform "Last Night I Said Goodbye to My Friend," a tribute to Sterling Morrison.

Nico—the chanteuse with the cheekbones

❶ 134

Even before joining the Velvets, Christa Päffgen (left) had a starry career. She modeled for Chanel, appeared in Fellini's *La dolce vita*, and had a child with Alain Delon. On exiting the band, she kick-started the teenage Jackson Browne's career with a cover of his "These Days" on her album *Chelsea Girl*. (Subsequent covers by her include Bowie's❶ "Heroes" and The Doors' "The End.") Nico's harmonium—which she was taught by free jazz pioneer Ornette Coleman—lent her music an even more somber air than that conjured by her heavy German accent. And although her career waned as her drug use escalated, she remained impressively authoritative. On tour with John Cale (above left), she campaigned to play last ("Who does he thinks he is? I'm a star, too"). This idiosyncratic icon met a suitably odd end: apparently clean of drugs, she fell off her bicycle and died of a brain haemorrhage, aged forty-nine, in July 1988.

Fleetwood Mac 1967–present

1967+ 1970+ 1977+ 1993+

Best known for blockbusters such as 1977's *Rumours* (and the surrounding soap opera), Fleetwood Mac are sometimes overlooked as a musical force. Yet they have exercised a major influence for more than four decades. Peter Green's bluesy incarnation of the band yielded gems such as "Oh Well"—covered by Jimmy Page with The Black Crowes, and a favorite of Joe Perry (who was lured to Aerosmith 154▶ after Steven Tyler saw him playing Mac's "Rattlesnake Shake"—a title later stolen by Mötley Crüe). And Mac's "Black Magic Woman" was made into a classic by Santana. Green befriended another Anglo-Jewish guitar god, Paul Kossoff, who formed Free; he gave a guitar to the teenage Gary Moore, later to play with Thin Lizzy; and the guitar on Pink Floyd's "Shine On You Crazy Diamond" is distinctly Green-esque. Mac rehearsals at the U.K.'s Headley Grange prompted Zeppelin 098▶ to record there, and the band also inspired Ozzy Osbourne of Black Sabbath 108▶. Not too shabby a legacy, considering that Green dismissed rock 'n' roll as "a joke invented by Mick Jagger and Keith Richards."

The Lindsey Buckingham and Stevie Nicks-led version of the band was also influential, although their mainstream supremacy at the time of punk meant few acknowledged it until recently. But their melodies and harmonies have been emulated by acts from Courtney Love to French stars Phoenix, while Buckingham's guitar has influenced Peter Buck of R.E.M. 204▶ to Jerry Cantrell of Alice in Chains. As Phil Oakey of The Human League said, "It must be incredible to be Fleetwood Mac."

April 1967

Drummer Mick Fleetwood joins bassist John McVie and guitarist/singer Peter Green in John Mayall's band, the Bluesbreakers. The union will be productive but very brief.

July 1967

Green and Fleetwood try in vain to entice McVie into their band, named partially after him. Fleetwood "Mac" will instead feature bassist Bob Brunning.

September 1967

McVie finally joins. The band will debut on vinyl, as Peter Green's Fleetwood Mac, in November, with "I Believe My Time Ain't Long" (a cover of a Robert Johnson song).

MARCH 2, 1968: *Fleetwood Mac* flies into the chart

Thanks to the British blues boom, and the band's live reputation, the Mac's self-titled debut album soared into the U.K. chart, peaking at No. 4 in its thirty-seven weeks on the listing. It was followed by hit albums (1968's *Mr. Wonderful* and 1969's *Pious Bird of Good Omen* and *Then Play On*) and smashes including "Albatross," "Need Your Love So Bad," and "Oh Well" (all minor successes in the U.S.A.). By the summer of 1968, Danny Kirwan had been added as a result of Green's frustration with guitarist Jeremy Spencer, and the band recorded in America with blues heroes including Willie Dixon (the original author of Zeppelin classics such as "Whole Lotta Love"). But their success did not suit Green (left) who, having converted to Christianity and given away much of his wealth, made 1970's hit "The Green Manalishi (with the Two-Prong Crown)"—later covered by Judas Priest—his swan song.

October 10, 1970

With Christine McVie now in the band, *Kiln House* hits the U.K. chart. It is the Mac's last new album to chart in the U.S.A. for six years.

February 1971

Spencer quits, apparently for religious reasons, and Green is drafted in for a U.S. tour. The remaining members will replace him with Bob Welch.

September 1971

Future Games keeps U.S. sales ticking over, as do 1972's *Bare Trees* and 1973's *Penguin and Mystery to Me*. Their sound will move toward "soft rock."

September 13, 1974

After a succession of lineup reshuffles, *Heroes Are Hard to Find* is released. It will be the band's first album to crack the U.S. top forty.

DECEMBER 1974: The fall and rise of the Mac

Even by the Mac's standards, 1974 was a nutty year. Bob Weston, who had replaced Kirwan, was fired after an affair with Fleetwood's wife. When Fleetwood canceled their tour, the band's manager assembled a "new" group (made of session musicians then working with Kirwan), and sent them on the road as Fleetwood Mac. The resultant legal war took its toll: despite the success of *Heroes Are Hard to Find*, guitarist Welch quit in December. His replacement was Lindsey Buckingham—who brought his partner, Stevie Nicks (left). The duo had recorded their own album in 1973, with little commercial success. But in 1975, they helped to secure their new band's first U.S. gold album. Thanks to the hit singles "Over My Head," "Say You Love Me," and "Rhiannon," *Fleetwood Mac* finally topped the chart in September 1976; this album eventually sold more than five million in the U.K. alone.

April 2, 1977

Rumours tops the U.S. chart for the first of thirty-one (non-consecutive) weeks. It will eventually sell more than nineteen million in the U.S.A.

February 17, 1978

"Jail Guitar Doors," a B-side by Buckingham's beloved The Clash, namechecks Peter Green: "Pete didn't want no fame / Gave all his money away."

June 1979

Green re-emerges with *In the Skies*, featuring Pink Floyd's tour guitarist, Snowy White. Green will make an uncredited cameo on the next Mac album.

November 10, 1979

Tusk tops the U.K. chart. Its U.S. sales are harmed by the entire album being aired on radio before its release. Bootleggers rejoice.

SEPTEMBER 5, 1981: *Bella Donna* tops the chart

Fleetwood Mac entered the Eighties as one of the world's biggest bands, but were riven by drugs and dissent. When Nicks' debut solo album *Bella Donna* hit the U.S. top spot—thanks in part to the Tom Petty duet "Stop Draggin' My Heart Around"—the writing was on the wall. Mac regrouped for 1982's excellent, U.S. chart-topping *Mirage* but, after an acrimonious tour, split to pursue solo projects (of which only Nicks' albums were major sellers). In August 1985, Christine McVie enticed Fleetwood, ex-husband McVie, and Buckingham to contribute to a cover of Elvis' ❶ "Can't Help Falling in Love." With Nicks back aboard, the band reunited for 1987's *Tango in the Night*, but Buckingham refused to tour and was replaced by Rick Vito and Billy Burnette. This new lineup scored a U.K. No. 1 with 1990's *Behind the Mask* but, when Nicks and Vito quit, it seemed Fleetwood Mac had finally ground to a halt.

January 13, 1993

Fleetwood, the McVies, Nicks, and Buckingham reunite to play "Don't Stop" at U.S. President Bill Clinton's inaugural ball.

July 21, 1994

Billy Burnette, Traffic's Dave Mason, and Delaney & Bonnie's daughter, Bekka Bramlett, join Fleetwood and McVie in a new lineup of the band.

October 21, 1995

Despite featuring cameos by both Christine McVie and Buckingham, the new band's *Time* spends just one week in the U.K. chart and flops Stateside.

May 7, 1996

The *Twister* soundtrack sees Nicks back with Fleetwood and Buckingham. Fleetwood and the McVies will later help on Buckingham's solo album.

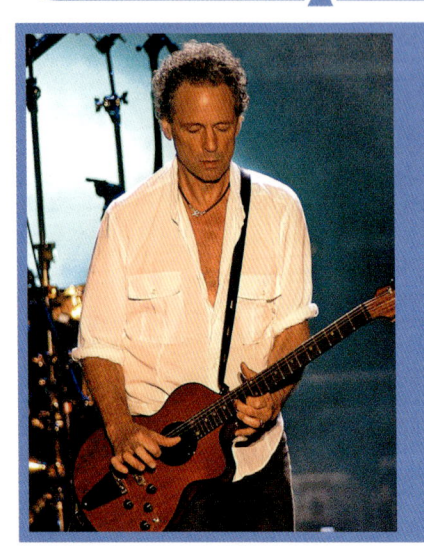

MAY 22 and 23, 1997: *The Dance* goes on forever

After months of rumors, Buckingham, Nicks, Fleetwood, and the McVies reunited in May 1997 for the MTV special *The Dance*. The album of the same name hit the U.S. No. 1 on its way to five million sales, as the band embarked on a hugely successful tour. After a selection of solo projects, they reunited again—minus Christine McVie—on January 6, 2001, at a show for out-going U.S. President Bill Clinton. McVie remained absent as the group recorded *Say You Will*, the 2003 album that occasioned another lucrative tour (including their first European dates in thirteen years). Having struck a balance between band and solo work, the Mac's only major controversy came when Nicks' pal Sheryl Crow prematurely announced that she would be replacing Christine McVie. Unamused, the band hit the road yet again, in 2009, without her, and mooted the latest recorded chapter in a story that seems to have no end.

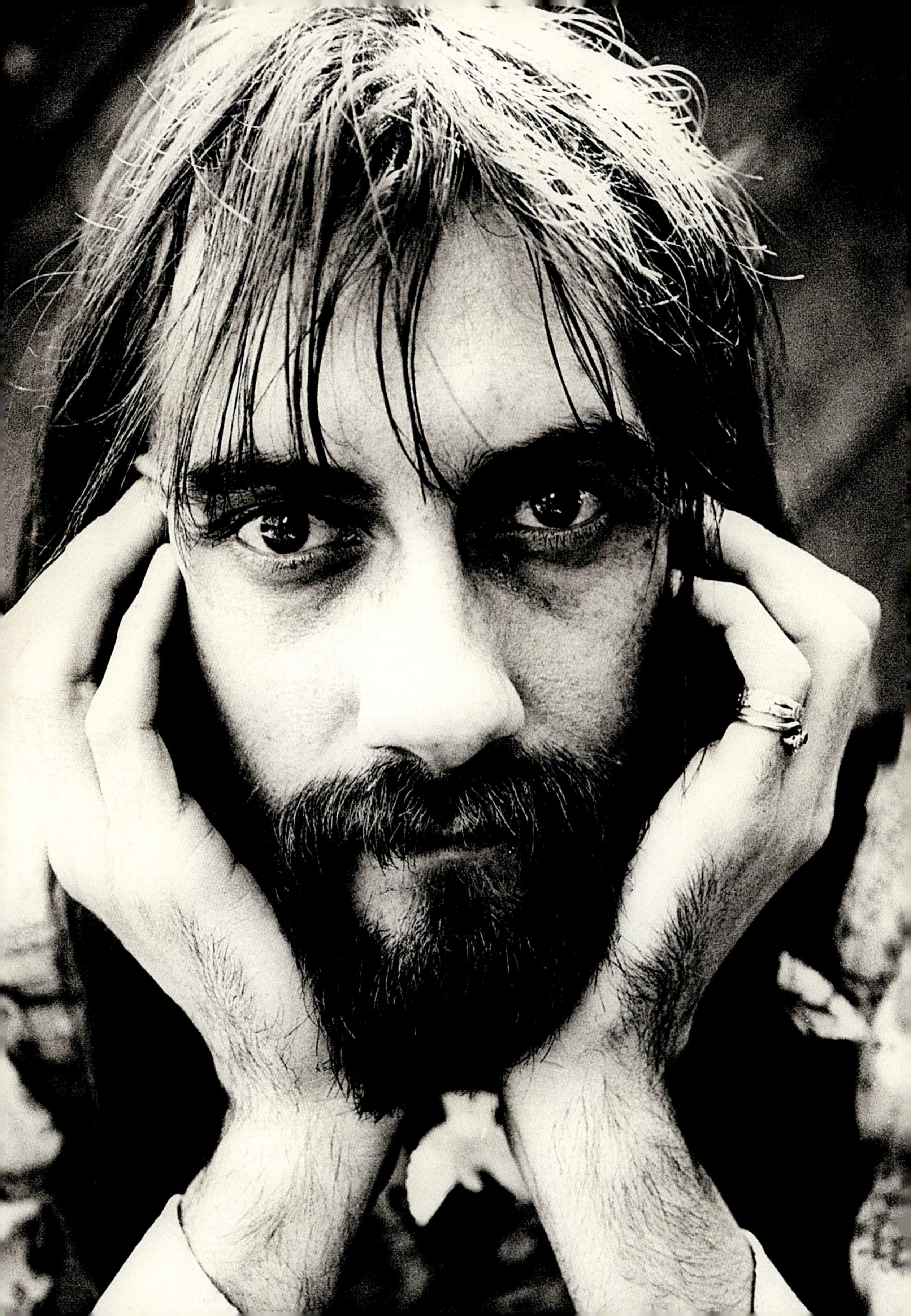

Led Zeppelin

1968–80

1944+ 1968+ 1971+ 1976+ 1993+

Though rooted in the Sixties, no rock band better defined the Seventies than Led Zeppelin. They sold albums and tickets in such quantities that promotion proved unnecessary. They wrote anthems on classic albums that became all-time best-sellers. They inspired more macabre rumors than any act bar The Beatles ◀044, sold more than the Stones ◀054, and had their own branded jet.

Friendship wasn't a factor. Guitarist Jimmy Page and singer Robert Plant didn't gel until, wandering in Welsh mountains, they bonded over a love of folk music. In 1973, bassist John Paul Jones—always the outsider—threatened to quit to become a choirmaster. "We would do the tours, we would do the recordings," he said, "then we wouldn't see each other at all. We weren't a band that socialized."

Nonetheless, Page, Plant, and drummer John Bonham attended a May 1974 Elvis Presley ◀012 show together at the Los Angeles Forum. "We've got Led Zeppelin out there," Presley told his band. "Let's try to look like we know what we're doing."

Their influence stretches from being sampled by Dr. Dre 256▶ ("Stranded on Death Row") to being named in a Nirvana 242▶ song title ("Aero Zeppelin"). "We went boldly where few men had been before, let's put it that way," remarked Page.

"The greatest hard rock 'n' roll band of all time," enthused Dave Grohl, who enticed bassist Jones to work on the Foo Fighters' *In Your Honor* album, then formed Them Crooked Vultures with him (and Josh Homme of Queens of the Stone Age) in 2009. "More than anything," he said, "they sounded fearless."

January 9, 1944

James Patrick Page is born in Middlesex, England. In twenty years, he will be an in-demand session guitarist—and, after turning them down once, will join The Yardbirds in 1966.

January 3, 1946

John Baldwin is born in Kent, England. As John Paul Jones, he will be a top session player, recording with many of the same acts as "Jimmy" Page.

1948

John Henry Bonham is born in Worcestershire (May 31) and Robert Anthony Plant is born in West Bromwich, England (August 20).

AUGUST 12, 1968: The New Yardbirds take flight

In July 1968, The Yardbirds❶—having changed the sound of British rock—split up. Inconveniently, they were still contracted to go on tour, obliging Jimmy Page and bassist Chris Dreja to scout for a new band. Procul Harum singer Terry Reid turned them down, but recommended Robert Plant, who brought along drummer John Bonham. There was one final reshuffle—Dreja was replaced by John Paul Jones (with whom Page had played on Jeff Beck's❷ "Beck's Bolero" in 1966, alongside The Who's❸ Keith Moon). The quartet convened for rehearsal in August 1968 and discerned that, despite having little personally in common, they had a musical spark. They recorded their first album in September and, having fulfilled their obligations as "The New Yardbirds," became Led Zeppelin (a name conceived by The Who's Moon and John Entwistle to describe an act that would go down like a lead balloon).

❶ 060
❷ 043
❸ 068

LED ZEPPELIN   99

November 23, 1968

On the recommendation of singer Dusty Springfield, Atlantic signs "the hot, new, English group." Thanks to manager Peter Grant, they secure a huge advance.

April 12, 1969

Led Zeppelin hits the U.K. chart, on which it will remain for seventy-nine weeks. It will hit No. 10 in the U.S.A. and go gold there in July.

April 18, 1969

Zeppelin begin a U.S. tour, on which Page plays a guitar once owned by future Eagles star Joe Walsh. They will record at various studios along the way.

June 13, 1969

A first headlining U.K. tour begins in the home of hard rock, Birmingham. It will climax at the prestigious Royal Albert Hall in London.

❶ 044
❷ 112

DECEMBER 27, 1969: Zeppelin beat The Beatles

In a symbolic twist of chart history, *Led Zeppelin II* knocked *Abbey Road* off the U.S. No. 1 at the end of the decade. (In September 1970, they would win "best band" at Britain's *Melody Maker* awards, ending The Beatles'❶ seven-year reign.) Having earned such a reputation that they could imperiously dismiss a request to play at Woodstock❷, the band laid waste to the U.S.A. and Europe, armed with new stormers such as "Whole Lotta Love." Now tagged—to Plant's (left) enduring annoyance—as heavy metal, they emphasized their folky side on *Led Zeppelin III* (although it also boasted the brutal "Immigrant Song"). "Musically," remarked Plant, "the whole Zeppelin thing came into full bloom at the beginnng of *Zep III*, when we went up into the Welsh mountains and I started taking Page around these places. We were on the trail of the Holy Grail!" The album duly hit No. 1 on both sides of the Atlantic.

March 23, 1971

Zeppelin play The Marquee on a U.K. club tour. Page fears they are "losing contact" with those who first supported the band.

December 4, 1971

The untitled fourth album, with "Stairway to Heaven," tops the U.K. chart. It is kept off the U.S. No. 1 by Sly & The Family Stone and Carole King.

March 28, 1973

Houses of the Holy is issued. It will top U.S. and U.K. charts. Despite later rumors, model and singer Samantha Fox is not one of the child cover stars.

May 5, 1973

Breaking a record set by The Beatles, a show at Tampa Stadium attracts the biggest U.S. audience (56,800) for a single act.

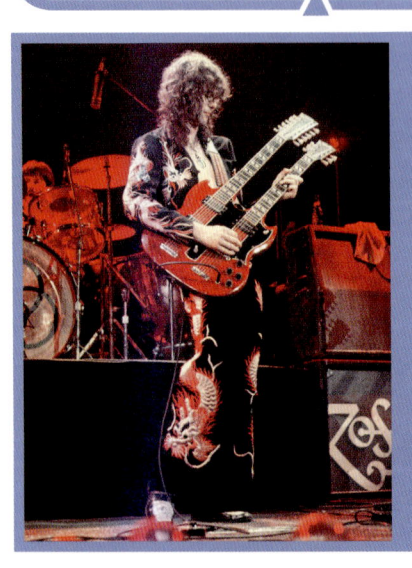

MARCH 1975: "Trampled underfoot"

Zeppelin's *Physical Graffiti* was intended to be the first album on their Swan Song label (launched in late 1974). But delays with its cover art meant Bad Company and The Pretty Things beat them to it, with the former's self-titled debut becoming the label's first U.S. No. 1. However, *Physical Graffiti* became another transatlantic chart-topper, and included "Kashmir"—reckoned by the band to be the quintessential Zeppelin song. Its success revived their catalog, making Zeppelin the first act to have six albums on the U.S. chart at the same time. They crowned the triumph with five shows at London's Earls Court (their last European concerts for more than four years). Then things began to go wrong. Plant and his family were injured in a car crash, forcing the cancellation of a U.S. tour. When Zeppelin reconvened to record in November, he was still on crutches—and angry to find Page (left) on heroin.

TURN ON, TUNE IN, DROP OUT

March 31, 1976

Presence hits No. 1 in the U.S. and U.K. Plant later hails the intense set (home of "Achilles' Last Stand") as *the* Led Zeppelin album.

October 19, 1976

Mick Jagger is among guests at the premiere of Zeppelin's concert movie (with fantasy sequences), *The Song Remains the Same*. An awful live album of the same title is also issued.

July 26, 1977

The death of Plant's young son from an infection causes the cancellation of the remaining dates on what will turn out to be Zeppelin's final U.S. tour.

August 4 and 11, 1979

The New Barbarians, led by Keith Richards and Ronnie Woods, are among support acts for Zeppelin's last U.K. shows, at Knebworth.

SEPTEMBER 25, 1980: "The coldness of my winter"

Recorded at Abba's❶ studios, 1979's *In Through the Out Door* gave the band a final, transatlantic chart-topper. The "Tour Over Europe" in 1980 suggested they might stride successfully into the new decade—but, during September rehearsals for a U.S. tour, Bonham (left) died of alcohol-induced asphyxiation. On December 4, owing to "the loss of our dear friend," Zeppelin disbanded. In August 1982, Plant earned his first solo gold disc for *Pictures at Eleven*, only to find himself sharing charts with a set of Zeppelin off-cuts, *Coda*. While Page's solo career moved in fits and starts, Plant streaked ahead, peaking with 1988's *Now and Zen* and 1990's *Manic Nirvana*. These triumphs helpfully eclipsed Zeppelin's shambolic reunions at Live Aid❷ in 1985 and Atlantic's❸ fortieth anniversary show in 1988. A better testimony came when Page launched a series of reissues with 1990's *Remasters*.

❶ 083
❷ 214
❸ 082

June 8, 1993

The album *Coverdale Page* unites, you guessed it, guitarist Jimmy Page with Whitesnake's David Coverdale and goes gold.

August 25–26, 1994

Plant and Page play shows for MTV, later released as *No Quarter*. They will begin a world tour in 1995 and release the album *Walking into Clarksdale* in 1998.

January 12, 1995

Aerosmith's Steven Tyler and Joe Perry induct Led Zeppelin into the Rock and Roll Hall of Fame. Tyler and Neil Young jam with them.

November 25, 1997

The ten-disc *The Complete Studio Recordings*, with sleeve notes by fan-turned-writer-turned-movie director Cameron Crowe, goes platinum in the U.S.A.

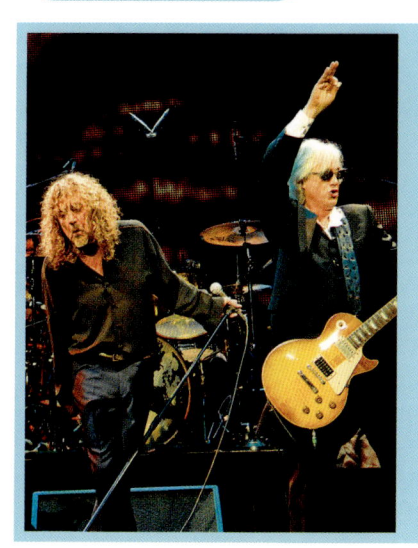

DECEMBER 10, 2007: It's been a long time . . .

The Zeppelin industry had long churned along to multi-platinum effect. To their unstoppable back catalog were added compilations—plus, more rewardingly, 1997's *BBC Sessions* and 2003's live *How the West Was Won*, with an accompanying DVD. Their success made the band the fourth best-selling act in U.S. history, behind only The Beatles❶, Garth Brooks, and Elvis❷. So, when they announced a show, at London's O2 (left), in 2007 (in honor of Atlantic❸ founder Ahmet Ertegun), it became the world's hottest ticket. The concert itself—with Bonham's son Jason on drums—was rapturously received and raised hopes of a longer-term reunion. To fans' frustration, but his own credit, Plant (then enjoying success with his Alison Krauss collaboration, *Raising Sand*) refused to play along. As the years pass, it seems ever more unlikely that Led Zeppelin will reform—an honorable conclusion to an amazing career.

❶ 044
❷ 012
❸ 082

LED ZEPPELIN 101

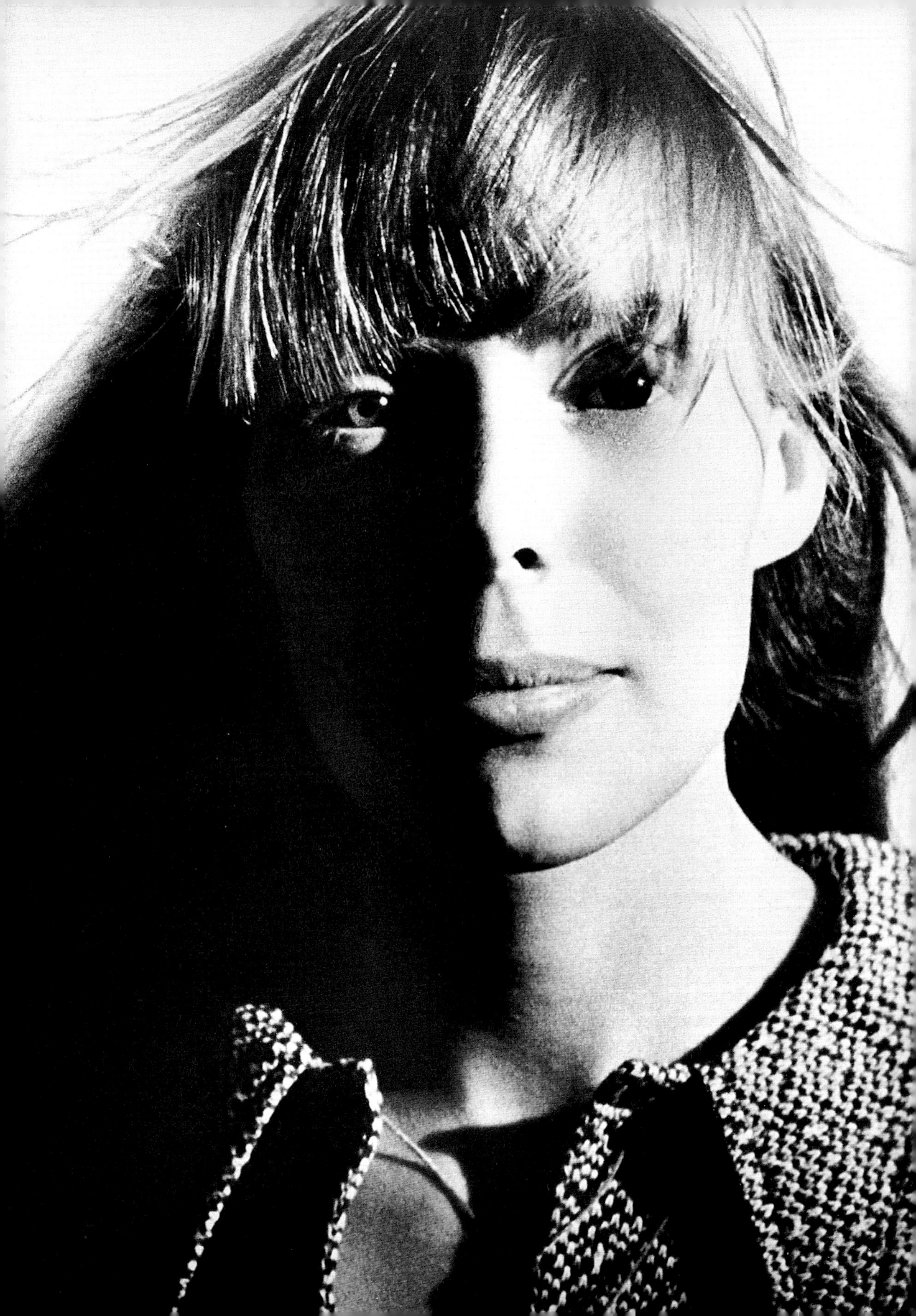

Joni Mitchell
1943–present

A friendly rival of Bob Dylan ◀062, a friend of Neil Young ◀078, tour bus listening for Pink Floyd ◀086, and an influence on Prince 174▶—Joni Mitchell has had an extraordinary career, founded not on rock 'n' roll hijinks and scandal, but four decades of superb songs and ambitious albums.

She has been immortalized in song by a diverse range of artists. "Joni Mitchell never lies," raps Q-Tip on Janet Jackson's "Got 'til It's Gone"—based on a sample of Mitchell's "Big Yellow Taxi." "To find a queen without a king / They say she plays guitar and cries and sings," gushes Robert Plant on Led Zeppelin's ◀098 "Going to California." And both Neil Young and Sonic Youth have tracks about her: "Sweet Joni" (only ever performed live) and "Hey Joni" (on 1988's *Daydream Nation*), respectively.

> *"I knew every word to* Court and Spark. *I worshipped her when I was in high school . . . She had the most profound effect on me."* —Madonna

Her songs have been covered by artists, from Bing Crosby ("Both Sides Now") to Bob Dylan ("Big Yellow Taxi"), from Herbie Hancock ("A Case of You") to Heart ("River"), and from Cyndi Lauper ("Carey") to Richard Thompson ("Woodstock").

Indeed, it was as a writer that Mitchell rose to prominence. Having switched from art to music, she graduated to New York folk clubs. Stars such as Tom Rush, Fairport Convention, and Buffy Saint-Marie discovered her material, while Judy Collins took "Both Sides Now" into the U.S. top ten in 1968.

Her solo career hit an early peak with *Ladies of the Canyon* (1970), featuring two of her best-known songs: "Woodstock" (a hit for Crosby, Stills, Nash & Young) and the eco-anthem "Big Yellow Taxi."

The starkly confessional *Blue* (1971) started the real superstar streak for Mitchell. From the simple singer-songwriter fare of *For the Roses* (1972), she progressed to the eerie majesty of *Hejira* (1976) and the jazzy experimentation of *Don Juan's Reckless Daughter* (1977). The oddest was *The Hissing of Summer Lawns* (1975), which deployed Burundi drums long before Adam & The Ants made them a much-imitated sound. "Prince was one of those people . . . who holed up in his room with *Hissing of Summer Lawns*," Mitchell reported after meeting him. "He became quite obsessive." (Prince even wrote a song for her, "Emotional Pump." She passed on it.)

Although her commercial standing waned, her talent rarely wavered. After Eighties albums that buried great songs beneath over-production, she stripped her sound back for gems such as *Night Ride Home* (1991) and *Turbulent Indigo* (1994). Recent efforts *Taming the Tiger* (1998) and *Shine* (2007) have, unusually among veteran performers, done nothing to tarnish her extraordinary legacy.

"She's a completely graceful performer," said Natalie Merchant in 1997, "and she's writing songs that are just as good as, if not better than, those that she wrote at twenty-five. And she's so wise."

If the thought of morose singer-songwriters or jazzy bohemians makes you run for cover, check out *Court and Spark* (1974). Its glorious classics include "Help Me" and "Free Man in Paris."

Chalk Mark in a Rain Storm (1988) features guests Peter Gabriel, Willie Nelson, Wendy & Lisa, Don Henley, Tom Petty, and Billy Idol—and a handful of Mitchell's greatest songs.

Mitchell and her princely fan

"I remember seeing him sitting in the front row [in 1976] when he was very young," Mitchell told *New York* magazine. "He must have been about fifteen. He was in an aisle seat and he had unusually big eyes. He watched the whole show with his collar up, looking side to side. You couldn't miss him—he was a little Prince-ling. [Laughs.] Prince used to write me fan mail with all of the "U"s and hearts that way that he writes. And the office took it as mail from the lunatic fringe and tossed it!" Undeterred, the maestro thanked her in the sleeve notes of *Dirty Mind* (1980), hid her name on the cover of *Controversy* (1981), titled his protégés The Time's *Ice Cream Castles* (1984) after a line in "Both Sides Now," namechecked her in "The Ballad of Dorothy Parker" (1987), and referred to her "The Circle Game" in his own "Circle of Amour" (1998). "He's a strange little duck," Mitchell reflected, "but I like him."

Joni Mitchell

November 7, 1943
Roberta Joan Anderson is born in Fort McLeod, Alberta, Canada. She will marry fellow musician Chuck Mitchell in 1965 and keep his surname after they separate in 1966.

1976 Influence

February 10, 1985
Mitchell joins Neil Young, Jane Siberry, Bryan Adams, Rush's Geddy Lee, and others to cut "Tears Are Not Enough"—the Canadian equivalent of "We Are the World."

May 1, 1969
Mitchell and Bob Dylan guest on *The Johnny Cash Show*. At a post-show party (which she attends with Graham Nash), Mitchell will have her "first official meeting" with Dylan.

February 13, 1978
Don Juan's Reckless Daughter—which features Chaka Khan, the Eagles' Glenn Frey, and J. D. Souther—becomes Mitchell's eighth consecutive gold album in the U.S.A.

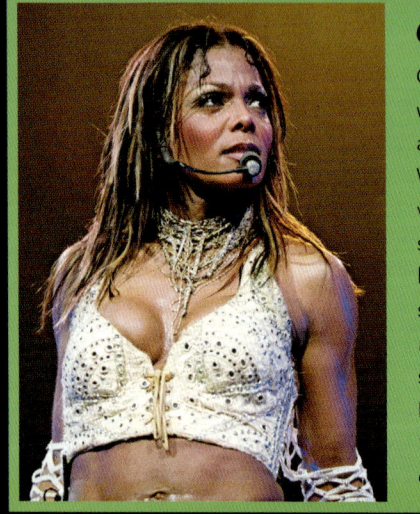

Influence 1988

Chalk Mark makes its mark on Janet

One of Mitchell's later albums that, to her frustration, made little impact was March 1988's *Chalk Mark in a Rain Storm*. Among the few paying attention was Janet Jackson, who rightly regarded "The Beat of Black Wings" as one of the writer's finest. The track was inspired by a Vietnam veteran, Mitchell told *Q*. "He said to me . . . 'You've got a lotta nerve, sister, standing up there and singing about love because there ain't no love and I'm gonna tell you where love went.' He ended up crying and shaking." "The Beat of Black Wings" "turned me around," Jackson told *Rolling Stone*, and "made me take music seriously." Janet covered the song for the unreleased tribute album *A Case of Joni* and consulted Mitchell herself for her 1997 hit "Got 'til It's Gone," which sampled "Big Yellow Taxi." "I sent her the tape," Jackson recalled, "and she called back and said she absolutely loved it and it was totally fine."

Tori Amos, the "Cornflake Girl"

"As I was growing up, I kept my ears open," Tori Amos (left) told *Rolling Stone*. "Whether it was Debbie Harry❶ or Laurie Anderson or Kate Bush❷ or Joni Mitchell, they all affected me." After Amos' 1991 debut *Little Earthquakes*, she was often compared to Mitchell. The link was made clear in January 1994, when one of the B-sides to her hit "Cornflake Girl" was a cover of Joni's "A Case of You"—from *Blue*. (She has also sung "River" and "The Circle Game" in concert.) "There's this jungle called 'Women in Music,'" Amos told ABC's *Nightline*, "and the women that come before you, they have their machetes . . . Joni Mitchell cleared a lot of brush away with her machete in the Sixties to make room for so many who have come after her. Joni Mitchell influenced bands of that time. It wasn't as if she had to be as loud as the band she inspired. They understood. It was about how powerful her content was."

❶ 172

❷ 049

May 20, 1988
Mitchell attends the opening of the first exhibition of her paintings, in Tokyo. She has painted several of her covers, claiming to be "a painter first, a musician second."

1994 Influence

May 17, 1999
In L.A., Stevie Wonder arrives in a big yellow taxi to sing "Woodstock" as the American Society of Composers, Authors & Publishers awards Mitchell its highest honor.

October 28, 2007
Mitchell, Chaka Khan, and Sting are among performers at a tribute show for Herbie Hancock in L.A. Mitchell once said that she and James Taylor refer to Sting as "their son."

September 18, 1989
Mitchell sings "Night Ride Home"—the title track of an album that will be released in 1991—on the latest show by Muppets creator Jim Henson, *The Ghost of Faffner Hall*.

May 22, 1994
The last of Mitchell's three nights at Japan's Alanoshi Festival is shown on TV. "They stuck Bob [Dylan] at the mic with me," she complains, "and he never brushes his teeth."

April 6, 2000
Elton John, Richard Thompson, and Cyndi Lauper are among performers at a tribute show for Mitchell at New York's Hammerstein Ballroom. The star of the show also sings.

Influence 2007

Sarah McLachlan follows in Joni's footsteps

From the ashes of the unreleased *A Case of Joni* rose the April 2007 album, *A Tribute to Joni Mitchell*. Among its stars were Emmylou Harris, Björk, Prince❶, k.d. lang, Sufjan Stevens, and Elvis Costello. Perhaps the most obvious inclusion, however, was Sarah McLachlan (left), singing Mitchell's "Blue." The cover was actually recorded in the early Nineties; since when McLachlan—another Canadian singer-songwriter—had evolved into a multimillion-selling superstar. Ironically, much of her success was based on a mainstream sound that wasn't far from Mitchell's Eighties style. But the latter had little time for her multi-platinum soundalikes, complaining, "I'd like to line *my* pocket a little." Still, McLachlan put her status to good use, conceiving the Lilith Fair: a barrier-busting, all-female festival. And, showing no hard feelings for Mitchell's dismissiveness, she covered her "River" in 2006.

❶ 174

Leonard Cohen 1934–present

1934+ 1989+

From *American Idol* to *Natural Born Killers*, Leonard Cohen's music has been pervasive. Besides the classic "Hallelujah" (see right), his songs have been covered by, among many others, Elton John **126▷** ("I'm Your Man"), U2 **192▷** ("Tower of Song"), Tori Amos ("Famous Blue Raincoat"), Martin Gore of Depeche Mode **196▷** ("Coming Back to You"), the Pixies **224▷** ("I Can't Forget"), Rufus Wainwright ("Chelsea Hotel #2"), and Don Henley ("Everybody Knows"). And R.E.M. **204▷** covered "First We Take Manhattan," as well as reworking Cohen's first single, "Suzanne," as "Hope" on the *Up* album.

Initially famed as a favorite of lovelorn students, thanks to albums such as *Songs from a Room* (1969) and *Songs of Love and Hate* (1971), Cohen's appeal narrowed as he issued just five albums from 1974 to 1984. But when Jennifer Warnes, his former backing singer, released a collection of his songs as *Famous Blue Raincoat* (1986), it reminded the world of his talent. Cohen then returned to form with *I'm Your Man* (1988), which was followed by the tribute albums *I'm Your Fan* (1991) and *Tower of Song* (1995). Sealing the comeback, *The Future* (1992) gave him his highest ever chart placing in his native Canada.

After years of meditation, during which he was ordained as a Buddhist monk, Cohen issued *Ten New Songs* (2001) and *Dear Heather* (2004), and, in 2008, he returned to the stage after fifteen years.

"He really seemed," enthused Nick Cave **202▷**, "to be the first person to approach a song . . . poetically and spend time . . . It takes a long time for his songs to form. They're really high art."

106 TURN ON, TUNE IN, DROP OUT

September 31, 1934

Leonard Norman Cohen is born in Montreal, Canada. He will publish a book of poetry and two novels before issuing his 1967 debut album, *Songs of Leonard Cohen*.

April 1, 1969

***Songs from a Room**—which includes the subsequently much-covered "Famous Blue Raincoat"—is released. It will become the star's highest-charting U.S. album.*

January 20, 1971

Cohen and John Lennon are among the artists featured in the dire cinematic collage *Dynamite Chicken*, which premieres in San Francisco.

NOVEMBER 17, 1977: *Death of a Ladies' Man*

❶ 028

❷ 062

"This isn't punk rock," declared producer Phil Spector❶ toward the end of making Cohen's 1977 album. "This is *rock punk!*" Spector's career had waned since his early Seventies work with George Harrison and John Lennon, but he had met Cohen in 1974, which led to the pair working on the songs that became *Death of a Ladies' Man*. "Some of his [Spector's] musical treatments are very foreign to me," Cohen told the *L.A. Phonograph*. "I mean, I've rarely worked in a live room that contains twenty-five musicians—including two drummers, three bassists, and six guitars." Spector's Wall of Sound also included Bob Dylan❷— who, in March, sang backing vocals on Cohen's "Don't Go Home with Your Hard-On." "Phil was frankly round the bend, mad as a hatter," Cohen told *Rock CD* in 1992. "It was a weird combination. There were a lot of guns around. He liked them, and so did I, but it was mayhem!"

November 10, 1989

After twenty-two years, *Songs of Leonard Cohen* is certified gold in the U.S.A. It will be one of only two such awards that Cohen receives.

September 13, 1993

Kurt Cobain sings "Give me a Leonard Cohen afterworld" on Nirvana's "Pennyroyal Tea." Cohen says, "I'm sorry I couldn't have spoken to the young man."

August 26, 1994

The movie *Natural Born Killers* premieres. It features three songs from Cohen's *The Future*, which director Oliver Stone was given during filming.

June 1, 2007

***Book of Longing*—Philip Glass' song cycle based on the poems and images of Leonard Cohen—has its world premiere in Toronto.**

DECEMBER 2008: "Hallelujah"!

❶ 157

❷ 090

❸ 062

"Hallelujah," from Cohen's *Various Positions* (1984), has been covered by acts from Bon Jovi❶ to Justin Timberlake. At the close of 2008, three versions were in the U.K. top forty: TV talent show victor Alexandra Burke's chart-topper; a 1994 reading by Jeff Buckley (left); and, bolstered by Burke and Buckley's race for No. 1, Cohen's original. It wasn't the first time the song had infiltrated the mainstream. The 2001 movie *Shrek* used a version by former Velvet Underground❷ man John Cale (from *I'm Your Fan*), although its soundtrack featured one by Rufus Wainwright. Bob Dylan❸ has also played it live. "Dylan and I were having coffee," Cohen recalled after one such performance. "He asked me how long it took to write it. And I told him a couple of years. I lied, actually. It was more than a couple of years. Then I praised a song of his, 'I and I,' and asked him how long it had taken and he said, 'Fifteen minutes.'"

LEONARD COHEN   107

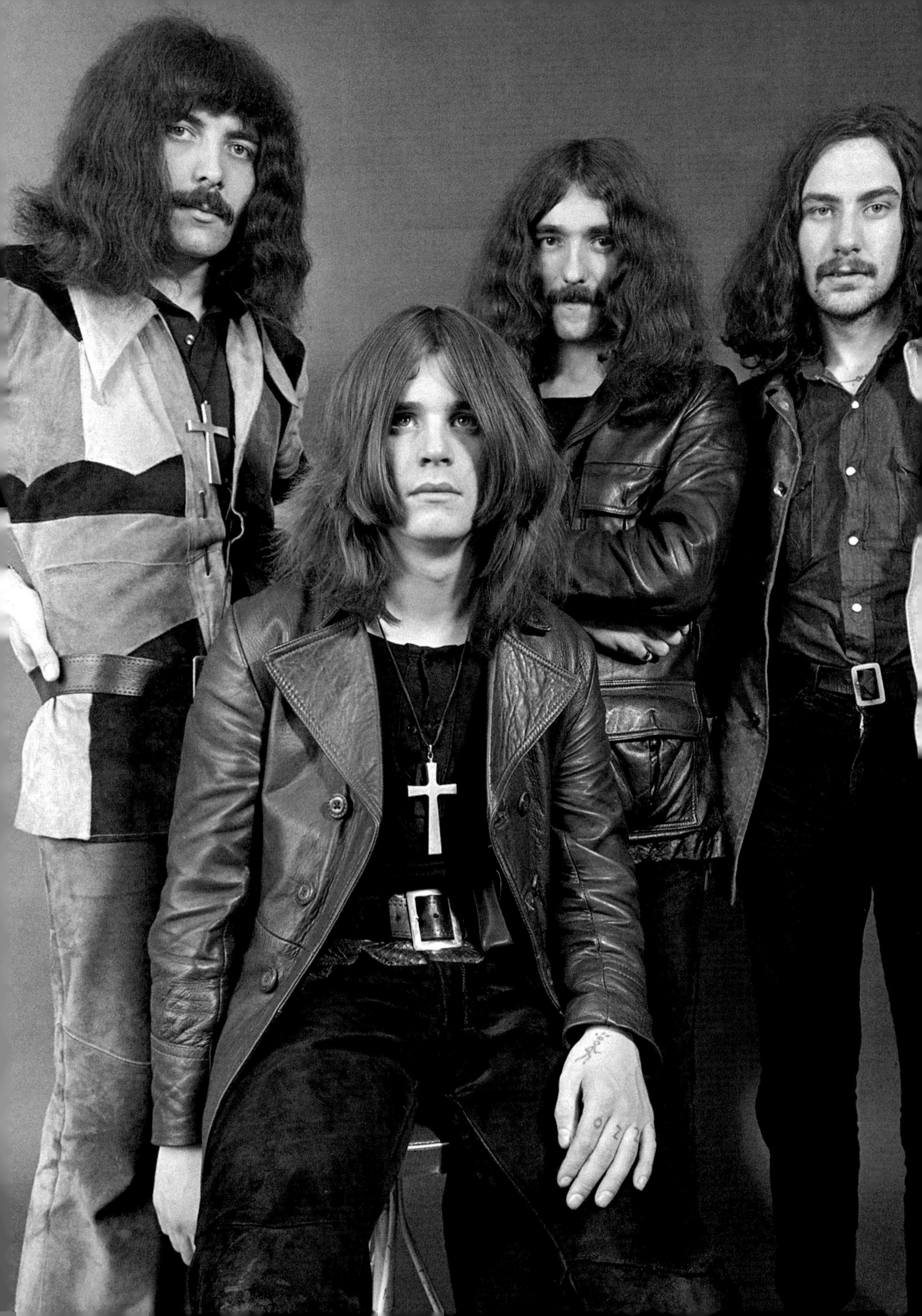

Black Sabbath
1968–2009

Historians may argue that The Kinks ◀066, Blue Cheer, or Jimi Hendrix ◀072 invented heavy metal. Yet fans point to Black Sabbath, who rolled hellraising riffs, blood-curdling vocals, and rock-hard bass and drums into one pulverizing package.

"The end of the Sixties," recalled front man Ozzy Osbourne, "it was all 'If you're going to San Francisco, be sure to wear a flower in your hair.' What a load of old fucking happy, hippy crap that is. Here's us living ninety-nine million miles away in Aston, Birmingham, industrial city, and the world wasn't happy. We used to rehearse across the road from a movie theater and [guitarist] Tony Iommi said to us, 'Isn't it weird how people like to go to the movies and get scared? Why don't we start making music that scares people?' And he came up with the heaviest fucking riffs of all time."

> *"I never was scramblin' around with Bob Dylan in mind. I was more concerned with Black Sabbath."* —Beck

Iommi's riffs are indeed the only constant in the band's catalog—of which the highlights include 1970's *Paranoid*, 1980's *Heaven and Hell*, and 1989's *Headless Cross*, and crucial cuts such as "Supernaut" (Frank Zappa's ◀076 favorite) and "The Mob Rules."

Convoluted lineup shifts over four decades have seen Ozzy Osbourne and his successors—Ronnie James Dio and Tony Martin—come, go, and come back (not to mention ex-Deep Purple singers Ian Gillan and Glenn Hughes, who lasted one album each, and David Donato, Ray Gillen, and Dave Walker, who failed even to make it that far).

At one soap operatic peak, Dio (in Sabbath for a second time in the Nineties) refused to play in a supporting role at Osbourne's Ozzfest, obliging the band to hire Judas Priest's Rob Halford instead.

Bassist Geezer Butler and drummer Bill Ward have also been in, out, and in again, with substitute skins-bashers including Carmine Appice's brother Vinnie, ELO's Bev Bevan, Kiss' Eric Singer, Faith No More's Mike Bordin, Rainbow and Whitesnake's Cozy Powell, and The Clash's 170▶ Terry Chimes. However, the band's squabbles have been outshone by their legacy. Critical loathing only made their fans—particularly in the U.S.A.—love them more. "Here's this band singing about being paranoid," recalled Billy Corgan of The Smashing Pumpkins, "and I'm like, 'Yeah, I know what you mean.'"

Their influence shows up in surprising forms. Red Hot Chili Peppers' 232▶ "Give It Away" ends with the riff from "Sweet Leaf." The Seattle grunge scene—led by Green River and popularized by Nirvana 242▶—was largely founded on Sabbath's sludgier riffs. And listening to the band was one of the crimes that got Bootsy Collins fired by James Brown ◀022.

Sabbath songs have been sampled by Cypress Hill, the Beastie Boys, and Busta Rhymes, and covered by acts from Pantera and Metallica 218▶ to Soft Cell, Mercury Rev, and The Cardigans. As Osbourne said, "If you're gonna do that heavy metal thing, never mind your half-baked imitators. The only people who could do that was Black Sabbath."

Sabotage (1975) is the original lineup's last classic and boasts the riff-driven gems "Hole in the Sky" (later covered by Pantera) and "Symptom of the Universe" (later covered by Sepultura).

Purists hated *Born Again* (1983) for no good reason other than that singer Ian Gillan was not Ozzy Osbourne or Ronnie James Dio. The album itself is very heavy and very excellent.

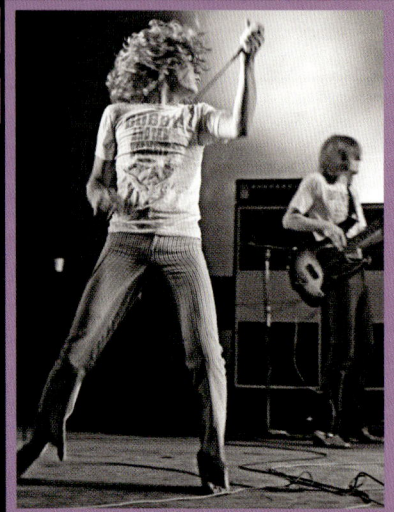

Zeppelin and Sabbath write the rules of rock

"I can remember walking through Birmingham with Geezer Butler . . ." Osbourne told *Spinner UK*, "and he knew Robert Plant (left). Plant was walking through the subway and I'd heard his voice. And Geezer says to him, 'What are you up to?' Plant says, 'Well, they asked me to join a band called the New Yardbirds.' And that was it . . . The first two [Zeppelin] albums had such an impact on my voice, and on my life—similar to The Beatles❶ when I first heard them." Zeppelin❷ tried to distance themselves from heavy metal: after their fourth album, claimed bassist John Paul Jones, "No one ever compared us to Black Sabbath." Nonetheless, the two pillars of hard rock jammed in 1975 at London's Morgan Studios, where Sabbath were recording *Sabotage*. "I have no idea if it was recorded though," Geezer Butler told *Classic Rock*. "I suspect it was, but what happened to the tapes . . . They might even have been wiped."

Black Sabbath

1968 Influence

November 19, 1969
Having performed in the U.K. and Germany as Earth, the Osbourne-led band changes its name to Black Sabbath—the title of a song of theirs that has wowed audiences.

August 29, 1970
"Paranoid" hits the U.K. chart and is soon to be Sabbath's biggest hit. It will be the first single purchased by Mark E. Smith of The Fall, who remarks, "He's a good singer, Ozzy."

Connection 1980

May 1, 1980
Sabbath release their first album with Ronnie James Dio, *Heaven and Hell*. Dio, Iommi, Butler, and Vinnie Appice will use its title as a band name when they reunite in 2006.

October 1983
The Ian Gillan-led Sabbath get ready for a U.S. and Canadian tour, only to find that their "Stonehenge" set—bigger than the real Stonehenge—does not fit into the venues.

The Ozzman cometh

"Black Sabbath were heavy," observed Lemmy of Motörhead, "but I never cared for them. I thought Ozzy's first album was better than all Sabbath's stuff put together." *Blizzard of Ozz* (1980) was indeed a revelation after the singer's dreary, final albums with Sabbath and—thanks in part to his new guitar hero, Randy Rhoads—established Osbourne (left, with Rhoads) as Sabbath's commercial superior for the next three decades. Their stories have often intertwined: Osbourne released the live *Speak of the Devil* (1982), packed with his old band's songs, as a spoiler tactic when the Ronnie James Dio-led Sabbath were preparing their own *Live Evil* (1983), and Geezer Butler joined Osbourne's band in 1988 and 1995. Ozzy himself, having unleashed classics such as "Crazy Train" and "No More Tears," became a TV star in 2002, thanks to *The Osbournes*, which even earned a namecheck from U.S. President George W. Bush.

Nirvana and the sound of Seattle

From Soundgarden to Screaming Trees, Seattle had no shortage of acts with a sonic debt to Sabbath. Although Kurt Cobain likened Nirvana to "Black Sabbath playing ["My Sharona" hitmakers] The Knack," little of Sabbath's influence could be heard in his work. However, producer Butch Vig recalled that, when they began *Nevermind*, "one of the first things Kurt said was, 'We want to sound slower and heavier than Black Sabbath. Turn the treble off on all the tracks.'" (Vig's studio boasted a console from London that was used by Sabbath and Zeppelin.) "I was talking to Dave Grohl," recalled Osbourne in 2007, "and he said, 'You probably don't remember this, but when you were in Devonshire Studios in the [San Fernando] Valley, me and Kurt were in the room where they had a pool table . . .' They'd both written 'OZZY' on their fingers in indelible ink. He said, 'We were both trying to hide our hands.'"

1989 Influence

June 15, 1997
Marilyn Manson joins the Ozzfest tour, headlined by Sabbath. "Their audience," he complains, "were drunk white guys wanting to beat me up for wearing pantyhose."

December 5–6, 1997
Iommi, Butler, Osbourne, and Ward play their first British shows together in nineteen years, in their hometown Birmingham's NEC (issued as the live album, *Reunion*).

March 13, 2006
Having previously asked to be taken off the ballot, Sabbath are inducted into the Rock and Roll Hall of Fame. Metallica play "Iron Man" and "Hole in the Sky" in their honor.

June 8, 1995
Sabbath's eighteenth studio album *Forbidden* is issued. Despite an Ice-T cameo, it is the band's poorest seller and will be their last studio album under the name Black Sabbath.

Connection 1997

September 5, 2000
Hip-hop giants Wu-Tang Clan team up with Osbourne and Iommi on a metallic overhaul of Wu-Tang's "For Heaven's Sake," released on the *Loud Rocks* compilation.

May 26, 2009
Osbourne sues Iommi, whom he accuses of claiming to be the sole owner of the band's name. Sabbath's legacy, Ozzy pleads, "should live on long after we have all gone."

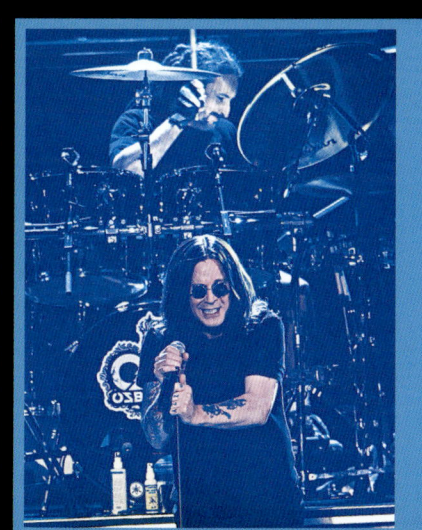

Mike Bordin gets back in Black

With Bill Ward not in a position to play with the reunited Osbourne, Iommi, and Butler, the Black Sabbath drumstool for the 1997 Ozzfest tour went to Mike Bordin of Faith No More (left). Fortunately, Bordin—whose early influences were Ward and Zeppelin's John Bonham—had already joined Osbourne's band (meaning he now had to play two sets per night). He already had experience of at least one Sabbath classic: Faith No More had released a live cover of *Paranoid*'s perennial "War Pigs" in 1989. Bordin once said, "Black Sabbath is the only band whose records I have actually worn out." (FNM guitarist Jim Martin agreed: "I've stayed into Black Sabbath for a long time.") Reflecting on his time with them, Bordin said: "I owe so much to Ozzy . . . Tony is a brilliant guitarist, maybe among the five best guitarists of all time . . . and also has a great sense of humor. And Bill Ward became a great friend, too."

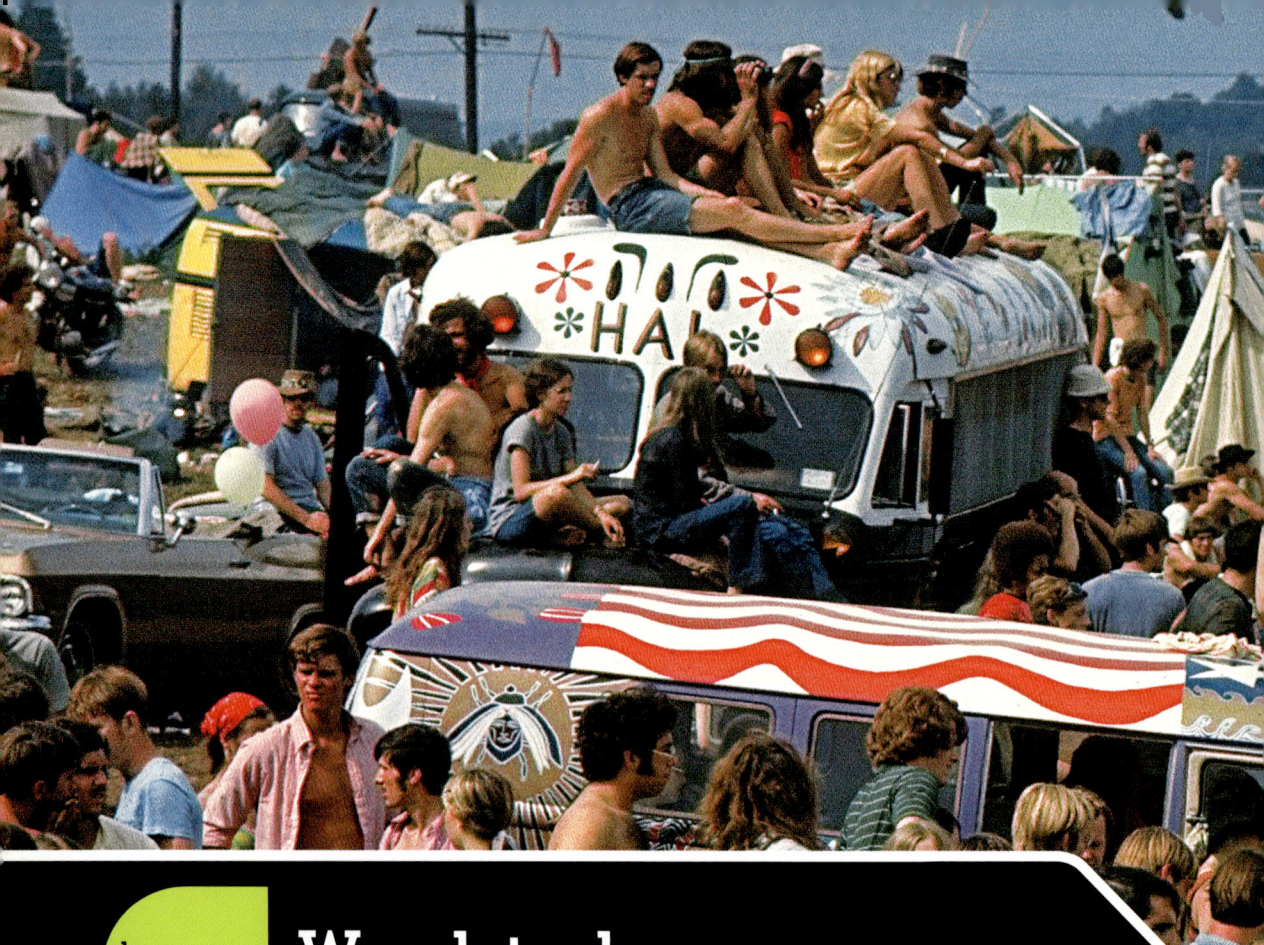

key festival

Woodstock
1969, 1994, and 1999

Commemorated as the greatest festival of the Sixties, Woodstock certainly featured several of the era's greatest acts, including Sly & The Family Stone, The Who ◀068, and Jimi Hendrix ◀072.

The music, however, ended up being secondary to the sheer scale of the event: half a million of the love generation made the pilgrimage between August 15 and 17, 1969—ten times more than anticipated. As *Life* reported, "Lured by music, the country, and some strange kind of magic ('Doesn't Bob Dylan ◀062 live in Woodstock?'), young people from all over the U.S.A. descended on the six hundred-acre [upstate New York] dairy farm."

As a huge jam built up on the New York State Freeway and thousands of people clambered over unfinished fences (due to a late venue change), the organizers declared it a free festival, despite more than 100,000 people having *bought* tickets.

Unmoved by such woes, The Grateful Dead and The Who demanded cash before going on. Karma dictated that the Dead played one of their worst sets, and The Who had no shortage of problems.

"Woodstock was a nightmare," recalled Roger Daltrey. "We got there at six, and didn't go on till six the next morning." And, noted John Entwistle, "Somebody put LSD in our water just before we were due onstage." When "Yippie" activist Abbie Hoffman clambered onstage to denounce the event as "a pile of shit," Pete Townshend bellowed "Fuck off my fucking stage," and clubbed him into the pit.

Other performances of note came from Jefferson Airplane, Country Joe & The Fish, Richie Havens, and Sly & The Family Stone. Most remarkable were Santana, who—though yet to release their debut album—dazzled for forty-five minutes on the hot Saturday afternoon (it poured the next morning).

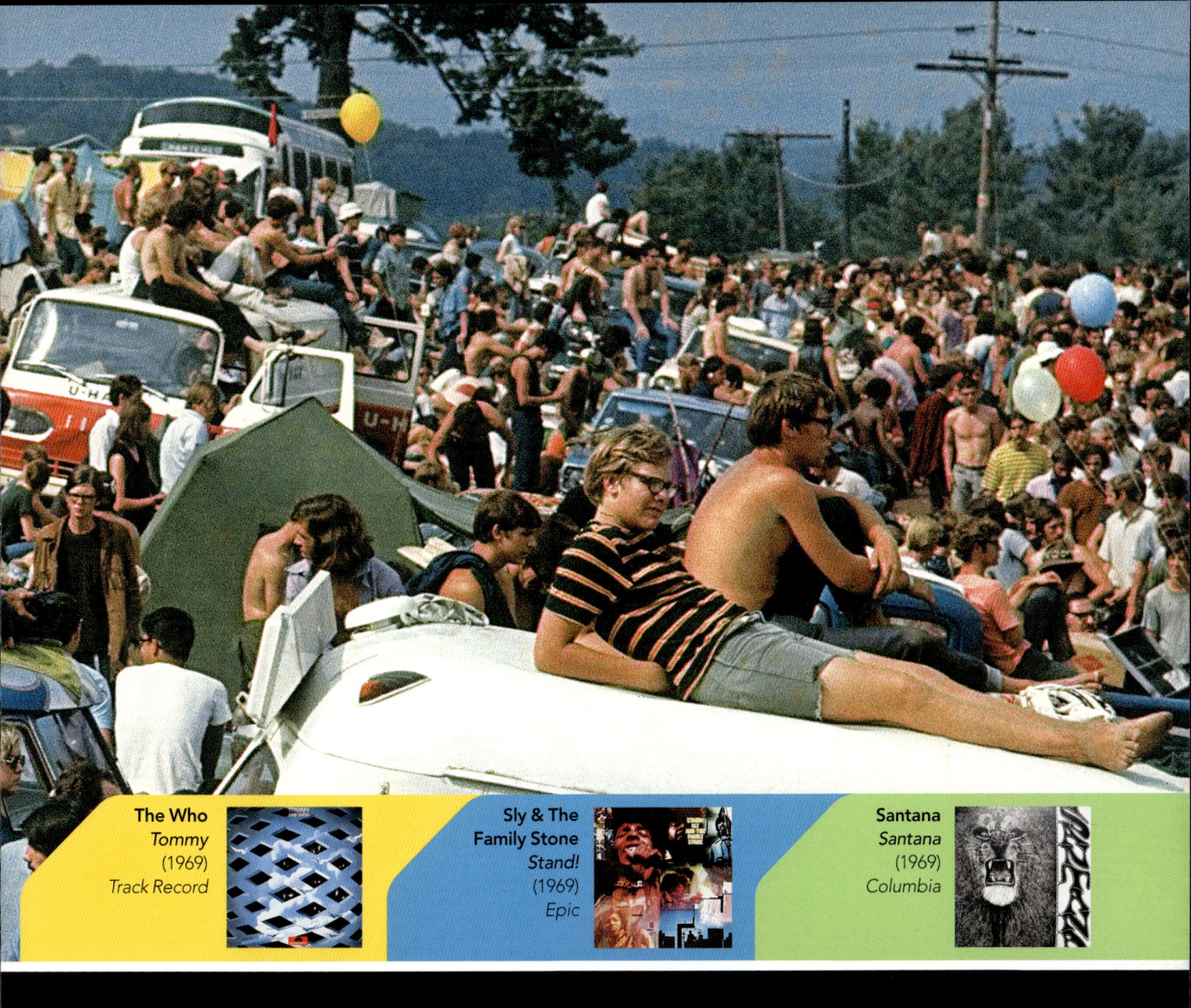

The Who	Sly & The Family Stone	Santana
Tommy	*Stand!*	*Santana*
(1969)	(1969)	(1969)
Track Record	Epic	Columbia

The "three days of peace and music" closed on Monday morning with Jimi Hendrix. "When Jimi was playing 'The Star-Spangled Banner,'" said John Sebastian, formerly of The Lovin' Spoonful, "most of the people had gone, and it looked like a battlefield out there." Steven Tyler of Aerosmith ◀154▶, who attended as a fan, concurred: "The fields all around looked like there'd been a war but with no bodies—sleeping bags instead of bodies."

The promoters' million-dollar loss was offset by a hugely successful movie and soundtrack of the event, which didn't stop them suing each other.

Also released in the aftermath was "Woodstock" by Crosby, Stills, Nash & Young (who played there), written by Joni Mitchell ◀102▶ (who didn't). But the writer was less rosy-eyed than her song suggested: "My generation was ready to change the world but, when the baton was passed to them . . . they didn't know what to do so they kind of degenerated into the greediest generation in the history of America."

An attempt at a commemorative event—held in 1979 on Long Island, featuring veterans of the first festival—was a flop. Then, in 1994, a twenty-fifth anniversary festival was held at Woodstock itself. Sixties stars Crosby, Stills, Nash & Young and Joe Cocker were overshadowed by acts such as Metallica ◀218▶, Aerosmith, and Green Day ◀258▶. And the highlight was Nine Inch Nails, whose mud-coated performance graphically embodied the nihilistic destructiveness that Mitchell had prophesized.

Even that paled beside Woodstock '99 (held in Rome, New York). Red Hot Chili Peppers ◀232▶, Limp Bizkit, Metallica, and Rage Against the Machine ◀254▶ unwittingly presided over a disaster, now infamous for its extreme violence. The "Devil's bargain" of Mitchell's song had become a horrifying reality.

Santana August 16, 1969 • August 14, 1994

A surprise hit of the first festival, Carlos Santana was a natural choice for the 1994 event (even though his astonishing commercial resurrection, courtesy of the *Supernatural* album, was still five years away). "I felt I was trying to accommodate Jimi Hendrix❶ and so many other people," he told Q. "Every note I was playing was coming from the root of my heart, rather than some disconnected place in my brain."

The Who August 17, 1969

"Throughout the entire day," Woodstock organizer Michael Lang remembered of Pete Townshend, "he was like the Grinch that stole Christmas. He was uptight, miserable, hated being there, and wanted to go home." Despite The Who's❶ misgivings, the event proved as pivotal to their legend as an appearance at the Monterey festival in 1967. Performing as the dawn broke, the band turned *Tommy* into a classic.

Woodstock
1969, 1994, and 1999

Sly & The Family Stone August 17, 1969

Despite performing at 3:30 A.M., Sly & The Family Stone❶ proved one of Woodstock's highlights. They had recently scored a smash with "Everyday People" and released the classic *Stand!*. Both helped to create a storming performance. "I got to witness the peak of the festival," recalled Carlos Santana, "which was Sly Stone. I don't think he ever played that good again—steam was literally coming out of his Afro."

Jimi Hendrix August 18, 1969

Festival co-creator Michael Lang had wanted the event to end with Roy Rogers singing "Happy Trails." Instead, it climaxed on Monday morning—nine hours after his scheduled stage time—with an era-defining set by Jimi Hendrix❶. His performance of the U.S. national anthem, "The Star-Spangled Banner," was full of screaming effects, evoking the Vietnam War. Hendrix never again played this piece more iconically.

Metallica August 13, 1994 • July 24, 1999

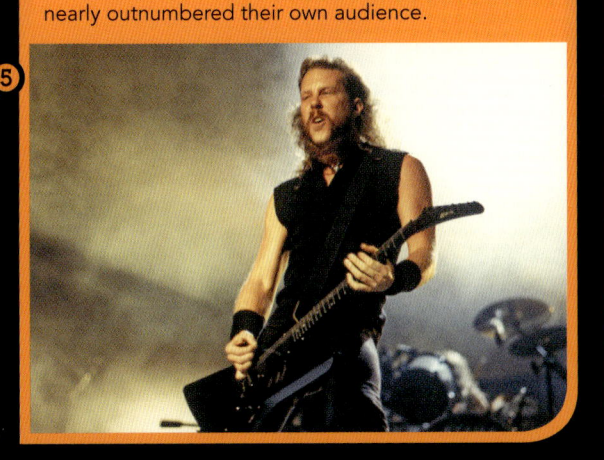

In 1994, Metallica❶ followed Nine Inch Nails—a task that might have proved tricky for anyone other than the biggest rock band on the planet. A pyrotechnic performance ensued. In 1999, they earned the best reviews of the festival (admittedly not hard, given the coverage), and drew so many people that The Chemical Brothers duo, playing the second stage, nearly outnumbered their own audience.

❶ 232

Red Hot Chili Peppers
August 14, 1994 • July 25, 1999

The Chili Peppers❶ would doubtless prefer to forget their Woodstock 1999 performance, with their cover of Hendrix's❷ "Fire" being taken as endorsement of the crowd's pyromania. But the 1994 event will forever be remembered for their lightbulb costumes (above); regarded with some bewilderment by guitarist Dave Navarro, who debuted with the band at this show.

❷ 072

Limp Bizkit July 24, 1999

Since riding to extraordinary fame on the coattails of nu-metal pioneers Korn (who played Woodstock the day before them), Limp Bizkit had shifted some three million copies of their album *Significant Other*. By the time they hit Woodstock's stage, the hot, dehydrated crowd had already turned violent. When the band—led by Fred Durst (above)—launched into "Break Stuff," the horrific outcome was inevitable.

Rage Against the Machine July 24, 1999

Rage❶ were one of the more thoughtful acts in 1999, although it's unclear how many watching perceived their burning of the U.S. flag as a comment on free speech. "The crass commercialism of the event and the greedy exploitation of these youngsters caught up with the vendors and promoters," opined guitarist Tom Morello. "Or maybe it was just a good old-fashioned healthy riot. One with a killer soundtrack."

❶ 254

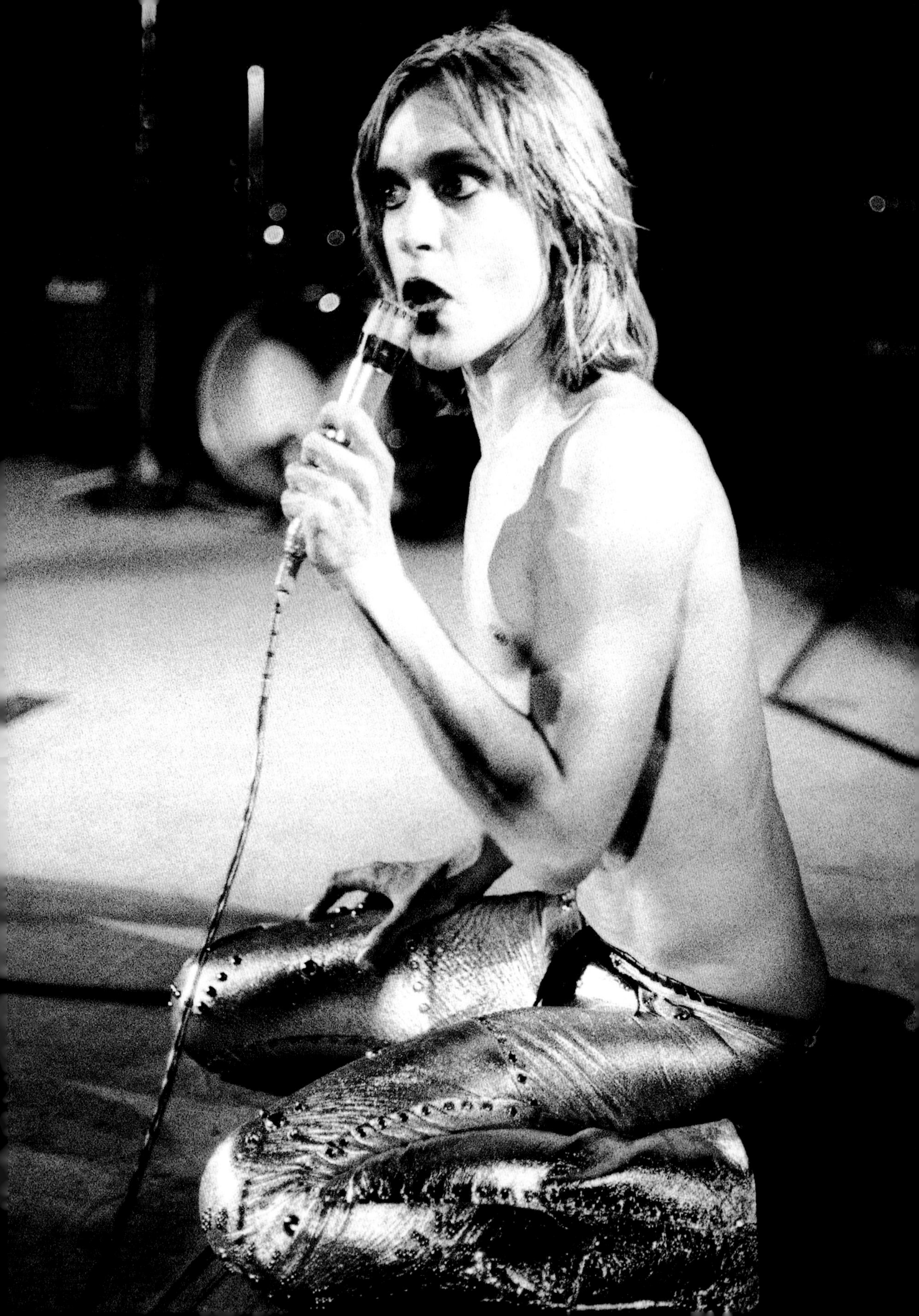

Iggy Pop
1947–present

Popular legend once held that, after a nuclear apocalypse, the only living things would be cockroaches and Keith Richards. To that list must be added Iggy Pop, who—in addition to making a handful of the most influential records in rock—has survived self-laceration, drug abuse, living on the street, mental breakdown, and playing in front of bemused Madonna 208◗ fans. And, unlike most of his contemporaries, he still makes vital music.

Iggy's legend could have rested on his very first album, *The Stooges*. With bassist Dave Alexander and guitarist and drummer Ron and Scott Asheton, he turned garage rock into proto punk, creating a masterpiece that has been plundered repeatedly, from the Sex Pistols 166◗ to The White Stripes 272◗.

> "He's such a fragile, sweet, soulful, honest, and sincere guy. I really love him a lot."
> —Slash, Guns N' Roses

Iggy concert-goers also got to encounter his uninhibited live persona: "Iggy," recalled Velvet Underground ◖090 man and Stooges producer John Cale, "had this way of threatening the audience and then embracing them the next minute. He was a chameleon." Alan Vega, of fellow influential cult band Suicide, witnessed The Stooges supporting the MC5: "What I saw that night was beyond anything I'd seen or heard before. It was like the new art form beyond music because the separation between performer and audience ended."

This manic persona fed into The Stooges' 1970 classic *Fun House*, a pivotal influence on the likes of Nick Cave 202◗. Another fan was David Bowie 134◗, who brought Iggy and his band (now the Asheton brothers and guitarist James Williamson) to the U.K. to create *Raw Power* (1973), after which the band collapsed and Iggy entered a mental hospital.

When Bowie and Iggy decamped to Europe, they made the 1977 classics *The Idiot* and *Lust for Life*. The latter was cut in Berlin, where they both lived with producer Brian Eno 138◗. Paul McGuinness, manager of U2 192◗ (who also worked in the German capital with Eno), recalled the producer describing the three of them in one squabblesome apartment: "There was constant fighting about socks . . . The three great men screaming at one another, 'You took my socks, you bastard!'"

Iggy toured with Bowie (and Blondie 172◗ supporting). Their songs proved pivotal influences on acts from Joy Division 184◗ to Nine Inch Nails, while Bowie himself had a worldwide smash with a cover of Iggy's "China Girl" (from *The Idiot*; recorded for *Let's Dance*, in a bid to boost Iggy's finances).

Iggy's later work has ranged from arty (*Zombie Birdhouse*) to slick (*Blah Blah Blah*), and from hard rock (*Naughty Little Doggie*) to jazz (*Préliminaires*). His collaborators have included electroclash queen Peaches, Blondie's Debbie Harry, Kate Pierson of The B-52's, and members of Guns N' Roses 228◗.

This icon even sells insurance in the U.K. "Ever since our first Stooges album," he said, "I thought, 'Why doesn't somebody hire me to do an advert? I can sell shit better than the zombies on TV!'"

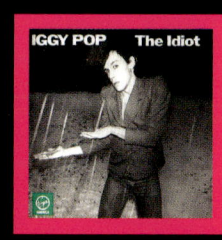

The Idiot (1977) was found on Ian Curtis' turntable after the Joy Division singer committed suicide. But this Bowie-helmed classic is packed with top tunes, such as "Nightclubbing."

From many "best ofs," *A Million in Prizes* (2005) stands out for its detailed sleeve notes and its fine Stooges and solo selections. Among many highlights is the spellbinding "Look Away."

Slash, the guitar hero

While shooting the movie *The Man Who Fell to Earth* in 1975, David Bowie❶ had an affair with his costume designer, Ola Hudson. She and her son, Saul, accompanied Bowie when he visited Iggy, then in a mental hospital. And that was how Saul—later Slash (left), guitarist with Guns N' Roses❷—met one of his heroes. More than fourteen years later, he and GNR bassist Duff McKagan contributed to four tracks on Iggy's best album in years, 1990's *Brick by Brick* (including "My Baby Wants to Rock & Roll," which the guitarist co-wrote). "That was great," said Slash. "We did that in one day and it kicked ass." (*Brick by Brick* producer Don Was promptly recruited Slash for Bob Dylan's❸ *Under the Red Sky*. Dylan, however, erased Slash's work because "it sounded like Guns N' Roses.") GNR themselves cut a sterling cover of Iggy's "Raw Power" for *The Spaghetti Incident?* (1993), prefaced with Axl Rose's gleeful "Yo Ig, check it out!"

Iggy Pop

April 21, 1947
James Newell Osterberg, Jr., is born in Ann Arbor, Michigan. Two decades later, his band The Psychedelic Stooges will make their live debut in Ann Arbor, on Halloween in 1967.

May 1970
Produced by Don Galluci of "Louie Louie"-hitmakers The Kingsmen, The Stooges record *Fun House*, a.k.a. "Osterberg's Fifth Symphony." Unlike their debut album, it fails to chart.

1975 Connection

June 1969
Signed to Elektra (the home of The Doors) and now called The Stooges, Iggy and the band record their self-titled debut album. It includes "I Wanna Be Your Dog."

September–October 1972
After a year of mowing lawns and improving his golf, Iggy moves to London and records "Gimme Danger," "Search and Destroy," and the title track for 1973's *Raw Power*.

Influence 1976

Never mind The Stooges, here's the Pistols

In 1975, Iggy was dragging himself out of the gutter. Meanwhile, in the U.K., four horrible urchins were forming The Stooges' spiritual heirs, the Sex Pistols❶. Even before they had released their first record, *Melody Maker* reported that "their dreadfully inept attempts to zero in on the kind of viciously blank intensity previously epitomized by The Stooges was rather endearing." (A description that best fit latterday Pistols bassist, and ardent Stooges fan, Sid Vicious.) The Pistols made the connection clear by covering Iggy's "No Fun" on the B-side of 1977's "Pretty Vacant" (it was also the last song they played before Johnny Rotten left the band in 1978). The Pistols' guitarist, Steve Jones (left), later worked with Iggy on *Blah Blah Blah* (1986) and *Instinct* (1988). Yet, despite all this, Iggy disdained his "godfather of punk" title: "I've been linked to a lot of movements but I never feel close to any of them."

Iggy on the silver screen

Iggy's acting career began with bit parts in 1986's *Sid and Nancy* and *The Color of Money*. By the Nineties, he had graduated to proper roles in *Cry-Baby* and *Dead Man* (in which he appeared with Johnny Depp; left). The latter's director, Jim Jarmusch, seized the opportunity to shoot one of his *Coffee and Cigarettes* shorts (compiled as a feature film in 2003), starring Iggy and Tom Waits. "It's exactly what you'd imagine Tom Waits and Iggy Pop hanging out to be like," the director said of the hilarious result. "It's exaggerated, but Tom has got a paranoid streak, and Iggy is very generous, so when Iggy says, 'Oh man, I saw this great drummer,' and Tom says, 'Well, what are you saying, my drumming sucks?,' it's very close." Iggy's résumé has since ranged from roles in *Tank Girl* and *The Crow: City of Angels*, to playing a Ferengi alien in *Star Trek: Deep Space Nine*, to voiceovers for *Persepolis* and *The Rugrats Movie*.

March 21, 1976
Iggy and David Bowie are busted for drugs in a New York hotel. They will promptly decamp to Berlin to make some of the most influential albums in rock history.

1986 Connection

November 4, 2003
The Stooges, Green Day, and Peaches guest on Iggy's new *Skull Ring*. It will be followed by the first Stooges concerts since the 1974 show captured on 1976's *Metallic K.O.*

November 2, 2009
Chrissie Hynde presents Iggy with the "Living Legend" title at the Marshall Classic Rock Roll of Honour awards. He dedicates it to Ron Asheton, who died on January 6.

December 1986
Iggy has one of his biggest hits with "Real Wild Child," a Bowie-produced cover of the Australian rock classic "Wild One" (previously recorded by Jerry Lee Lewis and others).

November 23, 1996
The nineteen-year-old "Lust for Life" hits the U.K. chart, thanks to its use in the movie *Trainspotting*. It will also appear, sung by Bruce Willis, in 2003's *Rugrats Go Wild*.

Connection 2008

March 15, 2010
At Iggy's behest, Green Day, plus Pearl Jam's Jeff Ament and Eddie Vedder, invade the stage when The Stooges are inducted into the Rock and Roll Hall of Fame in New York.

Madonna's stooge?

"She's from up the road," Iggy told *Classic Rock* of fellow Michigan native, Madonna❶, when asked why the pop idol selected The Stooges to play at her Rock and Roll Hall of Fame induction on March 10, 2008. "I think she wanted to keep it a little edgy." The band covered "Burning Up" and "Ray of Light," before Iggy recited lines from "Like a Virgin." "The Stooges represent everything that's against what she is," guitarist Ron Asheton told the *Free Press*. "I don't wish her ill . . . But I'd never even heard of these songs until I had to listen to a tape and figure out what's going on with them . . . Iggy said, 'We're gonna rock them up—just play 'em like Stooges songs . . .' I've actually enjoyed playing them." The Stooges previously supported Madonna at Ireland's Slaine Castle, described by Iggy as "Eighty-five thousand mentally-challenged people there to listen to her drum machine and watch one very overpaid person."

❶ 208

Sex, Drugs & Rock 'n' Roll

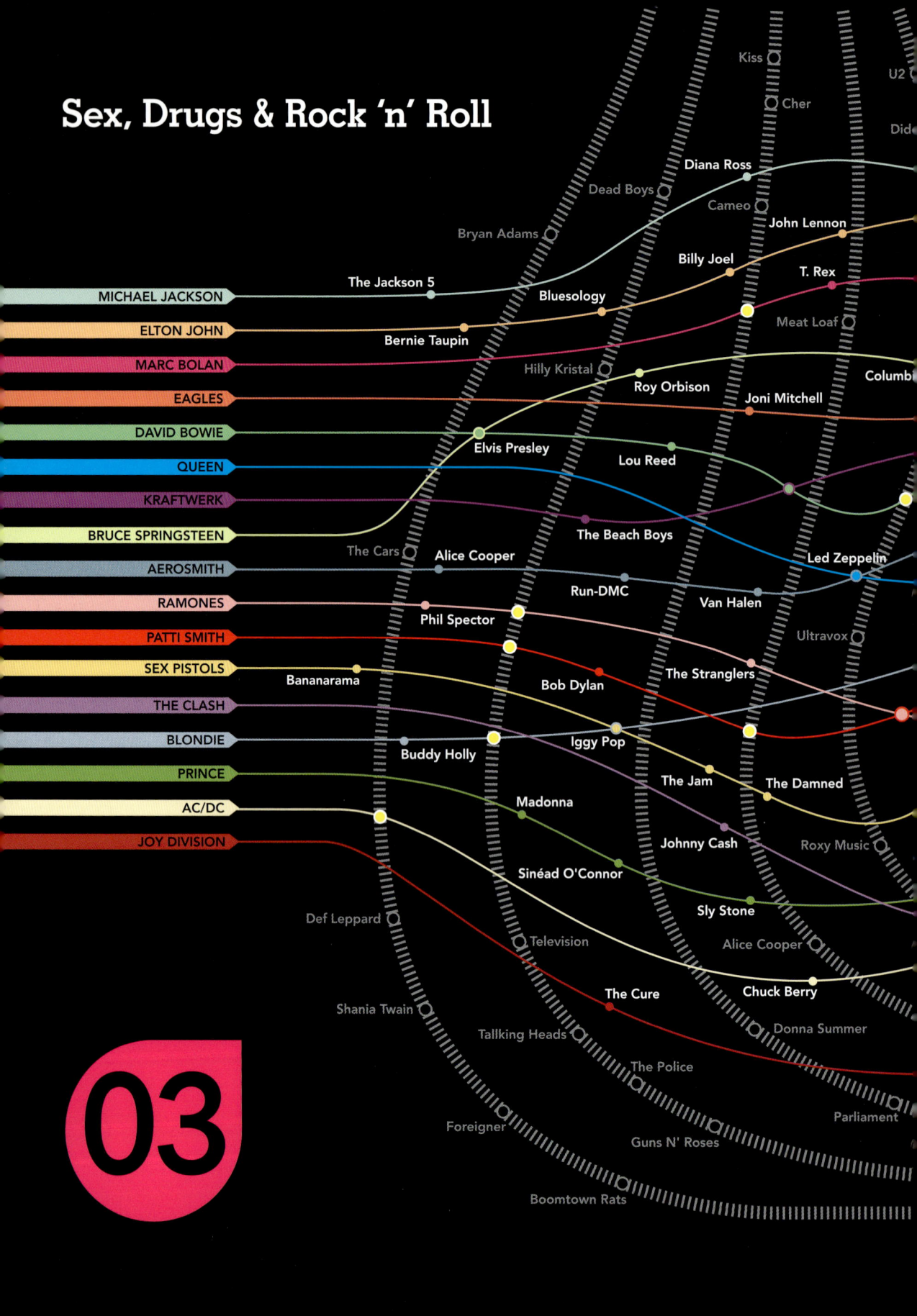

- MICHAEL JACKSON
- ELTON JOHN
- MARC BOLAN
- EAGLES
- DAVID BOWIE
- QUEEN
- KRAFTWERK
- BRUCE SPRINGSTEEN
- AEROSMITH
- RAMONES
- PATTI SMITH
- SEX PISTOLS
- THE CLASH
- BLONDIE
- PRINCE
- AC/DC
- JOY DIVISION

Kiss
Cher
U2
Dido
Diana Ross
Dead Boys
Cameo
John Lennon
Bryan Adams
Billy Joel
T. Rex
The Jackson 5
Bluesology
Meat Loaf
Bernie Taupin
Hilly Kristal
Roy Orbison
Joni Mitchell
Columbi
Elvis Presley
Lou Reed
The Beach Boys
Led Zeppelin
The Cars
Alice Cooper
Run-DMC
Van Halen
Phil Spector
Ultravox
Bananarama
Bob Dylan
The Stranglers
Buddy Holly
Iggy Pop
The Jam
The Damned
Madonna
Johnny Cash
Roxy Music
Sinéad O'Connor
Sly Stone
Def Leppard
Television
Alice Cooper
The Cure
Chuck Berry
Shania Twain
Talking Heads
Donna Summer
The Police
Parliament
Foreigner
Guns N' Roses
Boomtown Rats

03

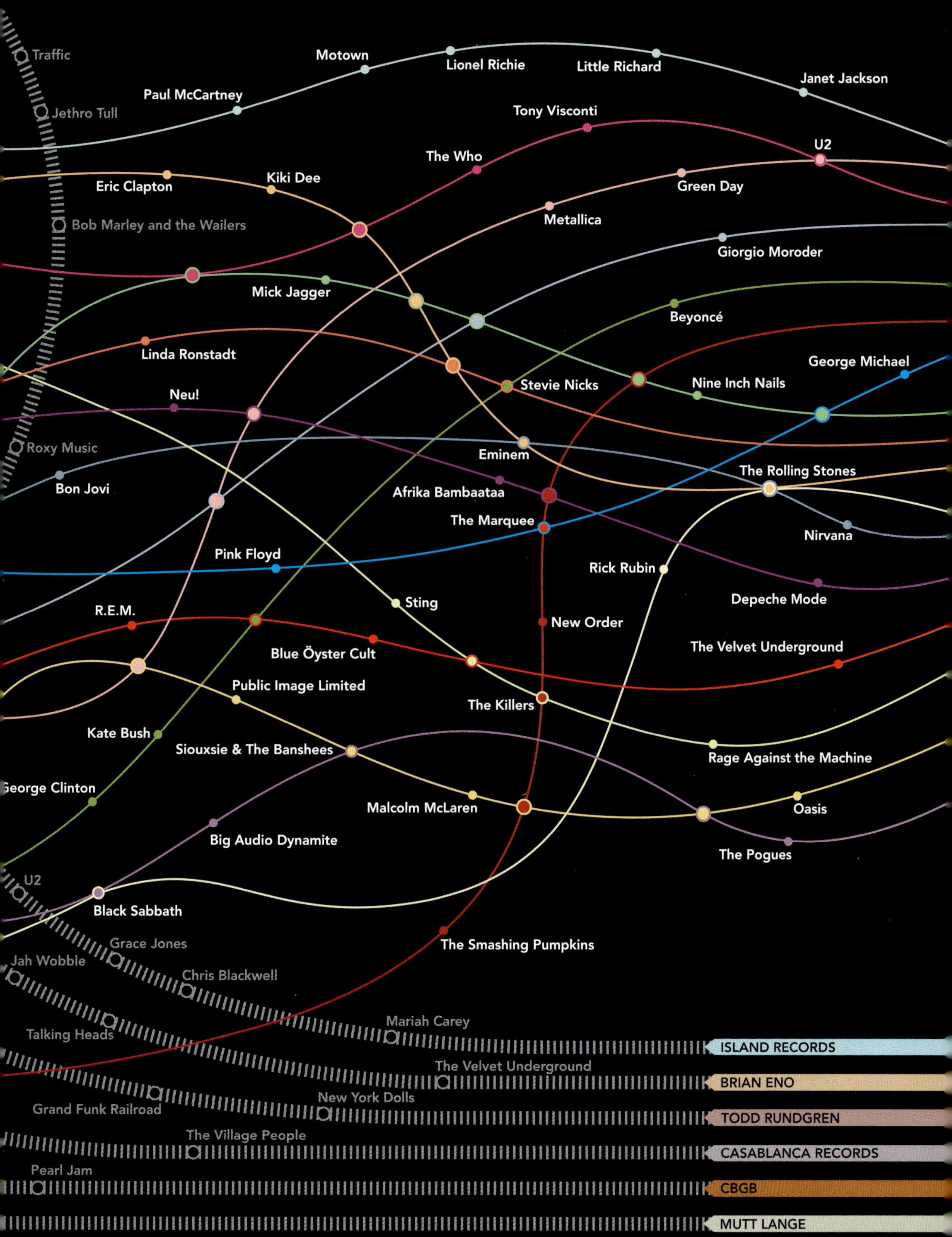
Traffic
Motown
Lionel Richie
Little Richard
Janet Jackson
Paul McCartney
Jethro Tull
Tony Visconti
U2
The Who
Eric Clapton
Kiki Dee
Green Day
Metallica
Bob Marley and the Wailers
Giorgio Moroder
Mick Jagger
Beyoncé
Linda Ronstadt
George Michael
Stevie Nicks
Nine Inch Nails
Neu!
Roxy Music
Eminem
Bon Jovi
The Rolling Stones
Afrika Bambaataa
The Marquee
Nirvana
Pink Floyd
Rick Rubin
Sting
Depeche Mode
R.E.M.
New Order
Blue Öyster Cult
The Velvet Underground
Public Image Limited
The Killers
Kate Bush
Siouxsie & The Banshees
Rage Against the Machine
George Clinton
Malcolm McLaren
Oasis
Big Audio Dynamite
The Pogues
U2
Black Sabbath
Grace Jones
The Smashing Pumpkins
Jah Wobble
Chris Blackwell
Mariah Carey
Talking Heads
ISLAND RECORDS
The Velvet Underground
BRIAN ENO
Grand Funk Railroad
New York Dolls
TODD RUNDGREN
The Village People
CASABLANCA RECORDS
Pearl Jam
CBGB
MUTT LANGE

Michael Jackson 1958–2009

1958+ 1971+ 1979+ 1984+ 1994+

Amid the hoopla of his life and hullabaloo of his death, Michael Jackson's true genius was often overlooked. Madonna 208▷ summed it up: "I've always admired Michael Jackson—the world has lost one of its greats, but his music will live on forever." A former collaborator, Slash from Guns N' Roses 228▷, added, "He was talent from on high."

Already having had phenomenal succcess with The Jackson 5 (his older brothers Tito, Jermaine, Jackie, and Marlon made up the rest of the quintet), Michael—with his incredible voice, astonishing dance moves, and undeniable star quality—launched his solo career at just thirteen, with "Got to Be There."

"Ben," an ode to a pet rat, was the first of many chart-topping singles, but it was the disco-laden grooves, soulful pop, and sublime ballads of 1979's *Off the Wall* that made him a global superstar.

"Michael Jackson," said producer Brian Eno ◁138 at the time, "has made much greater cultural breakthroughs than anyone else who's around."

Michael continued to record with his brothers but started branching out on his own and working with other artists too, including The Beatles' ◁044 Paul McCartney on "The Girl Is Mine," which appears on *Thriller*. Released in 1982, the latter became the biggest-selling album of all time.

Bad (1987), *Dangerous* (1991), *HIStory* (1995), *Blood on the Dance Floor* (1997), and *Invincible* (2001) were also incredible successes, spawning No. 1 singles and massive worldwide sales.

"The guy's a genius," said Neil Young ◁078. "They can say what they want about him, but he's burning a line across the sky forever, that guy. There's never gonna be another Michael Jackson."

August 29, 1958
Michael Joseph Jackson is born in Gary, Indiana. He is the seventh of nine children. He and four of his brothers will begin performing together in 1962.

May 16, 1966
Janet Damita Jo Jackson is born. She, too, will become a record-breaking solo singer, and her chart-topping duet with Michael, "Scream," will be released in 1995.

January 30, 1967
The Jackson 5's first single is issued on the Steel Town label—but, says brother Jackie later, "from the start we saw ourselves as being in the Motown mold."

❶ 033
❷ 032
❸ 030

JANUARY 31, 1970: The Jackson 5's first No. 1

Originally known as Ripples & Waves Plus Michael, then The Jackson Brothers, before settling on The Jackson 5❶, the group of brothers won an amateur talent competition in 1967 and gained an influential fan in Gladys Knight (for whom "I Want You Back" was originally intended). After being championed by Diana Ross❷, they were signed to Motown❸ and opened for the diva at a concert in L.A. in 1969. "I Want You Back" (ranked at No. 120 on *Rolling Stone*'s list of the 500 Greatest Songs of All Time) was the first Jackson 5 song to be released by Motown and, as 1970 got underway, it also became the group's first U.S. No. 1. Thanks to the subsequent "ABC," "The Love You Save," and "I'll Be There," the boys became the first pop group to have their opening four singles hit the top. By 1971, after four hit albums with his brothers, Michael was being prepped for solo success, while continuing to be part of the band.

122 SEX, DRUGS & ROCK 'N' ROLL

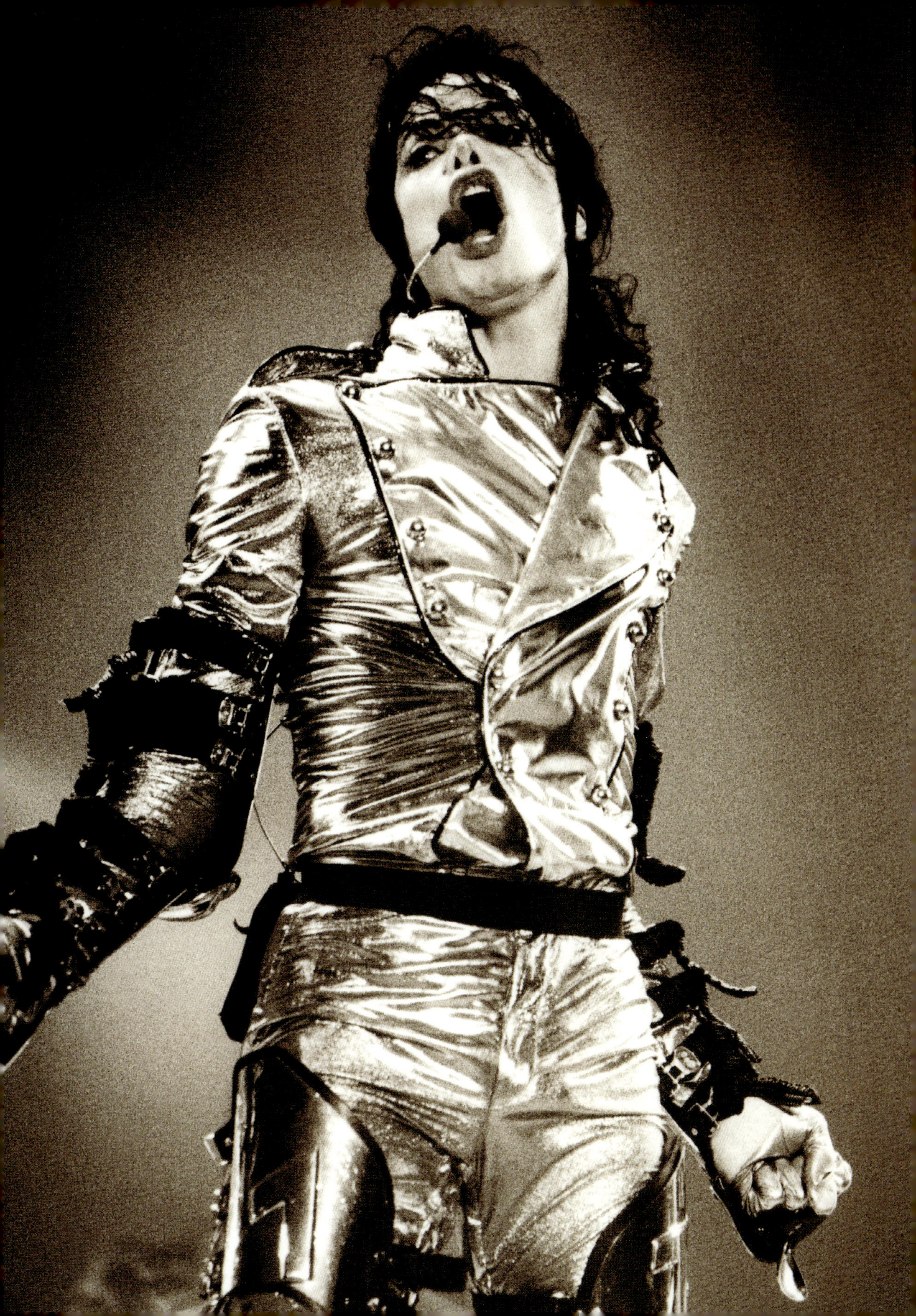

October 7, 1971

Michael's first solo single, the gorgeous "Got to Be There," is released. It will be a top five hit for the thirteen-year-old, and the first of over fifty international solo smashes.

June 23, 1972

The movie *Ben* is released, with a theme song performed by Michael. The track will reach No. 1 in the U.S.A. and Australia and be nominated for an Academy Award.

1976

The brothers (with Randy replacing Jermaine) sign to CBS. Motown retain rights to the name The Jackson 5, so they become—at Michael's suggestion—The Jacksons.

October 24, 1978

The Wiz, Motown's take on *The Wizard of Oz*, has its U.S. premiere. Making his film debut, Michael plays the part of the Scarecrow.

❶ 040
❷ 032

AUGUST 10, 1979: A superstar is born

Every superstar has a true classic, and *Off the Wall* is Michael Jackson's. Although Michael claimed that it was influenced by Little Richard❶, the album was a flawless blend of disco, pop, funk, and soul. Produced by Quincy Jones after the pair met while filming *The Wiz*, it featured songs by Paul McCartney and Stevie Wonder❷, as well as three by Michael himself, including the sublime "Don't Stop 'til You Get Enough." (McCartney's "Girlfriend" had been written with Michael in mind, but was first recorded on the composer's 1978 Wings album *London Town*.) Earning glowing reviews, *Off the Wall* made Michael the first solo artist to have four singles from the same album reach the top ten of the *Billboard* Hot 100 ("Don't Stop 'til You Get Enough" and "Rock With You" both hit No. 1). With over eight million copies sold in the U.S.A. alone, *Off the Wall* is an undisputed pop masterpiece.

August 29, 1979

Michael turns twenty-one and fires his father as manager. His later managers will include Frank DiLeo, a star of Martin Scorsese's classic movie *Goodfellas*.

December 10, 1979

Just four months after its release, *Off the Wall* goes platinum. Despite its massive success, Michael loyally remains part of The Jacksons.

February 27, 1980

"Don't Stop 'til You Get Enough" wins a Grammy but, to Michael's irritation, *Off the Wall* is not Album of the Year (that title goes to Billy Joel's *52nd Street*.)

October 18, 1982

"The Girl Is Mine," a duet with Paul McCartney, is released. Jackson tells a British magazine that his favorite English group will always be The Beatles.

❶ 157
❷ 030

1983: The year of *Thriller*

Released in December 1982, *Thriller* had a harder sound than *Off the Wall*. Eddie Van Halen❶ played guitar on "Beat It"—a role he reprised onstage with Michael in July 1984 (left). Producer Quincy Jones initially considered that "Billie Jean"—one of four songs penned by Jackson—wasn't strong enough. Yet it became the album's first No. 1, holding the top spot in the U.K. and U.S.A. in March 1983 (and, a month later, in Australia). During his performance of the song at the *Motown*❷ *25: Yesterday, Today, Forever* show in May of the same year, Michael caused a sensation when he did the moonwalk for the first time. It lasted only seconds but would become his signature move. *Thriller* spawned seven top ten hits—with a title track as famous for its video as for its music. The album topped the U.S. chart for thirty-seven weeks in total and by the end of 1984 had sold over twenty million in the U.S.A. alone.

SEX, DRUGS & ROCK 'N' ROLL

February 7, 1984

Thriller enters the *Guinness Book of World Records* as the best-selling record of all time. It will be the biggest-selling album in the U.S.A. until 1999, when the Eagles overtake it.

July 6, 1984

Michael begins a tour with The Jacksons. "I was invited . . ." says James Brown. "I don't want to distract attention away from him. Kids need to look at Michael, not me."

March 7, 1985

"We Are the World," which Michael co-wrote with Lionel Richie, and which features Dylan and Springsteen, is released. It will make the highest debut in the U.S. Hot 100 since "Thriller."

September 6, 1985

Jackson pays $47.5 million for ATV Music's publishing rights, including those for many songs by The Beatles. His friendship with Paul McCartney promptly cools.

SEPTEMBER 1987: The chart-topping *Bad*

In 1987, *Thriller*'s long-awaited follow-up, *Bad*, topped charts around the world (bar Australia, where Midnight Oil's *Diesel and Dust* kept it at bay). In the U.S.A., it became only the seventh album to debut at No. 1 and was the first to yield five No. 1 singles, of which "I Just Can't Stop Loving You" was the biggest-selling and "Man in the Mirror" ultimately the best-loved. The ensuing tour set new records for both attendance and financial success. 1991's *Dangerous* was another triumph. Although displaced from the U.S. top spot by Nirvana's ❶ *Nevermind* after just four weeks, it still sold four million within two months of its release. This success was hardly hindered by the chart-topping single "Black or White"—the video of which featured a then controversial crotch-grabbing sequence. This track also boasted guitar by Slash of Guns N' Roses ❷ (left), who played on "Give in to Me," too.

❶ 242
❷ 228

May 26, 1994

Pop royalty joins the rock 'n' roll aristocracy when Michael marries Lisa Marie Presley. They will divorce on August 20, 1996.

February 19, 1996

Jarvis Cocker, front man of British band Pulp, storms the stage when Jackson performs "Earth Song" at the Brit Awards in London.

November 2001

Invincible tops worldwide charts. Although its success is affected by a dispute over promotion with Sony, it will sell two million in the U.S.A. alone in under two months.

March 5, 2009

Michael announces a ten-date run of concerts in London. "This is it," he says. "I just want to say these will be my final show performances in London . . . I'll see you in July."

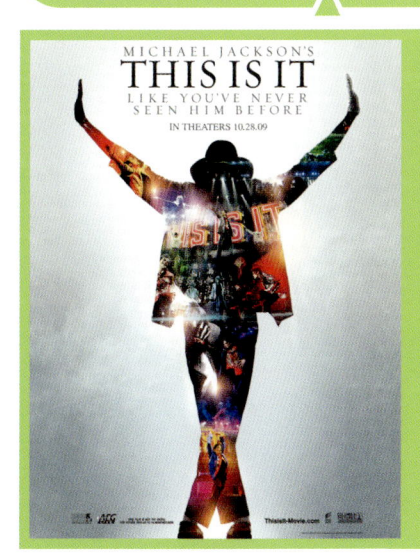

JUNE 25, 2009: The final curtain call

Less than three weeks before he was scheduled to perform his first comeback concert in London, Michael died after suffering a cardiac arrest. Concerns had already been raised about his appearance and health, particularly in light of the fifty concerts he was planning to perform. As news reached people of his untimely death, Internet traffic surged, distraught fans gathered outside his home, and sales boomed. Famous friends issued statements, including Paul McCartney, who said he was "privileged to have hung out and worked with Michael" and Quincy Jones, who called him "the consummate entertainer . . . his contributions and legacy will be felt upon the world forever." A star-studded memorial concert was organized and, within a few days, his albums occupied the top fifteen best-selling slots on Amazon. Sadly, it took his death to remind the world of the magnificence of his music.

Elton John 1947–present

Though never cool, Elton John has had amazing success and drawn many admirers. "He was so wonderful," gushed Kate Bush. "I'd play his records and dream of being able to play like him." "When I first heard 'Bennie and the Jets,'" said Axl Rose of Guns N' Roses ◁228, "I knew I had to be a performer."

Between 1972 and 1975, Elton John had seven consecutive, U.S. chart-topping albums. The last two entered the chart at No. 1 (making him the first artist to score two No. 1 albums in a calendar year).

In 1974, he enticed John Lennon onstage for the ex-Beatle's ◁044 last public performance. By 1975, the year he headlined a show at London's Wembley Stadium over The Beach Boys ◁050 and the Eagles 132▷, one in every fifty records sold was by him.

He has sung and played with stars including The Who ◁068, Aretha Franklin ◁084, George Harrison, Mary J. Blige, Brian Wilson, and 2Pac 262▷.

His songs—often co-written with lyricist Bernie Taupin—have been covered by Nickelback with Kid Rock ("Saturday Night's Alright for Fighting"), Beastie Boys ("Bennie and the Jets"), Red Hot Chili Peppers 232▷ ("Tiny Dancer"), Tina Turner ("The Bitch Is Back"), Dream Theater ("Funeral for a Friend/Love Lies Bleeding"), Rod Stewart ("Country Comfort"), Sandy Denny ("Candle in the Wind"), and Joe Cocker ("Sorry Seems to be the Hardest Word").

Elton has endorsed stars from George Michael to Ryan Adams, and the New York Dolls to the Spice Girls. Even his own stage name pays tribute to co-musicians: British R&B singer Long John Baldry, with whom Elton played piano in Bluesology (and who also launched Rod Stewart) and Elton Dean (Bluesology saxophonist, latterly of The Soft Machine). As Elton said, "The great thing about rock 'n' roll is that someone like me can be a star."

March 25, 1947
Reginald Kenneth Dwight is born in Middlesex, England. He will be playing with local band Bluesology by 1961.

January 1971
Composed in ten minutes, with lyrics by Bernie Taupin, "Your Song" is Elton's first transatlantic top ten hit.

February 5, 1972
"Levon" is a U.S. hit. Its title is inspired by Levon Helm of The Band, whose *Music from Big Pink* is a favorite of Elton's.

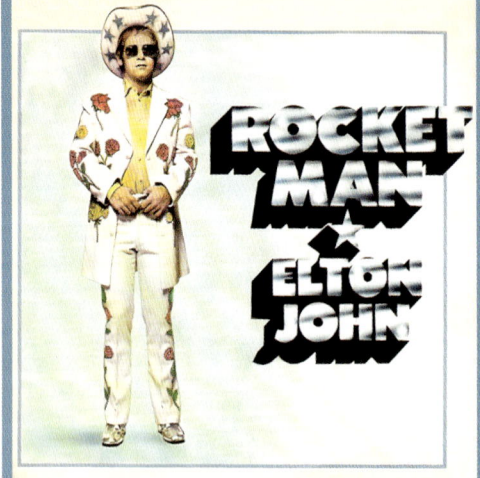

---

❶ 086
❷ 134
❸ 054

JULY 15, 1972: Elton topples the Stones

An astonishing run of success began when—thanks to the hit "Rocket Man"—Elton's *Honky Chateau* knocked The Rolling Stones' *Exile on Main Street* off the U.S. top spot. (The album was named after its studio, Château d'Hérouville, where Pink Floyd❶ made *Obscured by Clouds* and David Bowie❷ made *Low*.) The chart-toppers continued with 1973's *Don't Shoot Me I'm Only the Piano Player* and *Goodbye Yellow Brick Road*, 1974's *Caribou* and *Greatest Hits*, and 1975's *Captain Fantastic and the Brown Dirt Cowboy* and *Rock of the Westies*. Such was Elton's stardom that, in 1975, he insisted on guesting with The Rolling Stones❸ in Colorado, then refused to leave the stage. "If," remarked Mick Jagger, "it had been an American, like Stephen Stills, we'd have just kicked him off."

SEX, DRUGS & ROCK 'N' ROLL

January 4, 1975

Elton's version of "Lucy in the Sky with Diamonds" tops the U.S. chart. The Beatles cover boasts John Lennon, credited as Dr. Winston O'Boogie.

June 27, 1976

Elton meets Elvis Presley at a show in Maryland. Not having kept up with pop, the King is under the impression that the British star is a comedian.

July 24, 1976

"Don't Go Breaking My Heart"—with Kiki Dee—is Elton's first U.K. No. 1 single. (It also tops the U.S. chart.) The pair will later sing it at Live Aid.

October 7, 1976

In *Rolling Stone*, Elton says: "There's nothing wrong with going to bed with somebody of your own sex." The quote will cost him U.S. airplay.

NOVEMBER 3, 1977: Retirement blues

Exhausted from his extraordinary workload, and battered by the reaction to the *Rolling Stone* interview, Elton announced at a London show that he was retiring from touring. (This held true until 1979.) Although some distance from his Seventies heyday, the Eighties still saw relative successes, such as 1984's *Breaking Hearts*. In 1983, a reunion with Bernie Taupin for *Too Low for Zero* (after five years of sporadic collaboration, during which the lyricist co-wrote Alice Cooper's ❶ 1978 album *From the Inside*) yielded the hits "I Guess That's Why They Call It the Blues" and "I'm Still Standing." Most remarkably, on Valentine's Day 1984, Elton married female sound engineer Renate Blauel. "You may still be standing," observed Rod Stewart, "but we're all on the fucking floor!"

❶ 156

June 23, 1990

"Sacrifice" gives Elton his first U.K. No. 1 since 1976. Its parent album, *Sleeping with the Past,* will follow it to the top.

June 22, 1992

The One, featuring Eric Clapton and David Gilmour, is released. The double platinum album takes Elton back to the U.S. top ten.

March 23, 1993

The chart-topping 1974 set *Greatest Hits* passes ten million sales in the U.S.A. It will sell another six million over the next ten years.

June 1994

Disney's *The Lion King* opens in the U.S.A. The movie features songs by Elton such as "Can You Feel the Love Tonight" and "Circle of Life."

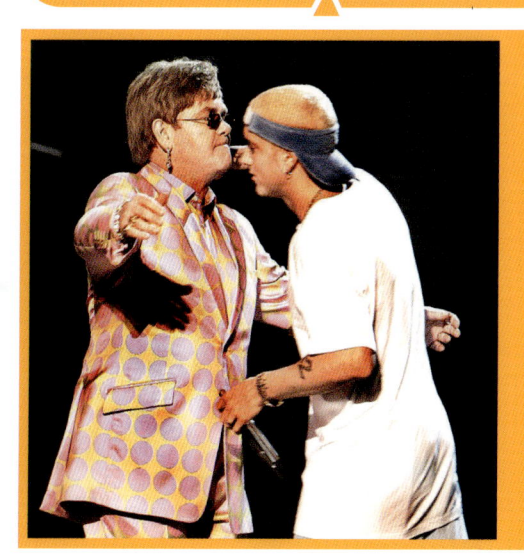

SEPTEMBER 6, 1997: "Candle in the Wind"

At the funeral of his friend Princess Diana—the British royal killed in a car crash on August 31, 1997—Elton sang a new version of 1973's "Candle in the Wind." The song topped charts around the world and took just over a month to become the best-selling single ever. Five months later, he was knighted by Queen Elizabeth, becoming Sir Elton John. Since then, he has duetted with Eminem❶ (at 2001's Grammys, left), had amusing wars of words with Madonna❷ and Keith Richards, and made the occasional album. A Las Vegas residency and tours (including several with Billy Joel) have kept the faithful happy. Meanwhile, renewed interest in his 1971 song "Tiny Dancer" —prompted by its use in the 2000 movie *Almost Famous*— was a stirring reminder of his true strength as a composer.

❶ 257
❷ 208

ELTON JOHN   127

Marc Bolan 1947–77

1947+   1972+

One of the U.K.'s best-loved pop legends, Marc Bolan worked hard for his fame and success. By the time he entered the top forty in 1968, he had moved to France and back, toyed with mod and folk styles, and seen six singles flop. These included three with John's Children, a psychedelic outfit with whom the future star supported The Who ◀068 in Germany. Bolan would later claim that the headliners "had us taken off the tour in the end because we upstaged them."

Back in London, he teamed with percussionist Steve Peregrine Took to form Tyrannosaurus Rex, and played the capital's hippy venues. "What the Pink Floyd ◀086 do electronically," he said, "we do acoustically." His friends included producer Tony Visconti and would-be pop star David Bowie 134▶.

When the relationship with Took disintegrated, Bolan united with Mickey Finn. After a third and final album as Tyrannosaurus Rex (*A Beard of Stars*), he abbreviated the name that "the BBC always had difficulty in pronouncing." T. Rex was born, and Bolan found the fame that he had always wanted.

By the time punk rock exploded onto the music scene, his star had waned. Unlike many of his contemporaries, Bolan embraced the young upstarts. "The [Sex] Pistols 166▶ are a bloody good mirror," he wrote. "Anyone who thinks things are not in a mess just does not look around." He signed The Damned to play on a T. Rex comeback tour and, had he lived, would doubtless have approved of covers of his hits by stars of the era, such as Siouxsie & The Banshees, and Bauhaus.

SEX, DRUGS & ROCK 'N' ROLL

September 30, 1947

Marc Feld is born in London, England. He will write early songs with local lad Keith Reid (later the lyricist for Procul Harum). The Decca label will change his name to "Bolan."

May 8, 1968

"Debora" is Bolan's first U.K. hit. In its wake, *My People Were Fair and Had Sky in Their Hair but Now They're Content to Wear Stars on Their Brow* will reach No. 15.

October 24, 1970

Having restyled Tyrannosaurus Rex into the electrified T. Rex, Bolan finally becomes a star: "Ride a White Swan" hits the chart and will peak at No. 2 during a twenty-week stay.

MARCH 20, 1971: T. Rextasy!

Bolanmania began in earnest when "Hot Love" topped the U.K. chart in March 1971. Nine further top ten hits followed, including the No. 1s "Get It On," "Telegram Sam," and "Metal Guru." Bolan also scored three chart-topping albums in four months: *Electric Warrior*, *Bolan Boogie*, and a Tyrannosaurus Rex repackaging. This success even crossed the Atlantic: "Bang a Gong" ("Get It On" retitled to avoid a clash with a song of the same name by Chase) hit No. 10, while 1972's *The Slider* made the top twenty. For the benefit of the press, he manufactured feuds with his friends David Bowie❶ (with whom he cut the flop single "The Prettiest Star" in 1970) and Elton John❷, and even earned a wry endorsement from The Who's❸ Pete Townshend: "I've always dug Marc Bolan and he knows it—and he also knows that I'd let him get away with murder because of what he's doing for rock 'n' roll."

❶ 134
❷ 126
❸ 068

December 18, 1972

Elton John and Ringo Starr are among guests in Bolan's movie *Born to Boogie*, intended to establish him as a major act in the U.S.A.

March 31, 1973

With four albums by rival David Bowie on the U.K. chart, T. Rex's *Tanx* reaches No. 4. In June, "The Groover" will be Bolan's final top ten hit.

April 9, 1977

Dandy in the Underworld hits the U.K. top thirty. Much better than 1976's *Futuristic Dragon*, its autobiographical title track ranks among his finest songs.

September 9, 1977

David Bowie films a song with Bolan for the latter's TV show, *Marc*. They are also working on other new songs together.

SEPTEMBER 16, 1977: Hidden riders of tomorrow

Bolan had once joked that were he to die in a car crash, "I'm so small, it would have to be a Mini." Sadly, this proved prophetic: returning from a London club in the early hours of September 16, 1977, his girlfriend Gloria Jones (who made "Tainted Love" a cult classic before Soft Cell made it a hit) crashed their Mini. She survived; Bolan did not. But his legacy endures. Acts who have sung his songs include Guns N' Roses❶ ("Buick Mackane"), Def Leppard❷ ("20th Century Boy"), and the Duran Duran❸ spinoff, The Power Station ("Get It On"). Bono sang "Children of the Revolution" in 2001, after U2❹ buried Bolan riffs on *Achtung Baby*. More blatantly, Oasis❺ turned "Get It On" into "Cigarettes & Alcohol." As Bolan's producer Tony Visconti remarked, "His music was 1950s-based, and he found a way of polishing that sound and making it fresh and timeless. There was some magical thing that he tapped into."

❶ 228
❷ 181
❸ 200
❹ 192
❺ 260

MARC BOLAN 129

legendary label

Island Records
1959–present

Having started as an essentially solo enterprise in Jamaica, Island has evolved into an extraordinary, multimillion-selling concern. Hailing from a wealthy Jamaican family, founder Chris Blackwell used a £1000 investment to set up a label distributing ska and rocksteady records (the precursor to reggae). In 1962, he moved Island to London and, two years later, scored a smash with Millie's "My Boy Lollipop" (licensed to the Fontana label, as Blackwell feared Island was not yet big enough to sustain a hit). Further releases on the label and its R&B subsidiary Sue became favorites of stars such as The Rolling Stones ◂054 (who would cover Bob & Earl's Sue single "Harlem Shuffle"), The Who ◂068 (whose Pete Townshend covered Robert Parker's "Barefootin'"), and The Beatles ◂044.

In the late Sixties, Blackwell swerved into rock, notably with Traffic—whose singer, Steve Winwood, he had long nurtured. Island's other rock successes included King Crimson, Jethro Tull, Roxy Music, Free, and Emerson, Lake & Palmer. In the folk arena, the label had huge success with Cat Stevens, some with Fairport Convention, and none at all with Nick Drake (whose impact has been felt posthumously).

In the Eighties, the company was buoyed by the success of U2 192▸, but its roster also boasted big sellers such as Anthrax and Robert Palmer. Blackwell sold the company in 1989; it has since appeared as Island Def Jam 222▸ (in the U.S.A.) and Island Universal (in the U.K.). Multi-platinum stars such as Bon Jovi, Mariah Carey, and Fall Out Boy have continued its success story into the current century.

1960+	**1960**	**September 6, 1969**	**February 7, 1972**
1974+	Blackwell issues his first LP, by Lance Haywood. Its catalog number, CB 22, refers to Blackwell's initials and age.	Jethro Tull's Island-issued *Stand Up* knocks Elvis Presley's *From Elvis in Memphis* off the top of the U.K. chart.	Traffic's *The Low Spark of High Heeled Boys* becomes the first of the band's three Island albums to go gold in the U.S.A.
1983+			

❶ 072
❷ 075
❸ 054
❹ 192

1973: Bob Marley—reggae's first superstar

Aiming to create "a black rock star as big as Jimi Hendrix❶," Blackwell gave Bob Marley and the Wailers £4000 to record their Island debut, 1973's *Catch a Fire*. Early albums made them a cult success, with endorsements from Eric Clapton❷ (who covered "I Shot the Sheriff") and The Rolling Stones❸ (who signed ex-Wailer Peter Tosh to their own label). International success came via 1975's live "No Woman, No Cry" and 1976's *Rastaman Vibration*. Until U2❹, Marley was Island's best-selling artist, and his posthumous 1984 compilation *Legend* has kept pace with the sales of U2's *The Joshua Tree*. His success opened the door for fellow Island signings, including Steel Pulse, and Toots & the Maytals—and turned reggae, once confined to Jamaica, into an international sensation.

SEX, DRUGS & ROCK 'N' ROLL

May 4, 1974

Sparks' "This Town Ain't Big Enough for Both of Us"—one of Island's stand-out singles—hits the U.K. chart. It will peak at No. 2.

June 15, 1974

The self-titled debut album by Bad Company (featuring Free's Paul Rodgers) hits the British chart. It will be the first of the rock legends' three top ten successes on Island.

December 1977

Grace Jones issues "La Vie en Rose," her first Island single, but it will be more than two years before this quintessential Island artist actually has a hit.

October 1979

Marianne Faithfull's *Broken English* marks her return from the wilderness and is the first of her fascinating albums for the label.

MARCH 23, 1980: U2 sign to Island

❶ 192

Impressed by a show in Dublin, Island's Nick Stewart signed U2 ❶—in a bathroom at London venue The Lyceum. "Signing your record deal in the ladies' toilet has a certain kind of rock 'n' rollness to it," observed bassist Adam Clayton. "But I don't think it affected the quality of the document." In 1984, the band was approached by other labels but chose to stick with Island—in the process, winning control of its songs' publishing, and upping its advances and royalty rate. Then, when Island proved unable to pay the royalties from 1984's *The Unforgettable Fire*, the band acquired a stake in the label instead—a deal that netted its members around twenty million pounds when the company was sold in 1989. U2 remains one of the biggest acts on Island, and on the planet.

September 1983

Swordfishtrombones begins a ten-year association with Tom Waits, including 1992's *Bone Machine*, featuring Keith Richards.

May 3, 1986

Robert Palmer's "Addicted to Love" tops the *Billboard* chart. It was intended to be a duet with Chaka Khan, but her label blocks the release.

May 19, 1988

Steve Winwood's *Chronicles* goes platinum. This "best of" his Island solo career is his last album for them before he departs to Virgin for *Roll with It*.

October 30, 1996

The Cranberries' *No Need to Argue*, with "Zombie," issued by Island in 1994, passes the seven million sales mark in the U.S.A. The Irish band is one of the label's biggest successes.

2003: Winehouse success story

Island has launched the careers of many impressive women—from Chris Blackwell's protégée Millie and folk star Sandy Denny, to the multi-platinum likes of Melissa Etheridge and Mariah Carey. But none have made such an idiosyncratic impression as Amy Winehouse. With just two albums—*Frank* (2003) and *Back to Black* (2006)—under her belt, she became a star, as famed for her wild behavior as her award-winning music. Island, she said in 2004, "has given me complete creative freedom. I wouldn't have released an album without it. I wouldn't be able to sing other people's songs . . . Obviously there are things on the promotional side that I can't say anything about, because I've never promoted an album before and they've done it millions of times."

ISLAND RECORDS

Eagles 1971–present

1971+ 1979+

Their country-rock sound became a worldwide hit and commercially they are one of the most successful groups ever, yet the Eagles' long career is littered with disputes. "Somebody asked my friend [singer-songwriter] Bob Seger, 'Why do you think the Eagles broke up?'" said co-founding guitarist Glenn Frey. "He said, *Hotel California*." The pressure of matching that chart-topping album's success caused the group to split three years after its release.

In the meantime, they became a byword for superstar success. "We are better than anyone, ain't we?" quipped Sid Vicious of the Sex Pistols 166▶ to one American audience. "Except for the Eagles—the Eagles are better than us." (To be fair, they had upstaged Elton John ◀126 at a 1975 London stadium show, even before *Hotel California* came out).

The Eagles were an integral part of the Seventies California scene, with connections galore. Glenn Frey dated Joni Mitchell ◀102, who wrote both "Help Me" and "Car on a Hill" (from *Court and Spark*) about him and his womanizing ways. Fleetwood Mac's ◀094 Stevie Nicks wrote the hit "Leather and Lace" about drummer Don Henley (who sang on it). "It became one of the most special love songs that I would ever write," said Nicks, who also composed "Rooms on Fire" about Eagles guitarist Joe Walsh.

The band were inducted into the Rock and Roll Hall of Fame in 1998. Twenty-three years after its release, *Their Greatest Hits 1971–1975* matched Michael Jackson's ◀122 *Thriller* as the all-time biggest-selling album in the U.S.A., with twenty-nine million copies sold in that country alone.

SEX, DRUGS & ROCK 'N' ROLL

1971

The original four "Eagles" (Frey, Henley, Leadon, and Meisner) meet in L.A. as part of Linda Ronstadt's backing band. They record their self-titled debut album in London.

1974

The band earn their first gold albums in the U.S.A., for 1972's *Eagles*, 1973's *Desperado*, and 1974's *On the Border*. The latter two will both go multi-platinum.

July 26, 1975

The Eagles achieve a first U.S. No. 1 with *One of These Nights*. "We were excited about getting more hard-edged," Henley recalls, "and more rock 'n' roll."

JANUARY 15, 1977: *Hotel California* hits No. 1

Guitarist Joe Walsh's (left) album debut with the Eagles proved to be the making of them. "Bernie [Leadon] had left the group and we left the country-rock material behind," recalled Henley. "The party line on Joe joining the group was that it made us a strong rock 'n' roll band but in fact he . . . presented ballads with a lot of harmonies in them." The album's title track, which was to be the band's only U.K. top ten single, began as a demo by guitarist Don Felder, which Henley listened to while driving around L.A. "I liked it because it was a nice synthesis of cultures . . . It was sort of a Latin reggae song." *Hotel California* became the Eagles' magnum opus, with more than seven million sales by the end of 1977. By 2001, it had achieved multi-platinum status, with a staggering sixteen million albums sold in the U.S.A. alone. "Every band has their peak," declared Henley. "That was ours."

November 3, 1979

Referred to by the band as "The Long One," as it has taken two hard years to make, *The Long Run* tops the U.S. chart.

July 1980

After a fractious couple of years, Frey calls Henley to announce the end. "I started a band," Frey will say later, "I got tired of it, and I quit."

March 1985

Frey hits U.S. No. 2 with "The Heat Is On" from the movie *Beverly Hills Cop*. He will match this success with "You Belong to the City" from *Miami Vice*.

April 9, 1985

Building the Perfect Beast turns platinum, thanks to "The Boys of Summer." It makes Henley the most successful former Eagle.

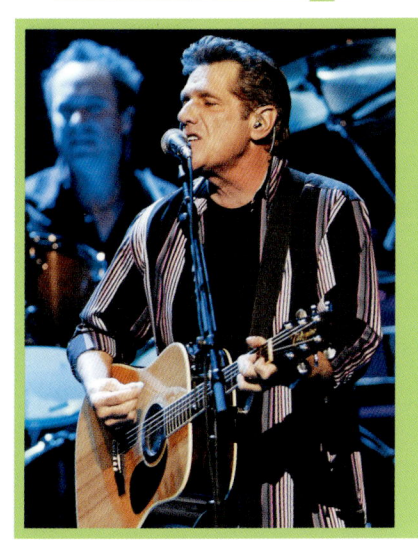

NOVEMBER 8, 1994: The Eagles reunite

Asked in 1982 when the band would reunite, Henley pulled no punches: "When hell freezes over." This became his standard response during the Eighties. Accordingly, *Hell Freezes Over*—containing eleven tracks recorded live for an MTV special and four new studio tracks, including the hit "Get Over It"—officially marked the reunion of the Eagles after they had reconvened for a track on 1993's country tribute album, *Common Thread*. "For the record," teased Glenn Frey (left), "we never broke up—we just took a fourteen-year vacation." Relations soured again when Don Felder was fired in 2001. (He sued for damages, but settled out of court.) However, 2007's *Long Road Out of Eden*, their first album of new material since 1979, debuted at No. 1 in the U.S.A. and elsewhere. It went multi-platinum, selling seven million, but Henley declared: "This is probably the last Eagles album that we'll ever make."

David Bowie 1947–present

1947+ 1969+ 1972+ 1977+ 1991+

At dinner with Guns N' Roses 228▶ one night, Bowie was, in the words of Axl Rose, saying "'One side of me is experimental and the other side of me wants to make something that people can get into, and *I don't know fucking why! Why am I like this?*' And I'm sitting there thinking, I've got twenty more years of *that* to look forward to?"

This "schizophrenia" has led to the most risk-taking of any star in his league (only Neil Young ◀078 has so consistently sidestepped expectations, but with less consistently rewarding results). Some of Bowie's best, most adventurous albums are also his least commercially successful (1977's *Heroes*, 1993's *The Buddha of Suburbia*, 1995's *1. Outside*). Yet he has also turned his peculiarities into hits, such as "Space Oddity," "Ashes to Ashes," and his two U.S. chart-toppers, "Fame" and "Let's Dance."

Aiming to rival Bob Dylan ◀062 and The Who ◀068, Bowie wound up leading British glam rock, along with Elton John 126▶ and Marc Bolan 128▶. He used his fame to bring influences such as Iggy Pop ◀116 and The Velvet Underground's ◀090 Lou Reed into the public eye, and has influenced generations of stars himself. His songs have been sung by an incredible variety of artists, from Lulu to Nirvana 242▶ ("The Man Who Sold the World"), from Bauhaus to Def Leppard ("Ziggy Stardust"), and from Barbra Streisand to The Dresden Dolls ("Life on Mars?").

His "Berlin" albums (*Low*, *Heroes*, *Lodger*) were as influential in their way as *Sgt. Pepper* and *The Velvet Underground & Nico*—as work by Joy Division 184▶, U2 192▶, Depeche Mode 196▶, and more proves.

So, was he an *artist*? Maybe. "You tell me what it means," he told one interviewer, "and I'll agree."

January 8, 1947
David Robert Hayward-Jones is born in London, England, twelve years to the day after Elvis Presley. Both singers will wind up recording for the RCA label.

June 5, 1964
"Liza Jane" by Davie Jones with The King Bees is released. An accompanying press release names Little Richard, Dylan, and John Lee Hooker as the singer's own favorites.

March 5, 1965
With The King Bees now split, The Manish Boys' "I Pity the Fool" is released. On August 20, "You've Got a Habit of Leaving" is the first single by Davy Jones & The Lower Third.

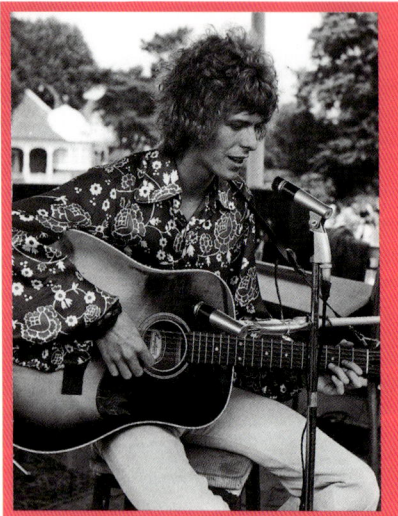

◀044 ❶
◀049 ❷

JANUARY 1966: The death of Davy Jones

For his fourth flop single—"Can't Help Thinking About Me"—Mr. Jones changed his name (his manager was keen to avoid confusion with Davy Jones of The Monkees). The singer selected Bowie (as in the Bowie knife): "I was into a heavy philosophy thing," he declared. "I wanted a truism about cutting through the lies." The name switch did nothing to boost his fortunes: his 1966 singles vanished into obscurity, as did 1967's "The Laughing Gnome," until a reissue came back to haunt Bowie six years later. Meanwhile, being released in the same month as The Beatles' ❶ *Sgt. Pepper* hardly improved the chances of his debut album, *David Bowie*. With no hits to promote, Bowie studied Tibetan Buddhism and mime (the latter taught by Lindsey Kemp, who later tutored Kate Bush ❷). In 1969, however, he conjured "a mixture of Salvador Dalí, *2001 [A Space Odyssey]*, and the Bee Gees" that would be his belated breakthrough.

SEX, DRUGS & ROCK 'N' ROLL

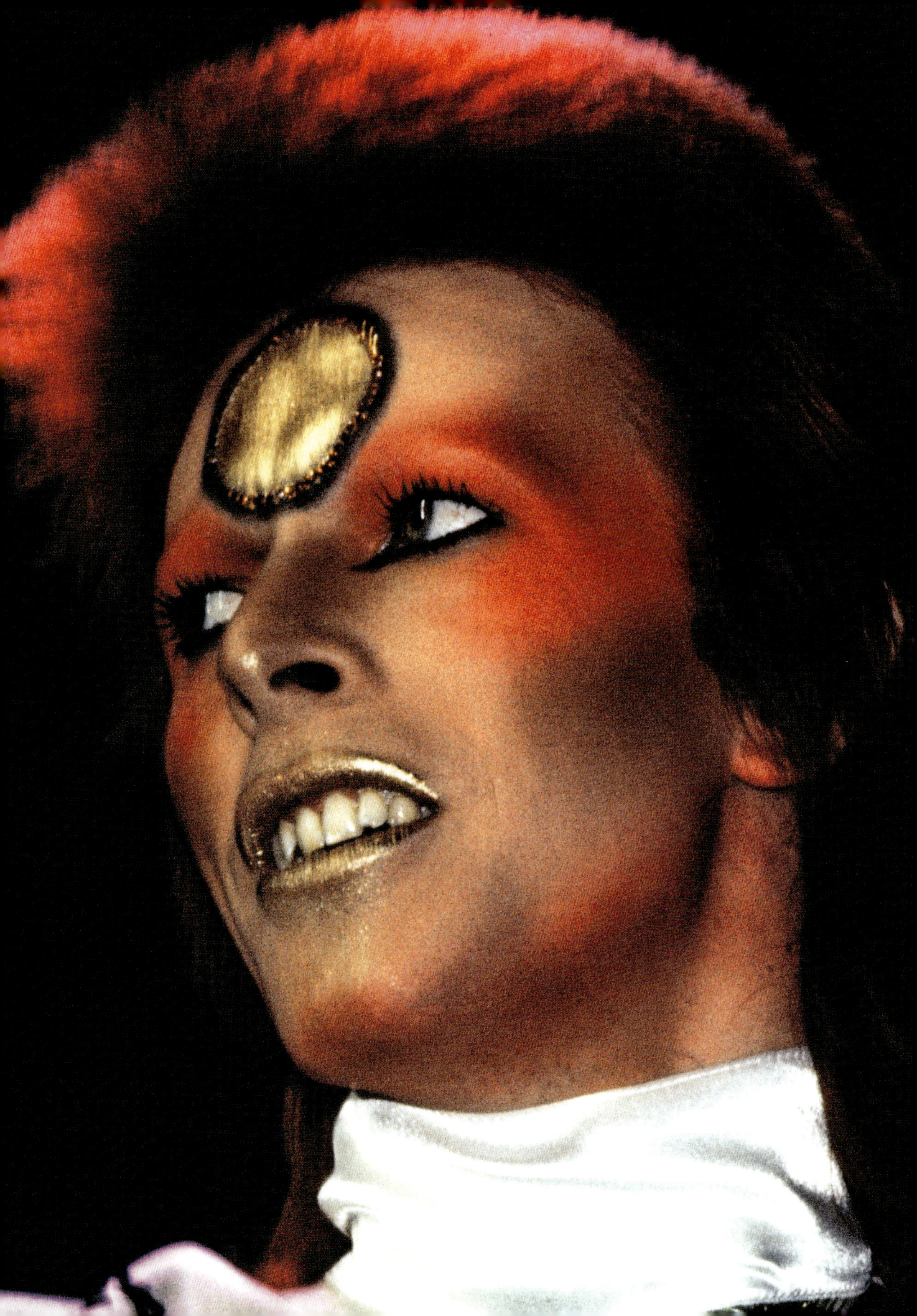

September 6, 1969

With the world gripped by the Moon landings, Bowie scores a first hit with "Space Oddity." It features future Yes member Rick Wakeman on keyboards.

November 1969

A second album entitled *David Bowie*—known in the U.S.A. as *Man of Words/Man of Music*—flops. However, it will chart in 1972, retitled *Space Oddity*.

November 1970

Five months before its release in the U.K., *The Man Who Sold the World* is issued in the U.S.A. Bowie's heaviest album, it will prove another flop until 1972.

November 1971

With homages to Dylan and Lou Reed ("Queen Bitch" will later inspire "Mr. Brightside" by The Killers), *Hunky Dory* fails to chart.

FEBRUARY 1972: Ziggy Stardust is born

In 1971, Bowie had formed a band called Hype, who—with guitarist Mick Ronson, bassist Trevor Bolder, and drummer Woody Woodmansey—became Arnold Corns, releasing "Moonage Daydream" and "Hang on to Yourself" as singles. The songs and musicians contributed to Bowie's most successful conceit: Ziggy Stardust. Reinventing himself as an orange-haired alien from the glam rock galaxy, Bowie and the band unveiled Ziggy Stardust on a 1972 British tour that paved the way for the hit "Starman" and the album *The Rise and Fall of Ziggy Stardust and the Spiders from Mars*. With Bowie's profile raised by an interview in which he had fancifully claimed to be gay (fueled by the original cover for *The Man Who Sold the World*, on which he posed in a dress), *Ziggy Stardust* shot into international charts, pulling Bowie's three previous albums in its wake. Six years after his first single, David Bowie was finally a star.

August 12, 1972

Mott the Hoople's Bowie-penned "All the Young Dudes" hits the U.K. chart. They had turned down Bowie's offer of the Ziggy cut "Suffragette City."

May 12, 1973

While Bowie's *Aladdin Sane* tops the U.K. chart, Lou Reed hits with "Walk on the Wild Side" (from *Transformer*), produced by Bowie.

November 3, 1973

With covers of Them, Pink Floyd, The Easybeats, The Mojos, The Yardbirds, The Kinks, The Who, and The Pretty Things, Bowie's *Pin Ups* tops the U.K. chart.

June 8, 1974

The George Orwell-inspired *Diamond Dogs* is Bowie's third U.K. No. 1 in just over a year. The cover artist also did The Rolling Stones' *It's Only Rock 'n' Roll* sleeve.

❶ 044
❷ 012

1974: Blue-eyed soul to Thin White Duke

As the tour for Bowie's eighth album, *Diamond Dogs*, wound its way across America in 1974, Bowie shed its theatrical trappings and introduced an R&B element to the music. This led to the spacey soul of 1975's *Young Americans,* which featured John Lennon on "Fame" and a cover of "Across the Universe" by The Beatles❶. Later that year, while Bowie was filming the movie *The Man Who Fell to Earth*, RCA reissued "Space Oddity" to U.K. chart-topping effect. Subsisting on cocaine and amphetamines, Bowie somehow managed to record one of his best albums, *Station to Station* (1976), whose "Thin White Duke" persona was inspired by his movie role as an alien. "Apparently Elvis❷ heard the demos," Bowie told *Blender*, "because we were both on RCA, and Colonel Tom (Parker) thought I should write Elvis some songs . . . But it never came to pass. I would have loved to have worked with him."

SEX, DRUGS & ROCK 'N' ROLL

January 1977

Started in France and finished in Germany, *Low* marks the start of the "Berlin trilogy." At the same time, Bowie makes Iggy Pop's *The Idiot*.

October 1977

Having toured with Iggy and made his *Lust for Life*, Bowie issues *Heroes*. The title track reaches only No. 24 in the U.K. and fails to hit the U.S. chart.

May 1979

Lodger is released. Though remembered as the runt of the Berlin litter, it was made in Switzerland and the U.S.A., and sold better than *Heroes*.

August 23, 1980

"Ashes to Ashes" tops the U.K. chart, as will *Scary Monsters . . . and Super Creeps*, featuring Pete Townshend, in September.

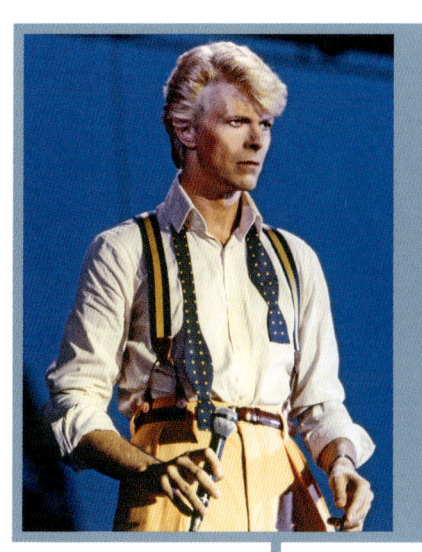

1983: Put on your red shoes and dance the blues

Bowie began the Eighties as a superstar. *Scary Monsters . . .* boosted his sales, a Broadway run in *The Elephant Man* was well reviewed, and the 1981 Queen❶ collaboration "Under Pressure" was a worldwide hit. But all that paled beside 1983's *Let's Dance*. When Bowie embarked on his first tour for more than four years, the title track had topped transatlantic charts and made the album his biggest ever. That summer, he held ten places in the U.K. Top 100. There were further successes with 1984's *Tonight* and 1985's "Dancing in the Street," with The Stones'❷ Mick Jagger, but his luck ran out with the preposterous *Glass Spider* tour that accompanied 1987's *Never Let Me Down*. "I didn't know my audience," he admitted, "and I didn't care about them." Seeking to reconnect, and inspired by guitar bands Sonic Youth and Pixies❸, Bowie formed Tin Machine, whose debut album overcame critical derision to sell well.

❶ 144
❷ 054
❸ 224

September 1991

Despite the success of 1990's compilation album *Changesbowie* and the Sound+Vision tour, *Tin Machine II* is a relative flop.

April 17, 1993

Black Tie White Noise hits U.K. No. 1. *The Buddha of Suburbia* will later be eclipsed by Nirvana's cover of "The Man Who Sold the World."

September–October 1995

Bowie tours concept album *1. Outside* in the U.S.A. with Nine Inch Nails, who play at the start of his set. Bowie and NIN front man Trent Reznor duet on "Hurt."

January 9, 1997

Lou Reed and members of the Foo Fighters, The Cure, Pixies, Smashing Pumpkins, and Sonic Youth guest at Bowie's fiftieth birthday show, at New York's Madison Square Garden.

FEBRUARY 2002: Never give up

Bowie had seen out the last century with the vibrant *Earthling* (1997) and the dour *Hours . . .* (1999), whose fleeting sales confirmed his apparently terminal disconnection from the mainstream. He remained cheerfully unconcerned and reunited with producer Tony Visconti, which yielded 2002's warm *Heathen*, Bowie's most internationally well-received album in nearly two decades. *Reality* (2003) was even better and occasioned his last major tour, which ended when he suffered a heart attack in 2004. He has since appeared with Arcade Fire in 2005 and Alicia Keys in 2006—the same year he made a surprise appearance at a David Gilmour show in London, to sing Pink Floyd's❶ "Comfortably Numb" and "Arnold Layne" (the latter later issued as a tribute to Pink Floyd founder and Bowie hero Syd Barrett). "He's probably in a reflective stage," Tony Visconti remarked in 2010, "but I wouldn't write him off."

❶ 086

DAVID BOWIE

super producer

Brian Eno
1948–present

Eno has been involved in several of rock's most influential albums, from the first two by Roxy Music, through his own classics like *Another Green World* and David Bowie's ❰134❱ "Berlin trilogy," to Talking Heads' *Remain in Light* and U2's ❰192❱ *The Joshua Tree*. He has collaborated with acts from punk-turned-world music star Jah Wobble to British indie band James (notably 1994's *Wah Wah*); from Bryan Ferry to Baaba Maal; and from Laurie Anderson to Dido. He was also executive producer for the 1995 charity set *The Help Album* (featuring Oasis ❰260❱ and Radiohead ❰264❱), has worked on albums with The Velvet Underground's ❰090❱ John Cale, and has been immortalized in song by MGMT ("Brian Eno").

As a guiding light behind Bowie's *Low*, *Heroes*, and *Lodger*, Eno was, said producer Tony Visconti, the singer's "Zen master." "I keep trying," Eno said, "to strip things back to something tense and taut, while Bowie keeps throwing new colors on the canvas. It's a good duet." Eno also co-produced Bowie's underrated *1. Outside* (1995).

Eno has had a well-received solo career. When, via Bowie, he met Iggy Pop ❰116❱, the latter sang Eno and Robert Fripp's 1973 instrumental work, *No Pussyfooting*. That album was a signpost to the ambient music that he would trademark with a series of albums from 1978. "I love [that year's classic] *Music for Airports*," enthused Joni Mitchell ❰102❱. "He is the champ of classical composition."

In 2008, Eno proved that even Coldplay ❰276❱ could be surprisingly versatile, producing the gem that is *Viva la Vida or Death and All His Friends*.

1948+
1974+
1983+

May 15, 1948
Brian Peter George St. John le Baptiste de la Salle Eno is born in Suffolk, U.K. He will later act as producer for the similarly long-named Dido Florian Cloud De Bouneville Armstrong.

December 25, 1968
Eno records a piece called "Ellis B. Compton Blues," with guitarist Anthony Grafton. The pair call themselves Maxwell Demon after a proposed thermodynamic experiment.

February 15–16, 1971
Eno takes part in the recording of *The Great Learning* by the British avant-garde composer Cornelius Cardew and his Scratch Orchestra.

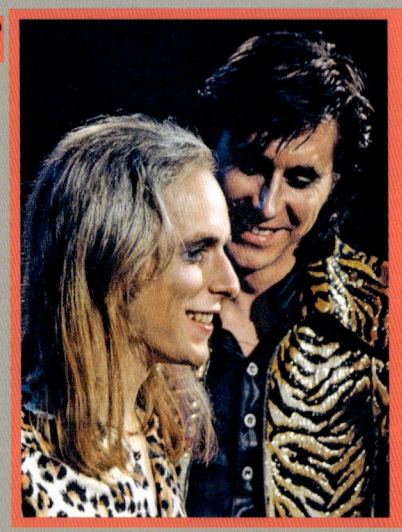

❰134❱

AUGUST 1972: Roxy Music hit the charts

"I started off mixing the band [Roxy Music] at the back of the auditoriums . . ." Eno told *Rock's Backpages*. "Then I started doing backing vocals as well, and it started getting a bit weird. The audience would wheel round to look at me." Onstage, Eno became a costumed icon. "What I do involves standing still a lot . . ." he explained, "so I thought it would make sense to wear garments that magnified my movements." After 1972's *Roxy Music* and 1973's *For Your Pleasure* (and supporting *Ziggy*-era Bowie❶), tensions between Eno and singer Bryan Ferry (left) escalated: "I got a lot more attention than I deserved, in the sense that I wasn't the writer, I hadn't been there at the beginning . . . the band wanted to do something else, too, and they did it really well. My favorite Roxy album, actually, is the third one [*Stranded*]. I love that record, and it might also be because . . . I wasn't involved in making it."

SEX, DRUGS & ROCK 'N' ROLL

December 1974

Eno helms an early session for Television. "Dreadful!" band member Richard Lloyd will recall. "Eno was warm and easy, but he hadn't gotten his feet yet as a producer."

September 1976

Eno's work on Bowie's *Low* begins. His "Warszawa" will be pivotal to its direction and inspires a Manchester group to call themselves Warsaw. They later become Joy Division.

February 25, 1977

Ultravox! (blessed with a Neu!-esque exclamation mark) issue their self-titled debut, on which Eno pioneers the use of drum machines in British music.

August 28, 1978

Devo release *Q. Are We Not Men? A. We Are Devo!*. "They were a terrifying group of people to work with . . ." Eno shuddered. "They were so unable to experiment."

1980: Getting together with Talking Heads

In May 1977, Talking Heads❶ were touring the U.K. with the Ramones❷, and John Cale❸ took Eno to see the show in London. That night, Eno invited Cale and Heads' mainman David Byrne to his apartment, where they listened to Nigerian musician Fela Kuti's 1973 album *Afrodisiac*. "I was very excited about this music at the time," Eno recalled, "and they were pretty excited, too—which was thrilling, because no one in England was at all interested." Eno had originally described Talking Heads as "music to do your housework by" but helmed an inventive series of albums for them, culminating in 1980's polyrhythmic masterpiece *Remain in Light* and the Byrne/Eno (left) collaboration *My Life in the Bush of Ghosts*. "A lot of the sample-based music that's happening now stems straight from that," enthused Kate Bush❹ about the latter. "Such a turning point—the whole use of repetition. It was a big influence on me, too."

❶ 162
❷ 158
❸ 092
❹ 049

July 1983

Apollo: Atmospheres and Soundtracks—Eno's lovely collaboration with his brother, Roger, and his partner on U2's material, Daniel Lanois—is released.

October 13, 1984

The Unforgettable Fire, Eno's first album with U2, tops the U.K. chart. His influence is evident on one of the album's signature songs, "Bad."

December 14, 1984

The movie *Dune* premieres, with an Eno song amid a soundtrack dominated by U.S. rock band Toto. Initially, it was to have had a Pink Floyd soundtrack.

October 23, 1995

Spinner, Eno's collaboration with Public Image Ltd bassist Jah Wobble, is issued, with drums by Jaki Liebezeit, who had played on Eno's *Before and After Science* (1977).

NOVEMBER 7, 1995: U2 become Passengers

By the mid-Nineties, Eno's association with U2❶ was a decade old. He had initially been reluctant to produce them: "He was intimidated by the lack of irony in what we were doing . . ." recalled The Edge. "He'd come from Talking Heads❷ . . . and here was this Irish band hitting everything full on—completely earnest, hearts on sleeves, no irony at all." But Bono (left, with Eno) charmed him into working with them, hence the classics *The Unforgettable Fire, The Joshua Tree, Achtung Baby*, and *Zooropa*. In 1995, they attempted a full-blown collaboration on the soundtrack to Peter Greenaway's movie *The Pillow Book*, which—when it fell through—evolved into the *Original Soundtracks 1* album, credited to Passengers. Eno, reported U2's manager Paul McGuinness, "found it frustrating that the band did not take it quite as seriously as him." But the album did yield two haunting classics: "Miss Sarajevo" and "Your Blue Room."

❶ 192
❷ 162

BRIAN ENO

super producer

Todd Rundgren
1948–present

Despite producing one of the all-time biggest-selling albums (Meat Loaf's *Bat Out of Hell*) and one of the most influential (the New York Dolls' self-titled debut), Todd Rundgren is a cult favorite. As with Frank Zappa ◀076, the quantity and diversity of his work makes him impossible to categorize.

Rundgren began in his native Philadelphia in garage band Nazz, whose "Hello It's Me" later became his biggest solo hit. Dissatisfied with Nazz's producer, Rundgren took over, having gained experience by engineering The Band's *Stage Fright* (1970). He also launched a solo career, under his own name, and was leader of Utopia. Hits included 1972's "I Saw the Light," a 1976 cover of The Beach Boys' ◀050 "Good Vibrations," 1978's gorgeous "Can We Still Be Friends," and 1980's "Set Me Free."

He has produced acts ranging from over-the-top glam punks The Tubes to hippy guitar guru Steve Hillage, from The Beatles' ◀044 protégés Badfinger to punk poetess Patti Smith 164▶, and from oddball popsters Sparks (then known as Halfnelson) to hard rock stars Grand Funk Railroad and Alice Cooper.

Rundgren also achieved more tangential links with rock's hierarchy. Scared by the drug excesses of Aerosmith's 154▶ Steven Tyler, the star's girlfriend Bebe Buell returned to her former boyfriend—Rundgren—who raised her daughter Liv as his own until Tyler's paternity was confirmed in 1991.

And, in the mid-Seventies, Rundgren was drawn into a war of words with John Lennon. One of Rundgren's albums was later found by police in the apartment of Lennon's killer, Mark Chapman.

1968+
1973+
1980+

October 1968
The self-titled debut album by the garage band Nazz, featuring the hit song "Hello It's Me" and mostly written by Rundgren, is released.

June 1970
Having left Nazz in 1969, Rundgren issues *Runt*. Thought of as his solo debut, it features brothers Hunt and Tony Sales, later of Tin Machine.

December 13, 1971
Finishing work started by The Beatles' George Harrison, Rundgren produces *Straight Up* for Badfinger. He will later work, briefly, on 1973's *Ass*.

1973: Grand Funk's *American Band*

"The Grand Funk Railroad album was one of the easiest things I ever did," Rundgren confessed to *Classic Rock*. "Grand Funk's manager insisted on producing their records, and he was terrible at it. So, by the time I worked with them, their expectations for the record were so low, I couldn't fail." *We're an American Band* duly became the group's ninth of twelve gold albums. "We wanted that commercial appeal Todd could give us with FM radio," explained drummer Don Brewer. "He really understood what the sound of the time was. When he came in, the magic was there." Indeed it was: the title track—sung by Brewer rather than, as was usually the case, guitarist Mark Farner (left, with Rundgren)—topped the U.S. chart on September 29, and became one of the biggest hits of 1973.

SEX, DRUGS & ROCK 'N' ROLL

February 1973
....
The Rundgren-produced *Mother's Pride,* by pioneering all-female band Fanny (whose fans include David Bowie and Keith Moon), is released.

March 1973
....
Rundgren unleashes the nutty, mescaline-fueled *A Wizard, A True Star.* Reviewer and friend Patti Smith will describe it as "rock and roll for the skull."

November 12, 1974
....
Hall & Oates' *War Babies,* produced by Rundgren, is released. It is much rockier than the soul sound with which they will find fame.

February 26, 1975
....
Something/Anything?, from 1972, becomes Rundgren's only solo album to earn gold status in the U.S.A., thanks to the enduring hits "I Saw the Light" and "Hello It's Me."

❶ 150

OCTOBER 21, 1977: The Meatloaf bat

Having "rolled on the floor laughing" the first time he heard the songs, Rundgren agreed to produce *Bat Out of Hell,* sung by Meat Loaf and written by Jim Steinman. (The latter hailed the producer as "the only genuine genius I've ever worked with.") "They did have a sort of Bruce Springsteen❶ influence," Rundgren told the BBC, "but it was all blown-up and melodramatic and comical to the extent that it didn't seem as though anyone would take it seriously." Rundgren played guitar on the title track, notable for its motorcycle-revving sonic effect. "The whole thing didn't take him more than forty-five minutes," marveled Meat Loaf. "The most astounding thing I have ever seen in my life." Rundgren also produced and played on Steinman's *Bad for Good* (1981).

June 13 1980
....
The *Roadie* movie opens, with two Rundgren-helmed songs by Alice Cooper. Rundgren says of the collaboration, "We used to do strange things together."

October 27, 1986
....
Skylarking by XTC is released. The Rundgren-produced album is reissued with another song he produced, "Dear God," one of XTC's best-received works.

October–December 1999
....
Rundgren helms *The New America* by Bad Religion, whose singer Greg Graffin is a Rundgren fan, but the union is not a happy one.

May 12, 2006
....
Led by Rundgren and Elliot Easton of The Cars, The New Cars begin a U.S. tour (with Blondie), showcasing Rundgren and Cars hits.

2009: Back in the New York Dolls groove

"The sessions involved politics, psychology, and crowd control," recalled Rundgren of having produced the New York Dolls' classic, self-titled debut in 1973. "I had to surrender to the process and accept that the surrounding insanity was going to be a part of the character of the record." Though hardly Rundgren's finest sonic triumph, the album proved immortal. Twenty-six years later, in 2009, he reunited with the band—whose habits had left them with just two original members— for *Cause I Sez So* (the second album since their return in 2004). "We know him and we know he's great," said singer David Johansen of the famously fast-working producer. "Since we wanted to do this thing really quick, it was the best idea. And, you know, Todd's fucking great."

TODD RUNDGREN   141

legendary label

Casablanca Records
1973–84

From Donna Summer—the queen of disco—to Kiss—the self-proclaimed "hottest band in the world"—Casablanca lived the Seventies dream like no other label. The company was set up by Neil Bogart, who, at previous organizations, had signed such diverse acts as Curtis Mayfield, ? & The Mysterians, and The Isley Brothers.

When Casablanca struck gold—with Kiss, then Parliament, Donna Summer, and The Village People—it occupied offices decorated in the style of the movie that inspired its name. Employees had their own Mercedes, and cocaine was snorted off desks.

A year after Kiss arrived, another leading light of glam rock came to the label: Marc Bolan ◀128. "I'm excited about the Casablanca deal," enthused the Boppin' Elf, "because it allows me to work with people who are excited about the kind of music I'm making." The label also took a chance on the all-female rock pioneers Fanny, to no commercial avail.

Casablanca began its golden years in 1975. One of the first labels to market twelve-inch singles commercially, they led the disco boom and bankrolled the massive hype and stage shows of Kiss and Parliament. After the label was bought by Polygram in 1980, ongoing success seemed assured. "Funkytown," by Lipps Inc., topped the U.S. chart, The Village People miraculously kept selling, and Motown ◀030 legends The Four Tops came aboard. But Donna Summer quit, disco died, Kiss stalled, and label founder Bogart died in 1982. After a final flare with the *Flashdance* soundtrack, Casablanca was closed. But it was fun while it lasted.

1973+
1975+
1977+

November 1, 1973
Kiss manager Bill Aucoin signs a deal with the label. Guitarist and singer Paul Stanley later recalls: "The industry called us 'Bogart's folly.'"

January 1974
"Virginia (Touch Me Like You Do)," by Canadian songwriter Bill (later Barbra) Amesbury, is Casablanca's first single.

December 5, 1974
Casablanca earns its first gold disc (and its last for almost a year), with *Here's Johnny—Magic Moments from The Tonight Show*.

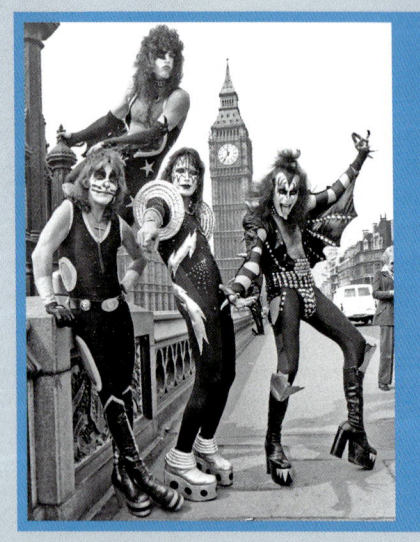

DECEMBER 4, 1975: Kiss go gold with *Alive!*

As Paul Stanley—co-founder of Kiss with Gene Simmons—remembered, Casablanca founder Neil Bogart "promised us enough things to put together the exact kind of show we always hoped for. It was actually like a dream come true." This nearly caused both the band and the label to fold—Kiss' albums didn't sell enough to keep their spectacular show on the road (their manager resorted to putting costs on his credit card). As a last resort, they capitalized on their live reputation with *Alive!*—which, to everyone's amazement, proved a huge success and yielded the hit "Rock and Roll All Nite." The subsequent hysteria peaked in 1978, when the label simultaneously issued solo albums by all four members of Kiss. All went platinum on their release, but on retailers' pre-orders rather than actual sales. As a somber footnote, Kiss dedicated their album *Creatures of the Night* to Bogart, who died on May 8, 1982.

SEX, DRUGS & ROCK 'N' ROLL

December 6, 1975

Donna Summer's single "Love to Love You Baby" is released. The sexy epic will kick-start her hit-making career on Casablanca.

April 22, 1976

Kiss' *Destroyer* goes gold, but will then stall until the band hits with "Beth." This ballad will revive interest in its parent album, which will go platinum in November of the same year.

1976

Angel issue their second album. The band—protégés of Kiss, dressed in white to contrast with their mentors' black—will be fondly remembered non-sellers.

1976

Casablanca's R&B subsidiary Chocolate City—named after a Parliament song—had launched in 1975 with a Cameo single, but gets into gear in 1976 with cult favorites such as Smoke.

SEPTEMBER 20, 1976: Parliament go platinum

George Clinton's (left) tangled family history of funk had involved doo-wop group The Parliaments and acid-fried rockers Funkadelic. In 1974, with another contractual wriggle, he had created Parliament—who, in their own way, were just as spectacular and influential as Kiss. Their first two albums, *Up for the Down Stroke* and *Chocolate City*, were packed with gems that would later be sampled endlessly, but it was *Mothership Connection* (1975) that proved the blockbuster and went platinum in 1976. Its guitar-fueled funk would inspire acts from Dr. Dre❶ and Ice Cube❷ to the Red Hot Chili Peppers❸ and The Black Crowes❹. Later classics included "Flash Light" and "Bop Gun," but Parliament and Casablanca ultimately collapsed in tandem, sunk by overspending and contractual squabbles. Sadly, this also meant that Neil Bogart's plans for a movie of their 1978 album, *Motor Booty Affair*, came to nothing.

❶ 256
❷ 257
❸ 232
❹ 223

June 30, 1977

Kiss' *Love Gun* is certified platinum on the day of its release. Alex and Eddie Van Halen had played on the album's demos.

June 8, 1978

Meco's discofied "Star Wars Theme/Cantina Band" single and *Star Wars & Other Galactic Funk* album go platinum.

May 3, 1979

Cher goes gold with *Take Me Home*. The singer is dating Kiss' Gene Simmons (until she introduces him to her friend, Diana Ross, to whom he quickly switches).

December 4, 1979

Cameo go gold with *Secret Omen*. The band, who blend funk, rock, and R&B, will crash the mainstream with 1984's "She's Strange" and, later, 1986's "Word Up!"

DECEMBER 11, 1979: Summer dims the lights

To promote Donna Summer's first Casablanca album, *Love to Love You Baby*, a life-size cake of her was made in Los Angeles, then flown—first class—to New York. It was a suitably indulgent start to a spectacular career that saw eight hit albums and fifteen dance chart No. 1s in just four years. Summer also sang backing vocals on the 1978 solo album by Gene Simmons of Kiss (the star-studded cast of which ranged from Joe Perry of Aerosmith❶ and Rick Nielsen of Cheap Trick to solo stars Janis Ian and Helen Reddy). Her success climaxed with three consecutive U.S. chart-topping albums: 1978's *Live and More* and 1979's *Bad Girls* and *On the Radio*. But the title of one of Summer's 1979 gold singles, "Dim All the Lights," was to prove prophetic: she launched a ten-million-dollar lawsuit against Casablanca (objecting that her manager was Bogart's wife, among other complaints) and decamped to Geffen.

❶ 154

CASABLANCA RECORDS 143

Queen 1970–present

1946+ 1974+ 1976+ 1980+ 1991+

Classic hits and globe-conquering live shows have etched Queen into rock legend, but their huge impact is best illustrated by the lineup at the Freddie Mercury tribute concert in 1992. It included members of The Who ◁068, Led Zeppelin ◁098, and Black Sabbath ◁108, as well as Elton John ◁126, David Bowie ◁134, Metallica 218▷, and Guns N' Roses 228▷.

Brian May was a fluid and influential guitarist, Roger Taylor a powerful drummer and singer, and John Deacon a talented bassist and versatile writer. Yet as accomplished as the band were, they would never have conquered the world without Mercury, rock's greatest front man. "I went to Ealing Art School a year after Peter Townshend left," he said in 1974. "The school was a breeding ground for musicians . . . Music is so interesting, dear."

Queen could only have been spawned in the Seventies: amid the madness of glam rock, Led Zeppelin fans singing Beach Boys' ◁050 harmonies didn't seem as nutty as it might have done before. Yet their legacy stretches across the decades. "If I didn't have Freddie Mercury's lyrics to hold on to as a kid," said Axl Rose, "I don't know where I would be. It taught me about all forms of music." Kurt Cobain of Nirvana 242▷ referenced Mercury in his suicide note, while his erstwhile colleague Dave Grohl has continually namechecked Queen as a touchstone for his own band, the Foo Fighters.

"We had a joke," said drummer Roger Taylor, "that we wanted to be the biggest. It was a joke, but underneath, it was really true. Number one is much better than number two." Mission accomplished.

September 5, 1946
Farrokh Bomi Bulsara is born in Zanzibar, Africa. He will join a band called The Hectics at school, before he and his family relocate to the U.K. in 1964, and he joins Wreckage.

July 19, 1947
Brian Harold May is born in Middlesex, England. At London's Imperial College, twenty-one years later, the guitarist will form Smile with bassist Tim Staffell.

July 26, 1949
Roger Meddows Taylor is born in Norfolk, England. Finding playing the guitar too difficult, he will switch to drums and join Smile.

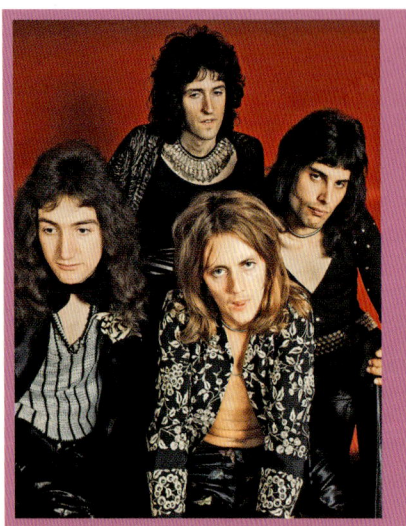

---

❶ 058
❷ 048
❸ 098

JUNE 1970: Smile—it's Queen!

Although signed to the Mercury label, Smile never amounted to much. Tim Staffell quit to seek fame with Humpy Bong, while May and Taylor teamed up with Bulsara—who renamed the band Queen (and himself Freddie Mercury). By July 1971, John Deacon (b. 1951) had joined on bass and, by the time they supported Sparks at London's Marquee club❶ in 1972, they had classics such as "Keep Yourself Alive" and "Stone Cold Crazy" in their sets. Signed to EMI❷ in 1973, they released a self-titled debut album. (That year also saw Mercury, as "Larry Lurex," issue a flop cover of The Ronettes' "I Can Hear Music," featuring May and Taylor.) Clearly demonstrating the influence of Led Zeppelin❸, *Queen* did nothing on the charts, but secured them a support slot with Mott the Hoople—while a half-formed "Seven Seas of Rhye" at the end of the album would be developed into their breakthrough.

SEX, DRUGS & ROCK 'N' ROLL

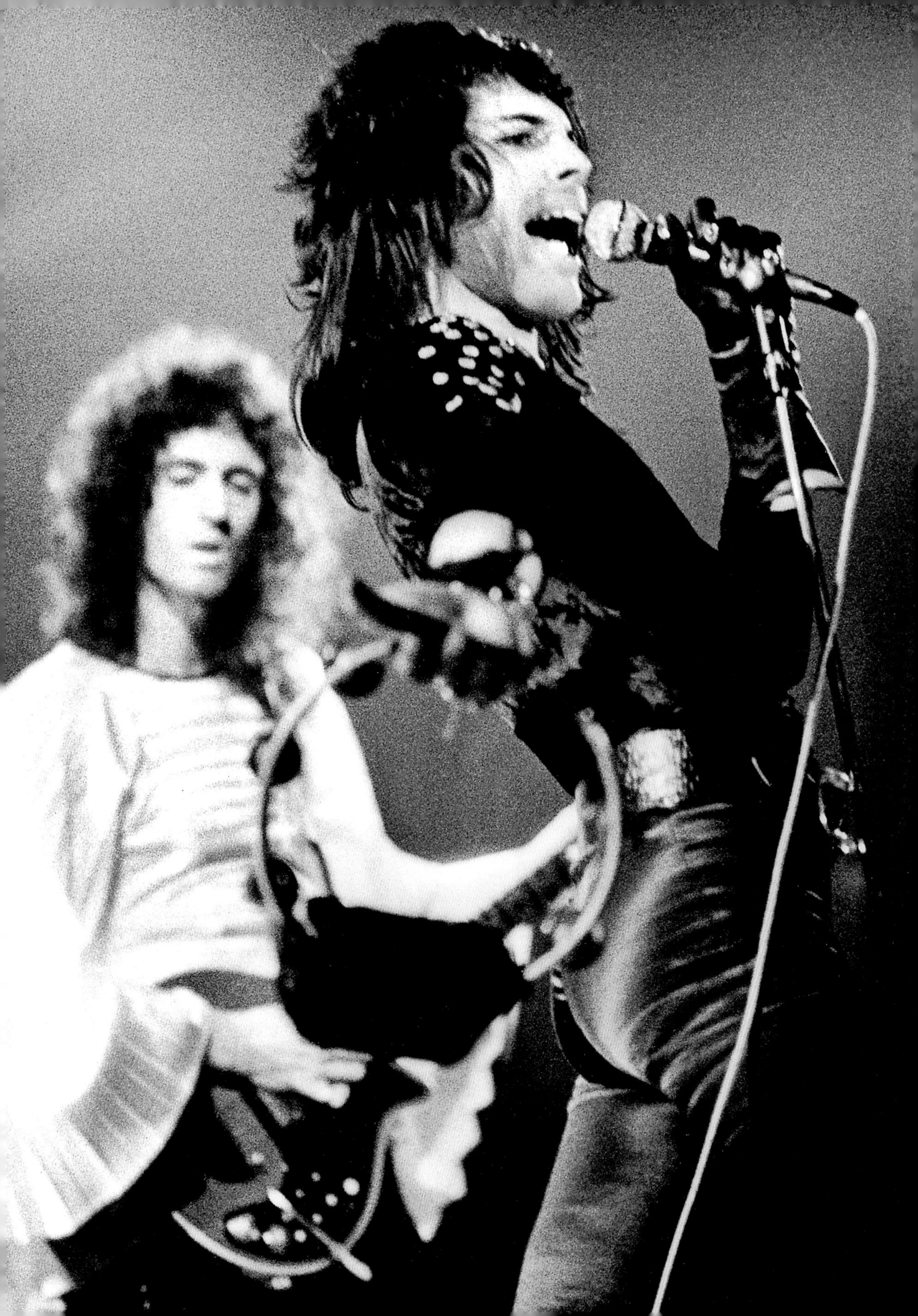

March 1974

The now fully formed "Seven Seas of Rhye" and *Queen II* give the band their first U.K. hits, dragging *Queen* into the chart behind them.

October 11, 1974

"Killer Queen" is released. It is, as May will observe, "the turning point"—Mercury's idiosyncratic song gives the band a first international hit.

November 23, 1974

Sheer Heart Attack hits the U.K. chart. The album is the first true representation of Queen's versatility (including "Stone Cold Crazy," later covered by Metallica).

May 1, 1975

The band's *Sheer Heart Attack* tour wraps up in Japan. Supporting acts have included future big sellers Styx and Kansas.

NOVEMBER 29, 1975: The reign begins

"It was just one of those pieces I wrote for the album," Mercury (left) said airily. "We started deciding on a single about halfway through. There were a few contenders—we were thinking of 'The Prophet's Song' at one point—but then 'Bohemian Rhapsody' seemed the one. There was a time when the others wanted to chop it around a bit, but I refused . . . People were all going, 'You're joking, they'll never play it. You'll only hear the first few bars and then they'll fade it out.' We had numerous rows." Yet as Christmas approached, "Bohemian Rhapsody" began a nine-week stay atop the U.K. chart. Meanwhile, both the song and its parent album, *A Night at the Opera*, soared up international charts, and Queen earned their first U.S. gold album, for *Sheer Heart Attack*. "If people don't like the songs we're doing at the moment," Mercury said, as the global conquest loomed, "we couldn't give a fuck."

December 25, 1976

A year after *A Night at the Opera* hit No. 1, *A Day at the Races* enters the U.K. chart. In two weeks, it will go gold in the U.S.A.

July–September 1977

In London, Mercury meets Sid Vicious, who asks, "Still bringing ballet to the masses?" "Ah, Mr. Ferocious," Freddie replies, "We are doing our best."

October 7, 1977

A single that couples "We Are the Champions" with "We Will Rock You" gives Queen their biggest international hit since "Bohemian Rhapsody."

December 28, 1977

News of the World earns Queen a first U.S. platinum disc. It will eventually sell four million there—equaled by 1980's *The Game*.

❶ 098
❷ 054
❸ 086

FEBRUARY 23, 1980: "Crazy little things"

Queen had finished the Seventies in style. *Jazz* (1978)—source of the much-loved "Don't Stop Me Now"—and the barnstorming *Live Killers* (1979) had been worldwide hits. Even a stunt involving nude girls on bicycles (for 1978's "Fat Bottomed Girls"/"Bicycle Race" single) had been largely laughed off. And, at the end of 1979, a rockabilly pastiche called "Crazy Little Thing Called Love," which Mercury (left) had written in the bath, climbed to No. 2 in the U.K. By the end of February 1980, it had become Queen's first U.S. chart-topper. "There we were with a No. 1 in America and no album," Taylor recalled. When *The Game* appeared, it became their first album to top the charts in the U.K., Australia, *and* the U.S.A., helped in no small part by another U.S. No. 1, "Another One Bites the Dust." With Led Zeppelin❶ about to disband and The Rolling Stones❷ off the road, Queen and Pink Floyd❸ were now rock's biggest bands.

146   SEX, DRUGS & ROCK 'N' ROLL

December 8, 1980

Flash Gordon is released and is a relative flop. A pioneering tour of South American stadia at the start of 1981 will be a more notable triumph.

November 21, 1981

Queen top the U.K. charts with the David Bowie collaboration "Under Pressure" and the hugely successful *Greatest Hits*.

June 1982

Despite MTV banning its video, "Body Language" hits U.S. No. 11. Other singles from the funky *Hot Space* will go largely unremarked.

1983

Riven by dissent and with *Hot Space* doing relatively badly, the band pursue solo projects. May enlists Eddie Van Halen for "Star Fleet."

JULY 13, 1985: We are the champions

❶ 214

The Works (1984) had restored Queen's fortunes, with a trio of hits led by Taylor's "Radio Ga Ga." The band had now scored smashes written by all four individuals, following Deacon's "You're My Best Friend" and May (left) and Mercury's various triumphs. They began 1985 headlining the huge Rock in Rio festival, but even that was eclipsed by a show-stealing set at Live Aid❶ in July. In just twenty minutes, Queen etched themselves into legend. They sealed their resurrection with a stadium tour for *A Kind of Magic* in 1986, climaxing in August with a final show in front of 120,000 in the U.K. (Largely recorded at that show, *Live Magic* stayed on the U.K. chart for forty-three weeks, a remarkable feat for a live album.) They saw out the Eighties with Mercury's duet with Monserrat Caballe ("Barcelona"), the formation of Taylor's band The Cross, and 1989's *The Miracle*. Then, in 1990, Mercury told his family that he was HIV positive and had AIDS.

January 26, 1991

The Led Zeppelin pastiche "Innuendo" gives Queen their first U.K. No. 1 since 1981's "Under Pressure." An album follows it to the top.

November 24, 1991

Two weeks after *Greatest Hits II* enters the U.K. chart at No. 1, Mercury dies. "Bohemian Rhapsody" will top the singles chart for a second time a month later.

February 14, 1992

Wayne's World premieres, sparking a U.S. revival with its headbanging "Bohemian Rhapsody" scene. *Classic Queen* will hit No. 4 there and sell millions.

April 20, 1992

George Michael steals the show at the Freddie Mercury tribute show in London. His "Somebody to Love" will fuel the U.K. chart-topping *Five Live* EP one year from now.

NOVEMBER 18, 1995: *Made in Heaven*

Slowed only briefly by Mercury's death, the Queen industry continued with 1995's chart-topping *Made in Heaven* (assembled from material recorded in the months before the singer's death, and previously). The years since then have seen several strong-selling live albums and hits sets, which have mollified purists appalled by the inexplicably successful musical *We Will Rock You*. With Deacon having distanced himself from the group, May and Taylor—having seen their solo careers meet with diminishing returns—reformed Queen, with Free and Bad Company singer Paul Rodgers (left). After a triumphant tour, the trio overplayed its hand with 2008's *The Cosmos Rocks,* whose failure led to an apparently amicable dissolution. (Rodgers promptly reformed Bad Company.) The legacy of Queen is too great to be tarnished by this minor blemish but, as Mercury had observed, "Sometimes it's best to leave well alone, dear."

Kraftwerk 1970–present

1970+ 1975+

From the same fertile, experimental rock scene as Can, Faust, Amon Düül, and Neu!, Kraftwerk are more than just German pop's biggest export; they are as influential as The Beatles 044, The Rolling Stones 054, or their own particular favorites The Beach Boys 050, and their legacy stretches from Dublin to Detroit, and from Depeche Mode 196 to Daft Punk 268.

"Kraftwerk were Europe's finest soul group," enthused Bono of U2 192, who covered *The Man-Machine's* "Neon Lights" in 2004. "They didn't have big voices, but their small voices really moved me. I responded to the pathos of their music." Others were more enticed by their electronic rhythms, such as Detroit techno pioneeers Derrick May, Juan Atkins, and Kevin Saunderson.

"This would pass for modern music nowadays," observed Coldplay's 278 Chris Martin of "Computer Love"—the song that his band borrowed for "Talk" — "yet they were doing it twenty-five years ago."

The band's musical innovation was matched by their increasingly unusual live shows. Milking their robotic reputation for all it is worth, the band have periodically replaced themselves with automatons, and played on calculators and, latterly, laptops. "There was so much showmanship involved," marveled Ed Simons of The Chemical Brothers. "People think it was all very boring—watching men play with computers and synths. It wasn't."

"Kraftwerk," said Madonna 208, who saw them live when she moved to New York in the Eighties, "blew me away . . . They were amazing."

1970
Organisation (Ralf Hütter and Florian Schneider) add drummers Klaus Dinger and Andreas Hohman to become Kraftwerk, whose self-titled debut appears in late 1970.

January 1972
With Dinger and the short-stayed Michael Rother having quit to form Neu!, Kraftwerk score a second German top forty album with *Kraftwerk 2*.

October 1973
Ralf and Florian is issued. Kraftwerk have largely discarded conventional instruments, bar the flute of Schneider and electric violin of Emil Schult.

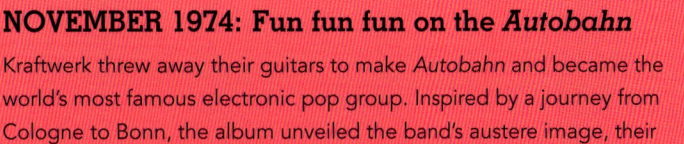

NOVEMBER 1974: Fun fun fun on the *Autobahn*

Kraftwerk threw away their guitars to make *Autobahn* and became the world's most famous electronic pop group. Inspired by a journey from Cologne to Bonn, the album unveiled the band's austere image, their new synthesizers, and Wolfgang Flur's homemade electronic drums. Charmed by its Beach Boys[1]-like "Wir fahr'n, fahr'n, fahr'n" hook, the pop-buying public sent the title track into international charts. The band were now bona fide pop stars—albeit very strange ones. David Bowie[2] duly cruised the streets of L.A. listening to them. "What I was passionate about," he recalled to *Uncut*, "was their singular determination to stand apart from stereotypical American chord sequences and their whole-hearted embrace of a European sensibility displayed through their music." Bowie's "V2-Schneider," on *Heroes*, is a tribute to Florian Schneider (left, with band co-founder Ralf Hütter).

[1] 050
[2] 134

October 1975
Radio-Activity is a somber follow-up to *Autobahn*. Only a hit in France, the title track later becomes a classic nonetheless.

May 1977
Kraftwerk namecheck David Bowie and Iggy Pop on the (later much-sampled) title track of the newly released *Trans-Europe Express*.

May 1978
The Man-Machine features "The Model" (a U.K. No. 1 on its 1982 re-release) and "The Robots," for which the band were replaced with dummies in concert.

May 1981
Computer World explores computer technology and represents a peak for the band. It will influence hip-hop and techno, and yield the hit "Computer Love."

1982: Adventures on "Planet Rock" and beyond

Grandmaster Flash had been playing "Trans-Europe Express" at block parties for years by the time Afrika Bambaataa's "Planet Rock" emerged. Fusing drums from *Computer World*'s "Numbers" to the melody from "Trans-Europe Express," producer Arthur Baker re-engineered rap with an electronic heart. (Unimpressed, Kraftwerk sued, settling out of court with Baker and Bambaataa.) As the decade progressed, sightings of the band became rare, and neither *Electric Cafe* (1986) nor *The Mix* (1991) did much for their reputation. But in 1997, after almost six years of near silence, they played a rapturously received set at a U.K. festival. The rehabilitated Kraftwerk released 2003's *Tour de France Soundtracks*, reissued much of their catalog, and returned to touring (latterly minus Schneider, leaving Hütter as the only original), often with little more than four laptops—commemorated by 2005's live *Minimum Maximum*.

KRAFTWERK 149

Bruce Springsteen 1949–present

1949+ 1975+ 1984+ 1999+

Bruce "The Boss" Springsteen is an American hero: like Bob Dylan ◁062 or Neil Young ◁078 to his fans; like Rambo or Mayor McCheese to his detractors. For all the apparent bombast of his concerts and most popular albums (*Born to Run* and *Born in the U.S.A.*), his songs are often thoughtful, moving, and intimate. They have been covered by an astonishing variety of artists: from Johnny Cash ◁018 ("Highway Patrolman") to Tori Amos ("I'm on Fire"), from David Bowie ◁134 ("It's Hard to be a Saint in the City") to Frankie Goes to Hollywood ("Born to Run"), and from Linda Ronstadt ("If I Should Fall Behind") to Rage Against the Machine 254▷ ("The Ghost of Tom Joad"). "The tabloids could never break news on Bruce," observed Bono of U2 192▷. "He had already told us everything in the songs."

Springsteen has never made any secret of his influences: he's wearing an Elvis ◁012 badge on the cover of *Born to Run*, sang with Roy Orbison on 1988's *A Black and White Night,* and emulated Phil Spector ◁028 on "Born to Run." He made a cameo on Lou Reed's "Street Hassle" and sang Tom Waits' "Jersey Girl" as if he'd written it himself.

Yet he has also created a readily identifiable sound of his own—one that has been echoed by Bon Jovi, The Hold Steady, and even The Killers 280▷, who accessed their inner Boss on the 2006 album *Sam's Town.* "I just fell in love with his music and it's been a real blessing," said Killers front man Brandon Flowers. "What struck me most forcefully about him is that I believe what he says. The guy is so incredibly sincere, whatever he sings."

September 23, 1949

Bruce Frederick Joseph Springsteen is born in New Jersey, U.S.A. In 1969, he will form Child, who evolve into Steel Mill, and then Dr. Zoom & the Sonic Boom.

January 9, 1972

With the Bruce Springsteen Band left behind (although most would be reinstated), Springsteen is signed to Columbia by John Hammond, who also signed Bob Dylan.

September 11, 1973

The Wild, The Innocent & The E Street Shuffle is released. Its song "Sandy" will be covered in 1975 by The Hollies, whose singer Allan Clarke is an early champion of Springsteen.

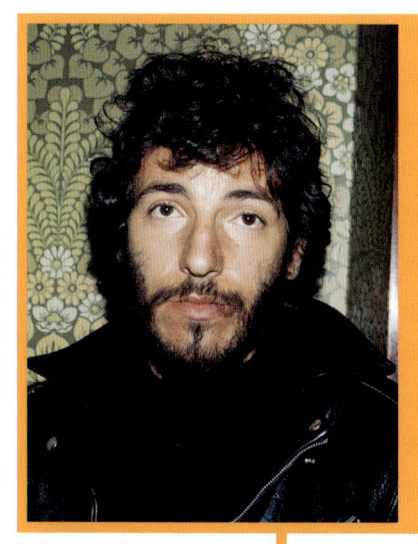

MAY 9, 1974: The future of rock 'n' roll

Although Springsteen's albums had made little impression, his shows were attracting rave reviews. Of one—a support slot for Bonnie Raitt on May 9, 1974—his future manager Jon Landau wrote: "I saw rock 'n' roll future and its name is Bruce Springsteen." This was duly adopted as a slogan by Columbia, while the star continued to win over audiences from coast to coast. He had begun recording his third album in January of the same year, but sessions stretched until July 1975. After his then-manager Mike Appel had begged Columbia to loan them $10,000, Springsteen endlessly reworked the songs, determined to create a hit. Meanwhile, the label, in Appel's words, "finally decided Bruce was their baby . . . We had a seasoned performer who could go out there and kick ass and had already done it in a lot of places. It was a known quantity and there was a readymade market for this record."

October 8, 1975

Born to Run earns Springsteen his first U.S. gold disc. Later this month, he appears on the covers of *Newsweek* and *Time*.

April 29, 1976

Springsteen and guitarist Steve Van Zandt jump a fence at Graceland in a doomed bid to see Elvis. The Boss explains: "I never liked going backstage."

November 26, 1976

Springsteen backs Patti Smith at a New York club. He will give her a song that she turns into the 1978 hit "Because the Night" (later sung by 10,000 Maniacs).

June 1977

After a year's absence from the studio caused by a legal dispute with his ex-manager Mike Appel, Springsteen resumes recording.

JUNE 27, 1978: Going platinum for the first time

Within a month of its release, 1978's *Darkness on the Edge of Town* became Springsteen's first album to go platinum. He was now a fully fledged star, albeit one who had yet to score a top ten hit. "Bruce was upset when The Pointer Sisters had a hit with his song 'Fire,'" said girlfriend Lynn Goldsmith. "It bothered him that others could have more success than he did with his own songs." For 1980's *The River*, he took no chances: having written "Hungry Heart" for the Ramones❶, he kept it for himself, sped the tape up to give his voice a more radio-friendly pitch, and hit No. 5; and the album itself became his first U.S. chart-topper. After a mammoth tour, Springsteen recorded 1982's *Nebraska* by himself. Despite its resolutely uncommercial sound, the album was another international success. Meanwhile, he returned to marathon recording sessions, punctuated by occasional New Jersey club gigs.

❶ 158

BRUCE SPRINGSTEEN

July 7, 1984

Born in the U.S.A. tops the U.S. chart. It will hit No. 1 around the world. At home, it will yield seven top ten singles and sell more than fifteen million copies.

November 29, 1986

Live/1975–85 is the first album to enter at the top of the U.S. chart in ten years. The five-record set will turn triple platinum in just two months.

November 7, 1987

Tunnel of Love, inspired by the collapse of his two-year marriage to Julianne Phillips, makes The Boss the only artist to score four U.S. No. 1 albums in the Eighties.

September 2, 1988

A tour in aid of Amnesty International—starring The Boss alongside Sting, Tracy Chapman, and Peter Gabriel—starts in London.

❶ 040
❷ 181
❸ 192

MARCH 31, 1992: Not so *Lucky Town*

Having had his fill of stardom, Springsteen (left, with Chuck Berry❶) began the Nineties raising a family with his new wife (backing singer Patti Scialfa), and was cheerfully unconcerned when 1992's simultaneously released *Human Touch* and *Lucky Town* were kept off the U.S. No. 1 by Def Leppard❷ (both went platinum anyway). Indeed, his only chart-topper of the decade was the 1995 blockbuster *Greatest Hits*, bolstered by 1994's Oscar-winning "Streets of Philadelphia." A defiantly electric set for MTV's *Unplugged* (1993) and the acoustic guitar-driven *The Ghost of Tom Joad* (1995) continued his niche success. Yet, as the decade drew to a close, his legend was recognized: first by the release of archive material on 1998's *Tracks*, then by his induction into the Rock and Roll Hall of Fame by Bono. "More than a boss," said U2's❸ singer, "he's the owner—because, more than anyone else, Bruce Springsteen owns America's heart."

April 9, 1999

An E Street Band reunion tour begins, despite Van Zandt now starring in *The Sopranos*. It will yield *Live in New York City* (2001).

August 11, 2002

The Rising returns The Boss to No. 1. It marks the start of a long association with Brendan O'Brien, producer for acts such as Rage Against the Machine.

February 23, 2003

Springsteen, Elvis Costello, and the Foo Fighters' Dave Grohl play The Clash's "London Calling" at the Grammys, in honor of that band's late Joe Strummer.

May 8, 2005

Arguably the least accessible of his acoustic albums, *Devils & Dust* is nonetheless the highest charting and hits No. 1.

❶ 062

2006–PRESENT: *Working on a Dream* and more

With a charming disregard for convention, Springsteen followed the grim *Devils & Dust* with 2006's much jollier, albeit seemingly equally uncommercial, *We Shall Overcome: The Seeger Sessions* (a tribute to Pete Seeger, the folk icon who inspired Dylan❶ and countless others). The album and its accompanying tour were only modest successes in the U.S.A., but rapturously received elsewhere. There was a more unanimous response to his next albums, with the E Street Band (left): 2007's storming *Magic* and 2009's quirky *Working on a Dream* both hit No. 1. The 2009 tour found the band playing several of their albums in full, including *Born to Run* and even *Greetings from Asbury Park, N.J.* "The nice thing about where we are now is that the rules are much fewer and further between," Springsteen declared. "I can do all these things now and really record whatever kind of music comes into my mind."

152   SEX, DRUGS & ROCK 'N' ROLL

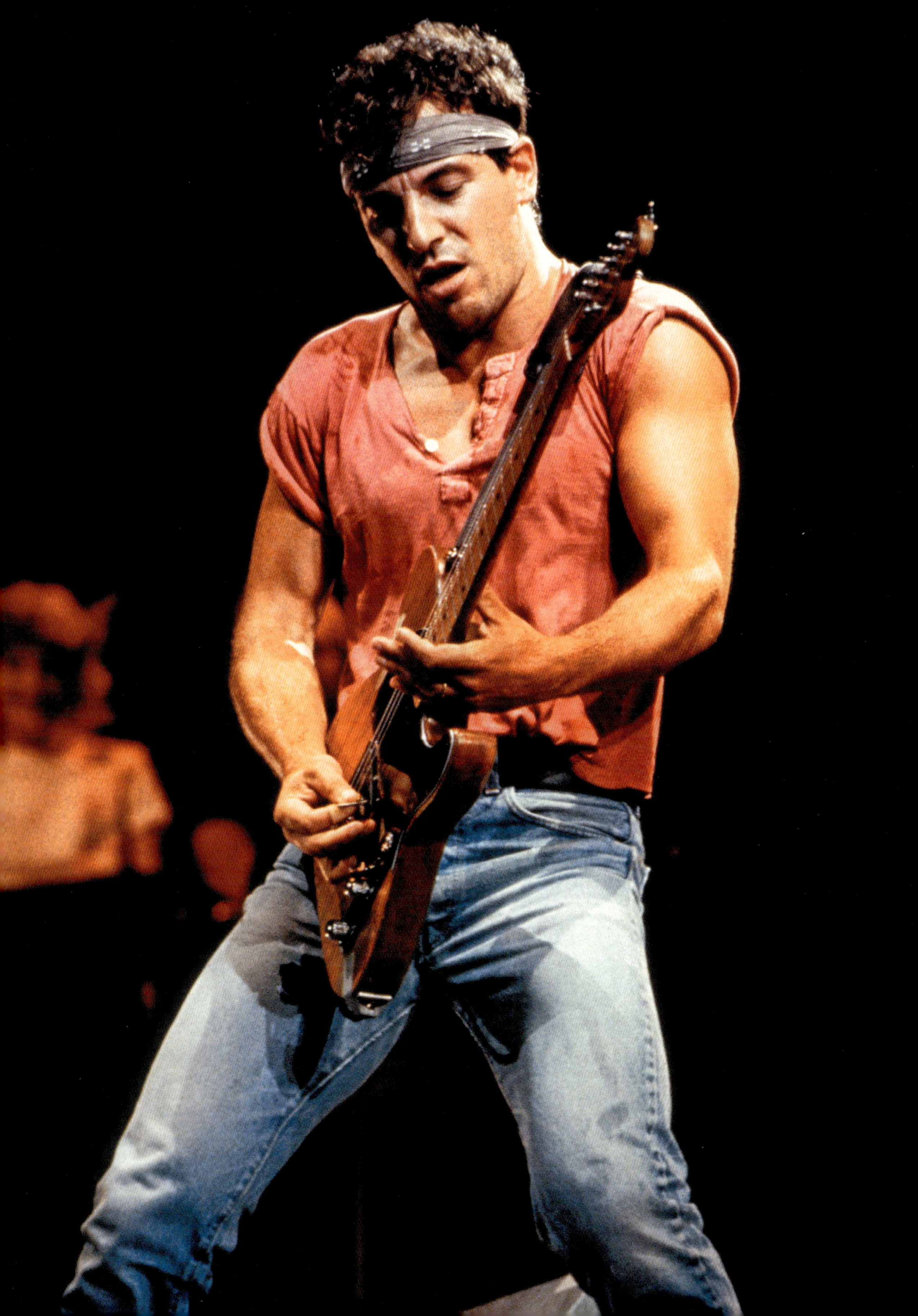

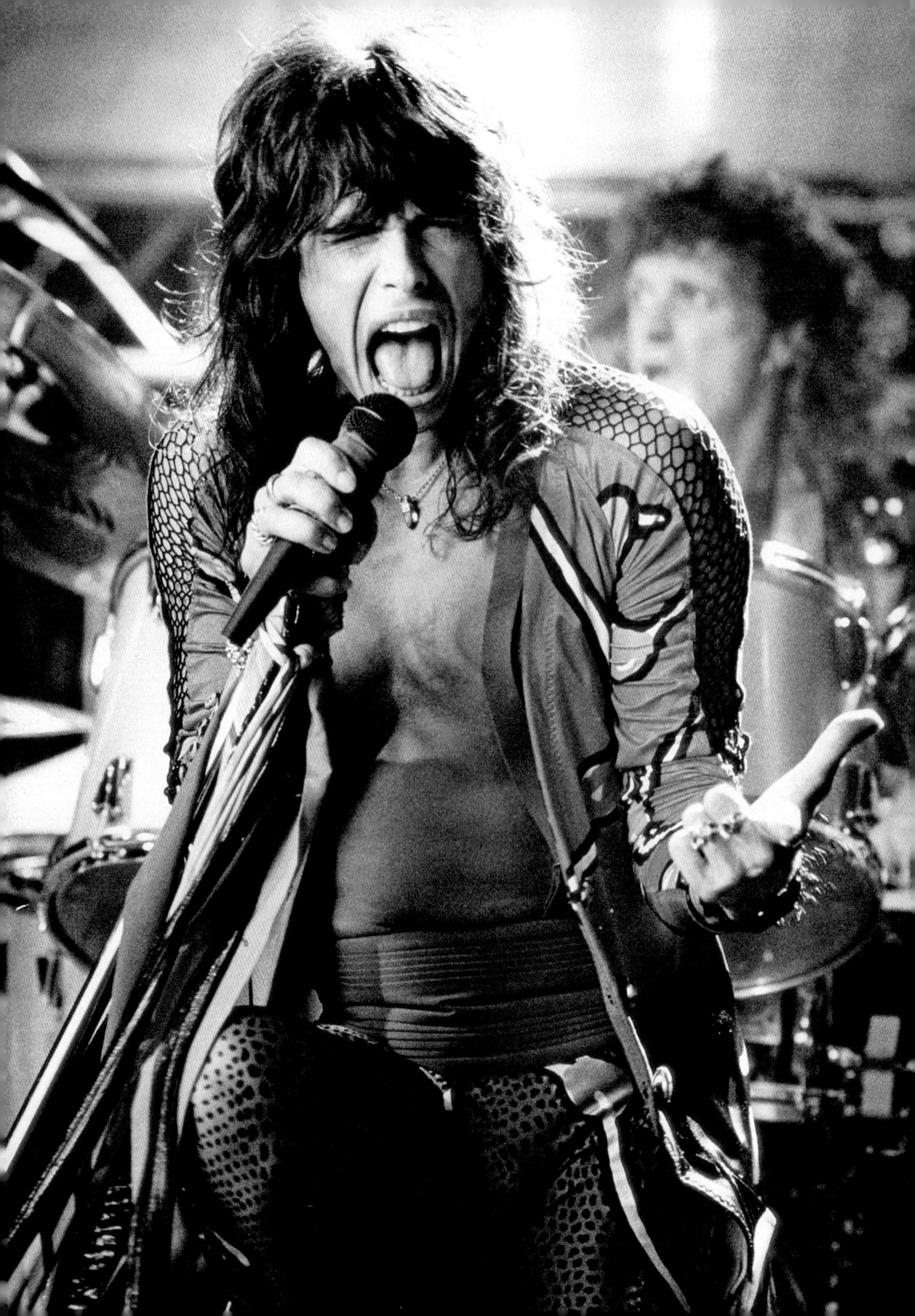

Aerosmith
1973–present

Bar The Rolling Stones ◀054—Aerosmith's obvious forebears—no other band has risen to such stadium-filling status, so spectacularly crashed and burned, yet come back to be bigger than ever before. It's a rare tale of rock 'n' roll redemption with a platinum-coated second chapter.

For all their success from the Eighties onward, it was the Seventies in which the legend of singer Steven Tyler, guitarists Joe Perry and Brad Whitford, bassist Tom Hamilton, and drummer Joey Kramer was founded. As The Smashing Pumpkins' Billy Corgan observed: "If you grew up in America, whether you like it or not you heard Aerosmith."

> "Aerosmith? Huge. It was the slime all over it that I liked."
> —Nikki Sixx, Mötley Crüe

The band were united by a love of the Stones, Peter Green's Fleetwood Mac ◀094, The Yardbirds, James Brown ◀022, Led Zeppelin ◀098, and other rock and R&B icons of the Sixties and early Seventies. (Led Zep's Robert Plant returned the favor, writing "Big Love" after hearing their "Love in an Elevator," and Jimmy Page often jammed with them.) Critics who identified these influences despised them. Fans, who couldn't care less about critics, thought they were the coolest band on Earth. "The classic thing happened one night," remarked Jeff Beck, "the audience recognized [The Yardbirds'] 'Train Kept a-Rollin'' . . . They thought it was an Aerosmith number . . . They were all cheering me for doing it."

Another elder statesman was less forgiving. "Oh Gawd, Aerosmith!" groaned Mick Jagger in 1977. "They're just rubbish . . . The singer's quite a nice guy, mind you. He's almost too bloody sweet. He's very kind to me, anyway . . . What can you do with him? Punch 'im in the mouth? ''Ere, what are you playin' at, fuckin' impersonatin' me?'—Slam!"

A younger generation disagreed. Their songs have been covered by Guns N' Roses 228▶ ("Mama Kin") and R.E.M. 204▶ (dismissed by Tyler as "white boys from the Midwest playing 'Toys in the Attic' real fast."), as well as sampled by Eminem. And, as Black Crowes star Chris Robinson said: "We see pictures of Aerosmith from around 1973 and think that looks much cooler than bands now in Spandex."

Nirvana's 242▶ Kurt Cobain specifically sought out producer Steve Albini because he had achieved, with the Pixies 224▶ and Breeders, a drum sound reminiscent of Aerosmith's 1976 classic *Rocks* (an album that so entranced Slash of Guns N' Roses that he missed a chance to lose his virginity because of it). Cobain also part-namechecked Aerosmith in the Nirvana title "Aero Zeppelin."

So, what are they like? Tyler, who did amyl nitrate on a big dipper with Hendrix ◀072? Perry, who memorably said they went from musicians dabbling in drugs, to drug addicts dabbling in music? Whitford, Hamilton, Kramer, who dubbed themselves the LI3 ("Less interesting three")? "They never make you feel they are who they are," commented Lenny Kravitz. "I went up to their house, hung out with their family and kids, ate together, cleaned up together. They're just guys."

The deliberately sloppy *Live! Bootleg!* (1978) features both thrilling arena recordings and vintage R&B cuts from a radio session. The mock-bootleg packaging is a treat, too.

Although made when the band, minus Joe Perry, were falling apart, *Rock in a Hard Place* (1982) is a vicious delight. Clues to their narcotic state abound, such as "Bolivian Ragamuffin."

The new kids on the block—Van Halen

Before they were discovered by Gene Simmons of Kiss❶, Van Halen were just another L.A. bar band, playing covers of favorites by the likes of Black Sabbath❷ and Aerosmith. But the rock-solid rhythms of Michael Anthony and Alex Van Halen, the charisma of David Lee Roth, and the jaw-dropping talent of Eddie Van Halen (left) made them stand out. In July 1978, Van Halen supported Aerosmith at the gigantic Texxas Jam and, although few realized it at the time, the baton was being passed. As the elder band stumbled, Van Halen entered the Eighties as America's favorite, homegrown hard rockers, a position they held until Aerosmith's renaissance later in the decade. Van Halen's supremacy even survived the departure of front man Roth, who figured "maybe in five years . . . we'll put the band back together." (In the end, it was twenty-one years before he reunited with them, in 2007.)

Aerosmith

January 13, 1973
Aerosmith's debut is released to, as guitarist Joe Perry will recall, "no fanfare, no critical accolades"—partly because CBS is busy with its other new signing, Bruce Springsteen.

1978 Influence

July 28, 1979
At a Cleveland show, Mrs. Perry throws milk over Mrs. Hamilton. In an ensuing row, Perry quits the band. Tyler later cracks, "We literally broke up over spilt milk."

July 9, 1976
Rocks earns Aerosmith their first platinum disc. "One of the records that sums up my taste in hard rock to this day," says Slash. It will also be one of Kurt Cobain's favorites.

Connection 1978

August 1, 1982
Their *Rock in a Hard Place* is released, the only album with Joe Perry and Brad Whitford's substitutes, Jimmy Crespo and Rick Dufay. It includes a cover of "Cry Me a River."

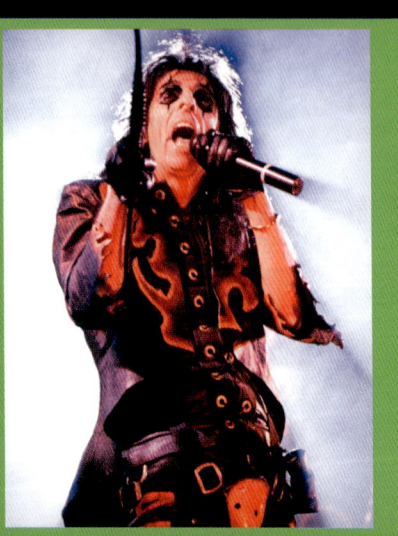

A man called Alice

Alice Cooper has a lot in common with Aerosmith. His early classics were closer to Aerosmith's Stonesy❶ "raunch 'n' roll" than the heavy metal that the Boston band helped spawn. Cooper's final album with his group—who bore his name before he took it for himself—was 1973's *Muscle of Love*, produced by Jack Douglas, who went on to produce five Aerosmith albums. Both Cooper and Aerosmith appeared in 1978's celluloid bomb *Sgt. Pepper's Lonely Hearts Club Band*. ("We and Alice Cooper were the bad guys," said Aerosmith drummer Joey Kramer, "which was great because everyone looked so silly that we looked cool when we wanted to kill them.") Both acts also employed producer and songwriter Desmond Child for late Eighties comebacks (Cooper's *Trash*, in 1989, featured Tyler). And in 1984, Joe Perry's work with Cooper inspired a jealous Tyler to call his old guitarist—and reform Aerosmith.

156 SEX, DRUGS & ROCK 'N' ROLL

Raising hell with Run-DMC

The reunited Aerosmith hit back with 1985's *Done with Mirrors*—a hard, Zeppelinesque❶ affair that did little to re-establish the band commercially. Yet salvation awaited in the form of Run-DMC (left), a New York trio who had made rock 'n' rap their stock in trade since 1984's "Rock Box." At their producer Rick Rubin's❷ behest, they added a cover of the Aerosmith classic "Walk This Way" to their 1986 album *Raising Hell*. "We didn't even know the name of the group," admitted Run. "All we knew was we liked the beat." Aerosmith's Tyler and Perry guested on the recording. "I loved sitting in the studio with Joe Perry," said Rubin, "having him do a solo, and being able to say, 'I know you can play it better.'" The result charted even higher than Aerosmith's 1975 original, assisted by a memorable video, again with Tyler and Perry. *Raising Hell* rocketed to triple platinum, and Aerosmith were back on the map.

❶ 098
❷ 226

1986 Connection

November 15, 1989
Led Zeppelin's main man Robert Plant sees the band play in London. "They've become born-again teetotallers," he says, "but they were great."

November 21, 1991
Aerosmith become the first band to guest on *The Simpsons*, with the episode "Flaming Moe's." "We were blown away that we were asked to do it," says Tyler.

September 5, 1998
"I Don't Want to Miss a Thing" is their first U.S. No. 1 single. "This," says composer Diane Warren (who wrote the song for Celine Dion), "is the best thing I've ever heard of mine."

September 15, 1988
The band's *Permanent Vacation* tour ends with Axl and Slash of support group Guns N' Roses guesting on "Mama Kin." A week later, *Appetite for Destruction* will hit No. 1.

Connection 1989

May 8, 1993
Aerosmith score a first U.S. No. 1 album with *Get a Grip*. Its sales of seven million are boosted by videos starring Alicia Silverstone and, in "Crazy," Tyler's daughter, Liv.

January 28, 2001
The band's Superbowl half-time show climaxes with "Walk This Way," starring Mary J. Blige, Nelly, and, in a very fetching Aerosmith T-shirt, Britney Spears.

Bon Jovi walk this way

While Aerosmith were in the doldrums in the early Eighties, a slew of bands copied them. Ratt were the most blatant (they even covered Rufus Thomas' "Walkin' the Dog," just like Aerosmith) and Mötley Crüe the most honest (they later recruited Tyler to sing on *Dr. Feelgood*). But Bon Jovi also borrowed from Boston's finest, as evidenced by several of their songs as well as by Jon Bon Jovi's early, scarf-bedecked stage appearance. "Steven Tyler certainly did have some influence on my live performance early on," admitted the singer (left with Tyler). "I admired him." Bon Jovi's multimillion sellers with writer-producer Desmond Child led to Child being assigned to work with Aerosmith—a writing partnership that gave them hits such as "Angel" and "Dude (Looks Like a Lady)." And in August 1989, Aerosmith's Steve Tyler and Joe Perry joined Bon Jovi at Milton Keynes Bowl in the U.K., performing the inevitable "Walk This Way."

Ramones 1974–96

1951+ 1989+

They never won a platinum album or cracked the top forty in their native U.S.A., but New York punks the Ramones are one of rock's most influential acts. Johnny, Joey, Dee Dee, and Tommy (who trained his own replacement, Marky, when he quit to be a producer) borrowed their shared group surname from a Beatles-era ◀044 pseudonym used by Paul McCartney. Other Brits such as the Dave Clark Five were among their influences, as were Phil Spector ◀028 and The Beach Boys ◀050.

"They're the crossroads . . . where everything comes together," observed Bruce Springsteen's ◀150 right-hand man Steve Van Zandt. "The Ramones listened to all the cool music that came before them and absorbed it. And they've been a huge influence on the bands that came after them."

Indeed, that influence has stretched from Kraftwerk ◀148 (whose "Ein, zwei, drei, vier" intro on "Showroom Dummies" was a pastiche of the Ramones' trademark count-in, "Onetwothreefour!") to U2 192▶. The Ramones' 1978 Dublin concert was, said The Edge, "the greatest show we'd ever seen."

Along the way, the Ramones got to work with some of their idols. When they met Spector to talk about working together on *End of the Century*, Dee Dee recalled, the producer's first words were, "My bodyguards want to fight your bodyguards."

The Ramones are now immortalized as a brand: their logo adorns many more people than actually bought their records. As Blondie's 172▶ Debbie Harry marveled, "The Ramones could never get on the radio, but now they're advertising a phone!"

158 SEX, DRUGS & ROCK 'N' ROLL

1951
Jeffry Hyman is born on May 19 in Queens, New York, and John Cummings is born on October 8 in Long Island. They will become Joey and Johnny Ramone, singer and guitarist.

1952
Tamás Erdélyi is born on January 29 in Budapest, later to become drummer Tommy. Douglas Colvin is born on September 18 in Virginia. He will become bassist Dee Dee.

March 30, 1974
Joey, Johnny, and Dee Dee debut as the Ramones at New York's Performance Studio. Joey realizes he can't drum and sing at the same time, so they enlist Tommy.

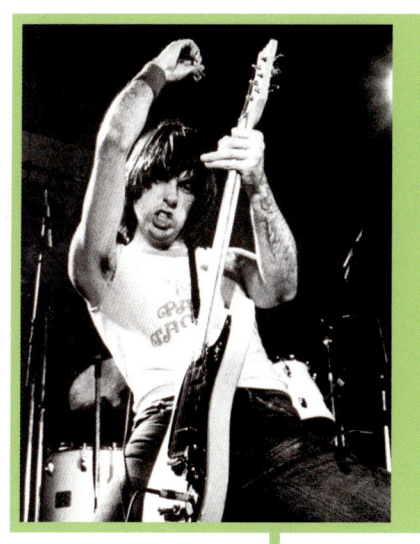

JULY 4, 1976: Punk!

Although it reached only No. 111 in the U.S.A. and didn't chart in the U.K., the Ramones' self-titled debut album, released in April 1976, proved a sensation. Heralded as the first punk album (if you don't count Patti Smith❶, whose *Horses* beat it by five months), it made the Ramones unwitting champions of the movement (they were horrified to find European fans spitting at them, emulating what had been misreported as a U.S. punk ritual). On Independence Day 1976, the band began their first British tour, supported by The Stranglers, and attended by members of the Sex Pistols❷, The Clash❸, The Damned, and future Pretender Chrissie Hynde. Although these acts all had roots ranging from The Kinks❹ to The Stooges❺, The Faces and beyond, there is no doubt that the Ramones galvanized many of them into action. Three further classic Ramones albums followed during the glorious Seventies.

❶ 164
❷ 166
❸ 170
❹ 066
❺ 116

May 18, 1989
Brain Drain is the band's last album with Dee Dee. It includes his "I Believe in Miracles," later covered in concert by Pearl Jam.

February 26, 1991
Motörhead release *1916*, with the tribute "R.A.M.O.N.E.S." "It was the ultimate honor," said Joey Ramone, "like John Lennon writing a song for you."

April 15, 2001
Joey dies of cancer. "He'll always be alive for me," says Debbie Harry, who writes "Hello Joe" for him. "I always loved that band and thought Joey was . . . a nice person."

March 18, 2002
Pearl Jam's Eddie Vedder inducts the band into the Rock and Roll Hall of Fame, while Green Day play in their honor. Dee Dee will die of a drug overdose on June 5.

FEBRUARY 11, 2003: *We're a Happy Family*

"The Ramones," remarked R.E.M.'s❶ Peter Buck, "made pretty perfect records." Admirers duly queued to rework their songs on a 2003 tribute, *We're a Happy Family*, helmed by metal star-turned-movie director Rob Zombie (who did the cover art, left). Among them were the Red Hot Chili Peppers❷, Metallica❸, U2❹, Kiss❺, Marilyn Manson, Green Day❻, The Pretenders, The Offspring, and Tom Waits, while Stephen King wrote the sleeve notes. The project was one of the last overseen by Johnny Ramone—the band's unofficial boss despite having barely spoken to Joey for years before they played a last gig in August 1996 (heard on *We're Outta Here!* and starring Pearl Jam's❼ Eddie Vedder, Motörhead's Lemmy, Soundgarden's Chris Cornell, and members of Rancid). Johnny was the last of the founding trio to die (of cancer) on September 15, 2004. As Vedder commented, "There'll never be another Ramones."

❶ 204
❷ 232
❸ 218
❹ 192
❺ 142
❻ 258
❼ 248

RAMONES   159

iconic club

CBGB
1973–2006

Other New York venues hosted punk pioneers (the New York Dolls at Mercer Arts Center; The Velvet Underground ◂090 and The Stooges ◂116 at Max's Kansas City). But CBGB was Punk Central, despite that not having been the initial idea.

Founder Hilly Kristal launched the downtown club—among flophouses on The Bowery—in 1973 as a Country, Blue Grass, and Blues venue, hence the acronym. (The rest of its name, OMFUG, stood for Other Music For Uplifting Gormandizers.)

While Kristal was up a ladder fixing the club's awning, he was approached by kids who asked him about the acronym and went on to tell him, "We play a little of that, a little rock, a little country, a little blues, a little bluegrass . . ." It was a lie, but Kristal booked them for a Sunday (a dead night).

They were Tom Verlaine and Richard Hell's Television and they stiffed—with Kristal: "Terrible: screechy, ear-splitting guitars, and a jumble of sounds that I just didn't get." Dee Dee Ramone remembered it differently: "Television were really special and created a real atmosphere of freedom."

Before long, Dee Dee's own band, the Ramones ◂158, were also appearing at the club. "They," shuddered Kristal, "were even worse than Television."

Other venues in the city had closed (the Electric Circus), fallen down (the Mercer Arts Center), or wouldn't host bands without a contract. So by 1974, bands playing abrasive guitars ("street rock") were heading to Kristal's Bowery hotspot, including Richard Hell (ex-Television) and his Voidoids; The Stilettos, featuring future Blondie 172▸ duo Chris Stein and Debbie Harry; and Patti Smith 164▸ (Kristal liked her). CBGB also attracted luminaries from previous countercultural waves, including The Velvet Underground's Lou Reed and John Cale.

SEX, DRUGS & ROCK 'N' ROLL

Ramones
Ramones
(1976)
Sire Records
Company

Blondie
Blondie
(1976)
Private Stock

Television
Marquee Moon
(1977)
Elektra

After that initial burst, Kristal gave the scene a boost with the Festival of Unrecorded Rock Talent, which ran from July 16 to August 2, 1975. *Rolling Stone, NME,* and *Melody Maker* covered the seventy-odd acts who appeared, including Television, the Ramones, and The Heartbreakers (starring Richard Hell and ex-New York Doll Johnny Thunders).

The next year saw influential synth duo Suicide at the club, and—to push bands that hadn't yet caught on—the recording of the compilation album *Live at CBGB*. (Acts to release material recorded at the club in later years include Social Distortion, Bad Brains, VAST, Agnostic Front, and Korn.) The venue's importance was becoming widely recognized —MCA even asked Kristal to showcase one of their new signings, Tom Petty & the Heartbreakers.

Although Punk's first rush was over by 1980, CBGB continued to host hardcore bands throughout the decade. Occasional violence led to Kristal banning such bands, but after a while he relented.

In 2005, a dispute arose over rent that Kristal allegedly owed to the local residents' committee. The end came on October 15, 2006, after a week in which veterans Blondie and The Dictators made appearances. Patti Smith closed the place out, with the Red Hot Chili Peppers' 232▶ Flea guesting. ("I liked every performance of Patti Smith," Kristal had said in 1998. "I think she was marvelous.")

Kristal had planned to shift his enterprise (along with many of the original features) to Las Vegas. "I am taking the bars with me," he said. "I am taking the stage. I'm taking the urinal that Joey [Ramone] pissed in." However, those plans had to be shelved permanently when the inspirational club founder passed away, from lung cancer, on August 28, 2007.

Television March 31, 1974

"At CBGB," remembered Ramones❶ bassist Dee Dee, "you couldn't imagine anyone else doing what they were doing." The members of Television were, however, frosty toward their contemporaries: "A strange bunch, pretty anti-social," recalled Joey Ramone. Indeed, the imperious quartet proceeded to make Blondie's❷ life somewhat of a misery when they toured the U.K. together in May 1977.

Ramones August 17, 1974

The awesome Ramones❶ debuted at the club in 1974. "At that first gig at CBGB," recalled club owner Kristal, "they were the most untogether group I'd ever heard." However, as front man Joey Ramone remembered in a *Q* magazine article, Kristal "knew we had something. Our first show was just the bartender and his dog, but then we got the Warhol, arty crowd. It always seems to be gays who pick up on things first."

CBGB
1973–2006

Talking Heads June 8, 1975

David Byrne, Chris Frantz, and Tina Weymouth of Talking Heads❶ first supported the Ramones❷ at the club. "Lou Reed❸ would take us aside and give us some hilarious tips," said Weymouth. "'David, you have to make a decision—are you going to wear long sleeves or short? Because you have pretty hairy arms.' And then he'd say, 'Smart move getting a chick in the band—wonder where you got that idea.'"

Blondie February 13–15, 1976

Although they ultimately outsold all their rivals, Blondie❶ were ridiculed at CBGB. "We weren't punk enough," said drummer Clem Burke in 1979. "But we never said we were, and that worked against us . . . We weren't intellectual enough . . . We liked the Bay City Rollers and that wasn't very chic. Now, because we *did* play CBGBs, people call us a punk band when all we're doing is making good pop records."

162   SEX, DRUGS & ROCK 'N' ROLL

Dead Boys July 22, 1976

"Johnny Thunders' band was playing so he invited me up," recalled front man Stiv Bators. "Joey [Ramone] helped me jive Hilly Kristal that we had a band." To Kristal, the Dead Boys—whose "Sonic Reducer" became a punk standard—symbolized "what a punk band should be. They were loud, raw, crass, with super high energy. They were outrageous and obscene, with excellent lyrics and music."

The Police October 27, 1978

Bassist Sting, guitarist Andy Summers, and drummer Stewart Copeland made their U.S. debut at CBGB. Copeland, who arrived before the others, recalled: "By the time they got through the customers, the club was already full . . . We went to the dressing room at the back which didn't have a door. Sting and Andy got their instruments and went straight on, plugged in, turned around, and 'Hello America.'"

Pearl Jam November 8, 1991

Given singer Eddie Vedder's hero worship of the Ramones[1], it was unsurprising that Pearl Jam[2] chose CBGB for a fan club show. The bulk of the set was from their debut album *Ten*, which had been released in August—including the future anthems "Black," "Even Flow," and "Alive." The closing "I Got a Feeling" was a Beatles[3] cover that had been a bonus track on the Japanese edition of *Ten*.

[1] 158
[2] 248
[3] 044

Guns N' Roses October 30, 1987

With *Appetite for Destruction* yet to make them superstars, Guns N' Roses[1] played a short, acoustic set at the club. They took the opportunity to play a trio of songs that would appear on *GN'R Lies* in 1988 (the controversial "One in a Million" and "Used to Love Her," and the hit "Patience"), one from *Appetite* ("Mr Brownstone"), and one from their debut EP, *Live ?!*@ Like a Suicide* ("Move to the City").

[1] 228

Patti Smith 1946–present

1946+   1977+

Poet is too ponderous a term for Patti Smith, who invested her Arthur Rimbaud and Baudelaire-influenced work with the vigor of the Stones ◁054▷. "She exemplified the sort of zest that these men characterized," said Sonic Youth's Kim Gordon, "and that's why she's a female icon. Even though her influences were all male and she related to men, she took that energy and that action."

The effect of these interpretations was immense. "*Highway 61 Revisited, Blonde on Blonde, Electric Ladyland*—I waited for those records, pored over them," she remembered. "It was inspiring . . . So, when we did *Horses,* I was really conscious of that responsibility. But I never dreamed it would have that kind of impact." Impressed listeners included future stars of U2 ◁192▷ and The Smiths ◁212▷.

Not everyone was as smitten. "Patti Smith was down on me, because she was very competitive," said Debbie Harry of fellow CBGB ◁160▷ graduates Blondie ◁172▷. Nonetheless, most were impressed by both her music and formidable presence. "Patti," said her producer—Velvet Underground ◁090▷ man John Cale—"had a preacher's verve."

At her 2007 induction into the Rock and Roll Hall of Fame, Rage Against the Machine's ◁254▷ Zach de la Rocha hailed her as "one of the sparks that set the punk prairie fire." Fittingly, her songs have been covered by acts as diverse as Morrissey ("Redondo Beach"), Marilyn Manson ("Rock 'n' Roll Nigger"), 10,000 Maniacs ("Because the Night"), Sammy Hagar ("Free Money"), Simple Minds ("Dancing Barefoot"), and Sandie Shaw ("Frederick").

164   SEX, DRUGS & ROCK 'N' ROLL

December 30, 1946

Patricia Lee Smith is born in Chicago. She will move to New York City two decades later and live there with controversial photographer Robert Mapplethorpe.

February 10, 1971

Smith performs for the first time with guitarist Lenny Kaye, with whom she will go on to form the Patti Smith Group. They will begin a residency at CBGB on February 1, 1974.

February 1973

Blue Öyster Cult issue *Tyranny and Mutation*, with "Baby Ice Dog," co-written by Smith. She was once mooted to be their singer but it never came about.

DECEMBER 13, 1975: *Horses* released!

❶ 192
❷ 090
❸ 204

"I'd play it to friends . . ." said U2's❶ The Edge, "and they hated it. Some of them claimed it actually made them want to throw up, which got me even more excited." *Horses* etched a new template for rock, despite its roots: it was produced by The Velvet Underground's❷ John Cale, quoted "Land of a Thousand Dances" (a hit for Wilson Pickett), and began with an interpretation of Van Morrison's garage rock staple "Gloria" ("One of the greatest openings to any album . . ." said The Edge, "beautifully streamlined and inspiringly uncomplicated"). "I was fifteen when I heard it," said R.E.M.'s❸ Michael Stipe, "and that's pretty strong stuff for a fifteen-year-old American middle-class white boy . . . It was like the first time you went into the ocean and got knocked down by a wave . . . I sat up all night with a huge bowl of cherries listening to Patti Smith, eating those cherries and going, 'Oh my God!' . . . Then I was sick."

January 23, 1977

On tour in Florida, supporting Bob Seger, Smith falls offstage and sustains injuries that will stall her for a year.

May 13, 1978

"Because the Night" enters the U.S. top forty. Based on a piece given to Smith by Bruce Springsteen, it will become her biggest hit.

May 19, 1979

Smith releases *Wave*. It is produced by Todd Rundgren, who plays bass on "Dancing Barefoot," which is later covered by U2, Alison Moorer, and Xymox.

September 1, 1979

After a final gig in Italy, Smith retires from music. She will settle in Detroit with her husband—former MC5 guitarist Fred "Sonic" Smith—and raise a family.

JANUARY 1, 1988: *Dream of Life*—the comeback

❶ 204
❷ 254
❸ 062
❹ 242

With *Dream of Life* and its stirring "People Have the Power," Smith returned to the spotlight in 1988. The deaths of her group's keyboardist Richard "DNV" Sohl, in 1990, and her husband, in 1994, later informed her 1996 *Gone Again* (with Jeff Buckley on backing vocals). The same year, she duetted on hit song "E-bow the Letter" by R.E.M.❶. Her *Peace and Noise* (1997) was followed by *Gung Ho* (2000) and *Trampin'* (2004). In 2005, she performed *Horses* in full in London, and, in 2007, she was inducted into the Rock and Roll Hall of Fame by Zach de la Rocha of Rage Against the Machine❷. She also staged shows with My Bloody Valentine's Kevin Shields, performing *The Coral Sea*, an elegy for photographer Robert Mapplethorpe. The covers set *Twelve* (2007) included songs by Dylan❸, with whom she toured in 1995, and Nirvana❹, whose Kurt Cobain is the subject of "About a Boy."

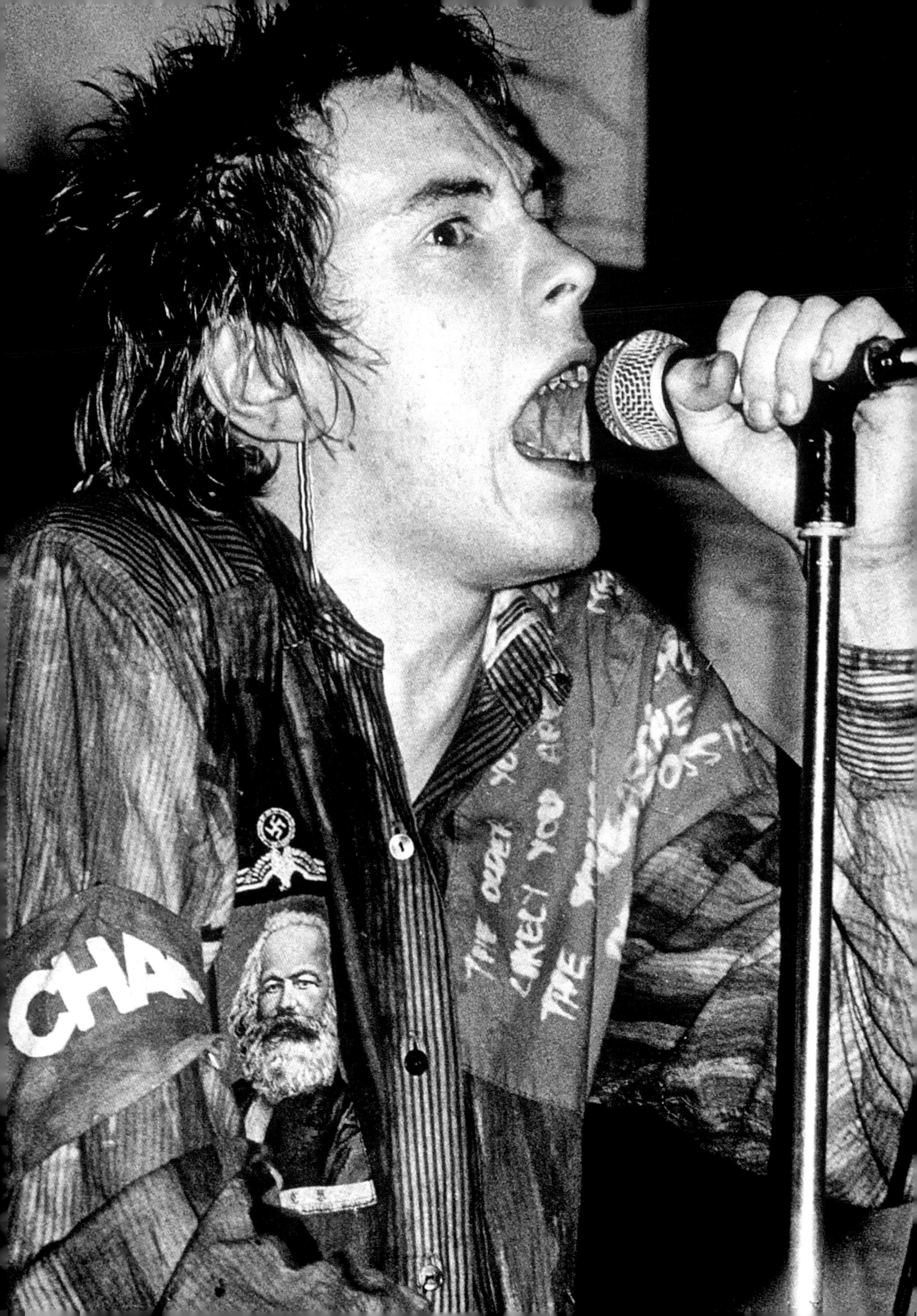
CHA

Sex Pistols
1975–present

The Rolling Stones ◀054 in their prime could probably have taken the Sex Pistols in a fight and, goodness knows, Elvis ◀012 was a lot better looking. But, in those "anything is possible" days of 1976 and 1977, the Pistols had to give ground to no one in terms of the moral panic they caused.

Malcolm McLaren, who had dabbled in music management with the New York Dolls, took on the nucleus of Steve Jones (singer), Paul Cook (drums), and bassist Glen Matlock. With Jones preferring the guitar to front man duties, the appearance in McLaren's clothes shop in London of John Lydon, a green-haired youth wearing an "I HATE Pink Floyd" T-shirt, grabbed the attention of like-minded folk. After Lydon auditioned, miming to an Alice Cooper song, it was decided that attitude was preferable to competence. (Ironically, Chris Thomas, who mixed Floyd's ◀086 *Dark Side of the Moon*, produced *Never Mind the Bollocks Here's the Sex Pistols*).

> "All the hype the Sex Pistols had was totally deserved—they deserved everything they got." —Kurt Cobain

The band's only studio album has a huge array of acolytes. In fact, anyone who picks up an instrument with the intention of making a noise that is likely to offend an older generation instantly qualifies for being influenced by it. "We've all got *Never Mind the Bollocks* . . . ," said Axl Rose 228▶. The songs have become touchstones, especially for U.S. rock acts. They have been covered with varying degrees of success by Anthrax ("God Save the Queen"), Velvet Revolver ("Bodies"), Mötley Crüe and Megadeth (both with "Anarchy in the U.K."), and Joan Jett ("Pretty Vacant"). U.K. acts from Motörhead to Lady Sovereign have also had a stab at them.

Every way they turned, the Pistols seemed to face a rock icon they despised, which was just how they liked it. Even before the album's release, the band outraged society with an expletive-laden appearance on the British TV show *Today* after Queen ◀144 pulled out. When "God Save the Queen" was released, alleged fixing kept Rod Stewart at the top of the U.K. singles chart. The replacement of Glen Matlock with Sid Vicious (once of Siouxsie & The Banshees) robbed the band of creative input but subsequently provided the press with more headline-making material than it knew what to do with.

Burning so brightly inevitably led to a short shelf life. The Pistols entered in a blaze, vomited all over the music scene for eighteen months, then departed in an unholy mess (their final show, in San Francisco on January 14, 1978, concluded with an encore of The Stooges' ◀116 "No Fun"). Since then, there have been intermittent reunions (1996, 2002–03, 2007–08) that have added little to the band's legacy.

That is not to say, however, that seeing them again has been a letdown. After a 1996 gig in Brixton, London, Alan McGee, the manager of Oasis 260▶, was moved to take out a full-page advertisement in the *NME*: "This band are our alternative royal family. God save the Sex Pistols."

Just one studio album—but *what* an album. The all-out assault of *Never Mind the Bollocks Here's the Sex Pistols* (1976) is the yardstick by which all punk albums are judged.

Put aside ideological objections to the resurrection of the Pistols and there is fun to be had with *Filthy Lucre Live*—the record of their return to the stage in London, in mid-1996.

❶ 086
❷ 116
❸ 044

The Damned—punks with a pinch of prog

Their "New Rose" may have beaten the Pistols to be the first U.K. punk single, but later in 1976, The Damned were booted off the Anarchy tour. "We wouldn't have filth like that in our coach," said Pistol front man Lydon. Enmity forgotten, The Damned regularly covered their "Pretty Vacant" (issuing a live version in 1985). If attitude was measured by the plug-it-in-and-turn-it-up ethos, they were the most punk of the lot, but morphed into the least. After their debut *Damned, Damned, Damned*, Pink Floyd's❶ Nick Mason produced the follow-up (the band wanted Syd Barrett), and they worked with Robert Fripp and included a seventeen-minute track on 1980's *The Black Album*. Covers have included Iggy Pop❷, The Sweet, and MC5 (which you might expect) and The Beatles❸, Love, and Jefferson Airplane (which you might not). Their most commercially successful period was topped by a cover of Barry Ryan's "Eloise."

Sex Pistols

1976 Connection

June 4, 1976
Future members of landmark Manchester bands The Fall, Buzzcocks, The Smiths, and Joy Division attend a Pistols show at the British city's Lesser Free Trade Hall.

December 18, 1976
The band's debut single, "Anarchy in the U.K.," enters the charts. In 2007, the surviving members (bar Glen Matlock) will re-record it for a *Guitar Hero* video game.

April 24, 1976
Talking of the early years, Glen Matlock says that the band's set consisted mostly of covers of The Who and the Small Faces. "But that didn't get us anywhere."

Connection 1976

October 15, 1977
"I didn't mind them nicking it —you've got to get your ideas from somewhere," says The Jam's Paul Weller of similarities between "Holidays in the Sun" and his own "In the City."

❶ 186
❷ 092
❸ 090

Siouxsie & The Banshees are howlingly good

After a first show consisting of a twenty-minute version of "The Lord's Prayer," with Sid Vicious on drums (no better than he was on bass), the only way was up. Siouxsie Sioux (left) trailed around after the Pistols in the early days and caught presenter Bill Grundy's attention during their notorious 1976 *Today* appearance. But, with bassist Steve Severin and drummer Kenny Morris (the latter replaced by Budgie, formerly of The Slits), her own band, the Banshees, were both fascinating and influential. *The Scream* (1978) was a fine, unsettling debut, while later releases made Siouxsie the queen of Goth. A fluid roster of guitarists included The Cure's❶ Robert Smith. John Cale❷ produced 1995's *The Rapture*, the Banshees having already covered his old band The Velvet Underground's❸ "All Tomorrow's Parties," as well as Cale's own "Gun." "Siouxsie," said Garbage's Shirley Manson, "embodied everything I wanted to be."

168 SEX, DRUGS & ROCK 'N' ROLL

❶ 054

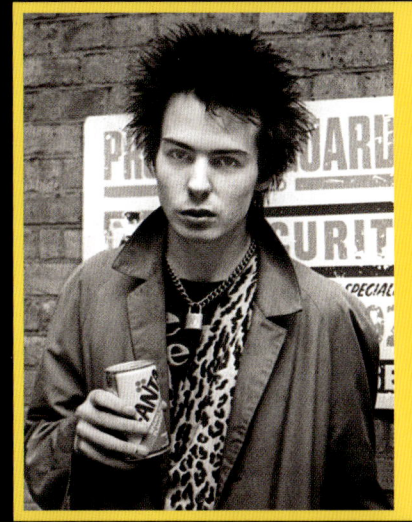

Sid sings but who's listening?

The boy born Simon John Ritchie, but better known as Sid Vicious, was almost a lot of things: he was almost lead singer of The Damned; he was almost bass player for the Pistols (Steve Jones played bass on the records); then, when Johnny Rotten started afresh as John Lydon, he was almost the new Pistols front man. Without noticeable songwriting talent, he also provided vocals on covers of the Sinatra standard "My Way" and Eddie Cochran classics "Something Else" and "C'mon Everybody." "I wouldn't piss on him if he was on fire," was his view of The Stones' ❶ Keith Richards, but the pair had one thing in common: heroin. "I could easily end up dead quite soon," he said. "But that's just my tough shit." The inevitable happened: he overdosed in February 1979. "Sid Vicious died for what? So that we might rock? It's garbage," said John Lennon. But the image lived on in the 1986 movie *Sid & Nancy*.

1979 Connection

1981
Cook and Jones discover the girl group Bananarama. Cook will help them record their debut single and produces their debut album. They will later cover "No Feelings."

June 23, 1996
Pistols idol Iggy Pop, with whom Steve Jones and Glen Matlock have already played, is chief support in London, at the band's first British gig since Christmas Day, 1977.

September 14, 2002
The Pistols headline a one-dayer in California that includes The Damned. It is the first time the bands have appeared on the same bill for more than twenty-five years.

June 5, 1980
The band's last official single for sixteen years is a cover of "(I'm Not Your) Stepping Stone" (made famous by The Monkees), from *The Great Rock 'n' Roll Swindle*.

Connection 1986

July 27, 2002
Hawkwind's "Silver Machine" is a shock choice of opening song for the Pistols at an all-day extravaganza held at London's Crystal Palace National Sports Centre.

March 13, 2006
Mysteriously unmentioned when the band are inducted into the Rock and Roll Hall of Fame is a note put up on the band's website that calls the museum "a piss stain."

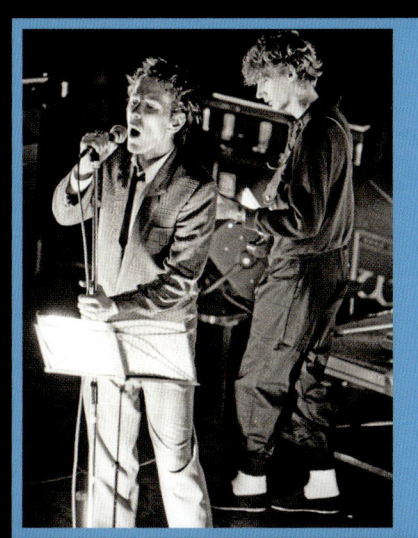

❶ 170
❷ 264

Public Image Limited—bolder and better

Where the Pistols inspired people to pick up an instrument, John Lydon's next band, Public Image Limited (or PiL) showed those same people how to think way beyond the three chords they had learned in 1976. With splintered six-string sounds from ex-Clash ❶ guitarist Keith Levene (left, with Lydon) and subterranean bass from Jah Wobble, the underrated first album and impossible-to-overrate *Metal Box* are still relevant today. Sonic Youth wanted their debut to sound like PiL, 3D of Massive Attack had his musical adolescence defined by the band, and James Murphy of LCD Soundsystem said simply: "Deep, strange, and scary." Variable later releases offered one last great offering in 1986's *Album*, featuring Ginger Baker, Steve Vai, and Ryuichi Sakamoto. Even now, musicians struggle to match the band's best work. "We could never do a record on a par with *Metal Box*," said Radiohead's ❷ Thom Yorke.

The Clash 1976–86

The Sex Pistols ◀166 made the biggest noise in British punk, but the coolest, most musically imaginative band were Joe Strummer, Mick Jones, Paul Simonon, and Topper Headon—The Clash.

"I know Elvis ◀012 didn't mean shit to [Public Enemy front man] Chuck D," said Bono of U2 ◀192▶, "but I'll bet The Clash did. They meant something to others as well: Manic Street Preachers, Rage Against the Machine 254▶, the Beastie Boys."

"I had great respect for Joe Strummer," agreed Chuck D. "How he used his music—incorporating a lot of black music, like hip-hop and reggae—was very different from the guys who invented rock 'n' roll: he always paid homage to those who came before him." (The band namechecked stars whose songs they covered and did much to popularize reggae and hip-hop with a white, rock audience.)

The Clash's songs have been covered by Bruce Springsteen ◀150 ("London Calling"), The Strokes ("Clampdown"), Silverchair ("London's Burning"), Annie Lennox ("Train in Vain"), and many others, and sampled by Cypress Hill, Will Smith, Beats International, and, most famously, M.I.A. (who used "Straight to Hell" on her "Paper Planes").

The band were distinguished by Headon's rhythmic inventiveness, Simonon's movie star looks, Jones' rock smarts, and Strummer's impassioned vocals. "Whatever he sang affected you," enthused Elton John ◀126, "because it was just so raw. His voice reeked of hurt and anger."

"When you listen to The Clash," observed Pete Townshend of The Who ◀068, "you're facing up to life, and at the same time being given strength to deal with it—which is what rock 'n' roll is about."

1952+
1977+
1980+

August 21, 1952
John "Joe Strummer" Mellor is born in Ankara, Turkey. On April 3, 1976, his band The 101'ers will be supported by the Sex Pistols, by whom Strummer will be inspired.

June 26, 1955
Michael "Mick" Jones is born in London, England. On April 21, 1976, he will meet Strummer and tell him that he likes his style but that The 101'ers are no good.

December 15, 1955
Paul Simonon is born in London. In March 1976, he will join Jones and guitarist Keith Levene in London SS, with Jones teaching him to play bass.

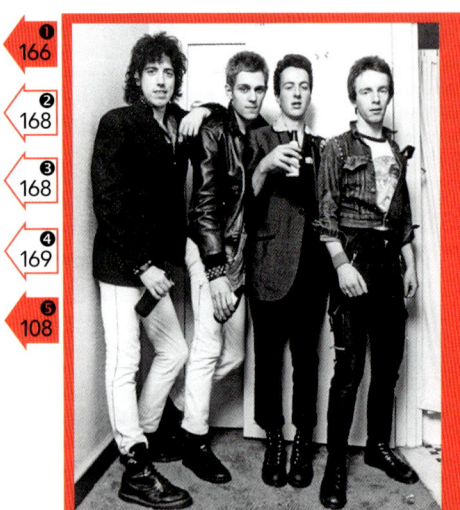

---

❶ 166
❷ 168
❸ 168
❹ 169
❺ 108

JULY 4, 1976: We are The Clash

Just three months after having his head spun by the Pistols❶, Strummer and his new band, The Clash (with Terry Chimes on drums), played their first show as support to Rotten & Co, in Sheffield, England, July 1976. The two bands played together several times over the ensuing months, notably at the Punk Festival (at the 100 Club, London) in September. The Clash (now trimmed to Strummer, Jones, Simonon, and Chimes) and Pistols played alongside The Damned❷, Buzzcocks, and Siouxsie & The Banshees❸ (featuring Sid Vicious❹). In December, they joined the Pistols' Anarchy tour (with Rob Harper on drums), then demoed future classics such as "White Riot" and "Janie Jones" (with Chimes). In January 1977, they signed to CBS and recorded their debut album. Chimes quit (later to return briefly, join Black Sabbath❺, and then become a chiropractor), and was replaced by Nicky "Topper" Headon, formerly of London SS.

170 SEX, DRUGS & ROCK 'N' ROLL

April 2, 1977

"White Riot" enters the U.K. chart. It is the first of numerous Clash singles to reach the top forty but miss the top ten.

April 30, 1977

The Clash's self-titled debut album hits the chart, to the envy of the Pistols (yet to finish theirs). According to Johnny Rotten, the band's appeal "is limited to England."

May 9, 1977

A White Riot tour date at London's Rainbow Theatre turns into a riot. The Jam promptly quit, leaving The Clash, The Subway Sect, and The Slits to continue.

April 30, 1978

The Clash headline a show in London for Rock Against Racism, founded in response to remarks made by Eric Clapton.

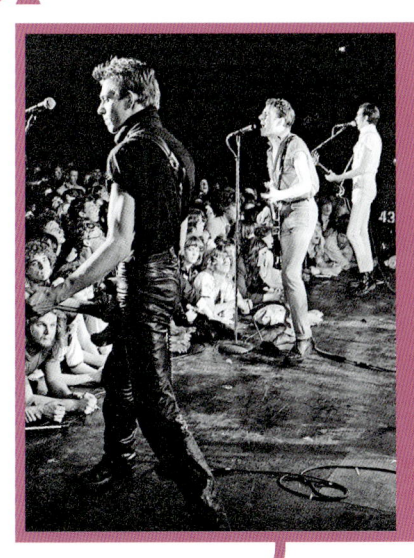

JUNE 16, 1978: "(White Man) In Hammersmith Palais"

❶ 044

Three months after the release of the dopey "Clash City Rockers," the Clash unleashed a single that demonstrated both their taste for ska and their musical superiority over their punk rivals: "(White Man) In Hammersmith Palais." Ironically, the eclectic tastes evident in this great track were submerged on the hard-rocking *Give 'Em Enough Rope*, produced by Blue Öyster Cult mastermind Sandy Pearlman (who didn't like Strummer's voice and mixed the drums higher). Nonetheless, the album just missed the top of the U.K. chart and, like their debut album, was well received across the Atlantic. The Clash played their first U.S. show on February 7, 1979, precisely fifteen years after The Beatles❶ had made their splash in the U.S.A.; their support was rock 'n' roll pioneer Bo Diddley. His influence and more fed into The Clash's masterpiece *London Calling*, released in December of the same year.

December 20, 1980

The dub-influenced triple album *Sandanista!* gets a baffled reception. "It was," Kurt Cobain will recall, "so bad."

April 1982

Headon is sacked for drug abuse. Ironically, his "Rock the Casbah" will be one of the most popular songs on their next album.

May 1982

Combat Rock is released. It will be their first album to go top ten on both sides of the Atlantic, spawn four hits, and be included in Kurt Cobain's top fifty albums.

October 12–13, 1982

The Clash support The Who at New York's Shea Stadium, famed for a 1965 Beatles concert (and closed in 2009 after star-studded Billy Joel shows).

MAY 28, 1983: The last gang in town

❶ 054
❷ 178
❸ 018

With Pete Howard replacing Terry Chimes (who had deputized for the sacked Headon), The Clash played a final show with Mick Jones in May 1983. Simonon and Strummer considered the band to have drifted too far from its ideals (hence the Stonesy❶ "Should I Stay or Should I Go"), and a makeshift lineup staggered through a final year, producing a classic in 1985, "This Is England." But *Cut the Crap* proved prophetic, and the band split in early 1986. Jones resurfaced with General Public (with members of The Beat and The Specials❷) and Big Audio Dynamite, and later produced The Libertines. Strummer scored movies, made solo albums, led The Pogues, and worked with artists including Johnny Cash❸. He was reunited with Jones onstage in London in November 2002, but hopes of a Clash reunion ended when Strummer died of a heart attack on December 22 that year, aged fifty.

THE CLASH 171

Blondie 1974–present

1974+   1983+

The band often deemed least likely to succeed out of their contemporaries—and looked down on by acts with whom they shared stages—wound up outselling them all. And—as the musical variety and image of Madonna ❿208▶, for example, prove—their influence was considerable, too.

Blondie were initially judged too poppy to thrive amid the angular guitars and harsh poetry of punk and new wave. In part, this lay with their influences—such as Buddy Holly ◀020❿, The Beatles ◀044❿, and The Shangri-Las. But there was also a backlash against Debbie Harry, whose gobsmacking beauty tended to overshadow both her songwriting and, to their enduring annoyance, that of her bandmates—early bassist Gary Valentine, for example, wrote the hit "(I'm Always Touched by Your) Presence Dear."

Blondie's repertoire ranged from rock to reggae, from rap to R&B. They proved to cynical executives that hip-hop and new wave-influenced music could compete in rock and disco-dominated charts. "We were," Harry observed, "fighting the idea that the only decent music was the Eagles ◀132❿ or Chicago."

Blondie hits have been covered by artists from The Smashing Pumpkins ("Dreaming") to Franz Ferdinand ("Atomic"). They, in turn, have sung the songs of Johnny Cash ◀018❿ ("Ring of Fire"), Buddy Holly ("I'm Gonna Love You Too"), David Bowie ❿134▶ ("Heroes"), and Marc Bolan ◀128❿ ("Get It On").

"Blondie I love," declared Annie Lennox. "For a certain type of sexual double entendre, Debbie Harry was very special for me—really special . . . more special than Madonna, definitely."

172 SEX, DRUGS & ROCK 'N' ROLL

August 1974
Debbie Harry, Chris Stein, and Fred Smith, formerly of New York bar band the Stilettos, form Angel & The Snake, soon to be renamed Blondie. (Smith will join Television in 1975.)

March 1, 1977
After a long battle to be taken seriously, Blondie release their self-titled debut album. They join Iggy Pop and David Bowie for the former's *The Idiot* tour.

November 1977
After October's *Plastic Letters*, the lineup solidifies around Harry, Stein, organist Jimmy Destri, drummer Clem Burke, bassist Nigel Harrison, and guitarist Frank Infante.

APRIL 28, 1979: "Heart of Glass" hits No. 1

When "Heart of Glass" topped the U.S. chart, it vindicated a band that had long been predicted to fail. But with that song's parent album *Parallel Lines* (1978), *Eat to the Beat* (1979), *Autoamerican* (1980), and *The Best of Blondie* (1981), the group outsold (on a multimillion scale) all of their CBGB❶ contemporaries. As brilliantly diverse as these albums were, Blondie are best remembered for their hit singles, including "Rapture" (the first rap-oriented U.S. No. 1), the reggae cover "The Tide Is High," and "Call Me," which producer Giorgio Moroder wrote with Harry after contractual issues prevented him working with Stevie Nicks❷. But the band were being torn apart by hard drugs, financial and managerial woes, and resentment of the focus on Harry and Stein. The singer's faltering solo career began with 1981's Chic-produced *Koo Koo*, before Blondie regrouped for the underrated *The Hunter*, then split in 1982.

❶ 160
❷ 095

February 4, 1983
Debbie Harry stars in the controversial movie *Videodrome*. Andy Warhol hails it as "a *Clockwork Orange* of the 1980s."

October 28, 1989
Def, Dumb & Blonde, the best of Harry's solo LPs, is issued. It reunites her with producer Mike Chapman, and Stein (who also worked on 1986's *Rockbird*).

June 28, 1990
Harry joins the Ramones and three of Talking Heads for a CBGB tour, and will report that Joey Ramone practices scales by singing his trademark "Hey ho, let's go!"

September 25, 1990
Debbie Harry and Iggy Pop's version of "Well, Did You Evah!" is a highlight of the Cole Porter covers album *Red Hot + Blue*, which also features U2 and Tom Waits.

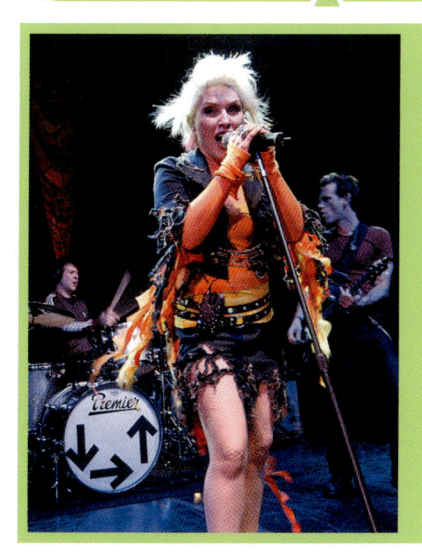

FEBRUARY 13, 1999: "Maria" and the comeback

"I never thought we would get back together," said Harry. "But Chris thought we'd regret not doing it before we were too old." Blondie—Harry, Stein, Burke, Destri, and hired hands—began a reunion tour in October 1998. The following February, "Maria" made them the first band to have U.K. chart-toppers in three different decades. The resurrection yielded *No Exit* (1999) and *The Curse of Blondie* (2003), after which Destri was cut from the touring lineup, reportedly because of substance abuse. In 2006, Blondie were inducted into the Rock and Roll Hall of Fame by Shirley Manson of Garbage, who called them "one of the coolest, most glamorous, most stylish bands in the history of rock 'n' roll." The night was blighted by grumbling from Frank Infante and Nigel Harrison, who had sued their former bandmates and found themselves unwelcome onstage. The band's legacy transcends such pettiness.

BLONDIE   173

Prince 1958–present

1958+   1980+   1987+   1996+

Over the years, Prince has played guitar like a god, danced in ways that made Michael Jackson ◁122 look, as one reviewer remarked, "nailed to the floor," and knocked Bruce Springsteen ◁150 off chart summits. However, only someone who has never heard Sly Stone or George Clinton would regard him as a one-off genius; both are influences whom he has frequently acknowledged.

"He's extraordinary," observed Bono of U2 192▷. "Add all those great tunes up." They include ones sung by Sinéad O'Connor ("Nothing Compares 2 U"), Chaka Khan ("I Feel for You"), Gary Numan ("1999"), the Foo Fighters ("Darling Nikki"), the Eels ("I Could Never Take the Place of Your Man"), Alicia Keys ("How Come U Don't Call Me Anymore"), Tina Turner ("Let's Pretend We're Married"), Cyndi Lauper ("When You Were Mine"), Richard Thompson ("Kiss"), Patti Smith ◁164 ("When Doves Cry"), and The Bangles ("Manic Monday"), to name but a few.

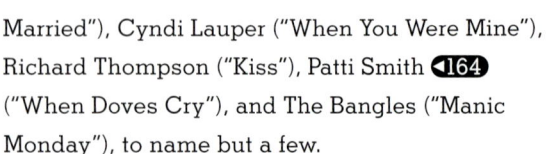

He has worked with Kate Bush, Sly Stone's bass player Larry Graham, Lenny Kravitz, Madonna, and talented protégés, including The Time (with future top producers Jimmy Jam and Terry Lewis), and Wendy & Lisa. "He definitely does things from the right attitude," said David Gilmour of Pink Floyd ◁086. "He goes out of his way to get the best people to do the best job, and thinks about every detail."

"He's so talented," enthused Kate Bush. "Very prolific, but very consistent." "A thoroughbred," said Miles Davis. "He's like an Arabian breed." Or, as Elton John ◁126 said, "He's a prat, but a clever prat."

SEX, DRUGS & ROCK 'N' ROLL

June 7, 1958

Prince Rogers Nelson is born in Minneapolis. To the dismay of future collaborator Madonna ("I couldn't stand Minneapolis"), he stays there.

June 25, 1977

Prince signs to Warner Bros., insisting: "If I deliver you rock 'n' roll, don't come back to me and say I can't do it because I'm black."

October 1, 1977

Recording begins on his debut *For You*. It will only be a minor success, but yields a hit—"Soft and Wet"—whose lyrics point where Prince will be heading.

FEBRUARY 21, 1980: *Prince* turns platinum

While 1977's *For You* had proved Prince's versatility, 1979's *Prince* showcased his songwriting (including "I Feel for You"). Bolstered by the infectious hit "I Wanna Be Your Lover," it earned Prince his first platinum disc the day before he began a U.S. tour supporting fellow funk rocker Rick "Super Freak" James❶. Despite their superficial similarities, the pair loathed each other: "Prince wasn't into [James'] world," said his drummer Bobby Z, "which was a lot of booze, a lot of pot, a lot of cocaine." James, in turn, sniped: "Long as he's in that pantyhose, he can *forget* it." Bob Marley❷ had a similar reaction when he met Prince at a Hollywood show in November 1979: associates had hoped that the two might work together, but Prince's attire—a leopard-print G-string—did nothing to put the reggae legend at ease, and nothing came of it. Not that this convinced the Minneapolis maestro to clean up his act.

❶ 080
❷ 130

October 8, 1980

A "thanks" to Joni Mitchell is the only tasteful aspect of *Dirty Mind*, which boasts songs about incest and oral sex. It is, naturally, brilliant.

January 14, 1982

Controversy turns gold. It has repaired the damage done by *Dirty Mind* and includes a song that will be a favorite of Kylie Minogue, "Private Joy."

January 1983

An uncredited Prince plays keyboard on Stevie Nicks' "Stand Back," inspired by "Little Red Corvette," from his latest hit album, *1999*.

August 20, 1983

Prince and Michael Jackson guest at a James Brown show at the Beverly Theater in L.A. "I think he was a little nervous," says Brown.

AUGUST 4, 1984: *Purple Rain* bumps The Boss

In the wake of Prince's first U.S. No. 1 single, "When Doves Cry," *Purple Rain* displaced Bruce Springsteen's❶ *Born in the U.S.A.* atop the album chart. Having spent twenty-four weeks at the summit, thanks to five hits and the movie that it soundtracked, *Purple Rain* was followed to the top less than four months after relinquishing its pole position by his *Around the World in a Day*—clearly indebted to the psychedelic soul of George Clinton❷ and Sly Stone❸. Thanks to "Raspberry Beret" and "Pop Life," this album went double platinum in just over a month. As the hysteria died down, the kaleidoscopic *Parade* (1986) and *Sign o' the Times* (1987) sold a mere million each at home, but "Kiss" topped the chart (keeping his "Manic Monday," sung by The Bangles, at No. 2). Meanwhile, Michael Jackson's❹ producer Quincy Jones tried to enlist Prince to duet on the title track of *Bad*. The response? "I just don't do that kind of stuff."

❶ 150
❷ 143
❸ 024
❹ 122

PRINCE 175

December 1, 1987

Prince cancels the release of his so-called *Black Album*, creating one of music's best-selling bootlegs. It will limp out in 1994 to fulfill his contract with Warner Bros.

May 21, 1988

Prince's poorest-selling album at home since 1980, *Lovesexy* —featuring the hits "Alphabet Street" and "Glam Slam"—is his first U.K. chart-topper.

April 22, 1989

Madonna's *Like a Prayer*, featuring Prince, tops the U.S. chart. She will (luckily for her) decline to appear in his forthcoming *Graffiti Bridge* movie.

July 22, 1989

Batman restores Prince to the top of the chart. It will yield the hits "Batdance" and "Partyman," and soon turn double platinum.

1990–96: *Chaos and Disorder*

Changing his name to an unpronounceable symbol and feuding with Warner Bros. did Prince's already eccentric image no favors. The nutty behavior masked moments of triumph: *Graffiti Bridge* (1990), *Symbol* (1992), and *Come* (1993) topped the U.K. chart; *Diamonds and Pearls* (1991) was his first Australian No. 1 album and yielded the U.S. chart-topper "Cream"; *The Hits* (1993) went platinum; and *The Gold Experience* (1995) was his best since *Lovesexy*. Even *Chaos and Disorder* (1996), issued to fulfill his contract, was better than its rush release suggested. Best was the soundtrack to Spike Lee's 1996 movie *Girl 6*, with rarities and classics such as Vanity 6's Prince-penned "Nasty Girl." However, Prince's crowning moments came courtesy of two hits: Sinéad O'Connor's reading of "Nothing Compares 2 U" (1990) and his first U.K. No. 1 single, "The Most Beautiful Girl in the World" (1994).

November 19, 1996

Emancipation, the artist's first post-Warner album, is released, with versions of hits by Bonnie Raitt, Joan Osborne, and The Delfonics.

January 29, 1998

His self-released *Crystal Ball* album rounds up previously unreleased material. Warner will follow suit in 1999 with *The Vault: Old Friends 4 Sale*.

December 10, 1999

Featuring Sheryl Crow, Eve, Gwen Stefani, Chuck D of Public Enemy, Ani DiFranco, and Maceo Parker, *Rave Un2 the Joy Fantastic* goes gold in the U.S.A.

November 20, 2001

Having changed his name back from the symbol, Prince issues *The Rainbow Children*, leading to the One Nite Alone . . . tour.

❶ 264

❷ 144

❸ 062

FEBRUARY 8, 2004: "Workin' up a black sweat . . ."

As a new decade dawned, Prince was adrift in what Thom Yorke of Radiohead❶ called "Prince territory . . . three albums a year [and] no quality control." Releases such as *N.E.W.S.* (2003) sold to a diminishing fan base while customers lapped up *The Very Best of Prince* (2002). But in 2004, he signaled his comeback, performing "Purple Rain" and "Baby, I'm a Star" with Beyoncé (left) at the Grammys. That year's *Musicology* crashed into the U.S. top three, as did *3121* (2006), *Planet Earth* (2007), and *LOtUSFLOW3R* (2009). In 2007, audiences thrilled to his Superbowl half-time show (featuring covers of Queen's❷ "We Will Rock You," Dylan's❸ "All Along the Watchtower," Creedence Clearwater Revival's "Proud Mary," and the Foo Fighters' "Best of You") and a record-breaking run at London's O2 arena. As he said, tongue (as ever) in cheek, at the Grammys, "Don't hate us 'cos we fabulous!"

SEX, DRUGS & ROCK 'N' ROLL

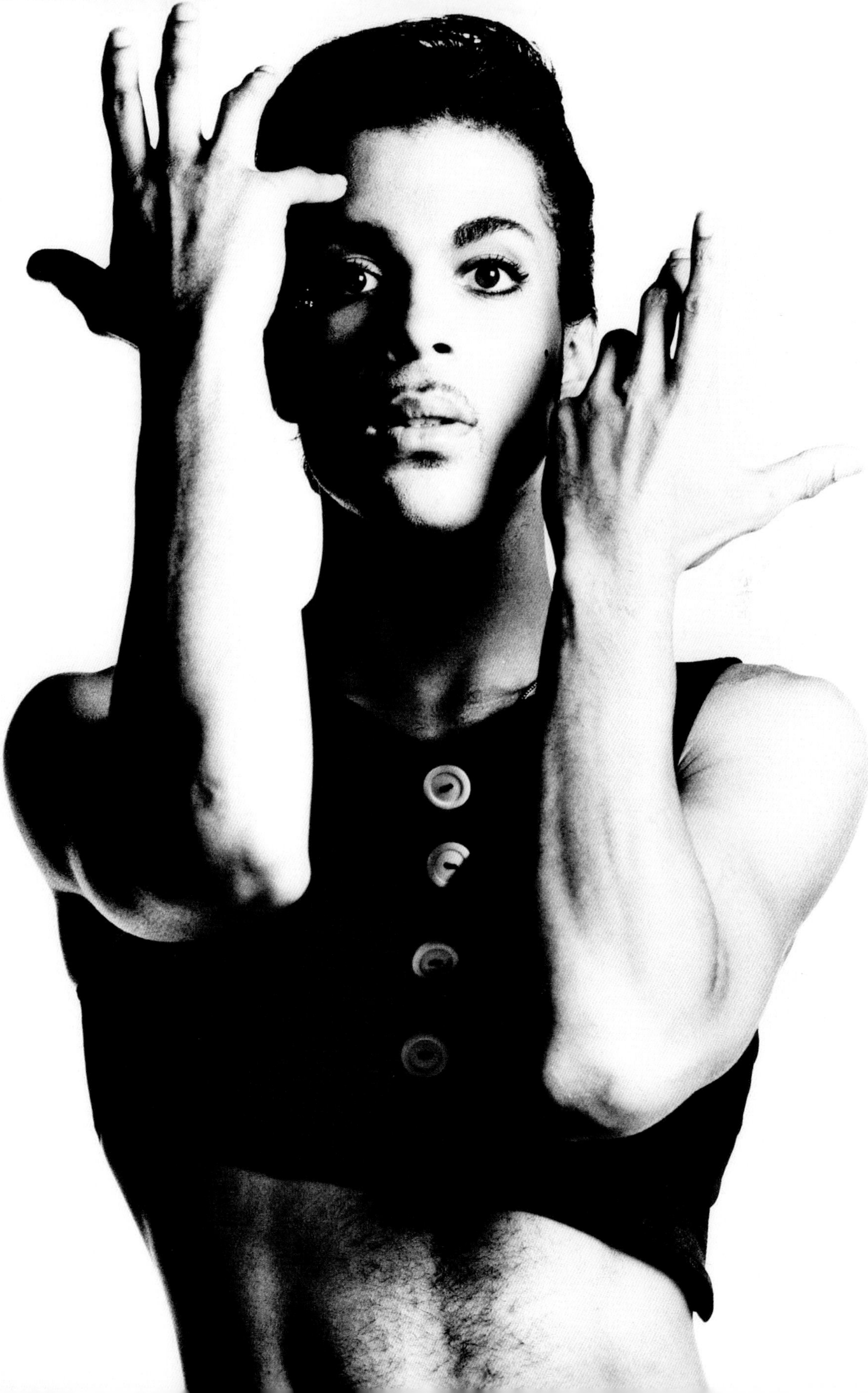

The Specials 1977–present

1977+ 1981+

The British blend of ska, punk, and pop called 2Tone spawned several fine bands, including The (English) Beat, The Selecter, and Madness. But the market leader was The Specials, a collective from Coventry in the U.K.'s West Midlands. And, for a very British band (despite their roots in Jamaica), The Specials had a far-reaching influence.

As a young girl growing up in Florida, Gwen Stefani listened to "Madness, The Specials, and The Selecter—it was really underground." (The impact of 2Tone is evident in Stefani's band, No Doubt.)

Having turned down production requests from U2 **192**, Madonna **208**, and David Bowie **134**, Liam Howlett of the Prodigy **252** said: "If [Specials singer] Terry Hall would have come up to me and said something, maybe I would have said, 'Yeah, great.'"

In 2009, Amy Winehouse made a long overdue live return—singing "You're Wondering Now" and "Ghost Town" with the band at a U.K. festival.

And The Specials almost had an even bigger link with rock royalty: Mick Jagger went to a show in May 1979, with a view to signing them to the Rolling Stones' **054** label. But legend has it that he was put out to discover the similarity of their "Little Bitch" to "Brown Sugar" and decided against it.

In some of the bravest singles to hit their home country's chart, The Specials tackled civil unrest ("Ghost Town"), Apartheid ("Nelson Mandela"), bigotry ("Racist Friend"), and rape ("The Boiler").

And, after their hard-fought but ultimately triumphant reunion, as Hall observed, "I'm now more aware of what The Specials mean to people."

1977

Organist Jerry Dammers, guitarist Lynval Golding, and bassist Horace Panter form The Coventry Automatics, who will become The Special A.K.A. the following year.

June 28, 1979

With guitarist Roddy Radiation and singer Terry Hall, the band begin a U.K. tour with The Clash and Suicide. Neville Staples will join the band in London.

November 3, 1979

Bolstered by their second top ten single ("A Message to You, Rudy"/"Nite Klub"), *Specials* (produced by Elvis Costello) begins a forty-five-week stay on the U.K. album chart.

FEBRUARY 2, 1980: Teen pregnancy goes to the top

The Specials' most extraordinary year began when *The Special A.K.A. Live! EP*—featuring the teen pregnancy warning "Too Much Too Young"—topped the U.K. chart. It was followed into the top five by "Rat Race," "Stereotype," "Do Nothing," and, in October, *More Specials*. However, the seeds of destruction had been sown at the start of the year, when the group played a punishing series of U.S. shows. "That really broke the spirit of the band," Dammers rued. "Everybody stopped getting on." An alcohol-fueled U.K. tour strained relations even further, and they were depressed by the violence that seemed to follow them. This helped inspire 1981's gothic dub masterpiece "Ghost Town" but, as that hit No. 1, the band splintered. Terry Hall, Lynval Golding, and Neville Staples formed Fun Boy Three, while Panter would resurface with The (English) Beat's Dave Wakeling in General Public.

June 12, 1981

The Go-Go's release "Our Lips Are Sealed." Its Terry Hall-penned lyrics draw on his relationship with Go-Go co-writer Jane Weidlin.

January 23, 1982

With singer Rhoda Dakar, The Specials scrape into the chart with "The Boiler." They will be eclipsed by smashes from Fun Boy Three (with Bananarama).

March 17, 1984

"Nelson Mandela" provides a rebirth for the Dammers-led Special A.K.A. It brings South African icon Mandela to public attention.

October 14, 2002

The Prodigy's cover version of "Ghost Town" gets a belated commercial release on the charity compilation album *1 Love*.

SEPTEMBER 6, 2008: The comeback kicks off

After Fun Boy Three faltered, Terry Hall (left) drifted through the indifferently received The Colourfield; Terry, Blair & Anouchka; and—with Dave Stewart of Eurythmics—Vegas. Cameos with the Lightning Seeds, Gorillaz❶, and Tricky maintained his elder statesman status. Meanwhile, Dammers translated his "Nelson Mandela" success into Artists Against Apartheid, which peaked with a seventieth birthday show for the by-this-stage free Mandela at London's Wembley Stadium in 1988. In 2003, attempts were made at a Specials reunion—but, as Lynval Golding told *Mojo*, "Jerry said that if we reformed the band without him in it, he was going to sue us." Ultimately, this was what they did—kicking off a well-received reunion at U.K.'s Bestival in 2008. "One or two barbed comments," remarked drummer John Bradbury, "have been trampled under the feet of the seventy thousand who were desperate to see us play."

❶ 274

THE SPECIALS 179

super producer

Mutt Lange
1948–present

To the public he is known (if at all) as the husband of country superstar Shania Twain. But to rock fans, Robert John "Mutt" Lange is the sonic wizard behind classic albums by AC/DC 182▶, The Cars, Def Leppard, and many more.

"The most easy-going dictator you'll ever meet," was Leppard guitarist Phil Collen's verdict on the publicity-shy producer. "He certainly knows how to stamp his foot if he wants to," declared Foreigner founder Mick Jones. To Meat Loaf's right-hand man Jim Steinman, whose productions are equally huge, "Mutt's like Frankenstein—he pieces little bits of skin together. I'm a big fan of the guy. I think he's one of the most brilliant producers in the world."

He is, if nothing else, spectacularly successful. Two of his productions—Twain's *Come on Over* and AC/DC's *Back in Black*—rank among the all-time top ten best-sellers, with U.S. sales alone topping, respectively, twenty and twenty-two million copies. Lange also co-wrote and produced Bryan Adams' Grammy-winning *Robin Hood: Prince of Thieves* theme "(Everything I Do) I Do It for You," one of the most successful songs of the past twenty years. Adams and Lange struck gold again with "Have You Ever Really Loved a Woman?". (Like "(Everything I Do) . . . ," this was written with Michael Kamen, the orchestrator who worked with the likes of Metallica 218▶ and Pink Floyd ◀086 before his death in 2003.)

Three decades ago, Lange even caught the eye of Michael Jackson ◀122, who recommended him to Kiss man Gene Simmons. Unluckily—for them—neither Jackson nor Kiss employed him.

1948+
1980+
1981+

November 11, 1948
Robert John "Mutt" Lange is born in Mufulira, Zambia. He will move to South Africa and, by 1970, be a sound engineer and a member of Hocus.

July 8, 1978
"5-7-0-5" is a British hit for City Boy. It is produced by Lange, who has moved to London and will produce the likes of Graham Parker.

November 18, 1978
The Lange-produced "Rat Trap" by the Boomtown Rats tops the U.K. chart. Main man Bob Geldof will later mastermind Live Aid.

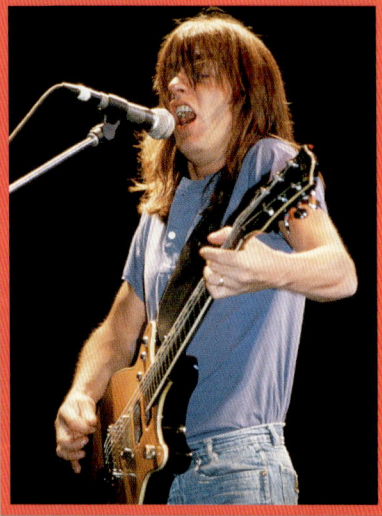

❶ 054
❷ 098
❸ 072
❹ 182

MARCH 18, 1980: AC/DC's platinum *Hell*

Despite working with The Rolling Stones❶, Led Zeppelin❷, and Jimi Hendrix❸, engineer-turned-producer Eddie Kramer did not gel with AC/DC❹. "We said to our manager, 'This guy's got to go, otherwise you're not going to have a band,'" guitarist Malcolm Young (left) told *Mojo*. The manager "did a bit of wheeling-dealing and got a tape to a friend of his, Mutt Lange. We [the band] told Kramer, 'We're having tomorrow off, we need a break,' and we went in and wrote nine songs in a day and whacked them off to Mutt. He got straight back and said he wanted to do it." The partnership was made in hard rock heaven. *Highway to Hell* (a phrase used by Malcolm's brother, Angus, to describe touring the U.S.A.) was a smash around the world—it has sold seven million in the U.S.A. alone—and paved the way for Lange's work on the band's *Back in Black* (1981) and *For Those About to Rock (We Salute You)* (1982).

180 SEX, DRUGS & ROCK 'N' ROLL

April–May 1980

AC/DC record the classic *Back in Black*. "Mutt helped with the arrangements," reported recording engineer Tony Platt, "and everybody pitched in a bit with lyrics."

October 13, 1980

Back in Black earns its first platinum award in the U.S.A. It will be ten times platinum by 1990, and twenty-two by 2007—the same year the title track turns double platinum.

June 22, 1981

"Urgent" is the first single on Foreigner's *4*. Produced by Lange, it features Junior Walker and Thomas Dolby, and will feature in 1985 film *Desperately Seeking Susan*.

July 11, 1981

Def Leppard release *High 'n' Dry*, their first album with Lange. It will go gold in the U.S.A. even before 1983's *Pyromania* turns the band into mega superstars.

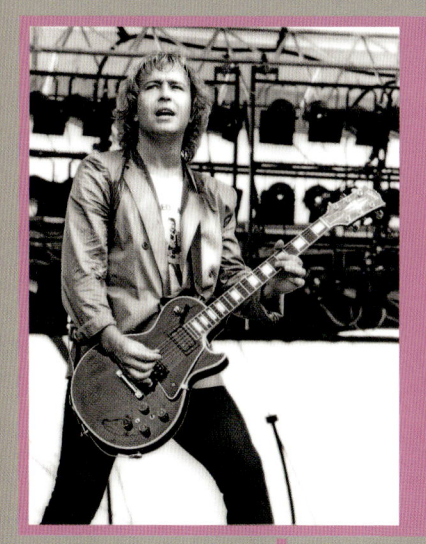

AUGUST 22, 1981: Foreigner top the U.S. chart

Eight months of hard work went into Foreigner's fourth album. "Not every day was total intensity," founder and guitarist Mick Jones (left) told *Sounds*, "but a good deal of that time was very, very intense, especially between Mutt Lange and myself. We just wouldn't let up on each other. He's very intense, and it's a question of durability—how much you can take of that kind of pressure and challenging each other all the time . . . I think it was the first time he'd ever worked with somebody in the way we worked together, on a kind of equal production basis, having to share the decision. It took us a little while to adjust, and what really kept the spark there was the fact that we just wouldn't let up on each other." The battle proved worthwhile: *4* spawned the hits "Urgent," "Waiting for a Girl Like You," and "Juke Box Hero." It was the band's only U.S. chart-topping album and sold six million copies in the U.S.A. alone.

December 26, 1981

AC/DC's *For Those About to Rock* hits the U.S. No. 1. The band had tried studios in Paris before recording in a rehearsal room that met Lange's sonic requirements.

May 1982

Written (but not produced) by Lange, "Do You Believe in Love?" is the breakthrough U.S. hit that Huey Lewis & The News have been looking for.

April 11, 1983

Pyromania by Def Leppard turns platinum in the U.S.A. (a feat it will achieve nine more times). The Lange-helmed gem will be held off No. 1 only by *Thriller*.

July 23, 1984

"Drive," from The Cars' *Heartbeat City*, is released. Produced by Lange, it will later soundtrack a moving video clip of the Ethiopian famine during Live Aid.

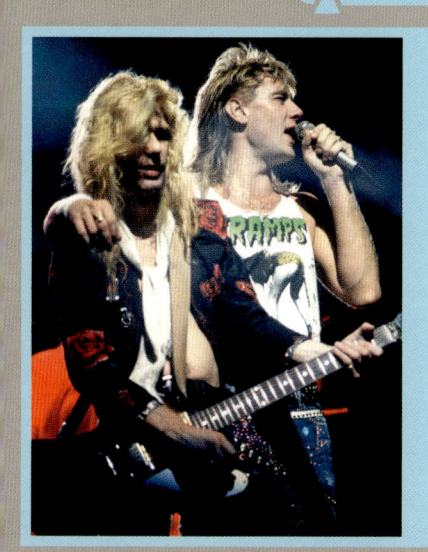

JULY 23, 1988: Leppard's *Hysteria* hits U.S. No. 1

The success of *Hysteria* was the culmination of years of turmoil for Def Leppard. In the aftermath of *Pyromania*, drummer Rick Allen had lost an arm in a car crash, while guitarist Steve Clark had become an alcoholic —reportedly leading Lange to use Clark's compadre Phil Collen for most of the album. Lange had declined to produce Leppard's fourth outing, citing exhaustion after years of nonstop work. But after the band had worked on it for more than a year—including three wasted months with Jim Steinman—he agreed to help salvage the project. Among his key contributions was to help vocalist Joe Elliott turn "Pour Some Sugar on Me" into a hit. "The album was doing well in America," said the singer (left, with Clark), "but, by the time 'Sugar' came out and really kicked in, [it] started selling almost a million copies a month for the next five months." It eventually went platinum twelve times.

AC/DC 1973–present

1973+ 1981+

AC/DC enjoy such a hallowed status that criticism seems heretical. This is due to their canon of classics and their unstinting faith in a formula —swaggering, rude, and very loud hard rock— that has endured for more than three decades.

Every metal band has a song that sounds like AC/DC, and everyone else likes at least one of their songs. "I'd love nothing better," said Joe Perry of Aerosmith ◀154, "than to play some AC/DC songs." Much of this affection is based on albums featuring singer Bon Scott, when the music was derived from the good-time boogie of Chuck Berry. "[Of] the early stuff," enthused Keith Richards of The Rolling Stones ◀054, "*Powerage* is the one. When everybody else was getting into cleverness and synthesizing . . . these cats [were] laying it out."

But the replacement of Scott with Brian Johnson hardly harmed the band's fortunes, with multi-platinum albums and sold-out tours remaining the norm. "I used to love AC/DC with Bon Scott," said Joey Ramone ◀158, "but the other guy is good, too. He looks like a cab driver, but he's a good guy."

The esteem in which they are held is not always reciprocal. In one interview with *Mojo*, band founder Malcolm Young—brother of the school uniform-clad Angus (and of George Young of The Easybeats, whose "Friday on My Mind was covered by David Bowie ◀134)—dismissed the Sex Pistols ◀166 ("couldn't fucking play"), The Faces ("a shit sound"), Iggy Pop ◀116 ("the talent wasn't there"), and Led Zeppelin ◀098 ("the singer's a bit of a bullshit artist, there's too much echo, and the fucking solos are too long").

182 SEX, DRUGS & ROCK 'N' ROLL

December 31, 1973

Angus and Malcolm Young play a first show together in Sydney. Their band will become AC/DC, and they will be the only members to appear on every album.

April 5, 1977

AC/DC begin a European tour supporting metal gods Black Sabbath. The new *Let There Be Rock* is their first album to chart in the U.K., Australian, and U.S. charts.

December 6, 1979

Highway to Hell earns AC/DC a first gold record in the U.S.A. The title track will be covered by acts ranging from Marilyn Manson to Maroon 5, and will be featured in *The Simpsons*.

FEBRUARY 19, 1980: Bon Scott—a touch too much

Since replacing original singer Dave Evans in 1974, Bon Scott (left) had defined the band as much as the Young brothers had with their earth-shaking riffs. From his lascivious lyrics on "Whole Lotta Rosie" to his bagpipes on "It's a Long Way to the Top (If You Wanna Rock 'n' Roll)," Scott embodied the mischief that distinguished AC/DC from their hard rock contemporaries. In his own words: "People say to me, 'Are you AC or DC?,' and I say, 'Neither—I'm the lightnin' flash in the middle.'" In 1980, he died after a night of drinking, etching himself into rock legend. "All people would say about Bon was that he was this creature from the gutter," Angus Young told *Kerrang!*. "No one would take him seriously. Then, after he died, all of a sudden he was a great poet. Even he himself would have been laughing at that." The band recruited Brian Johnson and made the greatest tribute of all: *Back in Black*.

March 9, 1981

More than seven months after its release, the U.K chart-topping *Back in Black* gives AC/DC a first No. 1 at home in Australia.

September 14, 1985

Rick Rubin attends an AC/DC show in New Jersey and plays the Beastie Boys' debut "Rock Hard" (which samples "Back in Black") to Angus and Malcolm.

September 26, 1995

Ballbreaker, co-produced by Rick Rubin, marks the return of drummer Phil Rudd, after twelve years in which Simon Wright and then Chris Slade had deputized for him.

January 22, 2001

Belated awards for *Flick of the Switch* (1983) and *Fly on the Wall* (1985) mean every AC/DC album issued in the U.S. is now platinum.

OCTOBER 17, 2008: *Black Ice* conquers the world

In the eight years since 2000's *Stiff Upper Lip* (the band's first album produced by George Young since 1978), AC/DC had been inducted into the Rock and Roll Hall of Fame by Steven Tyler of Aerosmith❶ ("Does it make you wanna boil your sneakers and make soup out of your girlfriend's panties? If it doesn't, then it ain't AC/DC") and played with The Rolling Stones❷, and Brian Johnson (left with Angus Young) had developed a musical about Helen of Troy. Then, in 2008, *Black Ice* topped charts in nearly thirty countries and, a month later, earned double platinum status in the U.S.A. (a year after *Back in Black* collected its twenty-second platinum award for U.S. sales alone). In 2010, after a spectacular tour, AC/DC assembled a greatest hits set in all but name for the *Iron Man 2* soundtrack. While Johnson has expressed doubts about how long he can continue as singer, this rock 'n' roll train, for now, keeps a-rollin'.

❶ 154
❷ 054

AC/DC 183

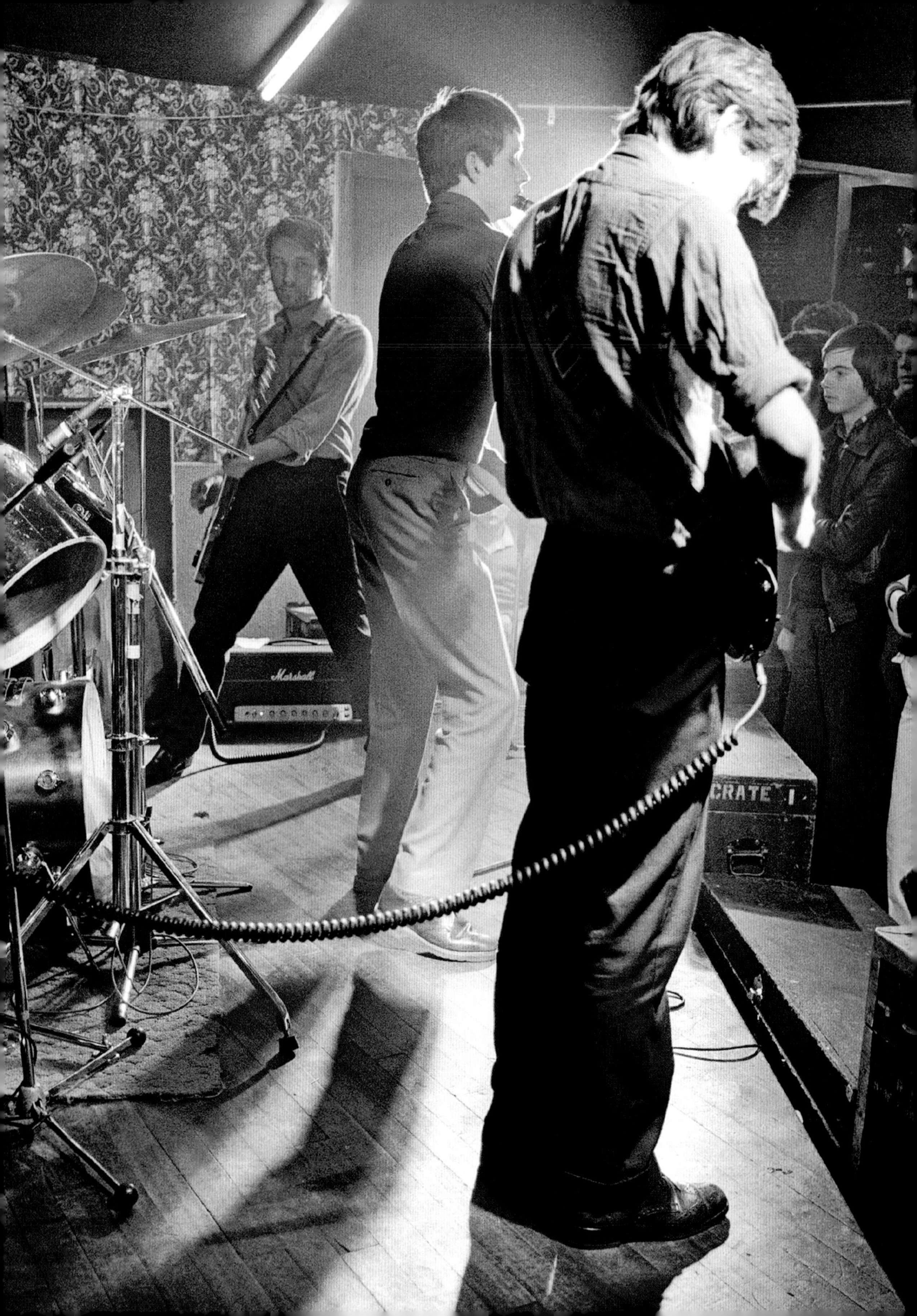
Marshall
CRATE 1

Joy Division
1976–80

Joy Division didn't explode on to the late Seventies post-punk scene; they electrified it. "It would be hard to find a darker place in music than Joy Division . . . Yet I sensed the pursuit of God, or light, or reason . . . or reason to be," recalled Bono of U2's 192▶ visit to the recording of Joy Division's seminal "Love Will Tear Us Apart." "In amongst the squalor of everyday life, they were building with their music some kind of cathedral." It was a dark, cavernous northern gothic cathedral, built on odes to bleak, postindustrial northwest England.

> **"'She's Lost Control'—that song meant so much to me when I was younger."**
> —Courtney Love

Their electro-gothic shadow continues to loom large three decades after their demise, influencing acts such as The Cure, The Smashing Pumpkins, Interpol, Editors, and White Lies.

Like many teenagers of the Seventies, the band's singer Ian Curtis was inspired by David Bowie ◀134, and he even named his band Warsaw after Bowie's "Warszawa" (from the album *Low*). Warsaw—soon to change their name to Joy Division (borrowed from a term for the prostitution wing of Nazi concentration camps)—had been inspired by two seminal Sex Pistols ◀166 gigs at Manchester's Lesser Free Trade Hall in the summer of 1976, described by bass player Peter Hook as "like a car crash. You had the blinding flash that you could do it."

Curtis' dark brooding lyrics—enhanced by Stephen Morris' relentless drums and Bernard Sumner and Peter Hook's trademark guitars—reflected his alienation and desperation to escape the band's bleak environment. Sumner, too, said, "For me, Joy Division was about the death of my community and my childhood."

Joy Division's early classic tunes included "Transmission" (covered by The Smashing Pumpkins) and "Dead Souls" (covered by Nine Inch Nails). As Anthony Wilson—founder of the legendary Manchester record label Factory, to which the band was signed—put it: "Punk enabled you to say 'Fuck you,' but somehow it couldn't go any further. Sooner or later, someone was going to want to say, 'I'm fucked,' and that was Joy Division."

While most of their peers were steeped in punk guitars, Joy Division—influenced by Kraftwerk ◀148—were among the first to incorporate primitive drum machines. This gave their music a relentless, hypnotic rhythm, which grounded their violent energy and Curtis' sometimes abstract words.

Yet just as the band's sound was evolving with the release of the landmark debut album *Unknown Pleasures* in 1979, Curtis began to fall apart. It was difficult to tell whether his whirling dervish stage performances were real or caused by the epileptic fits to which he became increasingly prone.

After listening continuously to *The Idiot* by Iggy Pop ◀116, and watching Werner Herzog's *Stroszeck* (about a musician who commits suicide), Curtis hanged himself in 1980. Sadly, his band's true importance was never revealed in his lifetime.

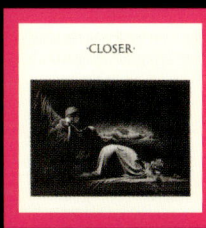

A somber synth classic, *Closer* (1980) reached No. 6 in the U.K., following its release soon after Curtis' death. Peter Saville's cover design, featuring a tomb, amplifies the funereal feel.

Still (1981), Joy Division's highest charting album (it reached No. 5 in the U.K.), is a collection of previously unused studio material and a recording of the band's last concert.

The Cure and Joy Division share the bill

If The Cure's Robert Smith (left) is to be believed, he didn't listen to his peers in the 1980s. "I would be more familiar with Janet Jackson [1] than I was with The Teardrop Explodes or Joy Division, because I didn't want to listen to my competitors for fear of nicking ideas off them," he told the *Guardian*. However, nods to Joy Division's doomed laments can be heard in The Cure's *Disintegration* (1989). Both bands released debut singles in 1978, but The Cure achieved success more rapidly: indeed, Joy Division supported them at London's Marquee club [2] in March 1979. The Cure also appeared to borrow an idea or two from New Order—on hearing the former's single "In Between Days," Peter Hook's mother told him, "You've got to sort this out, our Peter!" Robert Smith named Joy Division's "The Eternal" as one of his favorite songs of the Eighties, and The Cure have covered "Love Will Tear Us Apart."

Joy Division

1976
Inspired by seminal Sex Pistols gigs in Manchester, Bernard Dicken (later Sumner) and Peter Hook form Stiff Kittens. They will soon recruit vocalist Ian Curtis to form a new band.

May 1977
The band debuts as Warsaw, supporting the Buzzcocks in Manchester. Their star will rise as Joy Division—the name under which they will play their first gig in January 1978.

1979 Connection

July 1979
As their intense shows gain attention, the landmark debut album *Unknown Pleasures* (which includes "She's Lost Control") is issued to good reviews but negligible sales.

May 18, 1980
Shortly after the release of "Love Will Tear Us Apart," and two days before the group is due to embark on a tour of the U.S.A., Ian Curtis commits suicide, aged twenty-three.

Influence 1980

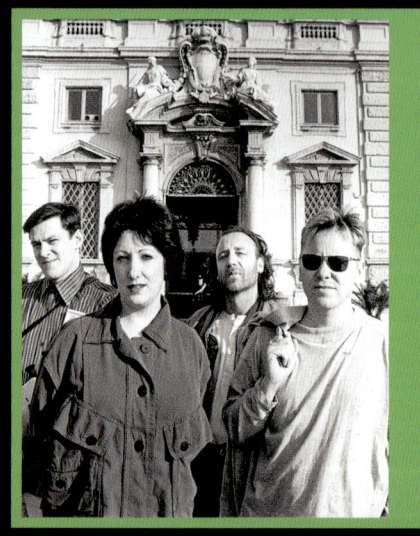

The emergence of a New Order

Out of Joy Division's ashes rose New Order (the name, chosen to imply change, drew the same accusations of fascism as their previous title), with the addition of Gillian Gilbert, Stephen Morris' girlfriend, on drums and keyboards. Initially, the group struggled to exorcise Ian Curtis' ghost. "For ages it just felt like a square peg in a round hole," admitted Barney Sumner of his first attempts to fill the singer's shoes. However, inspired by visits to New York and, later, Ibiza, they became more dance oriented, creating exemplary hits such as "Bizarre Love Triangle" (1986) and "True Faith" (1987). "Blue Monday" (1983) became the best-selling twelve-inch single of all time, the sales of which were used to keep afloat the Manchester club The Hacienda (co-owned by New Order). After a five-year hiatus from 1993, New Order reformed (and added Joy Division songs to their live sets), and then called it a day in 2007.

A Smashing Pumpkin tours the U.S.A.

Billy Corgan of The Smashing Pumpkins (left) was so enamored with Joy Division that he jumped at the chance to tour the U.S.A. with New Order in 2001. "Joy Division were a heavy metal band," he said later (they and the Pumpkins were Black Sabbath❶ fans). Like many a band before and since, the Pumpkins have covered "Love Will Tear Us Apart." They also borrowed the lesser known "Glass" (from *Still*) for a cut of their own, while their best-loved song, "1979," and several on 2000's *Machina*, owe a clear debt to the melancholy Mancunians. Another fan joining New Order on that tour was Moby. "We did a cover of 'New Dawn Fades,'" he told MTV. "It was the first time they had played it since Ian Curtis killed himself, so it meant a lot to me. We recorded it with Billy Corgan playing guitar and [Red Hot Chili Pepper❷] John Frusciante. It came out so well, we decided to put it on the *24 Hour Party People* soundtrack."

❶ 108
❷ 232

1993
In the documentary video *New Order Story* (featuring Quincy Jones and U2's Bono), Peter Hook is asked to name the laziest member of the band. "Ian Curtis," he replies.

2001 Connection

November 2002
"Love Will Tear Us Apart" is voted best single of all time by *NME*. It will be issued for a fourth time in 2007. Its title appears on the Macclesfield tombstone of Ian Curtis.

May 17, 2007
Joy Division photographer Anton Corbijn's directorial debut—the Ian Curtis biopic *Control* (based on *Touching from a Distance*)—premieres at the Cannes film festival.

1995
Ian Curtis' widow, Deborah, publishes her memoir *Touching from a Distance*, which details their difficult marriage, Curtis' affair, and the impact of his epilepsy.

February 13, 2002
The U.K. film *24 Hour Party People* premieres. It tells the story of the rise and fall of the Factory label, in comic style, bringing the once mythical Joy Division to a wider audience.

Connection 2007

September 7, 2007
Joy Division, Grant Gee's documentary about the band, premieres in Toronto, but coincides with a war of words between New Order's estranged Hook and Sumner.

The Killers in *Control*

Latter-day post-punk groups such as Interpol, Editors, and The Killers❶ are often compared with Joy Division, whether they like it or not (Interpol, for one, always brush off any such comparisons). The Killers have no option but to acknowledge the legacy because their name comes from that of a fictional band in a New Order video. "I'm a bigger New Order fan than Joy Division fan," confessed singer Brandon Flowers. "I got jealous when I heard a New Order album," he told *Rolling Stone*. "That was the starting point when I started really pursuing music." (He specifically cites "Shellshock" on the *Pretty in Pink* soundtrack.) Nonetheless, The Killers contributed a cover of Joy Division's "Shadowplay" to the soundtrack of the Ian Curtis biopic *Control* (2007). It was blasted by Joy Division fans at the time for being too upbeat, but that hasn't stopped The Killers including "Shadowplay" in the setlists of subsequent tours.

❶ 280

Big Hair & Big Hits

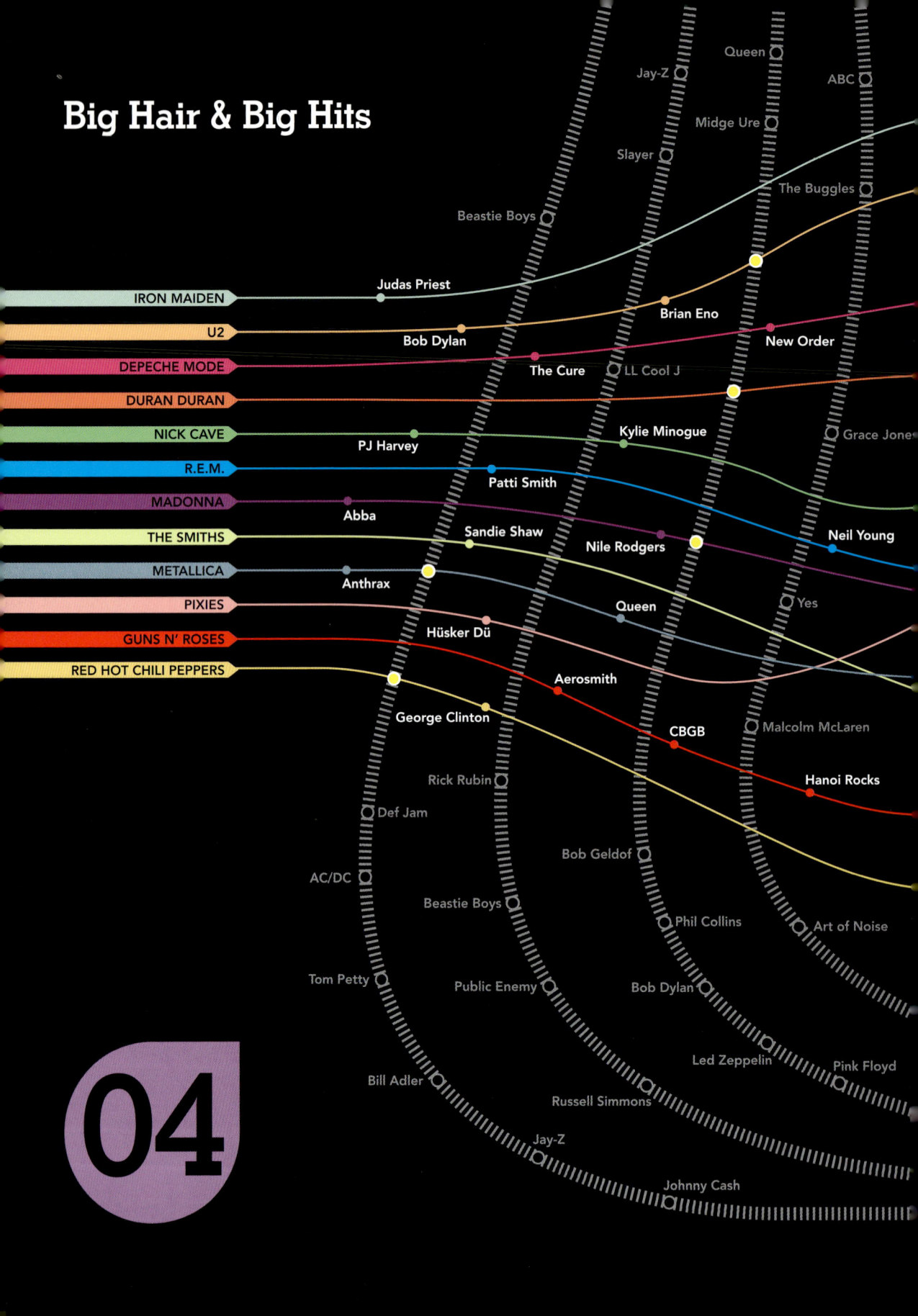

04

IRON MAIDEN
U2
DEPECHE MODE
DURAN DURAN
NICK CAVE
R.E.M.
MADONNA
THE SMITHS
METALLICA
PIXIES
GUNS N' ROSES
RED HOT CHILI PEPPERS

Judas Priest
Bob Dylan
PJ Harvey
Abba
Anthrax
Hüsker Dü
George Clinton

Beastie Boys
The Cure
Patti Smith
Sandie Shaw
Rick Rubin
Def Jam
AC/DC
Beastie Boys
Tom Petty
Public Enemy
Bill Adler

Queen
Jay-Z
Slayer
Brian Eno
LL Cool J
Kylie Minogue
Nile Rodgers
Queen
Aerosmith
CBGB
Bob Geldof
Phil Collins
Bob Dylan
Russell Simmons
Jay-Z
Johnny Cash

Midge Ure
The Buggles
New Order
Grace Jones
Neil Young
Yes
Malcolm McLaren
Hanoi Rocks
Art of Noise
Led Zeppelin
Pink Floyd

ABC

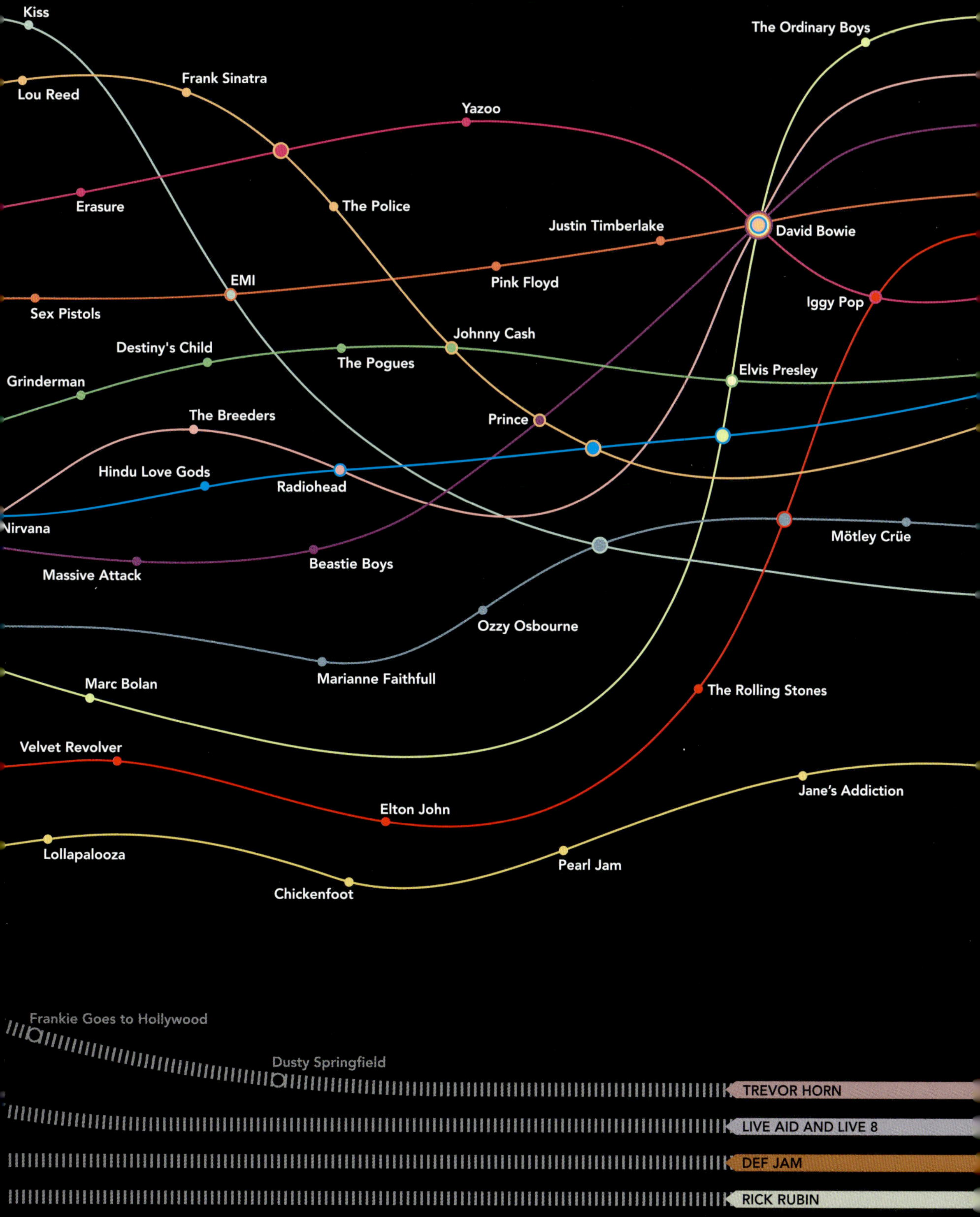
Kiss
The Ordinary Boys
Lou Reed
Frank Sinatra
Yazoo
Erasure
The Police
Justin Timberlake
David Bowie
EMI
Pink Floyd
Sex Pistols
Iggy Pop
Johnny Cash
Destiny's Child
The Pogues
Elvis Presley
Grinderman
The Breeders
Prince
Hindu Love Gods
Radiohead
Nirvana
Mötley Crüe
Massive Attack
Beastie Boys
Ozzy Osbourne
Marianne Faithfull
Marc Bolan
The Rolling Stones
Velvet Revolver
Elton John
Jane's Addiction
Lollapalooza
Pearl Jam
Chickenfoot
Frankie Goes to Hollywood
Dusty Springfield
TREVOR HORN
LIVE AID AND LIVE 8
DEF JAM
RICK RUBIN

Iron Maiden 1976–present

1956+ 1990+

British rock band Iron Maiden have never been "cool" but they have outlasted (and outsold) virtually all of their influences and contemporaries. Slayer started out playing Maiden covers, and Public Enemy producer Hank Shocklee marveled at how "the whole concept is built around that huge mummified figure [their mascot Edward the Head]."

Maiden was inspired by British twin-guitar bands such as Thin Lizzy and Judas Priest, as well as by the more conceptual Jethro Tull. The result was a "sort of semi-progressive metal," said Lars Ulrich of Metallica ❰218❱ (who spoofed Iron Maiden's "Run to the Hills" on the *Garage Days Re-Revisited* EP). But Maiden fused their epics with catchy choruses and sprightly riffs 'n' rhythms that distinguished them from the plodding metal of the early Seventies.

"My heart and soul were in England with Iron Maiden," said Lars Ulrich of his formative years. (Other stars who grew up listening to them include Slash of Guns N' Roses ❰228❱ and Marilyn Manson.)

Metallica covered their "Remember Tomorrow" for a 2008 tribute album (*Maiden Heaven*), which also featured Dream Theater, Coheed and Cambria, and Machine Head. Iron Maiden songs have also been covered by modern metal favorites such as Arch Enemy and Opeth, as well as by old school heroes Anthrax and Billy Corgan's Zwan.

"The only major arena rock concert I went to was Iron Maiden," recalled Nirvana's ❰242❱ front man Kurt Cobain. "People were shooting bottle rockets and throwing M-80s into the crowd all night, until they had to stop because the roof caught fire."

BIG HAIR & BIG HITS

1956

Steve Harris and Dave Murray are born in London (March 12 and December 23). They will be the only Maiden members to appear on every album.

February 23, 1980

"Running Free" is Maiden's first U.K. hit. They will be the first band to play live on the BBC TV show *Top of the Pops* since The Who.

September 1981

After tours with Judas Priest, Kiss, and UFO, and hit albums *Iron Maiden* (1980) and *Killers* (1981), singer Paul Di'Anno is replaced by Bruce Dickinson.

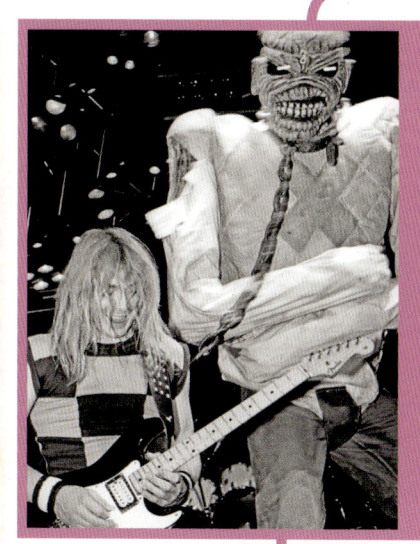

APRIL 10, 1982: *The Number of the Beast* hits No. 1

❶ 142

When *The Number of the Beast* smashed in at the top of the U.K. chart in April 1982, Maiden became the new kings of heavy metal. After years of lineup changes, the band solidified around bassist and chief songwriter Steve Harris, singer Bruce Dickinson, drummer Nicko McBrain, and guitarists Dave Murray and Adrian Smith. They scored hit after hit with *Piece of Mind* (1983), *Powerslave* (1984), *Live After Death* (1985), *Somewhere in Time* (1986), and *Seventh Son of a Seventh Son* (1988). Each album and single bore their zombie-like mascot Eddie, who regularly topped metal magazine *Kerrang!*'s "male sex symbol" poll. Meanwhile, the band's marathon tours became ever more spectacular. At the U.K.'s Monsters of Rock festival in 1988, they headlined over Kiss❶ (whom they had once supported), and, with their sound peaking at 124 decibels, earned a Guinness world record for the "largest front-of-house P.A."

October 13, 1990

No Prayer for the Dying hits the charts. Adrian Smith has been replaced by Janick Gers, who played on Dickinson's debut solo album.

January 5, 1991

Maiden knock fellow EMI artist Cliff Richard off the top of the U.K. chart with their first No. 1 single, "Bring Your Daughter . . . to the Slaughter."

May 23, 1992

Maiden score another U.K. No. 1 with *Fear of the Dark* but, after the ensuing tour, a frustrated Dickinson will quit for a solo career.

October 14, 1995

The X Factor hits the charts. It is Maiden's first album with singer Blaze Bayley (to be followed by 1998's equally poorly received *Virtual XI*).

JULY 11, 1999: Six (six six) piece back on the road

With ex-guitarist Smith and ex-vocalist Dickinson rejoining Harris, Gers, Murray, and McBrain, the six-man lineup hit the road in 1999, supporting their *Ed Hunter* computer game and then made *Brave New World* (2000). Chart positions instantly improved and got better still with *Dance of Death* (2003), *A Matter of Life and Death* (2006), and *The Final Frontier* (2010). Maiden have since settled into a routine of huge shows, occasional live albums, and a new "best of" every three years. While their albums have become more stately, their shows remain frenzied—and, as proven by 2009's *Iron Maiden: Flight 666* movie— attract crazed audiences from India to Australia. "Five years ago," remarked Harris in 2009, "we said we'd start easing back a bit . . . we thought that, by this age, we'd be needing to. But we don't need to— and the demand is there, so . . . What can you do? You keep on going."

U2 1978–present

1960+ 1983+ 1989+ 1997+

Drawing on influences ranging from The Beatles ◀044 and Bob Dylan ◀062, through Pink Floyd ◀086 and Patti Smith ◀164, to The Clash ◀170 and Joy Division ◀184, U2 have created a style all of their own—marked by Bono's soaring vocals, The Edge's ringing guitars, and Adam Clayton and Larry Mullen's rumbling rhythms. Bruce Springsteen ◀150 once described them as "the dark, chiming sound of heaven."

"It's not that it's old fashioned," said The Who's ◀068 Pete Townshend, "but it's the kind of music I relate to a lot . . . and I relate to the words as well." "I had the feeling when I bought the first U2 record," remarked Peter Buck of R.E.M. 204▶, "that they understood where they wanted to go . . . They wanted to be the biggest band in the world."

"For English bands to be super-big in America," sniffed Matt Bellamy of Muse 270▶, "you have to do the U2 class: a little bit of gospel, a little bit of country, a whisper of blues. I think Coldplay 276▶ watched *Rattle and Hum* a few times and found the key to American success." ("It's a great honor, I must say," responded Coldplay's Chris Martin, "to be compared to such an amazing band.")

Their songs have been covered by acts ranging from Johnny Cash ◀018 to Mary J. Blige (on whose 2005 version of "One" they guested) to the Pet Shop Boys. (The latter's lampooning of "Where the Streets Have No Name" in 1991 seemed prescient when U2 ditched their monochrome early image for the multicolored Nineties.) "If we get our songs right," Bono once said, "I think we could really be very popular."

192 BIG HAIR & BIG HITS

1960

Adam Charles Clayton is born in Oxfordshire, England (March 13), and Paul David "Bono" Hewson is born in Dublin, Ireland (May 10).

1961

David Howell "Edge" Evans is born in Essex, England (August 8), and Lawrence Joseph Mullen, Jr. is born in Dublin (October 31).

March 17, 1978

Formed by Mullen, the band (previously called Feedback and The Hype) shed Edge's brother Dick and become U2 for a talent show in Ireland.

JUNE 9, 1981: White men in Hammersmith Palais

Bruce Springsteen❶ (left with Bono) recalled: "I went with [The Who's❷] Pete Townshend—who always wanted to catch the first whiff of those about to unseat us—to a club in London. There they were: a young Bono, single-handedly pioneering the Irish mullet; The Edge—what kind of name was that?; Adam and Larry. I was listening to the last band of whom I would be able to name all of its members. They had an exciting show and a big, beautiful sound. They lifted the roof." Although they had barely charted outside Ireland, the band built up a devoted following in the U.S.A. and U.K. (their 1980 debut, *Boy*, scraped into the charts in 1981). Thanks to this burgeoning reputation, *October* (1981) just missed the U.K. top ten. On July 31, 1982, they played one of their final shows as a support act, to The Police❸ (with whom Bono sang "Invisible Sun"), and, in January 1983, released their first major hit, "New Year's Day."

❶ 150
❷ 068
❸ 163

March 12, 1983

War enters the U.K. chart at No. 1. "Sunday Bloody Sunday" will become a U2 anthem, despite not being a single in most territories.

June 5, 1983

A show at Denver's Red Rocks will be immortalized as the video *Under a Blood Red Sky* and contribute two songs to an album of the same name.

October 13, 1984

Bolstered by the hit "Pride (In the Name of Love)," *The Unforgettable Fire* tops the U.K. chart. It will also hit No. 1 in Australia.

July 13, 1985

U2 steal the show from everyone bar Queen at Live Aid. All of their albums will be back in the U.K. chart by the end of the month.

APRIL 25, 1987: The biggest band in the world?

On a 1986 tour for Amnesty International, U2 shared a bill with Lou Reed❶, Bryan Adams, Peter Gabriel, and Sting (sometimes with The Police❷). Then, with producers Brian Eno❸ and Daniel Lanois, the band created *The Joshua Tree*. In April 1987, the album knocked Beastie Boys❹ off the top of the U.S. chart, followed in May by the No. 1 single "With or Without You." As they sold out stadiums, it seemed U2 had become the biggest band in the world. Bob Dylan❺ duly joined them onstage in L.A. in April 1987 (left). "He sang beautifully," said Bono, "and the crowd went ballistic." Dylan reappeared on 1988's half-live, half-studio *Rattle and Hum*, which also featured a cover of Dylan's "All Along the Watchtower" and a collaboration with blues giant B. B. King. U2 performed five of the album's songs at a London club in October of the same year, with guests Keith Richards and Ziggy Marley.

❶ 092
❷ 163
❸ 138
❹ 222
❺ 062

U2 193

February 7, 1989

Roy Orbison's *Mystery Girl* is posthumously issued. Its beautiful "She's a Mystery to Me," written by Bono and Edge, turns out to be one of their finest songs.

December 31, 1989

Although they have four shows of their Lovetown Tour still to play, Bono tells a Dublin crowd that U2 must "go away and dream it all up again."

February 1990

A London stage version of *A Clockwork Orange* has a score by Bono and Edge that sees them evolving from U2's "three chords and the truth" formula.

September 25, 1990

A spooky "Night and Day," on the Cole Porter tribute *Red Hot + Blue*, is another clue to U2's new, electronic-oriented direction.

❶ 018
❷ 092
❸ 174
❹ 228
❺ 090
❻ 260

NOVEMBER 1991: ". . . If I could, I'd rearrange . . ."

"The Fly" signaled a new era in which U2 ripped up their self-imposed rule book and pursued whatever direction took their fancy. The results ranged from spectacular (1991's *Achtung Baby*, 1993's *Zooropa*, 1995's "Hold Me Thrill Me Kiss Me Kill Me") to interesting (1997's *Pop*) to near-disastrous (1995's *Original Soundtracks 1*). There were astonishing tours—such as *PopMart*—and fascinating collaborations: Frank Sinatra ("I've Got You Under My Skin"), Johnny Cash❶ ("The Wanderer"), Lou Reed❷ ("Satellite of Love"), Pavarotti ("Miss Sarajevo"), Prince❸ (with whom Bono duetted on "The Cross" at a Dublin show in March 1995), and Axl Rose (who showed up to hear "One" when U2's path crossed with Guns N' Roses❹, then appeared at a May 1992 show in Austria to sing "Knockin' on Heaven's Door"). U2 also had interesting support acts, from The Velvet Underground❺ in 1993 to Oasis❻ in 1997.

July 14, 1997

The video for "Last Night on Earth" features author William S. Burroughs, often credited with inventing the phrase "heavy metal."

December 8, 1997

The "If God Will Send His Angels" single features "Slow Dancing," with Willie Nelson, and "Two Shots of Happy . . ." (written for Frank Sinatra).

October 20, 1998

Dancers from *Riverdance* and Irish boyband Boyzone appear in the video for "Sweetest Thing," a 1987 B-side remade as a single for U2's first "best of."

March 15, 1999

Bono inducts Springsteen into the Rock and Roll Hall of Fame, then joins the all-star jam on Curtis Mayfield's "People Get Ready."

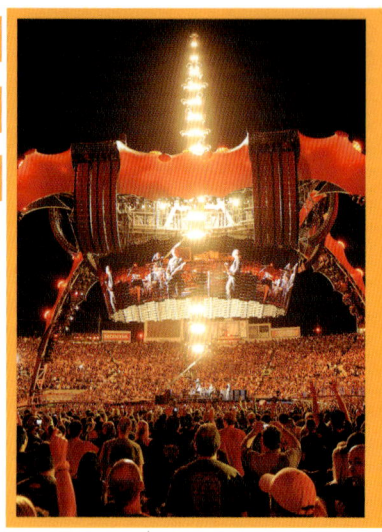

❶ 214
❷ 258
❸ 054

2000 ONWARD: "It's a beautiful day"

The U.K. No. 1 success of "Beautiful Day" confirmed the commercial wisdom of retreating from the experimentation of the past decade. "It was a very good idea to make a record that actually sounded like U2 again," remarked manager Paul McGuinness. "The album *[All That You Can't Leave Behind]* came out on October 31, 2000, and went straight to No. 1 in thirty-two countries." The pattern was repeated by 2004's "Vertigo" and *How to Dismantle an Atomic Bomb*. Even 2009's *No Line on the Horizon*, sandbagged by U2's worst opening single ("Get on Your Boots"), has its admirers. The band united with Paul McCartney in 2005 (to open Live 8❶ with "Sgt. Pepper's Lonely Hearts Club Band") and Green Day❷ in 2006 (for a cover of the Skids' "The Saints Are Coming"). Today, U2 are best experienced live (left), where their phenomenal success puts them just behind the Stones❸ as the decade's biggest band.

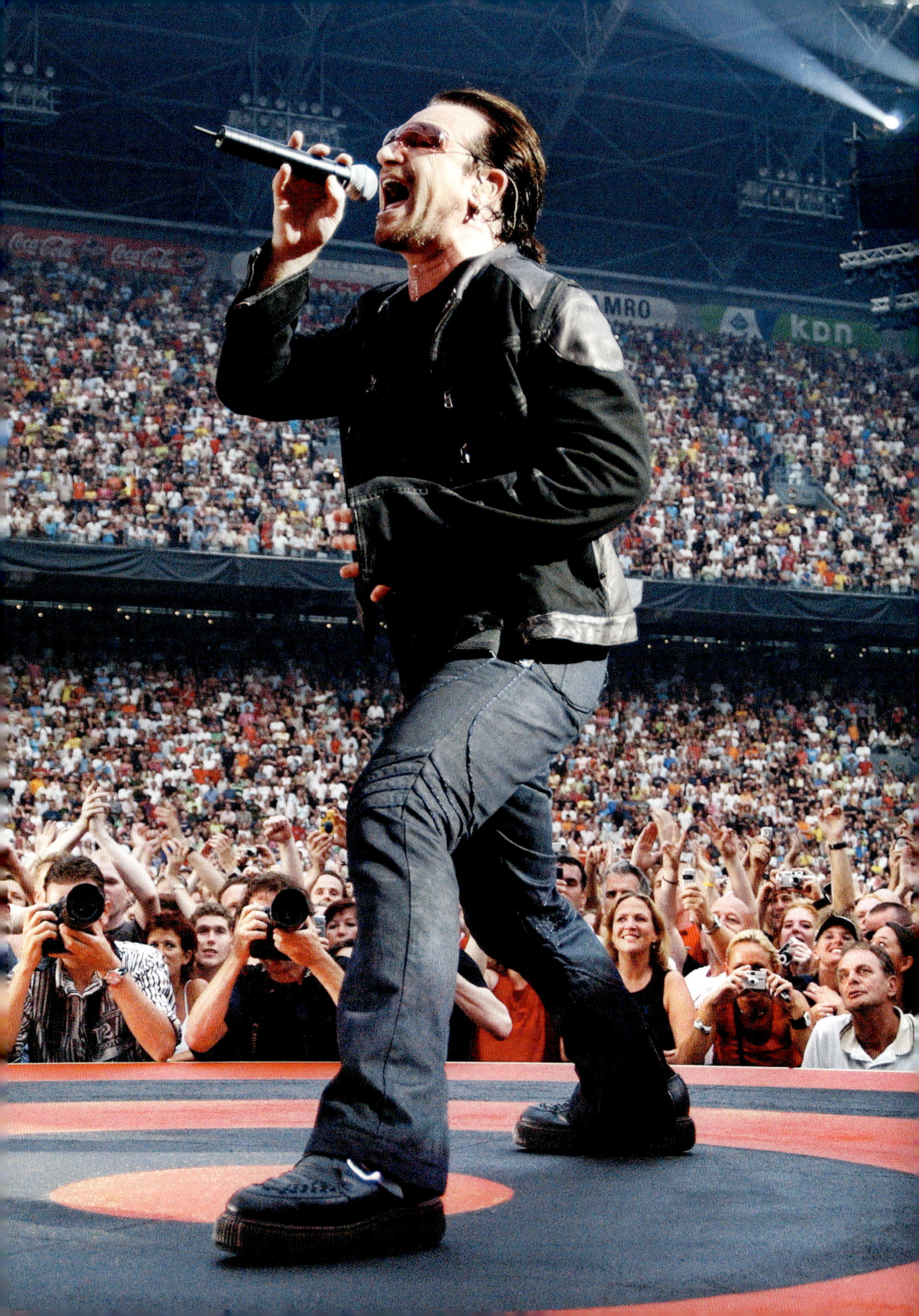
AMRO
kpn

Depeche Mode 1980–present

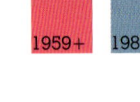

Before Nirvana 242▶ revived raging rock 'n' roll, it was British band Depeche Mode (with fellow British miserablists The Cure and New Order) who defined the glum sound of U.S. alternative radio. "The Eighties equivalent of one of those Italian, late Fifties, doo-wop groups, full of real teenage angst," remarked Neil Tennant of the chirpy Pet Shop Boys about the quartet.

Depeche's ubiquity in clubs and on U.S. college radio won them an unlikely cross-section of fans, from hip-hop diva Lauryn Hill and house pioneers such as Derrick May, to Trent Reznor of Nine Inch Nails and John Frusciante of the Red Hot Chili Peppers 232▶. Depeche, observed Elton John ◀126, "have got that synthesizer thing down to a fine art. I never used to like their records, but they grow on you." (In contrast, Phil Spector ◀028 kept Depeche waiting so long in 1987, after the band invited him to remix their songs, that they gave up on him.)

Their songs have been covered by Rammstein ("Stripped"), Johnny Cash ◀018 ("Personal Jesus," also sung by Marilyn Manson), Scott Weiland ("But Not Tonight"), The Smashing Pumpkins ("Never Let Me Down Again"), Placebo ("I Feel You"), Tori Amos ("Enjoy the Silence"), A Perfect Circle ("People Are People"), and The Cure ("World in My Eyes").

"I think Depeche Mode music somehow appeals to the oddball," said the band's singer Dave Gahan to actress Chloë Sevigny in *Interview*, "to the person who is looking for something a bit different." Sevigny objected that they have "sold a gazillion records." "There are a lot of freaks out there," he replied.

1959–62
Alan Wilder (June 1, 1959), Vince Clarke (July 3, 1960), Andy Fletcher (July 8, 1961), Martin Gore (July 23, 1961), and Dave Gahan (May 9, 1962) are born.

November 1981
Shortly after their debut *Speak & Spell* hits the U.K. top ten, songwriter Clarke quits. He will form Yazoo and, later, Erasure.

June 1984
With Wilder having replaced Clarke, and Gore in charge of writing, the fourth album *Some Great Reward* hits the charts. It will be their first album to go gold in the U.S.A.

MARCH 17, 1986: Let's have a *Black Celebration*

❶ 134
❷ 116
❸ 192
❹ 184

"Master and Servant" and "Blasphemous Rumours," from 1984's *Some Great Reward*, had highlighted just how far Martin Gore's writing had evolved from the poppier influence of Vince Clarke. While critics giggled at the clean-cut band's reinvention as black-clad purveyors of perversion, fans delighted at the ever-improving music and layers of lyrical meaning. Recorded at Hansa Tonstudio in Germany—also the setting for David Bowie❶ and Iggy Pop's❷ late Seventies masterpieces *Heroes* and *The Idiot*, and, later, U2's❸ *Achtung Baby*—1986's *Black Celebration* was, as *Uncut* mag observed, "a major step forward, oozing Berlin's brutalism and S&M gloom." It also marked the start of an association with Dutch video director Anton Corbijn—whose distinctive, black-and-white work with the likes of Joy Division❹ proved vital when he helped shape the images of both Depeche Mode and, with *The Joshua Tree*, U2.

September 28, 1987
Music for the Masses is released. It will be their top forty debut in the U.S.A., where "Strangelove" will head the dance charts.

June 18, 1988
A tour-closing show at the Pasadena Rose Bowl is filmed for *Depeche Mode 101* by D. A. Pennebaker, who shot Dylan's *Don't Look Back*.

January 23, 1990
"Personal Jesus" is the band's first U.S. gold single. Sales will be matched by "Enjoy the Silence," another hit from the forthcoming classic album *Violator*.

March 20, 1990
Thirty thousand fans turn up to a signing session at L.A.'s Wherehouse Records to launch *Violator*. It will duly reach the top ten.

1997: Depeche get back on track

❶ 186
❷ 054

The huge success of 1993's *Songs of Faith and Devotion* had confirmed Depeche as the world's biggest cult band. But as the ensuing tour wore on into 1994, the group had fallen apart: Fletcher took a leave of absence (replaced by Daryl Bamonte, brother of The Cure's❶ Perry), Gore (left) suffered seizures, Wilder quit entirely, and, worst of all, Gahan's heroin addiction escalated. However, after a near-fatal overdose in 1996, he cleaned up, and the band's next chapter began with 1997's *Ultra*. This kicked off a cycle of albums every four years—*Exciter* (2001), *Playing the Angel* (2005), and *Sounds of the Universe* (2009)—and mammoth tours, punctuated by solo outings from both Gahan and Gore. "I understand when people still go to see the Stones❷," said the singer in 2010. "I saw them in New York . . . and I was blown away by how good they were. But I was also thinking, 'Wow, I don't want to be doing this when I'm that old.'"

super producer

Trevor Horn
1949–present

From the Pet Shop Boys' *Introspective* to Paul McCartney's *Flowers in the Dirt,* from Rod Stewart's "Downtown Train" to Belle & Sebastian's "Step into My Office, Baby," from Marc Almond's *Tenement Symphony* to Mike Oldfield's *Tubular Bells II,* and from t.A.T.u.'s "All the Things She Said" to Seal's "Kiss from a Rose," Trevor Horn has worked with an astonishing range of artists.

This diversity emerged early in his career, when—in just four years—he graduated from The Buggles (the band's name an in-jokey reference to The Beatles ◀044) and Yes, to polished pop acts Dollar and ABC, then Malcolm McLaren's "Buffalo Gals."

"The first thing I did after leaving Yes was Dollar, which went down really well with the [notoriously iconoclastic British music paper] *NME,*" Horn marveled. "It never occurred to me that *NME* and [ABC singer] Martin Fry would be interested in it."

After huge success in the Eighties with Frankie Goes to Hollywood and in the Nineties with Seal, Horn maintained his prog rock credentials by helming a gorgeous 1997 remake of Genesis' 1974 gem "The Carpet Crawlers." Otherwise, his choice of clients testifies as much to his eye for a hit as to his artistic vision. The Pretenders, Cher, Tom Jones, Whitesnake's David Coverdale, and Tina Turner are among the many who have benefited from his touch.

The producer then diversified into soundtrack work. His celluloid CV includes *Toys* (1992), featuring Tori Amos, *Coyote Ugly* (2000), including LeAnn Rimes, and *Young Americans* (2010), inspired by the David Bowie ◀134 song of the same name.

1949+

1981+

1984+

July 15, 1949
Trevor Horn is born in Hertfordshire, England. By the late Seventies, he will be with Tina Charles, who topped the U.K. chart with the 1976 disco classic "I Love to Love."

January 1979
Horn forms The Buggles with Geoff Downes. They will top the U.K. chart in October with "Video Killed the Radio Star" (later the first song played on MTV).

October 20, 1979
Dusty Springfield has her first (albeit minor) U.K. hit in nine years with "Baby Blue," co-written by Horn. His other chart entries that year include songs by The Jags and Dan-I.

◀041

MARCH 1980: Just say Yes

Long-time fans of Yes❶, Trevor Horn and Geoff Downes had submitted a song to them when they found themselves recording in a neighboring studio in 1980. The pair were promptly persuaded to take the place of the newly departed Jon Anderson and Rick Wakeman. "Joining Yes was one of those stupid things that you do," Horn later reflected. "It was one of the two or three times in my life that I've done something that I knew was wrong." Although the association lasted under a year, they produced a hit album, *Drama,* and set a new record for shows at New York's Madison Square Garden. When the band split in December, Downes joined Yes' Steve Howe, ELP's Carl Palmer, and King Crimson's John Wetton in the staggeringly successful Asia. Horn renewed his acquaintance with Yes by producing their splendid reunion album *90125* (1983), featuring the hit "Owner of a Lonely Heart," as well as plenty of complicated key changes.

BIG HAIR & BIG HITS

1981

British pop duo Dollar score fantastic Horn-produced U.K. hits with "Hand Held in Black and White" (August) and "Mirror Mirror" (November).

July 3, 1982

ABC's *The Lexicon of Love* enters the British chart at No. 1. Produced by Horn, it features his three future Art of Noise cohorts.

January 15, 1983

Malcolm Mclaren's "Buffalo Gals," produced by Horn, enters the U.K. top ten, helping to usher hip-hop into the mainstream.

February 1983

Horn—with Gary Langan, J. J. Jeczalik, and Anne Dudley—begins recording *Into Battle with the Art of Noise*, the debut EP by Art of Noise.

JANUARY 28, 1984: Frankie hits No. 1

After the Liverpool band Frankie Goes to Hollywood cut sessions for influential British DJ John Peel and appeared on U.K. TV show *The Tube*, Horn snapped them up for his fledgling ZTT label. Their debut single, "Relax," crept into the U.K. chart in November 1983, then—thanks to a publicity-generating BBC ban—hit No. 1 in January of the next year. "Two Tribes" and "The Power of Love" followed, and Frankie became a global sensation. They hit a nutty peak with 1984's *Welcome to the Pleasuredome*, which featured covers of Bruce Springsteen's❶ "Born to Run," Dionne Warwick's "Do You Know the Way to San José," and Barrett Strong's "War," alongside originals that were largely created by Horn and the Art of Noise. The prevailing air of prog rock was cemented by cameos from Yes❷ guitarists Steve Howe and Trevor Rabin. Unfortunately, however, the Frankie and ZTT story ended in unseemly court wrangles.

❶ 150
❷ 041

November 17, 1984

Art of Noise's "Close (to the Edit)" begins a lengthy climb into the U.K. top ten. It will later be sampled on the Prodigy's "Firestarter."

December 15, 1984

Band Aid's "Do They Know it's Christmas?" enters the U.K. chart at No. 1. Approached to produce it, Horn instead took care of the spoken B-side.

March 1985

The Horn-produced "Cry" by Godley & Creme is released. Its video features a morphing effect seen again in Michael Jackson's "Black and White."

April 13, 1985

Two years since its release, Art of Noise's "Moments in Love" hits the U.K. chart. It will later be extensively sampled by hip-hop acts.

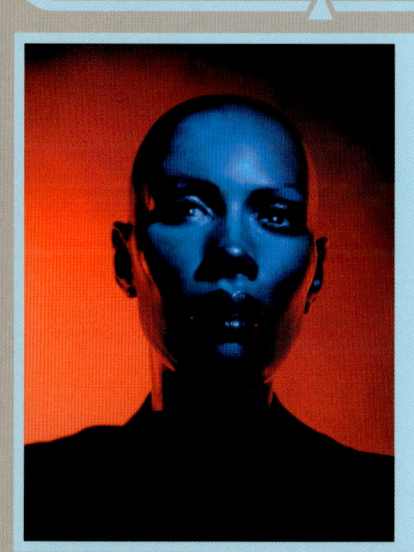

OCTOBER 12, 1985: The rhythmical Grace Jones

"Slave to the Rhythm" had initially been intended as the follow-up to "Relax" by Frankie Goes to Hollywood. However, Horn—convinced the song could be one of his greatest creations—held onto it, then bequeathed it to post-disco diva Grace Jones. The track, which hit the charts in 1985, was just a slice of an album comprised of variations on the same song. Among its musicians was Pink Floyd's❶ David Gilmour, who told *Q*: "I never met Grace Jones. I was approached by Trevor Horn and went down to their studio . . . Trevor had terrible food poisoning and was throwing up every three minutes—lying on the floor trying to produce a record and chucking up into a bin! Mostly they sampled anything I did into a Synclavier and tried to make some sort of sense out of it later." The hard work proved worthwhile. "Still to this day," remarked Horn more than two decades later, "it's one of my favorite records."

❶ 086

TREVOR HORN

Duran Duran 1978–present

1978+ 1987+

Aiming to be a cross between Chic and the Sex Pistols ◁166, Duran Duran wound up as a poppy Roxy Music, with a Bowie ◁134-inspired image. But they mitigated the ludicrousness of this with hit songs that made them leaders of a second "British Invasion" in the early Eighties and gave them success that has lasted three decades.

Their songs have been covered by acts including Nirvana 242▷ ("Rio"), Deftones ("The Chauffeur"), Hole ("Hungry Like the Wolf"), Lostprophets ("A View to a Kill"), Girls Aloud ("Girls on Film"), and Jimmy Eat World ("New Religion"), and sampled by The Notorious B.I.G. 262▷ ("Notorious").

For an unashamed pop band, Duran are awash in rock connections. Their offshoots have featured stars such as David Gilmour of Pink Floyd ◁086, Robert Palmer, Steve Jones of the Sex Pistols, and Matt Sorum and Duff McKagan of Guns N' Roses 228▷. Guitarist Andy Taylor guested with Rod Stewart and was replaced by Frank Zappa's ◁076 ex-sideman Warren Cuccurollo. Vocalist Simon Le Bon was part of a drinking collective, The Lead Singers' Club, with INXS' Michael Hutchence and U2's ◁192 Bono. Even their much-lambasted covers album *Thank You* enjoyed an endorsement from the Velvets' ◁090 Lou Reed.

"Their records still sound fresh," said The Killers' 280▷ Brandon Flowers, "which is no mean feat as far as synths are concerned." "They were cursed by what we can call the 'Bee Gees curse,'" observed Moby: "Write amazing songs, sell tons of records, and consequently incur the wrath or disinterest of the rock-obsessed critical establishment."

April 5, 1978

Keyboardist Nick Bates (later Rhodes), guitarist Nigel (later John) Taylor, and bassist/singer Stephen Duffy play a first gig as Duran Duran (a name taken from the 1968 film *Barbarella*).

July 9, 1980

The new "fab five" lineup—Rhodes, Taylor, singer Simon Le Bon, guitarist Andy Taylor, and drummer Roger Taylor—debut at the Rum Runner club in Birmingham, England.

December 4, 1980

Duran sign to EMI, despite better offers elsewhere. "We were patriotic," Rhodes said. "We thought, 'EMI, English company, the Beatles . . .' We got appallingly ripped off."

JULY 13, 1985: The fab five fall apart

Duran scored a U.S. chart-topper on July 13, 1985, with the James Bond theme "A View to a Kill." (This crowned a triumphant four years that had seen smashes such as "Hungry Like the Wolf," "Rio," "The Reflex," and "The Wild Boys.") But on the same day, at Live Aid❶, the classic lineup played its final show for eighteen years. The band splintered: John and Andy Taylor formed The Power Station with singer Robert Palmer and Chic drummer Tony Thompson (left), while Rhodes and Le Bon united as Arcadia. Roger Taylor contributed to both. "It wasn't an album," he said of Arcadia's *So Red the Rose*, "it was a scene. Sting, Grace Jones❷, [Pink Floyd's❸] Dave Gilmour were there. Mick Jagger came down just to hang out. It was ridiculous." By 1986, Roger and Andy had quit. The remaining trio enlisted producer Nile Rodgers—hot from David Bowie's❹ *Let's Dance* and Madonna's❺ *Like a Virgin*—for 1986's *Notorious*.

❶ 214
❷ 199
❸ 086
❹ 134
❺ 208

August 31, 1987

After supporting Bowie on the *Glass Spider* tour, Duran and Nile Rodgers guest with Lou Reed at a charity show in New York.

March 19, 1993

Now featuring former Zappa guitarist Warren Cuccurollo, Duran score their first big hit in years: "Ordinary World," from a self-titled new album.

March 22, 1994

Duran's cover of Zeppelin's "Thank You" graces the soundtrack of *With Honors*. It will reappear on the Led Zep tribute *Enconium* and Duran's own *Thank You*.

June 28, 1995

John Taylor plays with Guns N' Roses' Duff McKagan and Matt Sorum, and Sex Pistols guitarist Steve Jones at The Viper Room in L.A.

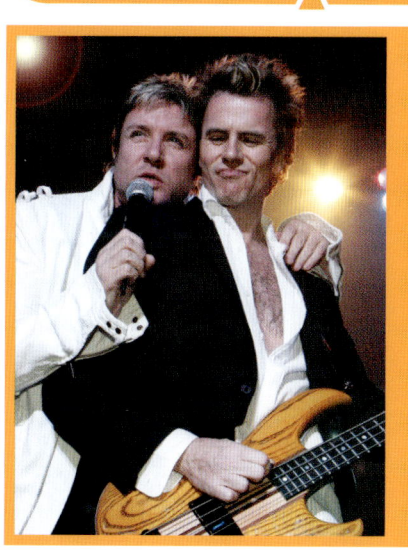

JULY 2003: The ragged reunion

❶ 076

Duran Duran's future looked poor. John Taylor had quit during the making of *Medazzaland* (1997) and busied himself with side-projects such as Neurotic Outsiders. Le Bon, Rhodes, and Cuccurollo plodded on with *Pop Trash*, although the latter was distracted by a reunion of Missing Persons, the Eighties band formed of fellow Zappa❶ graduates. But in 2001, the inevitable occurred: the "fab five" reunited, hitting the road to a rapturous response in 2003 (left—Simon Le Bon and John Taylor onstage), and issuing their most successful album in a decade, *Astronaut*. Equally inevitably, the temperamental Andy Taylor quit again, in 2006. The remaining four replaced a planned album, *Reportage*, with *Red Carpet Massacre* (2007), featuring Justin Timberlake. "People begrudge us anything," grumbled John Taylor. "The intelligentsia throws down the gauntlet to us every time we make an album. Well, we're picking it up."

DURAN DURAN 201

Nick Cave 1957–present

1957+   1997+

With a career that spans gothic punk with The Birthday Party, a blues-gospel-rock hybrid with the Bad Seeds, and anarchic sleazy blues with Grinderman, it would be hard to find a more eclectic and revered musician than Nick Cave.

A fan of Johnny Cash ◁018 and Bob Dylan ◁062, Cave has always been upfront about his influences. The covers set *Kicking Against the Pricks* (1986) included songs made famous by Jimi Hendrix ◁072 and The Velvet Underground ◁090. Another hero, Elvis ◁012, got the Cave treatment on 1984's "In the Ghetto." The same album, *From Her to Eternity*, also included Leonard Cohen's ◁106 "Avalanche." Cave's cover version bug had begun when he was in The Birthday Party, with one of their shows consisting solely of Stooges ◁116 songs.

As Cave's writing matured, the admiration was returned. In 2000, Johnny Cash covered "The Mercy Seat" and, two years later, Cash and Cave recorded a cover of Hank Williams' "I'm So Lonesome I Could Cry" together. After Cash's death, Cave wrote "Let the Bells Ring" as a tribute to him.

Religion, death, love, and violence inform much of his material. A break-up with British musician PJ Harvey partly inspired 1997's *The Boatman's Call*. (The previous year, Cave and Harvey had duetted on "Henry Lee," from *Murder Ballads*.) In 1997, he performed his song "Into My Arms" at the funeral of his friend, INXS singer Michael Hutchence. Like a beautiful, modern-day hymn—but for the secular as well as the religious—it would be hard to think of a more apt choice of tribute.

September 22, 1957

Nicholas Edward Cave is born in Warracknabeal, Australia. At school he will meet Mick Harvey, his future partner in The Birthday Party and Bad Seeds.

April 18, 1986

Kicking Against the Pricks is issued, with songs by Roy Orbison, Gene Pitney, and Johnny Cash. The Bad Seeds include future film composer Barry Adamson.

July 4, 1994

"Loverman," from the Bad Seeds' eighth studio album, *Let Love In*, is issued as a U.K. single. It will later be covered by Depeche Mode's Martin Gore and Metallica.

OCTOBER 2, 1995: Dark duet with Kylie

❶ 216

Cave always had an eye for a collaboration, but it was a surprise when he united with pop princess—and fellow Australian—Kylie Minogue (left) on the haunting murder ballad "Where the Wild Roses Grow." But, as he said, "I'd wanted to write a song for Kylie for many years. I had a quiet obsession with her for about six years." (He had, indeed, been pictured with a "Kylie" bag.) Via Minogue's boyfriend, Michael Hutchence of INXS❶, a beautiful duet was born. Inspired by the folk ballad "Down in the Willow Garden"—about a man awaiting execution for his lover's murder—Cave rearranged the dialogue to be between the killer and his sweetheart. The sumptuous strings, the incongruous singers, and the gorgeously gothic video—plus Minogue's popularity—led to his most commercially successful single. Despite this, Cave later said, "We thought it would be one of the world's great flops."

September 22, 1997

"Into My Arms" is up for for Single of the Year at the ARIA Awards. It is one of the songs that Cave is most proud of writing.

July 24, 2007

Grinderman, Cave's new band, open for The White Stripes at Madison Square Garden in New York, then embark on their own tour.

July 27, 2007

Jello Biafra, of the Dead Kennedys, and Henry Rollins, a long-time pal of Cave's, join Grinderman onstage in San Francisco to perform "Deanna."

December 2009

Cave confesses to Q that his favorite song of the decade is "Bootylicious," the Stevie Nicks-sampling smash by Destiny's Child.

MARCH 8, 2010: Spellbinding with MacGowan & co

❶ 062

❷ 170

The respect that Cave (left) inspires in musicians reached far and wide, including Pogues front man Shane MacGowan, with whom he united on a cover of Bob Dylan's❶ "Death is Not the End," as well as a cover of Louis Armstrong's "What a Wonderful World." Cave had also recorded The Pogues' "Rainy Night in Soho." In January 2010, moved by the devastating earthquake in Haiti, MacGowan joined forces with friends and former collaborators—including Cave, Primal Scream's Bobby Gillespie, the Pretenders' Chrissie Hynde, The Clash❷'s Mick Jones, and (on guitar) Johnny Depp—to create a new version of Screamin' Jay Hawkins' "I Put a Spell on You" in aid of Concern Worldwide's work in the disaster-struck country. Hawkins had died ten years to the day before the earthquake hit Haiti. The gutsy, impassioned take on the much-covered classic was released on March 8, 2010, via download only.

NICK CAVE   203

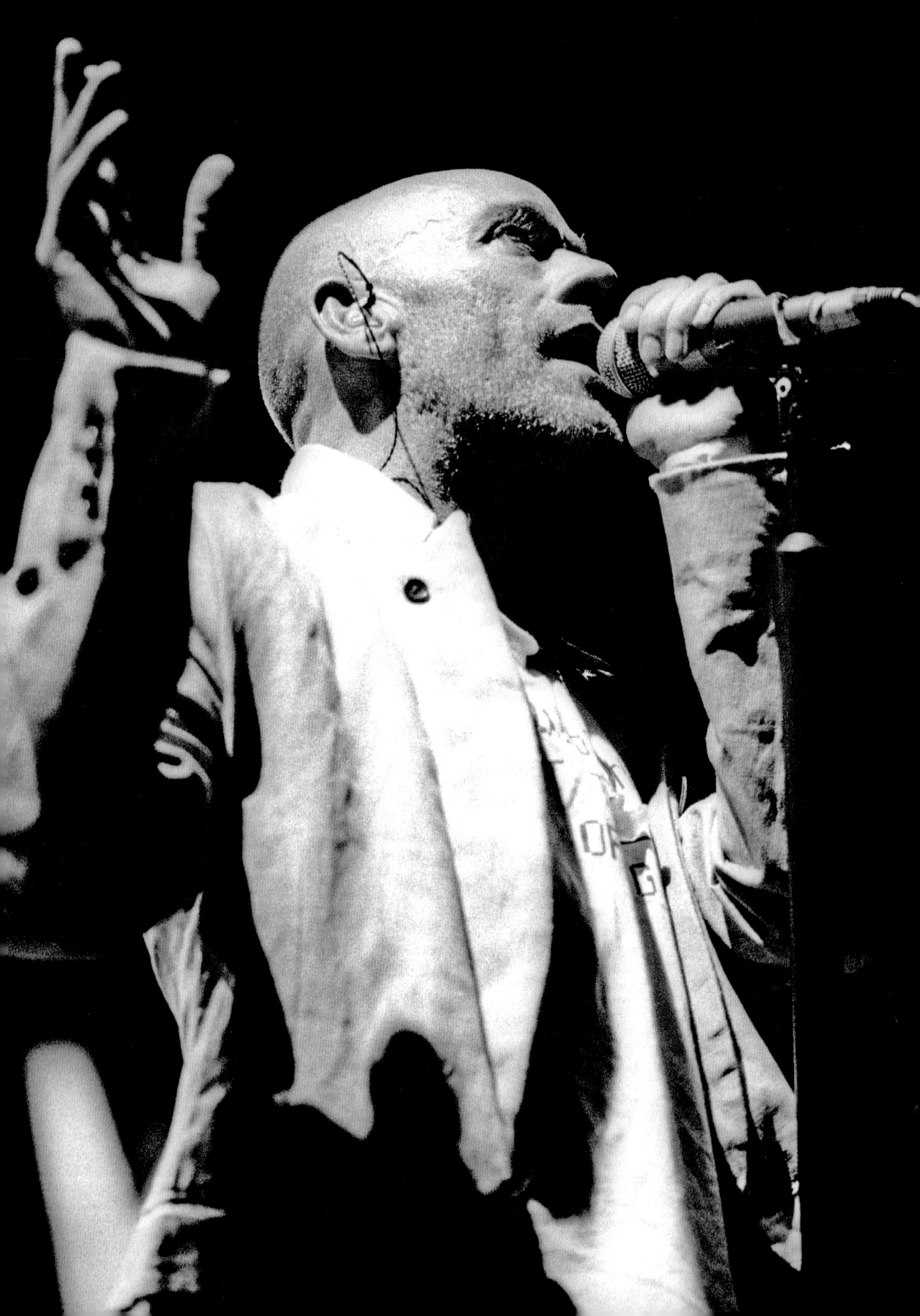

Having ascended to playing arenas, drummer Bill Berry, guitarist Peter Buck, bassist/keyboard player Mike Mills, and singer Michael Stipe could have further mined the radio-friendly seam that yielded "The One I Love" and "Stand." Instead, they took five years off touring, added a mandolin, and made one of the modern era's most oblique hits, "Losing My Religion." This topsy-turvy progress led one of the planet's biggest cult bands to a whole new level of superstardom. "In a fair world," Zeppelin's ◀098 Robert Plant had remarked in 1988, "Let's Active should be No. 1, R.E.M. should be No. 2, and . should be in there somewhere behind them . . ."

"I would go to school and kids would laugh at me because I listened to those 'new wave' bands U2 ◀192 and R.E.M.," recalled Billy Corgan of The Smashing Pumpkins. "That sounds completely funny now. But, to me, I could not understand why they were not the biggest bands in the world." (Corgan later enlisted R.E.M.'s Mike Mills to play piano on "Soma," on the Pumpkins' album *Siamese Dream*.)

"We've ripped off R.E.M. blind for years, you know."

—Thom Yorke, Radiohead

R.E.M.'s jingly-jangly early albums—which fused the poetic drama of Patti Smith ◀164 with the rock n' roll smarts of the likes of Big Star—made them college radio favorites. Across the Atlantic, their appeal was mirrored by The Smiths 212▶ whose singer Morrissey befriended Michael Stipe. "Music doesn't ever come into it," Morrissey declared. "We don't ever talk about R.E.M. or whatever it is I do . . . Who knows, we may even get a cover on *Hello!*."

For others, there was a more tangible musical connection. Elton John ◀126 wanted to duet with Stipe, remarking that R.E.M. "made consistently great records." Neil Young ◀078 planned a whole album with them in the mid-Eighties, before legal ties put a stop to it. (R.E.M., toying with signing to Young's then-bosses Geffen, chose Warner instead when their hero was sued for making unrepresentative records. "Geffen actually lost R.E.M.," Young later cackled, "simply for suing me!")

This acclaim occurred without the band sticking to one style ("They're more a folk band," suggested Pet Shop Boy Neil Tennant) or Stipe singing lyrics that made sense to anyone other than himself. But they achieved an emotional resonance that has prompted covers from Tori Amos ("Losing My Religion"), Joe Cocker ("Everybody Hurts"), 10,000 Maniacs ("Don't Go Back to Rockville"), Weezer ("Oddfellows Local 151"), Editors ("Orange Crush"), and The Replacements ("Radio Free Europe").

"Truly all-encompassing," observed Pearl Jam's 248▶ Eddie Vedder, inducting the band into the Rock and Roll Hall of Fame in 2007. "They've used every color on the palette, they've invented colors of their own, and they've painted this huge mural of music and sound and emotion that is as big as buildings. And they're still adding, to this day." And how can you get them to play in your garage? Simple, according to Homer Simpson: "I told them it was a benefit. They think they're saving the rain forest!"

Out of Time (1991) fused the band's formative jingle-jangle with somber lyrics and dreamy music—a beautiful blend that, thanks to "Losing My Religion," made them superstars.

Up (1998) was R.E.M.'s divorce from the mainstream—neither it nor any subsequent album has gone platinum at home. But it is as fascinating and heartrending as *Automatic for the People*.

Supporting U2

In June 1985, remarked U2's❶ Bono (left, with Stipe), R.E.M. were "very, very hot . . . extremely hip, better reviewed than us in the U.K. for their albums, and starting to really happen." The bands met when the Athens quartet supported the Irish stars at a show in Milton Keynes, England. Backstage, said Bono, "I saw this odd-looking bohemian with tiny little plaits in his hair . . . That was the moment I met Michael Stipe." While the singers remained friends, other links were formed. Pat McCarthy, a tape operator on sessions for U2's *The Joshua Tree*, wound up as R.E.M.'s producer from *Up* to *Around the Sun*. On January 20, 1993, Stipe and Mills united with Larry Mullen and Adam Clayton as Automatic Baby, to perform U2's "One" at U.S. President Bill Clinton's inaugural ball. And, in April 2002, a stirring testimony from Bono at a London court helped the "famously peaceful" Peter Buck to be cleared of a 2001 air rage charge.

April 5, 1980
Covers of songs by The Velvet Underground, The Troggs, and others dominate as the band play their first show together. Two weeks later, they will be calling themselves R.E.M.

June 9, 1984
At a New Jersey concert that is filmed for MTV, R.E.M. are joined by their jingly-jangly forefathers: The Byrds' Roger McGuinn and The Lovin' Spoonful's John Sebastian.

1985 Connection

R.E.M.

March 1, 1982
R.E.M. sign to I.R.S. Records, set up by Miles Copeland. They will support The Police—featuring Copeland's brother Stewart on drums—at Shea Stadium in August 1983.

April 22, 1985
At a warm-up for their *Fables of the Reconstruction* tour (in their hometown of Athens, Georgia), Big Star legend (and R.E.M. inspiration) Alex Chilton is the support act.

Connection 1987

"Good time" for the Hindu Love Gods

Bill Berry, Peter Buck, and Mike Mills united with Warren Zevon (left, formerly The Everly Brothers' musical director; latterly a singer-songwriter best known for "Werewolves of London") and singer Bryan Cook in the side-project Hindu Love Gods. Their diminutive discography amounted to one single: a cover of The Easybeats' "Gonna Have a Good Time Tonight" (written by AC/DC❶ producers Harry Vanda and George Young), backed with the R.E.M.-penned "Narrator." The Gods (minus Cook) jammed on further covers in 1987—from Robert Johnson's "Travelin' Riverside Blues" (previously covered by Led Zeppelin❷) to The Georgia Satellites' "Battleship Chains." The most notable was what Warren Zevon described as "quite a nice version" of Prince's❸ "Raspberry Beret," which became a single when the recordings—never intended for release—were issued as an album in 1990, to cash in on R.E.M.'s post-*Green* renown.

Close to Nirvana

❶ 248
❷ 242

R.E.M., observed Pearl Jam's❶ Eddie Vedder, cut "a path for alternative music, for bands like Nirvana❷." Kurt Cobain (left) approached R.E.M. producer, Scott Litt, to work on *Nevermind* in 1991—a job that went to Butch Vig. Nirvana did, however, enlist Litt later to remix songs from 1993's *In Utero*, produced by Steve Albini. "I'd been listening to *Automatic for the People*," explained Nirvana's Krist Novoselic, "and I really liked what Scott did with it." In the meantime, R.E.M.'s Stipe befriended Cobain. "I know what the next Nirvana recording was going to sound like . . ." the singer said. "Very quiet and acoustic, with lots of stringed instruments. It was going to be an amazing record, and I'm a little bit angry at him for killing himself. He and I were going to record a trial run of the album . . . At the last minute he called and said, 'I can't come.'" "Let Me In" (on *Monster*) was R.E.M.'s bittersweet response.

January 25, 1988

Document earns R.E.M. their first U.S. platinum award. It features future anthems "It's the End of the World as We Know It (and I Feel Fine)" and "The One I Love."

1991 Influence

October 15, 1994

Though never as popular as its predecessor, 1992's *Automatic for the People, Monster* (a mix of Marc Bolan and Iggy Pop) is the band's only album to enter the U.S. chart at No. 1.

October 1, 1997

In the wake of a potentially fatal brain aneurysm in March 1995, Berry announces that he is leaving the band. His final album is 1996's underrated *New Adventures in Hi-Fi*.

June 1988

R.E.M. sign to Warner Bros. Asked why, Stipe will reply, "Bugs Bunny." *Green* (1988) will be the first of four multi-platinum U.S. albums that they record for the label.

March 23, 1991

Out of Time enters the U.K. chart at No. 1. In May, it will knock Mariah ("rhymes with 'pariah,'" notes Stipe) Carey off the top of the U.S. chart and soon sell four million.

Connection 1995

October 2004

R.E.M. are second on the bill to Bruce Springsteen on the U.S. Vote for Change tour. The Boss calls the band "the pearls before the swine," and joins them on "Man on the Moon."

Radiohead board the R.E.M. train

❶ 264

"I remember when R.E.M. put out *Out of Time* . . ." said Radiohead's❶ bassist Colin Greenwood. "Around the same time, I.R.S. re-released [R.E.M.'s] *Murmur* and the *Chronic Town* EP and *Fables* and stuff . . . a lot of people got into R.E.M. around then." In 1995, Radiohead were the support act on the *Monster* tour, R.E.M. having been impressed by the British quintet's *The Bends*. Singers Thom Yorke (left) and Stipe formed a master-pupil relationship that led to the former contributing to the Stipe-produced movie *Velvet Goldmine*. As the association continued, Stipe eulogized Radiohead's *OK Computer*, and Yorke singled out gems from R.E.M.'s catalog, such as *Up*'s "Sad Professor." There have been onstage collaborations, too, such as when Stipe sang "Lucky" with Radiohead in 1998 at a Washington club, the day before Yorke sang "You and Me" and "E-bow the Letter" with R.E.M. at the RFK Stadium.

Madonna 1958–present

1958+ 1985+ 1991+ 2000+

When Madonna had a thirty-seventh U.S. Hot 100 top ten hit with "4 Minutes" in 2008, she beat Elvis Presley's ◀012 record of the most top ten hits in *Billboard* history. This was apt, considering that he had died on her nineteenth birthday and in one interview she described him as "God."

Madonna grew up listening to Joni Mitchell ◀102 and Motown ◀030. She snuck out of her parents' home to go to her first concert, David Bowie ◀134, in 1973: "He blew my mind. Ziggy Stardust in Detroit. What he did on stage was so inspiring, because he was so theatrical." Bowie would namecheck her in his 1989 song "Pretty Thing," on *Tin Machine*.

Like Bowie, the Queen of Pop has constantly reinvented herself, working with cool producers and artists to ensure that she stays at the top of the pop game. She has always known how best to make a statement, choosing Iggy Pop ◀116, for example, to perform at her induction into the Rock and Roll Hall of Fame in 2008. "I think she felt conflicted about the Hall of Fame thing," Iggy observed, "and thought, 'Well, if you want me, you're gonna get this . . .'"

Madonna's influence is undeniable. Gwen Stefani said of her early days with No Doubt that, "Madonna had just come out. Her early tracks were so wicked!" Other famous fans include Elton John ◀126—despite a war of words after he accused her of lip-synching—and Bono ◀192; she has hung out with Michael Jackson ◀122; she has worked with Prince ◀174; and even Bob Dylan ◀062 has praised her: "Madonna's good, she's talented, she puts all kind of stuff together, she's learned her thing."

208 BIG HAIR & BIG HITS

August 16, 1958

Madonna Louise (Veronica, her confirmation name, will be added later) Ciccone is born in Michigan. At nineteen, she will move to New York City to study dance.

May 31, 1984

Madonna earns a first gold album, for her self-titled debut. Its hit "Holiday" had originally been offered to soulster Phyllis Hyman and ex-Supreme Mary Wilson.

September 14, 1984

Wearing a wedding dress, atop a giant wedding cake, Madonna performs "Like a Virgin" at the MTV Video Music Awards. The song will become her first U.S. No. 1.

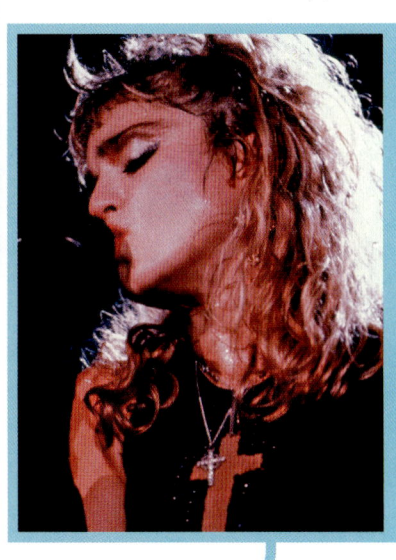

FEBRUARY 9, 1985: Virgin queen topples Prince

❶ 174
❷ 222
❸ 122

Prince's❶ 1984 masterpiece *Purple Rain* had been No. 1 in the U.S. *Billboard* album chart for twenty-four weeks when Madonna's second album, *Like a Virgin*, knocked him off the top spot. Chic's Nile Rodgers produced it, having seen her perform in 1983: "I loved her stage presence . . . I kept thinking to myself, 'Damn, is she a star,' but she wasn't at the time." It contained hit after hit—the title track, "Material Girl," "Angel," and "Dress You Up." ("Into the Groove"—her first U.K. No. 1, from her 1985 movie *Desperately Seeking Susan*—made it onto the album's re-release.) Two months after hitting the top spot, Madonna began her first U.S. tour, The Virgin Tour (left), with the Beastie Boys❷ supporting. During it, she sung a verse from "Billie Jean" as part of "Like a Virgin"— a wry nod to her pop rival, Michael Jackson❸, thirteen days her junior. (Madonna, Prince, and Jackson were all born in the summer of 1958.)

July 13, 1985

After her own set at Live Aid, Madonna joins The Thompson Twins and Nile Rodgers to perform The Beatles' "Revolution."

July 12, 1986

True Blue enters the U.K. chart at No. 1. It will be the year's biggest seller in the U.K. Its "La Isla Bonita" had been meant for Michael Jackson's *Bad*.

August 29, 1986

Shanghai Surprise opens in the U.S.A. The doomed comedy features Madonna and Sean Penn, with a cameo by George Harrison, whose company produced it.

September 1987

Madonna dedicates "Papa Don't Preach" to Pope John Paul II on her Who's That Girl World Tour, after he urges fans to boycott her.

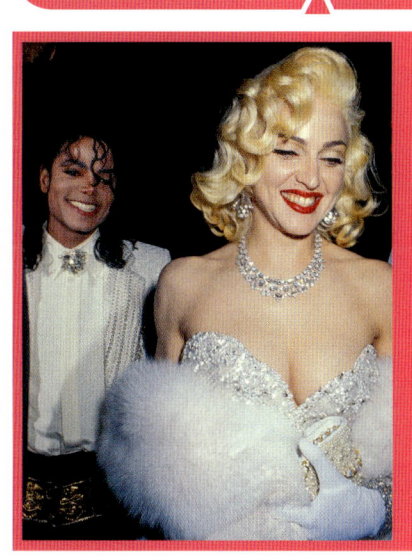

APRIL 1989: *Like a Prayer* conquers the world

❶ 174
❷ 122

"It was a real coming-of-age record for me emotionally," Madonna said of *Like a Prayer*. It was certainly her most personal album up until that point, with a dedication to her mother—who died when she was six and shared her first name—on the sleeve. It featured a collaboration with Prince❶, "Love Song" (lines from which spawned her 2005 "Hung Up"), as well as the smashes "Express Yourself" and "Cherish," but the title track was the biggest and most controversial hit. The video featured an interracial love story, a scene where Madonna develops stigmata, and burning crosses. In 2006, it was voted the most groundbreaking video of all time by MTV viewers. By the time the Eighties were drawing to a close, she was the most successful U.S. female artist of the decade, with three No. 1 albums and seven No. 1 singles under her famous Boy Toy belt. Only Michael Jackson❷ (left, with Madonna in 1991) was bigger.

MADONNA

January 18, 1991

The Immaculate Collection, including recent U.S. No. 1s "Vogue" and "Justify My Love," earns the first of the ten platinum awards that it will win in the U.S.A.

October 1992

The first print-run of Madonna's controversial photo-book, *Sex,* sells out in three days. An accompanying album, *Erotica,* will also sell in the millions.

February 20, 1995

Madonna performs at the Brit Awards, in London, for the first time. She sings "Bedtime Story," written by Björk. Its remixes include one by Orbital.

December 25, 1996

Alan Parker's film *Evita,* with Madonna in the title role, is released. She learns she is pregnant midway through production.

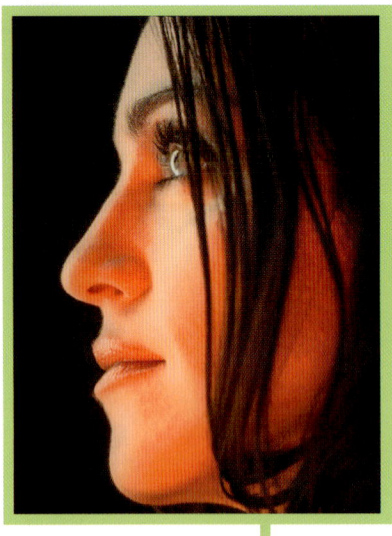

➊ 036

MARCH 3, 1998: Another successful re-invention

A very different Madonna was unveiled with her seventh studio album, *Ray of Light,* in March 1998. This Madonna had toned down the raunch, discovered the mystical teachings of Kabbalah, and given birth to a daughter, Lourdes. Madonna's voice, honed into shape during her work on *Evita,* was further nurtured by producer William Orbit. The album (later included in *Rolling Stone*'s 500 greatest of all time) was partly influenced by Massive Attack, with whom Madonna had worked in 1995 on a Marvin Gaye➊ cover, "I Want You." (Massive Attack member Mushroom also offered her the song that became their hit "Teardrop.") Although *Ray of Light*'s title track lost out to Celine Dion's "My Heart Will Go On" for Record of the Year at the 1999 Grammy Awards, and the album was denied the U.S. No. 1 by the *Titanic* soundtrack, it still revived her sales around the world, hence 2000's international chart-topper, *Music.*

March 3, 2000

Madonna issues a cover of "American Pie" in the U.K. Writer Don McLean calls it a "gift from a goddess" and "mystical and sensual."

April 2000

The video for "Music" stars Ali G (a.k.a. U.K. comic Sacha Baron Cohen) and goes on to win several awards. The single also tops the U.S. charts.

November 18, 2002

The James Bond movie *Die Another Day* premieres in London. Madonna sings the hit title song and makes an uncredited appearance as fencing instructor Verity.

August 28, 2003

In the wake of another hit album, *American Life,* an MTV awards show sees the star kissing Britney Spears and Christina Aguilera.

➊ 083
➋ 143
➌ 174

AUGUST 16, 2008: The Queen of Pop reigns

If anyone thought Madonna was going to slow down when she reached fifty in 2008, they were wrong. Toward the end of 2005, *Confessions on a Dance Floor*—a return to disco-pop form after a run of diverse albums—had topped charts in forty-one countries (a new record). Artists sampled on it included Abba➊ (the normally sample-resistant composers said "yes" this time "because we admire Madonna so much and always have") and Donna Summer➋. The star's next album, 2008's *Hard Candy,* featured Justin Timberlake on its first single, "4 Minutes." With her finger on the pulse as always, the album also featured Timbaland, Pharrell Williams, and Kanye West, with guitarist Wendy Melvoin—a former member of Prince's➌ old band, The Revolution (and a co-writer on *Ray of Light*)—featured on "She's Not Me." Madonna had reached half a century, but she was still sounding as relevant as ever.

210   BIG HAIR & BIG HITS

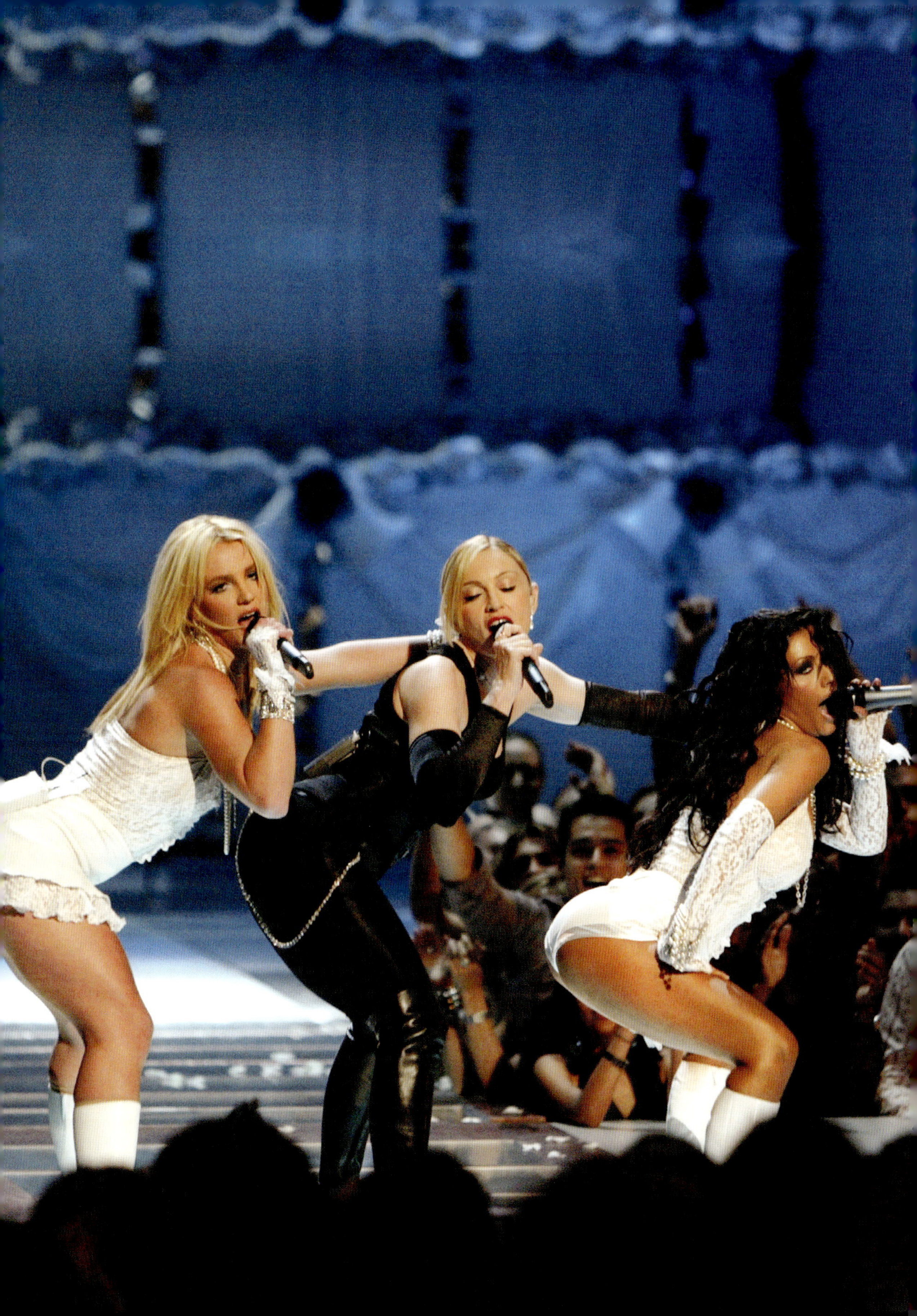

The Smiths 1982–87

1983+ 1986+

A devoted fan of the glam-rocking likes of Bowie ◁134 and Bolan ◁128 (not to mention the New York Dolls, whose reunion in 2004 was organized by The Smiths front man), Stephen Morrissey wound up leading an equally iconic act (after passing through the ranks of Ed Banger & The Nosebleeds, featuring future Cult guitarist Billy Duffy). Along with guitarist Johnny Marr, bassist Andy Rourke, and drummer Mike Joyce, Morrissey formed a band whose unique twist on rock (ambiguous sexuality, wry poetry, Byrdsy guitars, and Elvis ◁012-esque rhythms) influenced acts from Oasis 260▷ to The Killers 280▷.

The band made an impact despite lasting barely six years. "The Smiths released two albums a year, plus singles and fresh B-sides," observed Brandon Flowers of The Killers. "That's just incredible to me."

Their songs have been covered by acts including Dinosaur Jr.'s J. Mascis ("The Boy with the Thorn in His Side"), Everclear ("How Soon Is Now"), Jeff Buckley ("I Know it's Over"), Eurythmics ("Last Night I Dreamt that Somebody Loved Me"), Muse 270▷ ("Please Please Please Let Me Get What I Want"), Anthrax ("London"), Mark Ronson ("Stop Me If You Think You've Heard This One Before"), and Death Cab for Cutie ("Sweet and Tender Hooligan").

This passionate band provoked passionate reactions. "The Smiths came on *Top of The Pops* . . ." recalled Oasis' Noel Gallagher (who has covered "There Is a Light that Never Goes Out"). "From that day on," he said, "I wanted to *be* Johnny Marr." In contrast, The Cure's Robert Smith declared: "I hate The Smiths and everything they've ever done."

May 13, 1983

The Smiths debut with "Hand in Glove." ("It reminded me of Joy Division," Noel Gallagher will recall.) Less than a year later, they will remake it with Sixties singer Sandie Shaw.

1984

The band scores two U.K. top ten albums: their self-titled debut (March, No. 2) and the B-sides and radio sessions collection, *Hatful of Hollow* (November, No. 7).

February 23, 1985

Meat Is Murder enters the British chart at No. 1. A later U.S. version will include "How Soon Is Now" (to be covered by Love Spit Love in 1996 for *The Craft* and TV's *Charmed*).

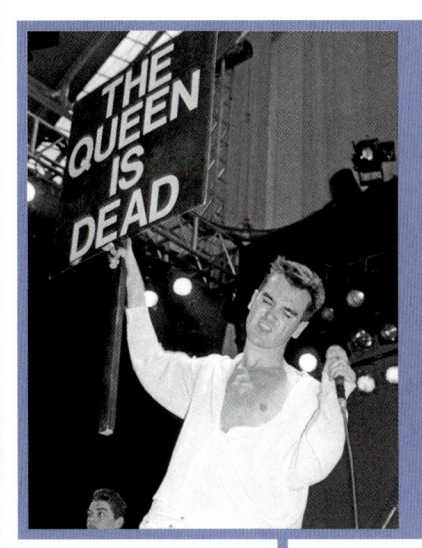

JUNE 28, 1986: *The Queen Is Dead*

Although Morrissey (left) and Marr maintain that 1987's *Strangeways, Here We Come* is The Smiths' masterpiece (and although Genesis'❶ *Invisible Touch* kept it off the top of the U.K. chart), *The Queen Is Dead* was the band's finest hour, despite being conceived in chaotic circumstances: everyone was exhausted, Marr was in a car crash, and Rourke's heroin problems were escalating to the point where he would be fired (briefly) in early 1986 (and replaced by Craig Gannon). Nonetheless, the album was superb: from the rollicking title track, through "Bigmouth Strikes Again" and "The Boy with the Thorn in His Side," to the beautiful "There Is a Light that Never Goes Out" and "Some Girls Are Bigger than Others." A tenth anniversary tribute collection in 1996, *The Smiths Is Dead*, featured the entire album, reworked by voguish acts such as The Boo Radleys, Placebo, Therapy?, Supergrass, and The Divine Comedy.

❶ 061

October 23, 1986

The Smiths play a London show later immortalized as the fine album *Rank*. It includes "His Latest Flame," originally sung by Elvis.

1987

Two more compilation albums hit the U.K. chart: *The World Won't Listen* (March, No. 2) and the U.S. import *Louder than Bombs* (May, No. 38).

July 1987

Exhausted and no longer in tune with Morrissey, Marr quits. The band will be over by the time *Strangeways, Here We Come* is issued in September (hitting No. 2).

March 26, 1988

Morrissey's first solo album, *Viva Hate,* enters the U.K. chart at No. 1. Its song "The Ordinary Boys" will inspire the name of a British band.

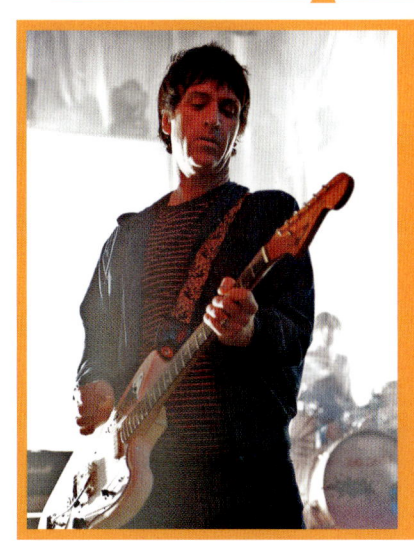

MARCH 1995: "There Is a Light that Never Goes Out"

In the wake of the band's dissolution, Morrissey and Marr (left) both enjoyed interesting careers. The singer issued regular albums, notably 1992's *Your Arsenal* (produced by former David Bowie❶ and Ian Hunter guitarist Mick Ronson), and the U.K. chart-toppers *Vauxhall and I* (1994) and *Ringleaders of the Tormentors* (2006, produced by Bowie and Bolan❷ producer Tony Visconti). Meanwhile, Marr has played with a bewildering variety of acts, including The Pretenders, The The, Electronic (with New Order's❸ Bernard Sumner), and Modest Mouse. But affection for The Smiths has never subsided. In 1992, *Best . . . 1* topped the U.K. chart. Then, in March 1995, the band held seven positions in the chart, with *Singles*, and reissues of their albums. However, Morrissey and Marr have stoically resisted all attempts to reunite the band that made them much-loved legends. "I do not," said the singer airily, "see the point."

❶ 134
❷ 128
❸ 186

THE SMITHS 213

key festival

Live Aid and Live 8
July 13, 1985 and July 2, 2005

For all the cultural, charitable, and technological significance of 1985's Live Aid, its most immediate impact was on the charts. In the U.K., for example, *No Jacket Required* by Phil Collins (who played on both sides of the Atlantic on the same day) and Madonna's ◀208 *Like a Virgin* leapt back into the top ten. Queen's ◀144 three-year-old *Greatest Hits* rose fifty-five places into the top twenty, followed by Freddie Mercury's *Mr. Bad Guy*. Most notably, every U2 ◀192 album returned to the chart. Then, after 2005's Live 8, The Who ◀068, Pink Floyd ◀086, U2, and The Killers 280▶ saw *their* sales surge. (David Gilmour pledged to donate the resultant profits to charity and was then obliged to explain that he wasn't speaking for the rest of Pink Floyd.)

Both events were the brainchild of Bob Geldof, front man of punk pop band The Boomtown Rats. Moved by the famine in Ethiopia, he and Ultravox front man Midge Ure had written the Band Aid smash "Do They Know It's Christmas?" in 1984. From this evolved worldwide charity records, such as USA for Africa's "We Are the World," and, in July 1985, the mammoth Live Aid concerts at London's Wembley Stadium and Philadelphia's JFK Stadium.

"Bob was being catapulted into the media every day, all day," recalled Geldof's keyboard player Johnny Fingers. "And no one mentioned The Boomtown Rats." (The Rats did, however, contribute to one of the day's memorable moments: Geldof's dramatic pause in their hit "I Don't Like Mondays.")

Queen
Greatest Hits
(1981)
EMI Records

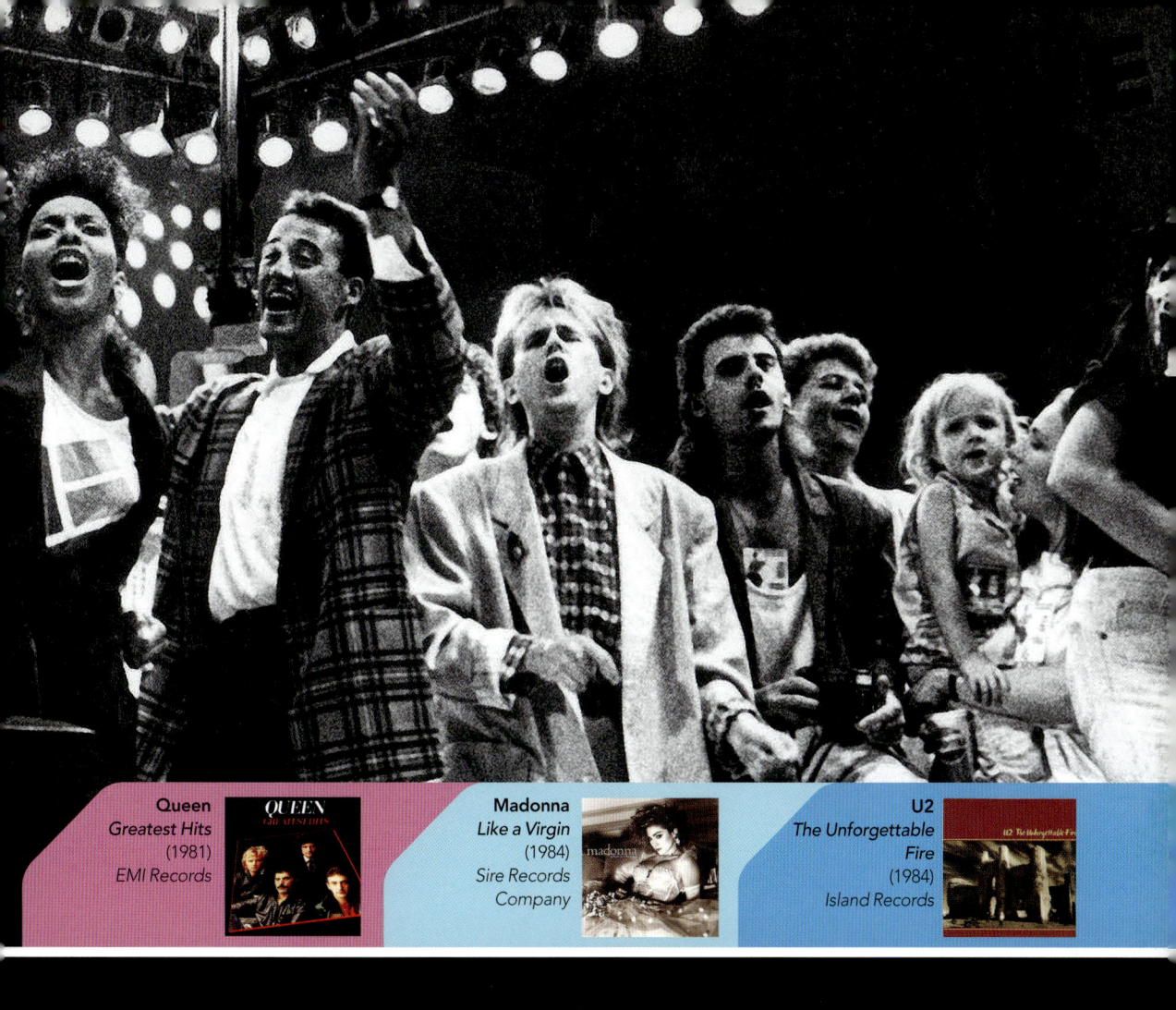

Madonna
Like a Virgin
(1984)
Sire Records Company

U2
The Unforgettable Fire
(1984)
Island Records

The 1985 event reunited Led Zeppelin ◀098, the original Black Sabbath ◀108, and The Who. David Bowie ◀134 turned "Heroes" into an anthem and duetted with The Rolling Stones' ◀054 Mick Jagger on a specially created video for the event: a cover of the Motown ◀030 classic "Dancing in the Street."

The 2005 sequel—played in venues around the world but focused on London's Hyde Park—reunited the estranged classic Pink Floyd lineup. When guitarist Gilmour was persuaded to participate by his old foe, bassist Roger Waters, a delighted Geldof (who had starred in Floyd's movie *The Wall*) told him, "You've made an old man very happy."

Gilmour was one of a number of people to play in both 1985 and 2005, as were Duran Duran ◀200

Bryan Adams, Sting, U2, and Paul McCartney. The latter had suffered a failed microphone at Live Aid but fared better when opening Live 8 with U2. The Who also did better in 2005 than at the earlier show, during which Pete Townshend had fallen over.

Greatest progress was made by Madonna. In 1985, *Penthouse* and *Playboy* were competing to print old nude pictures of her. "I ain't takin' shit off today," she quipped in Philadelphia. "They might hold it against me ten years from now." By 2005, the pop queen had become a global goddess. Her linked arms with Birhan Woldu—the now adult Ethiopian whose younger image had played a pivotal role in bringing attention to her country's famine—was one of the day's defining images.

INXS Melbourne 13:06 GMT

Oz for Africa, the Australian leg of Live Aid, kicked off twelve hours before London, making it the first event of the day. Headlining were INXS—heroes at home and soon to be superstars in the U.S.A. Their twenty-two-minute set featured four Australian hits ("Original Sin," "Listen Like Thieves," "Kiss the Dirt," and "Don't Change") and one—"What You Need"—that would take them into the U.S. top five in 1986.

David Gilmour London 16:07 GMT

Bryan Ferry's set (below) united his guest guitarist, Pink Floyd's ❶ David Gilmour, with keyboardist Jon Carin, who would deputize for Rick Wright in the revived Floyd. This incarnation enraged former leader Roger Waters, making the Floyd's Live 8 reunion in 2005 particularly noteworthy. Gilmour later emailed Waters: "Hi Rog, I'm glad you made that phone call. It was fun, wasn't it?"

Live Aid
July 13, 1985

U2 London 17:20 GMT

"Freddie Mercury pulled me aside," recalled U2's ❶ Bono. "I was up against a wall and he put his hand on the wall and was talking to me like he was chatting up a chick . . . David Bowie ❷ came over to me. And I was like, 'David Bowie just came to talk to me!' And then we started walking together and I turned to ask him something, and I was wearing that ridiculous hat with the wide brim, and I nearly took his eye out."

Queen London 18:44 GMT

In six songs ("Bohemian Rhapsody," "Radio Ga Ga," "Hammer to Fall," "Crazy Little Thing Called Love," "We Will Rock You," and "We Are the Champions"), plus an awe-inspiring Freddie Mercury singalong, Queen ❶—who had initially not wanted to play at the event—sealed their immortality. "It was the perfect stage for Freddie," observed Bob Geldof. "He could ponce about in front of the whole world."

216 BIG HAIR & BIG HITS

David Bowie London 19:02 GMT

"Bowie❶ was very busy filming *Labyrinth*," keyboard player Thomas Dolby told *The Quietus*. "We had to grab a few hours here and there to rehearse. But he kept changing his mind about what to play . . . He settled on the four final songs ["TVC15," "Rebel Rebel," "Modern Love," and "Heroes"] the evening before the show." Bowie sacrificed some of his time to play a heartrending video set to The Cars' "Drive."

Madonna Philadelphia 21:27 GMT

"We are thrilled," announced Bette Midler at Live Aid, "to introduce to you today a woman whose name has been on everyone's lips for the last six months. A woman who pulled herself up by her bra straps—and who has been known to let them down occasionally." Twenty years later, Geldof gave Madonna❶ an equally tongue-in-cheek tribute: "The queen bee of rock 'n' roll . . . she gives me a terribly hard time."

Led Zeppelin Philadelphia 01:13 GMT

"We virtually ruined the whole thing . . ." Zeppelin's❶ Robert Plant told *Q*. "I was hoarse and couldn't sing and Page was out of tune and couldn't hear his guitar. But on the other hand it was a wondrous thing because it was a wing and a prayer . . . They were still chanting for us fifteen minutes later and there were people crying all over the place . . . It was something far more powerful than words can convey."

Bob Dylan Philadelphia 03:39 GMT

Just before the Philadelphia finale, Dylan❶ (above, with Tina Turner, Mick Jagger, and Madonna❷) appeared with Ronnie Wood and Keith Richards of the Stones❸. (Jagger and Turner duetted separately before them.) Dylan tried to spring a last-minute setlist change on his cohorts, then a backstage rehearsal of "We Are the World" meant the trio couldn't hear what they were playing. "A great night," said Wood, wryly.

LIVE AID AND LIVE 8   217

Metallica 1981–present

1962+   1984+   1989+   1993+

The list of top twenty biggest sellers in U.S. recording history has obvious inclusions (Elvis ◀012 and The Beatles ◀044), surprises (before his death, Michael Jackson ◀122 had only just outsold George Strait), and hard elements (AC/DC ◀182 and Aerosmith ◀154). However, with the exception of Pink Floyd ◀086, none have made it on to the list with such an uncommercial sound as Metallica.

"A band like Metallica were basically taking our sound," noted Joey of the Ramones ◀158, "but they're sort of the new tip. The thing I like about bands like Metallica . . . is that they're doing it their way. There's an honesty. There's an excitement. There's an energy. There's a brashness that they're sayin,' 'Fuck you. This is us.' And their kind of hardcoreness, you know what I mean?"

Metallica have an enviably broad fan base. Even before their mainstream breakthrough, Tom Petty said they "have something going on," Johnny Cash ◀018 saw them in concert, and Black Francis of the Pixies 224▶ reported they were "pretty cool." "Early Metallica I like a lot," admitted Nick Cave ◀202.

"The fella that sings lead," remarked Iggy Pop ◀116, "he projects that uncompromising quality." "Macho about their work ethic and dedicated to their fans," observed Slash of Guns N' Roses 228▶. To Jon Bon Jovi, they were "bigger than God."

"I was a huge Metallica fan from the first album," Nirvana's 242▶ Dave Grohl told *Q*. "And as much as I've worn out my Beatles records and my Pixies records and the Zeppelin records ◀098 . . . that's the band that I've probably listened to the most."

218   BIG HAIR & BIG HITS

1962
Clifford Burton (February 10), Robert Trujillo (October 24), and Kirk Hammett (November 18) are born in California. They will join in 1982, 1983, and 2003, respectively.

1963
Jason Newsted (March 3), James Hetfield (August 3), and Lars Ulrich (December 26) are born, in Michigan, California, and Gentofte, Denmark, respectively.

December 1982
After fourteen months of shifting lineups, Metallica solidify around singer and guitarist Hetfield, drummer Ulrich, bassist Burton, and guitarist Dave Mustaine.

JULY 29, 1983: *Kill 'Em All*

By the time Metallica's debut *Kill 'Em All* emerged (its mooted title, *Metal Up Your Ass*, was vetoed by the Megaforce label), Dave Mustaine was out. James Hetfield, the guitarist reported, "kicked my dog and I punched him in the mouth." While Mustaine licked his wounds and later founded Megadeth, Metallica (with Cliff Burton, left) recruited Kirk Hammett—who, like Zappa❶/David Lee Roth/Whitesnake string-slinger Steve Vai and Rage Against the Machine's❷ Tom Morello, was a student of guitar god Joe Satriani. With their labelmates Anthrax, Metallica led a wave of thrash metal: a fiery blend of Motörhead-fueled rock and punky attitude that was at odds with prevailing trends in metal, epitomized by Mötley Crüe and Def Leppard❸. This style won Metallica loyal fans; when they supported W.A.S.P., the headliners were pelted and spat at. (Even worse awaited W.A.S.P. when they hired Slayer as support.)

❶ 076
❷ 254
❸ 181

July 27, 1984
The sophisticated *Ride the Lightning* (with Mustaine's final writing credit) proves that the band are starting to leave thrash behind.

August 1985
Metallica appear low on the bill at the U.K.'s Monsters of Rock (headliners: ZZ Top) and California's Day on the Green (headliners: Scorpions).

March 27, 1986
The band begins a tour with Ozzy Osbourne that breaks them into the big time. On November 4, the *Master of Puppets* will earn them their first U.S. gold album.

September 27, 1986
Cliff Burton is killed when Metallica's bus crashes in Sweden. Mustaine will pay tribute with Megadeth's "In My Darkest Hour" in 1988.

NOVEMBER 8, 1986: New Kid on the block

❶ 190

Less than six weeks after Burton's death, Metallica were back on the road with new bassist Jason "New Kid" Newsted (left), of Flotsam & Jetsam. His first recording with the band was the fantastic *The $5.98 E.P.: Garage Days Re-Revisited*, featuring songs originally by Diamond Head, Holocaust, Killing Joke, Budgie, and The Misfits (plus a closing parody of Iron Maiden's❶ "Run to the Hills"). Its gutsy immediacy gave way to weirdly produced progressive metal on 1988's *...And Justice for All*, which mysteriously mixed Newsted's bass to near inaudible levels. Nonetheless, with little airplay and no hit single ("One" didn't chart until 1989), the album entered transatlantic top tens and went platinum in the U.S.A. With the band now an arena-filling sensation, four Metallica shows were attended by a Californian teen by the name of Cameron Diaz. "They play some good, hard, speed rock 'n' roll," the actress later reported.

METALLICA 219

February 22, 1989

At the Grammys, Metallica are up against Mötley Crüe and Jethro Tull for the Rock award. To what Mötley's Tommy Lee describes as "fucking horror," Tull win.

January 1990

Metallica cut Queen's "Stone Cold Crazy" for a compilation. Hetfield will sing it with Tony Iommi and Queen at the 1992 Freddie Mercury tribute show.

February 26, 1991

Kill 'Em All turns platinum in the U.S.A. (every album has sold at least a million in the U.S.A. alone). It will also earn gold status in the U.K., despite never charting.

August 17, 1991

For their third appearance at the U.K.'s Monsters of Rock, Metallica are second on the bill to AC/DC. They will finally headline in 1995.

❶ 228

AUGUST 1991: *Metallica* conquers the world

"We had taken the progressive, complicated side of Metallica as far as we could," Lars Ulrich (left) told *Billboard*'s Craig Rosen. "We really needed to make a major change." Impressed by his work with Mötley Crüe, the band hired producer Bob Rock, with whom they spent nine months crafting a classic. It was time well spent: 1991's *Metallica*—a.k.a. "The Black Album"—crashed the U.S. and international charts at No. 1, en route to becoming one of the decade's biggest sellers (it has since sold fifteen million in the U.S.A. alone). The band spent much of the next two years on the road, including a tense co-headliner with Guns N' Roses❶. In Montreal on August 8, 1992, an exploding stage effect sent Hetfield to hospital, and a riot ensued when Guns went on three hours late, then cut their show short. "I couldn't," said Slash, "look James, Lars, or anyone from their band in the eye for the rest of the tour."

November 23, 1993

The CD/video set *Live Shit: Binge & Purge* is released. Including Queen, Diamond Head, and Misfits covers, it will be another huge seller.

April 10, 1996

Metallica attend the taping of *Unplugged* by Alice in Chains, who play snippets of "Enter Sandman" and "Battery" to the audience's amusement.

August 12, 1996

Load, a belated follow-up to "The Black Album," goes triple platinum in just over two months. The following year's *ReLoad* will be another multimillion seller.

November 11, 1997

"The Memory Remains" is released as a single. Guest vocalist Marianne Faithfull reports: "They're all nice boys—good to their mums."

❶ 108
❷ 202
❸ 226

JANUARY 2001: Difficult times ahead

As a new decade dawned, Metallica's most recent albums had been a covers collection, from Black Sabbath❶ to Nick Cave❷ (1998's *Garage Inc.*) and a symphonic live experiment (1999's *S&M*). Although both were successful, they suggested stagnation. The discomfort was compounded by Lars Ulrich's battle with the file-sharing service Napster. Then, in 2001, tired of being treated as a junior partner, Jason Newsted quit. The ensuing turmoil—including Hetfield's stint in rehab, the near split of the band, and the appointment of Newsted's replacement, former Ozzy Osbourne bassist Rob Trujillo (left)—is documented in the 2004 movie *Some Kind of Monster*. Metallica re-emerged with 2003's *St. Anger*, while 2008's Rick Rubin❸-produced *Death Magnetic* made Metallica the first band to have five consecutive studio albums enter the U.S. chart at No. 1. Their reign as the world's biggest metal band shows no signs of ending.

220   BIG HAIR & BIG HITS

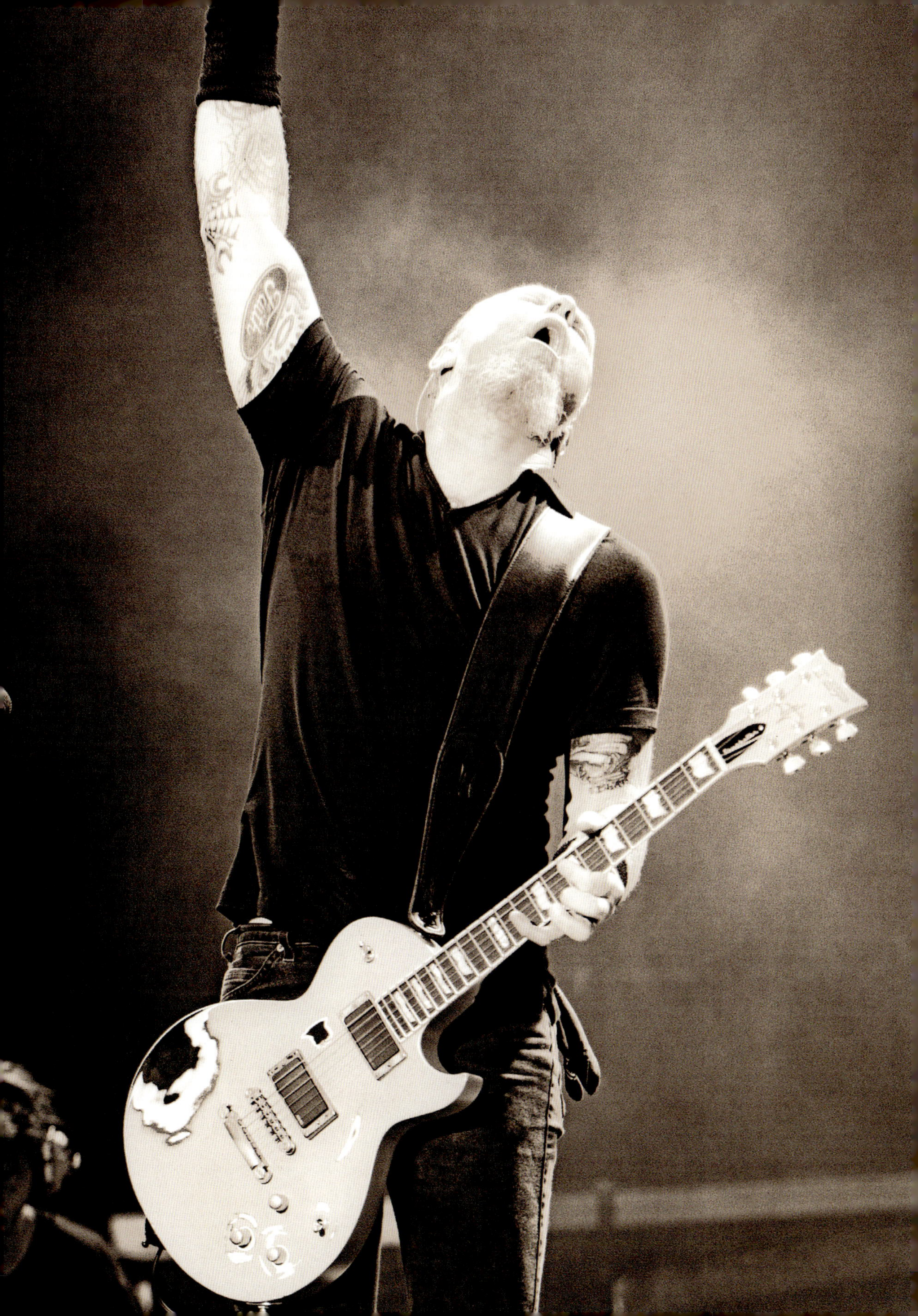

legendary label

Def Jam / American Recordings
1984–present

Though primarily associated with hip-hop, Def Jam's roster—and that of its co-founder Rick Rubin's ◁226▷ next venture, American Recordings—has been entertainingly diverse: from Public Enemy to Slayer, from the Beastie Boys to Mariah Carey, and from Johnny Cash ◁018▷ to System of a Down.

"I made [T La Rock and Jazzy Jay's 1984 single] 'It's Yours,'" Rubin explained to *Rolling Stone,* "and was planning to release it on an independent label myself, which was going to be called Def Jam . . . It took about nine months until it caught on. That's when I met Russell Simmons. He was shocked that I was white and had made that record. I was really excited about meeting him, because he had made a bunch of records I liked." (Simmons had helmed records by his brother Joseph's band, Run-DMC.)

Still in their twenties, Rubin and Simmons were to revolutionize the music industry. "The first Public Enemy record, the first LL [Cool J] too—each of these records doesn't sound like anybody else's record," Simmons mused. "You create your own musical identity and do something special."

"Def Jam has basically changed my life," said LL. The label even impacted on the generation whose records it sampled: Rick Rubin produced AC/DC ◁182▷, whose "Back in Black" and "TNT" were the basis of early cuts by the Beastie Boys. Meanwhile, the Beasties' sampling of Led Zeppelin ◁098▷ riffs on their debut album inspired Robert Plant to dust off his old band's songs in concert: "I thought to myself that, if Def Jam can do it, so can I. Maybe Rick Rubin will sue me for it!"

1984+
1987+
1992+

1984
Although T La Rock and Jazzy Jay's "It's Yours" is the first release with the Def Jam logo, LL Cool J's "I Need a Beat" is the first on the label itself.

November 18, 1985
Now distributed by Columbia, Def Jam issues what will be its first U.S. gold album: LL's Cool J's *Radio*. He will still be going gold two decades later.

October 7, 1986
Slayer's *Reign in Blood* has a Def Jam label, but its lyrics lead Columbia to refuse to handle it, and Geffen end up distributing it.

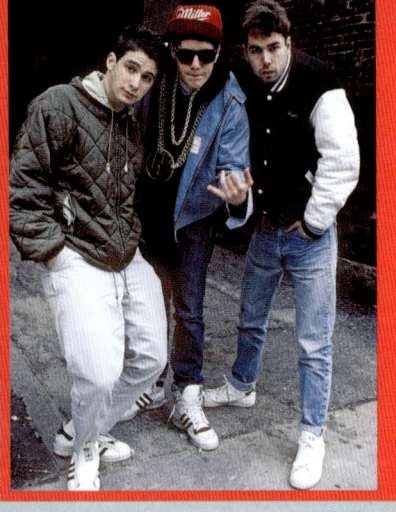

❶ 182
❷ 208
❸ 157
❹ 226
❺ 022
❻ 098

MARCH 7, 1987: The Beastie Boys hit No. 1

Adam "King Ad-Rock" Horowitz, Mike "Mike D" Diamond, and Adam "MCA" Yauch (left) had begun as a hopeless hardcore band, before trading punk for hip-hop. Their "Rock Hard," based on an AC/DC❶ loop, was a pivotal single in Def Jam's formative discography, yet Columbia hardly had high hopes for the trio when they took over the label's distribution. "They looked at us," said Mike D, "as the curse of the whole deal." But they honed their craft on tour with Madonna❷ and Run-DMC❸ (the latter also produced by Rick Rubin❹, and featuring Russell Simmons' brother, Joseph), and scored the first chart-topping rap album with *Licensed to Ill*. "The way black kids who grew up with James Brown❺ used his stuff, the Beastie Boys used Led Zeppelin❻," recalled Simmons. "They used what they liked about Run-DMC . . . and what they didn't like, they made fun of it. They made it cool."

BIG HAIR & BIG HITS

November 6, 1987

Less than Zero premieres. Its Def Jam soundtrack includes Roy Orbison singing a song by Danzig, and The Bangles covering Simon & Garfunkel.

September 26, 1988

Public Enemy's classic *It Takes a Nation of Millions to Hold Us Back* (which samples "Angel of Death" by Slayer and "Flash" by Queen, and namechecks Anthrax) goes gold.

October 23, 1989

3rd Bass release *The Cactus Album*, which samples Pink Floyd's "Time" and bears the hit "Pop Goes the Weasel." 3rd Bass will also help launch the career of rapper Nas.

June 7, 1990

Public Enemy's transatlantic top ten album, the fantastic *Fear of a Black Planet*, goes platinum less than three months after its release.

1991: Def American goes platinum

"While at Def Jam," Rick Rubin❶ told *Rolling Stone*, "I was responsible for LL Cool J, the Beastie Boys, Public Enemy❷. At that time, Russell had brought in mostly R&B stuff . . . We each ran our own team, really . . . and when he would question what I was doing—'Why are you doing Public Enemy?'—it was frustrating." Rubin duly left Def Jam to set up Def American (later to become American Recordings). "We don't have Slayer anymore—that's how much it affected us," sniffed Russell Simmons. On January 8, 1991, the new label scored its first platinum smash with The Black Crowes' (left) *Shake Your Money Maker*, and enjoyed ongoing success with Slayer, Sir Mix-A-Lot, System of a Down, and a career-revitalizing series of albums by Johnny Cash❸. Rubin also made a spectacular contribution to a later Def Jam release, producing the incredible "99 Problems" on Jay-Z's❹ 2003 *The Black Album*.

❶ 226
❷ 025
❸ 018
❹ 266

September 22, 1992

Whut? Thee Album is the first smash by Redman. His success will hit a peak with 1999's *Blackout!*, featuring Wu-Tang's Method Man.

August 24, 1994

Warren G's *Regulate . . . G Funk Era* goes platinum. Dr. Dre's stepbrother will sell another two million albums over the next year.

June 29, 1995

Method Man and Mary J. Blige's Motown-based "I'll Be There for You" goes platinum. Meth's *Tical* will do the same, despite not featuring the hit single.

June 6, 1998

DMX's debut *It's Dark and Hell Is Hot* enters the *Billboard* chart at No. 1, as will his next four albums (of which 1999's . . . *And Then There Was X* will be his multi-platinum champ).

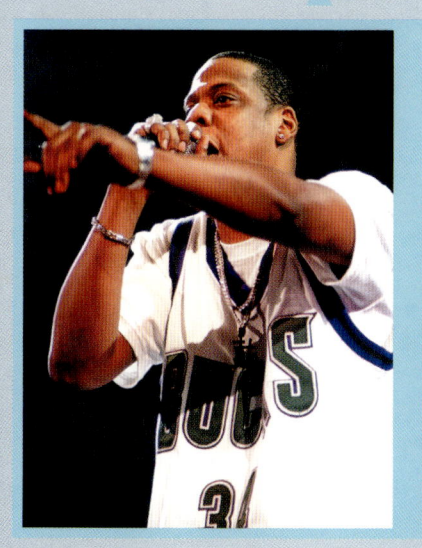

OCTOBER 17, 1998: Jay-Z hits No. 1 for the first time

With *Vol 2 . . . Hard Knock Life*, Jay-Z❶ scored the first (and best-selling) of eleven U.S. No. 1 albums, breaking a record held by Elvis Presley❷. During his short-lived retirement from recording and touring, the rap star was even appointed head of Def Jam in 2004. Not everyone was pleased: "I wish Rick [Rubin]❸ and Russell [Simmons] was back," LL Cool J grumbled on 2007's "Queens." "I miss the old Def Jam / 'cause them new monkeys act like they don't know who I am." The following year's *Exit 13* became his twelfth U.S. top twenty album on the label, including six that have topped the R&B chart. LL was the only constant in the label's evolution: the twenty-first century Def Jam is far removed from the business first run out of Rubin's dorm room. It can hardly hope to be as innovative as when it began, but artists such as Kanye West, Mariah Carey, and Rihanna ensure that it remains a force to be reckoned with.

❶ 266
❷ 012
❸ 226

DEF JAM 223

Pixies 1986–present

1961+   1988+

They have scored only two gold albums in their native U.S.A., where they never rose above No. 70. Their biggest single peaked at No. 28, and for more than a decade, from 1993, they didn't even play together. Yet the Pixies are among the most influential acts of the past quarter century, with fans ranging from David Bowie ◀134 to Radiohead 264▶.

Nirvana's 242▶ Kurt Cobain wrote that the 1988 classic *Surfer Rosa* "made me finally admit that I'm a music lover. Their music reminded me of the music that I always wanted to do." "Smells Like Teen Spirit" was, as Cobain conceded, an attempt to sound like the Pixies, whose loud-quiet-loud formula influenced them, among many grunge stars. (Nirvana drummer Dave Grohl named *Trompe le Monde* as his favorite album of all time and has sung bits of "Cactus" live.)

The Pixies' songs have been covered by David Bowie, Pearl Jam 248▶, TV on the Radio, Placebo, Weezer, and Belle & Sebastian. Bob Mould of Hüsker Dü (a pivotal influence on the Pixies themselves) paid tribute with his band Sugar's "A Good Idea." And a video of Israeli teens miming to "Hey" has now got nearly thirty million views on YouTube.

"We were ripping off the Pixies when we started," remarked Radiohead's Thom Yorke, "or trying to." "One of the bands that really blew my mind when I first moved to L.A. and started to discover cool music," said Weezer's Rivers Cuomo. Ultimately, the band's importance outweighs statistics. As another fan—Chris Martin of Coldplay 276▶ (who sang "Debaser" at soundchecks)—noted, "The best bands aren't necessarily the biggest—like the Pixies."

1961

Kim Deal (June 10, Ohio) and David Lovering (December 6, Massachusetts) are born. They will meet at Deal's wedding and she will put him forward for the band that she's in.

1965

Charles Thompson IV (April 6, Massachusetts) and Joey Santiago (June 10, Philippines) are born. They will be roommates at the University of Massachusetts.

1986

Thompson and Santiago advertise for a bassist who is into "Hüsker Dü and Peter, Paul & Mary." They duly recruit the only applicant: Kim Deal, a.k.a Mrs. John Murphy.

MARCH 1987: The purple patch begins

Guitarist and singer Thompson (left, now calling himself "Black Francis" in homage to "funny, corny, pompous stage names like Iggy Pop❶ and Billy Idol"), lead guitarist Santiago, bassist Deal, and drummer Lovering convened in July 1986 and made their live debut in Boston six months later. "Possibly the worst gig in the history of rock," Lovering recalled. "All our friends came to see us and laughed their asses off." But by March 1987, they had their act together and recorded the so-called "Purple Tape," including future favorite "Here Comes Your Man" and a cover of "In Heaven (The Lady in the Radiator Song)" from David Lynch's movie *Eraserhead*. Ivo Watts-Russell of U.K. independent label 4AD (best known for the Cocteau Twins) was so impressed that he issued eight of these demos as 1987's *Come On Pilgrim*. It would be another two years before the Pixies charted at home but, in Europe, they became cult heroes.

❶ 116

March 21, 1988

Surfer Rosa is released. It is dominated by Francis' off-kilter songs, but will attract attention for "Gigantic," co-written by Deal.

April 29, 1989

Awash with classics (including "Debaser," "Here Comes Your Man," and "Monkey Gone to Heaven"), *Doolittle* enters the U.K. chart at an amazing No. 8.

August 13, 1990

Two months after *Pod*, the debut of Deal's other band The Breeders, *Bossanova* is issued. It will be the Pixies' highest charting album on both sides of the Atlantic.

October 5, 1991

Trompe le Monde becomes the band's third U.K. top ten album. But their days are numbered, owing to tension between Francis and Deal.

DECEMBER 1992: Frank Black and The Breeders

"Everybody was under the impression that we were taking a year off," Santiago told *Mojo*, "but it never came to that. Charles started doing his own album (as Frank Black), and Kim started doing The Breeders (left). Three or four months later, Charles called, out of the blue, at my girlfriend's house, to say he was splitting the band." In the wake of the split, *Frank Black* and The Breeders' "Cannonball" hit the mainstream. Amid succeeding solo projects, the Pixies legend was nurtured by superstar namechecks, reissues, and the use of "Where Is My Mind" at the climax of 1999's *Fight Club*. In 2004, the band reunited for the first in a series of well-received tours, but Francis was skeptical about a new album: "It feels funny to make a record to take advantage of this situation. Whatever box we were performing or writing within before, it's really gotta break through all that and just be upside down."

super producer

Rick Rubin
1963–present

Despite establishing a guru-like reputation, Rick Rubin has plenty of people prepared to pay tribute to his idiosyncratic approach. "He was, very self-consciously, an enfant terrible," reported his Def Jam-era associate Bill Adler. "He was loud, he was slobbish, he was rude, he was overbearing, he was condescending, he was dismissive . . ."

By the Nineties, the producer's behavior had improved, but the complaints continued. "He isn't very easy to work with," observed Malcolm Young of AC/DC **182**, whose *Ballbreaker* (1995) Rubin produced. "*You've* got to be understanding to work with *him,* not the other way around. But he's good and he sticks to his plan. And he's the first producer we've ever worked with who hasn't said, 'Where's the single?' That's a big plus."

"He certainly wasn't easygoing in the studio," agreed Neil Diamond, whose career underwent a spectacular revival thanks to the Rubin-produced *12 Songs* (2005) and *Home Before Dark* (2008), the latter the singer's first U.S. No. 1 album. "He's a passionate, obsessive person . . . But I have so much respect for the guy. He's talented, and he knows music, and he brings a fresh perspective."

Rubin's multi-platinum, extraordinarily diverse discography ranges from Slayer to Shakira, Justin Timberlake to Weezer, Sir Mix-a-Lot to Nusrat Fateh Ali Khan, and Slipknot to the Dixie Chicks. "The songs always feel better after his suggestions," said System of a Down front man Damon Malakian. "And so do you. He's just so easy to be around. That's why people keep going back to him."

1963+
1987+
1994+

March 10, 1963
Frederick Jay Rubin is born in Long Island, New York. "From an early age," he will recall to Q magazine, "The Beatles came my way, and I was obsessed with them."

1981
At New York University, Rubin forms Hose, who issue a 1981 single and 1982 mini-album on his label Def Jam Recordings (although neither will actually count as a Def Jam release).

1984
Rubin meets Russell Simmons, with whom he forms Def Jam, and Adam Horovitz, via whom he meets the Beastie Boys.

---

❶ 222
❷ 222
❸ 025
❹ 157
❺ 154

1986: "Walk This Way"

At Def Jam❶, Rubin presided over Slayer's *Reign in Blood* and debuts by LL Cool J, the Beastie Boys❷, and Public Enemy❸. Yet his most important work was with Run-DMC❹ (signed to Profile)—particularly their 1986 album *Raising Hell*, with an inspired reworking of "Walk This Way" by Aerosmith❺. "To me, rap sounded like an offshoot of the blues," Aerosmith guitarist Joe Perry (left, with DMC) told *Classic Rock*, "so it seemed like a very natural thing for us to play on it. When Rick Rubin said, 'Come on over and sit in,' we thought, 'This seems like another adventure, let's see how it turns out.' It was pretty thrown together but, as it turned out, it really did seem to set the course for the kind of music that's popular today." Rubin worked with Aerosmith again on the *Less Than Zero* (1987) soundtrack, which also found him producing Roy Orbison (covering a Danzig song), The Bangles, Poison, and Joan Jett.

BIG HAIR & BIG HITS

April 1987

The Cult's Rubin-produced, AC/DC-inspired *Electric* is unleashed. Rubin's rock leanings will flourish on his new label, American, thanks to acts like Masters of Reality.

September 24, 1991

Red Hot Chili Peppers release *BloodSugarSexMagik*, the first of five albums with Rubin. "They were really ready," he will recall, "to do what it took to make a great record."

March 24, 1993

Mick Jagger's *Wandering Spirit* goes gold in the U.S.A. It features Flea of the Chili Peppers and begins Rubin's reputation for kick-starting flagging superstar careers.

June 18, 1993

Last Action Hero premieres. Its soundtrack features "Big Gun," produced by Rubin, who has finally got a chance to work with his "favorite band of all time"—AC/DC.

MAY 13, 1994: The return of the legendary Cash

When Rubin first proposed to Johnny Cash❶ (left, with Soundgarden's Kim Thayil and Nirvana's❷ Krist Novoselic) that he sign and produce him, the beleaguered star's response was "What for?" As his champion explained: "I thought it would be a challenge to find a true legend who wasn't doing his best and see if we could change that. Johnny was the first person I thought of: someone without peer, still capable of good work. He felt lost artistically." Over seven albums—the first of which, *American Recordings*, hit charts in May 1994—Rubin achieved his goal in style: cajoling Cash to sing songs old and new (including ones by Depeche Mode❸, Nick Cave❹, U2❺, and the Eagles❻) and to write new material. "My fondest memories are just of hanging out and hearing his stories," Rubin told *Q*. "He didn't speak much, but . . . he seemed to know everything. He was shy and quiet, but a wise, wise man."

❶ 018
❷ 242
❸ 196
❹ 202
❺ 192
❻ 132

November 1, 1994

Wildflowers is the first of Rubin's three albums with Tom Petty; it is followed by 1996's soundtrack *She's the One* and 1999's *Echo*.

December 5, 2000

Rage Against the Machine issue the largely Rubin-helmed *Renegades*. He will later work with three of the band again when they form Audioslave.

September 22, 2001

Toxicity is the first of three U.S. chart-topping albums by System of a Down (all produced by Rubin); it is followed in 2005 by both *Mezmerize* and *Hypnotize*.

November 3, 2003

Johnny Cash's version of Nine Inch Nails' "Hurt," produced by Rubin, is his final single. Rubin had long been a friend and mentor to NIN's Trent Reznor.

NOVEMBER 14, 2003: Back to the rap attack

"I had stopped listening to rap around the time of the first Public Enemy❶ album," Rubin informed *Rolling Stone* in 1990. It was a genre he returned to infrequently after leaving Def Jam❷, notably with the blood-soaked Geto Boys and party-hardy Sir Mix-a-Lot. But in 2003 he was enticed to contribute to Jay-Z's❸ *The Black Album*, and the result was a career high for both the producer and artist (left): "99 Problems" (in whose video he appeared). Of his subsequent work, most attention has been focused on Weezer's 2005 return to commercial form (*Make Believe*), and Metallica's❹ international chart-topper *Death Magnetic* (2008). Unfortunately, U2❺—bemused by the producer's hands-off approach—dispensed with his services after just one collaboration, on their 2006 single with Green Day❻, "The Saints Are Coming." "I don't know what their perspective was," Rubin informed *Q*. "I thought we had fun."

❶ 025
❷ 222
❸ 266
❹ 218
❺ 192
❻ 258

RICK RUBIN

Guns N' Roses 1985–present

1962+   1986+   1988+   1990+   1993+

While the rock intelligentsia was blown away by the Pixies ◀224, the rest of the world had its socks knocked off by two Indiana country boys, a pair of L.A. addicts, and a Johnny Thunders fan from Seattle: Guns N' Roses. In the aftermath, only Nirvana 242▶ would have such an explosive effect, and even they never sold albums or tickets on the same scale.

"They don't kiss ass," noted Joey of the Ramones ◀158. "I like their attitude cause it's real rock 'n' roll . . . I don't like all this drug shit—the fuss they make about drugs and all that stuff. And the way they're going, I don't see them being around in five years. But they write great songs and they have the right attitude and they look good and they're a *band*. They're a good, rowdy band. They're role models for the world, especially America . . . kids look at Guns N' Roses and put together a real rock 'n' roll band."

"They're an interesting band," agreed Don Henley, formerly of the Eagles ◀132, in 1990. "It's gonna be interesting to watch them now, to see how they grow . . . Getting that hot that fast can be hard on your head. Selling eight million copies of your first album will mess you up." Success did indeed ruin Guns N' Roses, but not before they had nearly eclipsed Aerosmith ◀154—the band that had inspired them, played with The Rolling Stones ◀054, and forged links with everyone from Michael Jackson ◀122 (for whom Slash played guitar) to Iggy Pop ◀116 (on whose *Brick by Brick* Slash and Duff guested).

Alice Cooper—an early champion—was once asked his biggest regret. His answer: "I wasn't born at the right time and at the right place to be the lead singer of Guns N' Roses." But considering how the story has unfolded, perhaps he still has a chance . . .

1962
William "W. Axl Rose" Bailey (February 6) and Jeffrey "Izzy Stradlin" Isbell (April 8) are born in Indiana. They will meet as teenagers and both move to L.A. in the Eighties.

February 5, 1964
Michael "Duff" McKagan is born in Washington. He will play with bands in Seattle before moving to L.A. and joining Road Crew with Slash and Steven Adler.

1965
Steven Adler (January 22, Ohio, U.S.A.) and Saul "Slash" Hudson (July 23, Stoke-on-Trent, U.K.) are born. They meet as kids and begin to play music.

❶ 144
❷ 054
❸ 154
❹ 142
❺ 141

JUNE 1985: Pistol-packin' punks in bloom

Having played together—on and off, in different bands—for sixteen months, vocalist Axl (left), guitarists Slash (who had also auditioned for Poison) and Izzy, drummer Steven, and bassist Duff united in 1985 to form the classic GNR lineup. "The first rehearsal day that we had as the five guys was at a studio in Silver Lake [in L.A.]," Duff recalled. "Playing the first few chords was like . . . lightning had hit the room. That day was probably the most important day of the five of our lives, as players and musicians." They were unabashed about their influences, ranging from Queen❶ and The Rolling Stones❷ to Aerosmith❸ and Kiss❹; although the most obvious influence was Hanoi Rocks—the Finnish, early Eighties, glam rock heirs of the New York Dolls❺. (Sadly, Hanoi fell apart after their drummer died in a car crashed by Mötley Crüe's Vince Neil. But singer Mike Monroe reappeared on GNR's "Bad Obsession" and "Ain't it Fun.")

228   BIG HAIR & BIG HITS

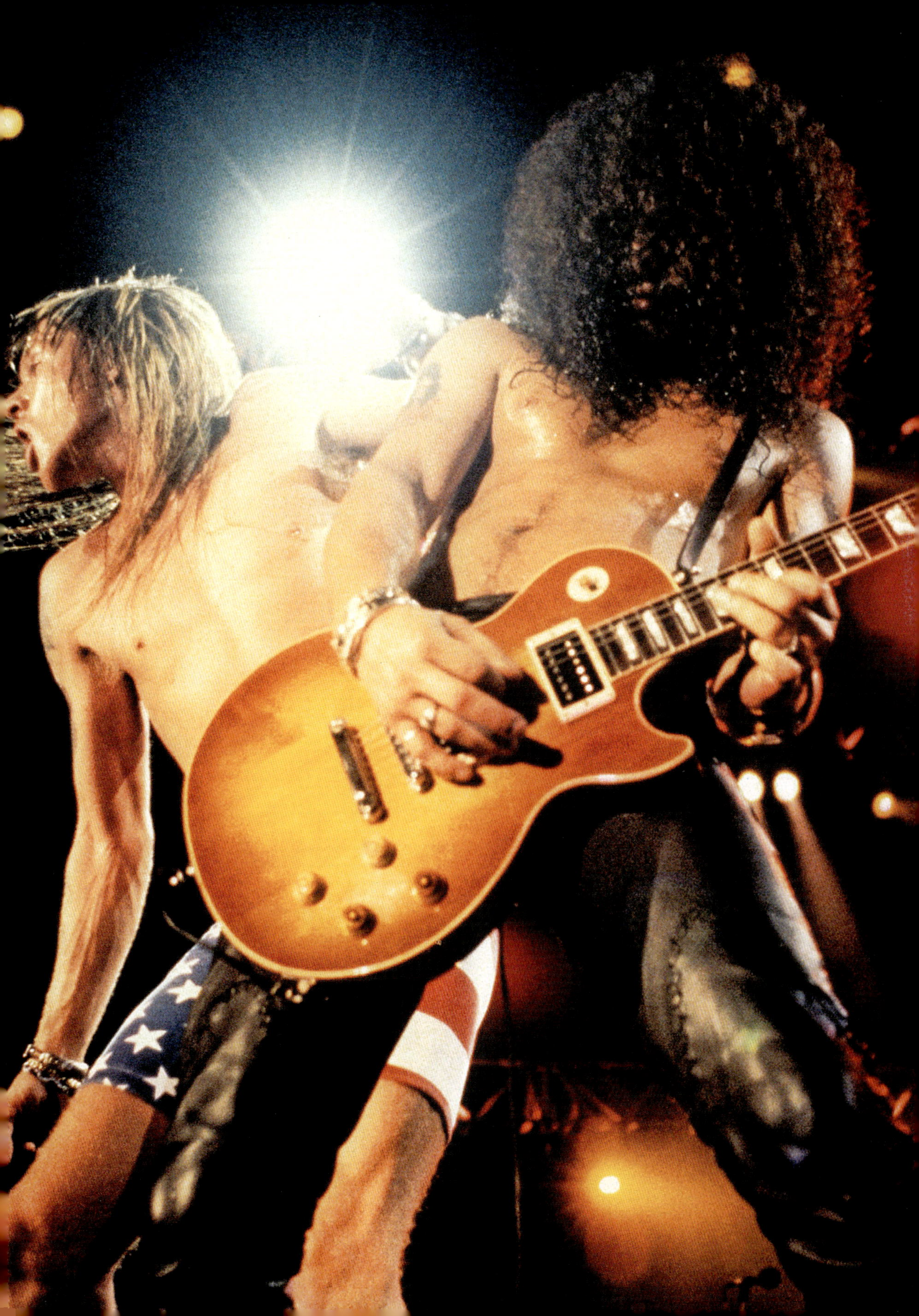

March 25, 1986

GNR are signed to Geffen by A&R man Tom Zutaut, who will later try in vain to enlist Kiss' Paul Stanley and Mötley Crüe's Nikki Sixx to produce GNR's first album.

August 29, 1986

Sid and Nancy premieres. The Sid Vicious biopic includes Slash as an uncredited extra (all five Guns had been cast but only Slash stuck around).

December 16, 1986

Four GNR demos (including Rose Tattoo's "Nice Boys" and Aerosmith's "Mama Kin")—with dubbed crowd noise—are released as the *Live ?!*@ Like a Suicide* EP.

December 21, 1986

Having opened for the Chili Peppers, Alice Cooper, and Ted Nugent in breaks from recording their first album, GNR support Cheap Trick.

JULY 21, 1987: *Appetite for Destruction* unleashed

❶ 190
❷ 154
❸ 049

One of rock's most successful debuts was issued to what Slash (left) recalled as "little or no fanfare at all." Outside the metal fraternity, *Appetite for Destruction*'s lurid cover attracted more attention than its music. GNR spent the rest of 1987 on tour with U.K. rockers The Cult, then with fellow L.A. hellraisers Mötley Crüe. In February 1988—thanks in part to MTV belatedly putting "Welcome to the Jungle" into heavy rotation—*Appetite* went gold in the U.S.A. By April, it had gone platinum. And by the time GNR finished playing with Iron Maiden❶ and launched into an Aerosmith❷ tour, "Sweet Child o' Mine" was heading to No. 1, and the now chart-topping *Appetite* was up to a million a month. On August 16, 1988, they were bottom of the bill to Aerosmith and Deep Purple❸ at Giants Stadium in New Jersey (where the "Paradise City" video was shot), but were arguably the most popular band in the U.S.A.

August 20, 1988

GNR open for Megadeth, David Lee Roth, Kiss, and Iron Maiden at the U.K.'s Monsters of Rock festival. While Axl appeals for calm, two fans die in the crush.

December 1988

With the release of *GN'R Lies*, the band become the only act of the Eighties to place two albums in *Billboard*'s top five at the same time.

January 30, 1989

With Axl having guested on his forthcoming solo album, Don Henley, of the Eagles, deputizes on drums when GNR play "Patience" at the American Music Awards.

September 11, 1989

At an MTV award show, Axl joins Tom Petty to perform Petty's "Free Fallin'" and Elvis' "Heartbreak Hotel," and Izzy is punched by Mötley Crüe's Vince Neil.

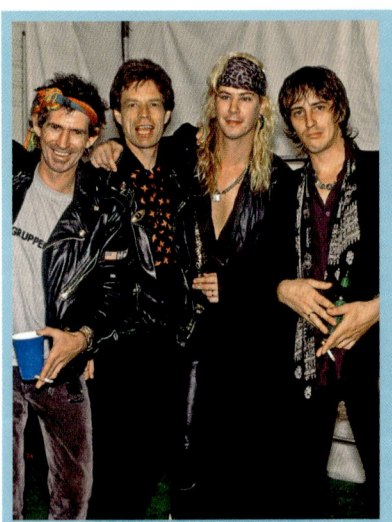

OCTOBER 1989: Dancin' with Mr. Brownstone

❶ 054
❷ 134

When GNR opened for The Rolling Stones❶ (left) in October 1989, they had been off the road all year. Despite doing virtually nothing, they continued to sell millions, fueled by re-released singles. When they shot a video for "It's So Easy"—more than two years since its original release as the first *Appetite* single—Axl nearly fought with a visiting David Bowie❷, who the singer adjudged to be too friendly with his girlfriend, Erin Everly (daughter of Don, of The Everly Brothers). Meanwhile, the band, particularly Slash, descended into narcotic and alcoholic excess. At the first Stones show, Axl told the audience, "Unless certain people in this band get their shit together, these will be the last Guns N' Roses shows you'll fucking ever see." While Izzy cleaned up, and Slash made a token effort, Steven Adler never won back the singer's confidence. A Farm Aid show on April 7, 1990, would be his last with the band.

230   BIG HAIR & BIG HITS

July 11, 1990
Adler is fired. When rehearsals with the Pretenders' Martin Chambers prove fruitless, The Cult's Matt Sorum is drafted. His first GNR session is Dylan's "Knockin' on Heaven's Door."

July 24, 1990
"Civil War," the first new GNR song since *GN'R Lies*, appears on *Nobody's Child: Romanian Angel Appeal*, a charity album compiled by ex-Beatle George Harrison and his wife Olivia.

November 9, 1990
Axl, Slash, and Duff jam with Skid Row's Sebastian Bach and Metallica's Kirk Hammett, Lars Ulrich, and James Hetfield at a party for *RIP* magazine at the Hollywood Palladium.

January 20, 1991
Sorum and keyboard player Dizzy Reed make their live debuts with GNR at the Rock in Rio festival. The band's first headlining world tour will kick off on May 24.

OCTOBER 5, 1991: Double chart success

With 1991's *Use Your Illusion I* and *II*, GNR became the first act since Jim Croce in 1974 to hold the top two places on the U.S. chart. (As in the U.K. and Australia, *II* was No. 1.) When their tour resumed (the first leg had concluded at London's Wembley Stadium in August), Gilby Clarke had replaced Izzy, who had tired of Axl's iron grip on the band and temperamental unreliability. The tour was one of the most eventful in history, including riots in St. Louis and Montreal, a co-headlining leg with Metallica❶, and Izzy returning for five 1993 shows after Gilby broke his wrist. In 1992, GNR appeared at London's Freddie Mercury Tribute Concert, where Axl sang "Bohemian Rhapsody" with Elton John❷ (left); Axl joined U2❸ onstage in Austria; and Aerosmith's❹ Steven Tyler and Joe Perry joined GNR onstage in Paris, as did Queen's❺ Brian May in London. The tour finished, after nearly 200 shows, in July 1993.

❶ 218
❷ 126
❸ 192
❹ 154
❺ 144

November 23, 1993
"The Spaghetti Incident?" is released, with covers of the Sex Pistols, Marc Bolan, Iggy Pop, Charles Manson, The Dead Boys, and others.

January 20, 1994
Axl inducts Elton John into the Rock and Roll Hall of Fame and duets with Bruce Springsteen on The Beatles' "Come Together."

December 1994
A cover of the Stones' "Sympathy for the Devil" is Slash's last GNR release (and the band's last until 1999). Slash will quit the band in 1996, as will Duff in 1997.

August 25, 1996
The Stone Roses headline the U.K.'s Reading Festival. "Slash offered to play guitar for us," singer Ian Brown will report. "I wish we'd taken him on . . . It would have been amazing."

2000 ONWARD: The Axl Rose roadshow

❶ 122

Bar the retrospective *Live Era: '87–93* and new "Oh My God" on the *End of Days* soundtrack (both 1999), little was heard of GNR after their messy disintegration. Axl toiled on a new album, with innumerable producers (including Moby) and musicians (including Brian May). But in 2000, he unveiled new hired hands—notably guitarist Buckethead—for the first of several tours over the next decade (with occasional cameos by Izzy). Slash played with acts from Michael Jackson❶ to Carole King, before forming Velvet Revolver (left) with Duff, Matt Sorum, and Stone Temple Pilots' Scott Weiland. Their *Contraband* (2004) entered the U.S. chart at No. 1—a feat that Axl's overcooked *Chinese Democracy* failed to emulate when it limped out in 2008. Velvet Revolver have since split, Axl still tours as GNR, and the sense of wasted opportunity remains—as does, fortunately, their original, six-year legacy of thrilling rock 'n' roll.

GUNS N' ROSES

Red Hot Chili Peppers

1983–present

1961+ 1984+ 1991+ 1998+

Funk rock never seemed likely to take over the world. An amalgam of George Clinton-inspired funk and punk-fueled rock didn't sit well on segregated airwaves, even after Aerosmith ◁154 teamed up with Run-DMC. But relentless touring and freak hits eventually made stars of the likes of Faith No More, Primus, and biggest of all, the Chili Peppers.

Their rubbery sound made them a novelty on the metal scene with which they were first associated. "If you wanna hear a good rap band, go and see the Red Hot Chili Peppers," enthused Iron Maiden's ◁190 Bruce Dickinson. Even ex-Smiths ◁212 star Morrissey—not, it's safe to assume, a fan of funk—marveled, "When something like the Red Hot Chili Peppers becomes successful, the nation is aghast that it just isn't the same old tawdry regurgitation."

"The Red Hot Chili Peppers are good," observed Fleetwood Mac ◁094 founder Peter Green. "I like their bass player, good guitarist, too. He's got a lot of energy." That bassist—the astonishing Flea—has played with Patti Smith ◁164 (her movie *Dream of Life*), Johnny Cash ◁018 (*Unchained*), Radiohead's 264▷ Thom Yorke, and Pink Floyd's ◁086 Roger Waters (demos for *Amused to Death*), and inducted Metallica ◁218 into the Rock and Roll Hall of Fame.

Even drummer Chad Smith, the most overlooked Chili, has had his day in the sun: playing in big sellers Chickenfoot alongside Joe Satriani, and Van Halen's Sammy Hagar and Michael Anthony.

The Chilis also achieved the remarkable feat of offending Marilyn Manson, albeit in 1989, when he was a geeky journalist. They have since apologized.

232 BIG HAIR & BIG HITS

October 25, 1961

Chad Gaylord Smith is born in Minnesota. He will join in 1988 and become the Chilis' fourth drummer after Jack Irons (later to join Pearl Jam), Cliff Martinez, and D. H. Peligro.

1962

Hillel Slovak (April 13, Acre, Israel), Michael "Flea" Balzary (October 16, Melbourne, Australia), and Anthony Kiedis (November 1, Michigan, U.S.A.) are born.

March 5, 1970

John Frusciante is born in New York. He will follow Hillel Slovak, Jack Sherman, and DeWayne McKnight on guitar. His replacements include Dave Navarro and Josh Klinghoffer.

1983: From Mayhem Masters to Chili Peppers

"The miracle of manipulating energy and tapping into an infinite source of power, and harnessing it in a small space with your friends," wrote Anthony Kiedis, "was what I had been put on this earth to do." Such was his feeling after the first show by Tony Flow and the Miraculous Masters of Mayhem—comprising himself and his high school friends Flea and Slovak (left), as well as the drummer from Slovak's band What Is This?, Jack Irons. The quartet duly evolved into the Red Hot Chili Peppers ("A derivation of a classic, old-school Americana blues or jazz name," said Kiedis in his autobiography, *Scar Tissue*. "There was even an English band that was called Chilli Willi and the Red Hot Peppers, who later thought we had stolen their name"). However, when What Is This? got a record deal, Slovak and Irons opted to remain with them, obliging Kiedis and Flea to hire drummer Cliff Martinez (far left) and guitarist Jack Sherman.

August 1984

After the Andy Gill (Gang of Four)-produced *Red Hot Chili Peppers* is issued, John Lydon tries to poach bassist Flea for Public Image Ltd.

August 16, 1985

With Slovak back in the band, P-Funk legend George Clinton producing, and covers of cuts by The Meters and Sly Stone, *Freaky Styley* is released.

September 29, 1987

With drummer Irons back, and a cover of Bob Dylan's "Subterranean Homesick Blues," *The Uplift Mofo Party Plan* is released. It will be their first success.

June 25, 1988

Slovak dies of an overdose in L.A. His last release was 1988's *The Abbey Road* EP, featuring a cover of his idol Jimi Hendrix's "Fire."

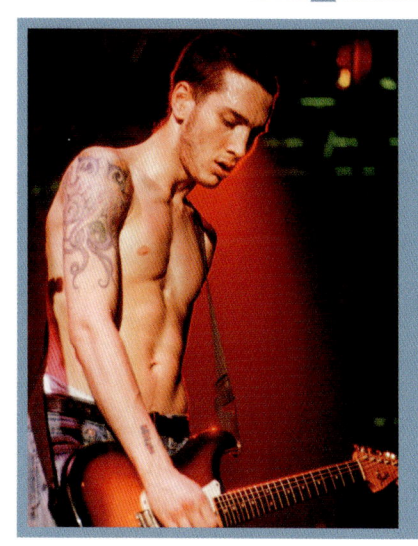

1989: Rebirth with *Mother's Milk*

In the aftermath of Slovak's death, Irons quit, unwilling "to be part of something where my friends are dying." Flea and Kiedis hired drummer D. H. Peligro and guitarist DeWayne "Blackbird" McKnight, before replacing them with Chad Smith and John Frusciante (left), who, though still in his teens, had auditioned for Frank Zappa's ❶ band, but figured that freedom, drugs, and girls would be more abundant as a Chili Pepper. *Mother's Milk* was their first great album, bolstered by a trio of hits: the Slovak tribute "Knock Me Down," "Taste the Pain," and a cover of Stevie Wonder's ❷ "Higher Ground." It duly earned their first gold award, in March 1990. EMI ❸ relinquished the band to Warner Bros., and the Chilis teamed up with producer Rick Rubin ❹ to create *BloodSugarSexMagik* (1991). As "Give It Away" became a hit, the band set off on tour with two promising new bands: The Smashing Pumpkins ❺ and Pearl Jam ❻.

❶ 076
❷ 032
❸ 048
❹ 226
❺ 187
❻ 248

RED HOT CHILI PEPPERS 233

December 27, 1991

Nirvana, a week away from going double platinum, join the tour. Kurt Cobain will be referenced in the Chilis' "Tearjerker" (1995) and "Californication" (2000).

April 1, 1992

Thanks in part to their latest hit, "Under the Bridge," the Chilis earn their first platinum award, for *BloodSugar*. It will sell seven million in the U.S.A.

May 7, 1992

Frusciante quits, asking his manager to announce that he has gone insane. He is replaced (fleetingly) by Zander Schloss, then, until 1993, by Arik Marshall.

July 18, 1992

The Chilis are headliners as Lollapalooza begins. The tour also boasts Pearl Jam and the then little-known Rage Against the Machine.

❶ 240
❷ 228
❸ 112

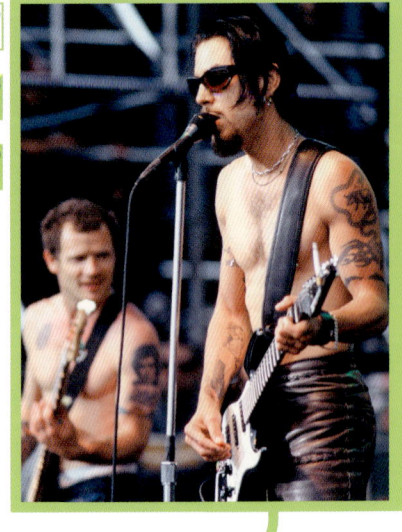

AUGUST 14, 1994: Another lineup debut

Chilis guitarists had become like Spinal Tap drummers. In little more than a year, the role was filled by Zander Schloss, Arik Marshall (who lasted just long enough to appear with the Chilis on *The Simpsons*), and Jesse Tobias (later to play with Alanis Morissette). In September 1993, they settled on former Jane's Addiction❶ man Dave Navarro (left, with Flea). (After that band's implosion in 1991, the latter had missed out on joining Guns N' Roses❷ by failing to turn up for auditions.) The new Chilis lineup debuted in August 1994 at Woodstock II❸, wearing light bulb-shaped head gear. The new guitarist, Kiedis noted approvingly, "didn't complain at all." With Navarro, the Chilis made their most underrated album, *One Hot Minute* (1995), yet never caught fire as they had done with Frusciante. In July 1997, they played their final show with the guitarist—who, just two months later, was on the road, with Flea, as part of the reunited Jane's Addiction.

April 28, 1998

The Chilis announce that Frusciante—who has spent much of the past six years with a near-fatal heroin habit—is back in the band.

June 14, 1998

The reunited band's first major show is the Tibetan Freedom Concert in Washington, D.C., an event they had also played in 1996, in San Francisco.

July 22, 1999

Just six weeks after its release, *Californication* turns platinum in the U.S.A. Three days later, the Chilis will headline the disastrous Woodstock '99 show.

February 13, 2001

Frusciante's *To Record Only Water for Ten Days* is the third of his ten solo albums from 1994 to 2009, and his first on a major label.

❶ 022
❷ 143
❸ 086
❹ 242
❺ 126
❻ 094

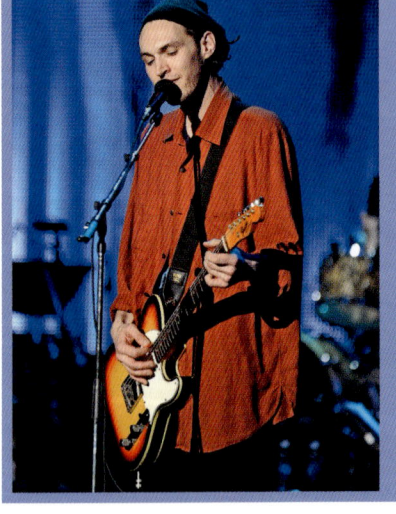

JULY 2002: "Standing in line to see the show tonight"

With 2002's *By the Way*—arguably their finest album—the Chilis set the seal on their resurrection. It narrowly missed the top of the U.S. chart (and nonetheless went platinum in a month), but hit No. 1 elsewhere around the world. On the subsequent tour, massive shows at London's Hyde Park found them supported by James Brown❶. In 2006, *Stadium Arcadium* debuted at No. 1 in the U.S.A. and every other major territory. Its "Dani California," "Snow," and "Tell Me Baby" became three of the band's biggest singles. On the ensuing tour, Frusciante—whose cover of Donna Summer's❷ "I Feel Love" was a long-standing live highlight—sang songs by Pink Floyd❸, Nirvana❹, Elton John❺, Fleetwood Mac❻, and others. In 2009, the idiosyncratic Frusciante amicably parted ways with the band again. Now with a ninth guitarist, Josh Klinghoffer (left), the Chilis look set to ride their roller coaster into the next decade.

234 BIG HAIR & BIG HITS

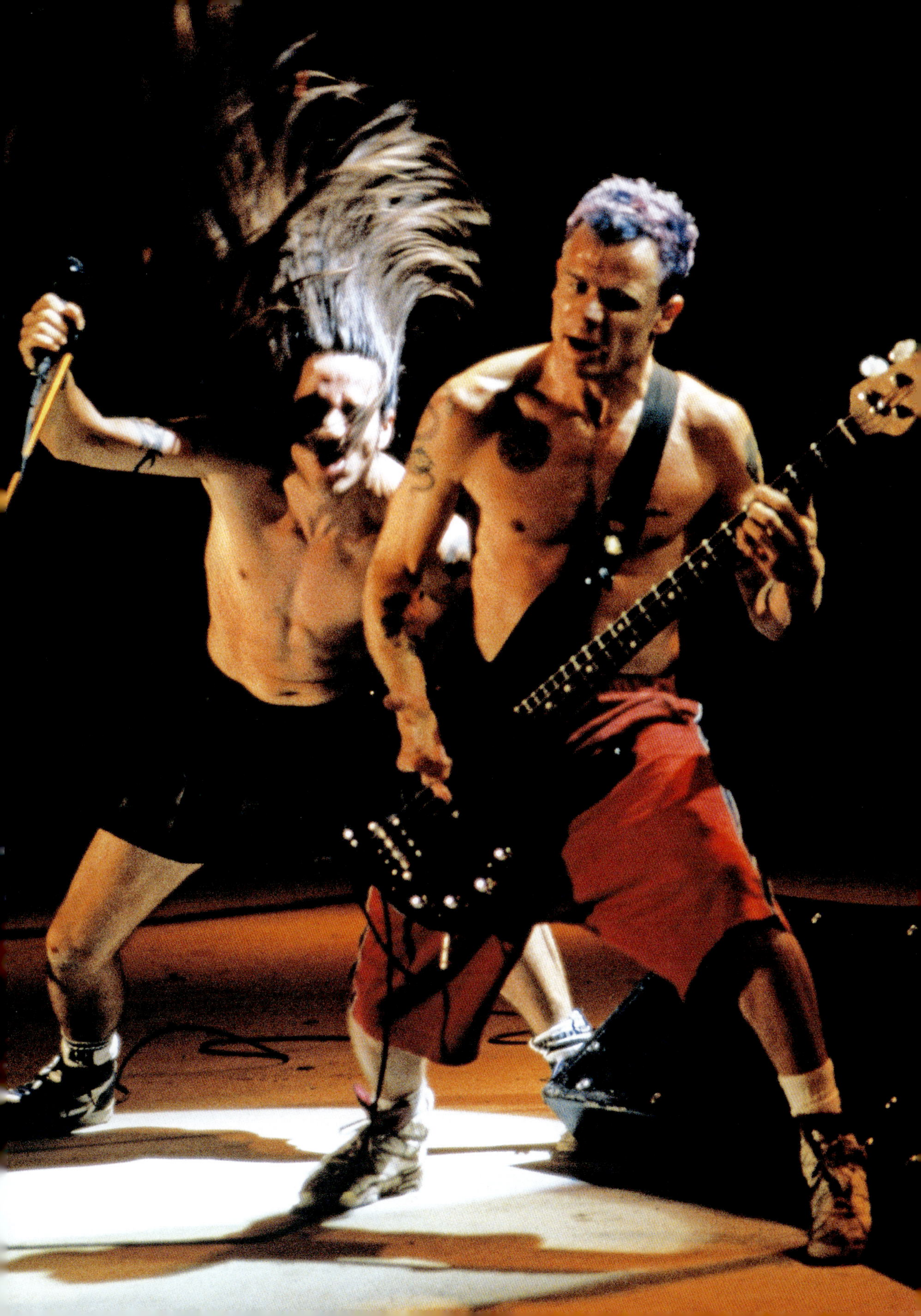

Here We Are Now, Entertain Us

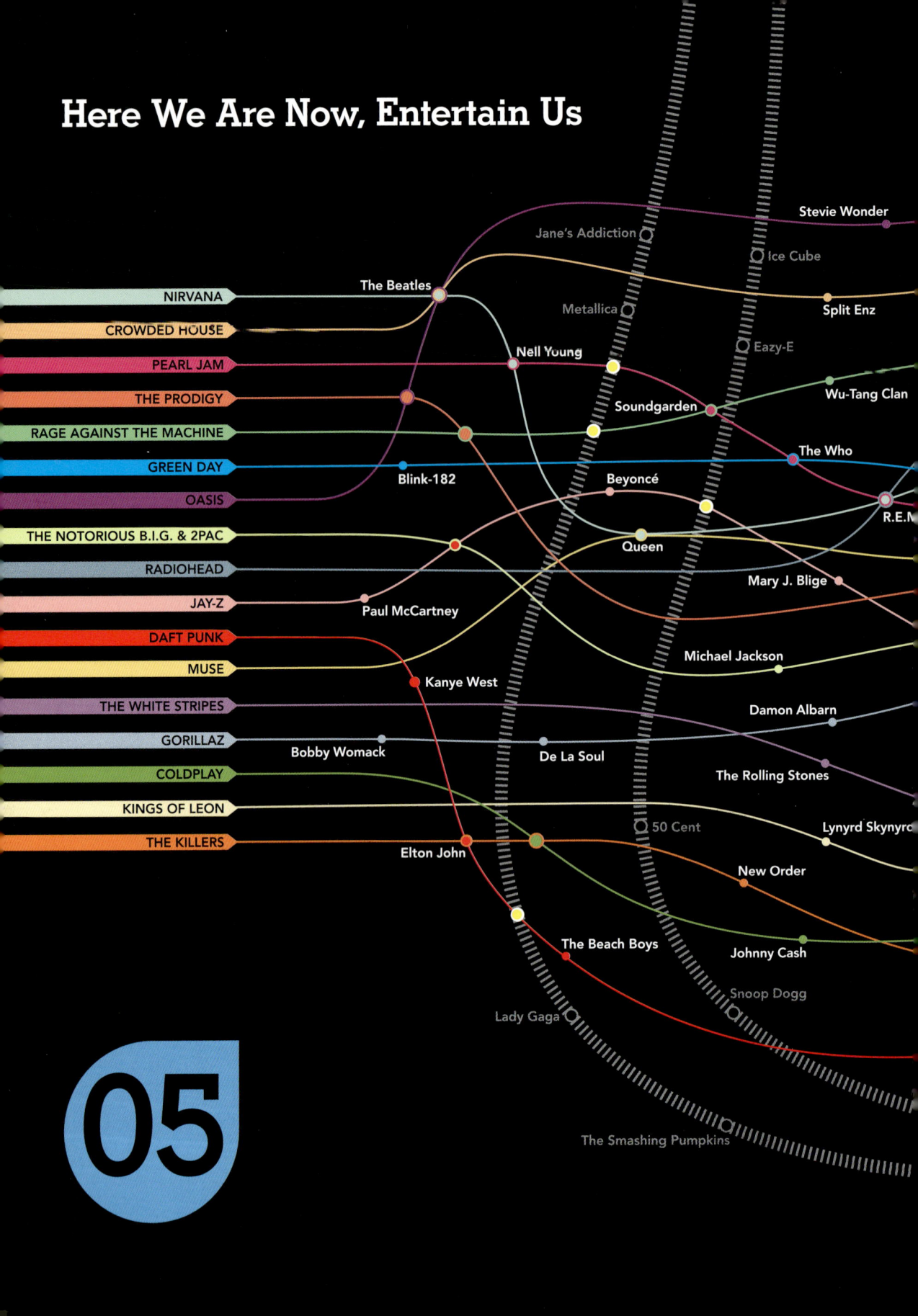

05

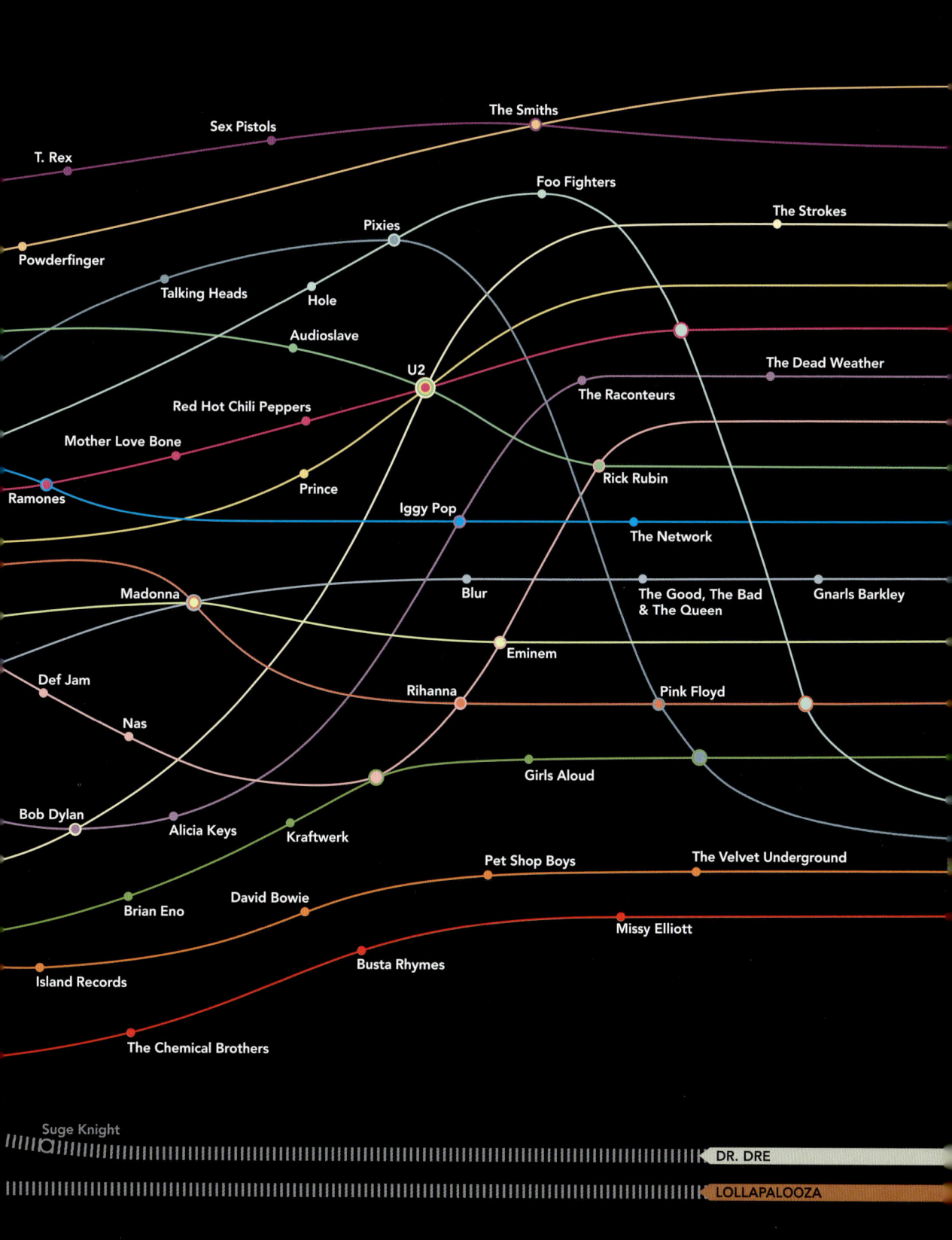

T. Rex
Sex Pistols
The Smiths
Foo Fighters
The Strokes
Pixies
Powderfinger
Talking Heads
Hole
Audioslave
The Dead Weather
U2
Red Hot Chili Peppers
The Raconteurs
Mother Love Bone
Rick Rubin
Prince
Ramones
Iggy Pop
The Network
Madonna
Blur
The Good, The Bad & The Queen
Gnarls Barkley
Def Jam
Eminem
Nas
Rihanna
Pink Floyd
Bob Dylan
Girls Aloud
Alicia Keys
Kraftwerk
The Velvet Underground
Pet Shop Boys
Brian Eno
David Bowie
Missy Elliott
Island Records
Busta Rhymes
The Chemical Brothers
Suge Knight
DR. DRE
LOLLAPALOOZA

key festival

Lollapalooza

1991–present

Before Nirvana (242▶), alternative rock rules were simple. "Get bigger than Sonic Youth," recalled Courtney Love, "but you couldn't get bigger than Jane's Addiction." Persuaded by Jane's drummer Stephen Perkins' joyous account of U.K.'s Reading Festival in 1990 (headlined by the Pixies ◀224), Jane's front man Perry Farrell created a traveling extravaganza—Lollapalooza—for the band's farewell tour in 1991. The bill was bravely diverse, given that the last attempt at something similar in the U.S.A.—1988's Monsters of Rock tour—was a strictly metal affair. "You had Ice-T, Butthole Surfers, us, Living Colour," said Siouxsie Sioux of the Banshees. "Yet everyone got on backstage. It was sort of like a traveling circus." "A fabulous experience," agreed Banshees drummer Budgie, "seeing six other bands going through the day, struggling against all the things that you thought only ever happened to you."

Lollapalooza became annual, and the 1992 tour —headlined by the Red Hot Chili Peppers ◀232 —was perhaps its defining hour. Its second stage featured two bands—Stone Temple Pilots and Rage Against the Machine 254▶—who would go on to become multi-platinum superstars. But the most spectacular success was enjoyed by Pearl Jam 248▶, who, by the end of the tour, had sold three million copies of their debut album *Ten*.

Successive years rode the wave of alternative rock's multi-platinum mainstream success. The tours featured a blend of newly crowned stars and hip legends, such as in 1994 when The Smashing Pumpkins and Beastie Boys shared a bill with funk lord George Clinton. The Pumpkins also featured in *The Simpsons'* spoof, "Homerpalooza," alongside others who had graced the real event: Cypress Hill and Sonic Youth (plus rock veteran Peter Frampton).

Jane's Addiction
Ritual de lo Habitual
(1990)
Warner Bros.

Pearl Jam
Ten
(1991)
Epic

Rage Against the Machine
Rage Against the Machine
(1992)
Epic

But not everyone was won over. Nirvana pulled out of headlining, while Nick Cave ◀202 recalled the 1994 tour as "the most destructive thing I've ever done in my career." William Reid of The Jesus & Mary Chain, who played in 1992, agreed: "We always felt our music was huge, and there it just felt tiny . . . We thought, 'Okay, we really cannot compete.'" (Mercury Rev fared even worse in 1993: they were kicked off the tour for bad behavior.)

The 1996 tour sounded the death knell for the event's alternative status, with established stars Metallica ◀218 and Soundgarden headlining. Yet it still had its defenders. "Those kids are lucky," said Mark Lanegan of Screaming Trees (enjoying their biggest success with *Dust* when they played that year). "They're fucking lucky . . . They're lucky to see the Ramones ◀158, they're lucky to see You Am I, they're lucky to see Metallica, for that matter."

After the 1997 tour, featuring The Prodigy 252▶, Lollapalooza ground to a halt until 2003, when it showcased the re-formed Jane's Addiction. It was later reinvented as a two-day event at Chicago's Grant Park. This has featured the Pixies and The Killers 280▶ (2005), Kanye West and Patti Smith ◀164 (2006), Daft Punk 268▶, Muse 270▶, and Pearl Jam (2007), Rage Against the Machine and Radiohead 264▶ (2008), Depeche Mode ◀196, Tool, and Kings of Leon 278▶ (2009), and the re-formed Soundgarden with Green Day 258▶ (2010).

Despite its now stationary status, Lollapalooza confirmed that the touring festival concept could work in the U.S.A. Among those to follow its lead were Ozzy Osbourne's Ozzfest, Blues Traveler's H.O.R.D.E., and Sarah McLachlan's Lilith Festival. Perry Farrell, McLachlan observed, "had a great idea, and more power to him for going for it."

Jane's Addiction 1991 · 2003 · 2009

Jane's Addiction front man Perry Farrell (below) chose the name "Lollapalooza" after hearing it on U.S. TV's *The Three Stooges*. "It means someone or something great, and/or wonderful," he explained to *Q*. "That's from Webster's dictionary." As for his earnings from the festival, he added: "In my day—the great days—I made two million dollars a year and, in the lean years, a quarter of a million. Pretty okay money, huh?"

Henry Rollins 1991

"Really good," said Henry Rollins (above, with Ice-T) of the very first Lolla show, on July 18, 1991, in Phoenix, Arizona. "Rollins was phenomenal," recalled booking agent Marc Geiger. "The band was so good and so powerful that everybody was scared to go on after them." The show took place in 110-degree heat. "It's about the hottest thing I've ever done," Rollins noted, "next to stealing Edie Brickell's underthings."

Lollapalooza
1991–present

Red Hot Chili Peppers 1992 · 2006

The Chilis' [1] 1992 Lolla headliner was a trial by fire for new guitarist Arik Marshall. "I just thought it would be great if we wore helmets that belched fire (above)," wrote front man Anthony Kiedis. "Our tour manager was, in some ways, the original Homer Simpson, so imagine Homer with a full, fire-retardant outfit trying to get it together to turn the right knobs and light the fire. It's amazing we got through that tour alive."

Rage Against the Machine
1992 · 1993 · 1996 · 2008

After a lowly slot at Lollapalooza in 1992, Rage Against the Machine [1] rose to headlining the very next year. Their guitarist Tom Morello became a Lolla regular, after four years with Rage, as well as, in 2003 —alongside Soundgarden's Chris Cornell—as part of Audioslave (below, at a Californian amphitheater where Rage had shot a video for their cover of Bruce Springsteen's [2] "The Ghost of Tom Joad" in 1997).

HERE WE ARE NOW, ENTERTAIN US

The Smashing Pumpkins 1994

As well as playing on the 1994 Lollapalooza tour (see bassist D'Arcy Wretsky below, at the Shoreline Amphitheater in San Francisco Bay Area), the Pumpkins❶ graced "Homerpalooza," *The Simpsons'* 1996 pastiche. "My kids think you're the greatest," Homer informs Pumpkins main man Billy Corgan. "And, thanks to your gloomy music, they've finally stopped dreaming of a future I can't possibly provide."

Hole 1995

After showing up in 1994 to discuss the death of Kurt Cobain❶, Courtney Love (above) took her band Hole on 1995's Lolla tour, headlined by Sonic Youth (whose Kim Gordon co-produced Hole's debut album). "It's all Sonic Youth approved," Love grumbled to *Rolling Stone*. "Still, I would rather be here with Sonic Youth. I don't want to be out there in the world with Billy [Corgan] and Trent [Reznor] and Eddie [Vedder]."

Metallica 1996

Metallica's❶ headlining status at Lolla 1996 signified the apogee of their ill-fated attempt to align themselves with alternative rock. "It doesn't matter how short my hair is," snapped bassist Jason Newsted (below, at the New York date of the tour, with James Hetfield, Lars Ulrich, and Kirk Hammett), "[or] how many times Kirk modifies himself. What matters is what's comin' out on tape and how we're able to back it up."

Lady Gaga 2007 · 2010

Stefani Germanotta—who took her stage name from Queen's❶ "Radio Ga Ga"—was hidden on a second stage when she played Lolla in 2007 (above). By 2010, she was a superstar, billed beneath only Green Day❷ and Soundgarden. "It's very difficult to see anybody breaking through within a year out of nowhere to headline," said Jane's Addiction's Perry Farrell. "This is the first time in ten years [that's happened]."

Nirvana 1987–94

1967+ 1990+ 1992+ 1994+

The Rolling Stones' ◀054 Keith Richards might have dismissed them as "an upstart pop band that will come and go," but no band from the last twenty years has had the same influence, or the same impressive rock connections, as Nirvana.

Front man Kurt Cobain's interest in music accelerated when he was given a guitar for his fourteenth birthday. He was a fan of The Beatles ◀044, Led Zeppelin ◀098, Black Sabbath ◀108, and Queen ◀144—who influenced Nirvana's early work. His love for Neil Young ◀078 has also been well documented, with Cobain quoting one of the latter's lyrics in his suicide note. He once named *Raw Power* by The Stooges ◀116 as his favorite album of all time, and the band's admiration for the Pixies ◀224 is evident throughout their recordings.

Love for them was huge among fellow musicians. "Nirvana were fantastic," said Elton John ◀126. "You play that stuff and it just gets better all the time for me." They turned down support slots with Guns N' Roses ◀228, Metallica ◀218, and U2 ◀192, as they didn't want to be associated with them. But, with fellow Seattle scenesters Pearl Jam 248▶, they supported Red Hot Chili Peppers 232▶ in 1992. After Cobain's suicide in 1994, R.E.M. ◀204 wrote and recorded "Let Me In" as a tribute. And in 2007, Patti Smith ◀164 recorded a cover of their seminal "Smells Like Teen Spirit" (as had Tori Amos in 1992).

Of the many accolades both before and after Cobain's death, one of the most profound and moving came from Bob Dylan ◀062. After hearing "Polly," he said simply, "That kid has heart."

February 20, 1967

Kurt Donald Cobain is born in Washington. "He was singing Beatles songs from the age of two," his aunt will say. His parents get divorced when he is just eight years old.

1987

Nirvana form (although the name comes later): Cobain, Krist Novoselic (bass), and Aaron Burckhard (drums; quickly replaced by Dale Crover, then Dave Foster).

November 1988

Nirvana—now featuring Chad Channing on drums—release their debut single, "Love Buzz," a cover of a Shocking Blue song. (The Prodigy will later sample the original.)

JUNE 15, 1989: Nirvana debut unleashed

❶ 204
❷ 044

Nirvana's debut album *Bleach*—made for about $600, over a matter of days—initially sold just 30,000 copies. (It was finally certified platinum in the U.S.A. in 1995.) One of the stand-out tracks—later revisited on *MTV Unplugged in New York*—is "About a Girl," allegedly written after Cobain (left, with short-stayed guitarist Jason Everman, who funded the recording of *Bleach*, drummer-for-two-years Chad Channing, and bassist Krist Novoselic) spent an entire afternoon listening to *Meet The Beatles!*. He later told *Rolling Stone* that, "to put a jangly, R.E.M.❶ type of pop song on a grunge record, in that scene, was risky." Butch Vig, soon their producer, saw it as a sign that there was more to Nirvana than just grunge. "Everyone talks about Kurt's love affair with . . . the whole punk scene, but he was also a huge Beatles❷ fan, and the more time we spent together the more obvious their influence on his songwriting became."

April 1990

The band record with Butch Vig for the first time. He is informed that, "if you saw Nirvana here in Seattle, it's like Beatlemania!"

September 22, 1990

Dave Grohl sees Nirvana for the first time and soon joins the band. "We knew in two minutes that he was the right drummer," says Novoselic.

October 1990

Heaven and Hell—A Tribute to The Velvet Underground is released, with Nirvana's "Here She Comes Now." They will also contribute to a Kiss tribute album.

November 27, 1991

A performance of "Smells Like Teen Spirit" on British TV show *Top of the Pops* includes the lyric, "Load up on drugs, kill your friends."

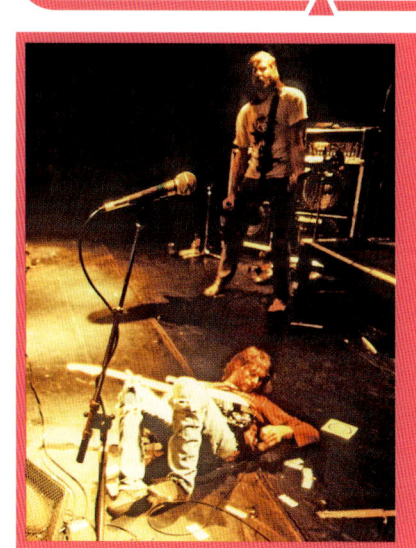

JANUARY 11, 1992: Grunge topples pop

❶ 122
❷ 224
❸ 248

When *Nevermind* knocked Michael Jackson's❶ *Dangerous* off the top of the *Billboard* chart, it was seen as a triumph for alternative music. Building on the back of their massive "Smells Like Teen Spirit" (Cobain remarked that he had been "trying to write the ultimate pop song . . . I was basically ripping off the Pixies❷"), *Nevermind* popularized the Seattle grunge movement and made alternative rock truly mainstream. Not that Cobain was happy about their success. As his aunt later said, "Music was, for Kurt . . . a way to express what was inside himself. It was an understanding friend . . . When he became famous, music was no longer an escape for him—it was a nightmare of scheduled 'creativity.'" Nirvana opened the floodgates for other bands such as Alice in Chains, Pearl Jam❸, and Soundgarden to enter the charts (Cobain had once considered joining the latter Seattle pioneers).

NIRVANA 243

August 18, 1992

Having married Cobain on February 24, Courtney Love (of the band Hole) gives birth to a daughter, Frances (named after The Vaselines' guitarist) Bean.

August 30, 1992

Nirvana's stunning set forms the climax of U.K.'s Reading Festival. The previous year, they were sixth on the bill, on a day headlined by Iggy Pop.

November 18, 1993

The band perform for *MTV Unplugged*, playing a lovely cover of Bowie's "The Man Who Sold the World" and spotlighting the Arizona band Meat Puppets.

November 30, 1993

In Utero goes platinum in the U.S.A. Recorded by Pixies producer Steve Albini, it was "softened" by R.E.M. producer Scott Litt.

❶ 144
❷ 078

APRIL 8, 1994: Death of a legend

Cobain's battle with depression and heroin had been well documented, despite attempts to keep overdoses and suicide attempts hushed up. The music world went into mourning when he was discovered dead at his home in Seattle, on April 8, having taken his own life (apparently while listening to R.E.M.'s *Automatic for the People*). His suicide note revealed his torment about being famous—"It doesn't affect me the way in which it did for Freddie Mercury [Queen❶], who seemed to love it, relish in the love and adoration from the crowd, which is something I totally admire and envy"—and ended with a line from Neil Young's❷ "Hey Hey, My My (Into the Black)": "It's better to burn out than fade away." Young responded by writing 1994's "Sleep with Angels" about him, later saying that, "he really, really inspired me. He was so great. Wonderful . . . Kurt was one of the absolute best of all time for me."

April 1994

Plans to issue *In Utero*'s Leonard Cohen-referencing "Pennyroyal Tea" as a single are scrapped in the wake of Cobain's suicide.

January 5, 1995

Just weeks after its release, and featuring only two hits ("Come As You Are" and "All Apologies"), *MTV Unplugged in New York* goes platinum.

October 19, 1996

Live compilation *From the Muddy Banks of the Wishkah* is Nirvana's third consecutive No. 1 album in the U.S.A., and displaces Celine Dion for one week.

February 27, 1998

Nick Broomfield's film *Kurt & Courtney* premieres. It investigates claims that Cobain was murdered, but concludes that his death was almost certainly suicide.

❶ 150
❷ 108
❸ 098
❹ 144
❺ 086
❻ 044

2000 ONWARD: Grohl and his many connections

Having formed Foo Fighters after declining an offer to join Tom Petty's band, ex-Nirvana drummer Grohl has become rock royalty. He has performed with Bruce Springsteen❶ (at the 2003 Grammys), Black Sabbath's❷ Tony Iommi (on 2000's *Iommi*), Motörhead's Lemmy (on Grohl's 2004 side-project Probot), and acts from Cat Power to Nine Inch Nails. His latest venture, Them Crooked Vultures, features Queens of the Stone Age's Josh Homme and Led Zeppelin's❸ John Paul Jones (who worked on the Foos' *In Your Honor* and guested onstage with them in 2008). Among Grohl's inspirations is Queen❹, with whom he sang at their Rock and Roll Hall of Fame induction in March 2001 (Brian May also graced the Foos' cover version of Pink Floyd's❺ "Have a Cigar"). Factor in playing Beatles❻ and Wings songs with Paul McCartney in Liverpool 2008 (left), and you have one well-connected rock star.

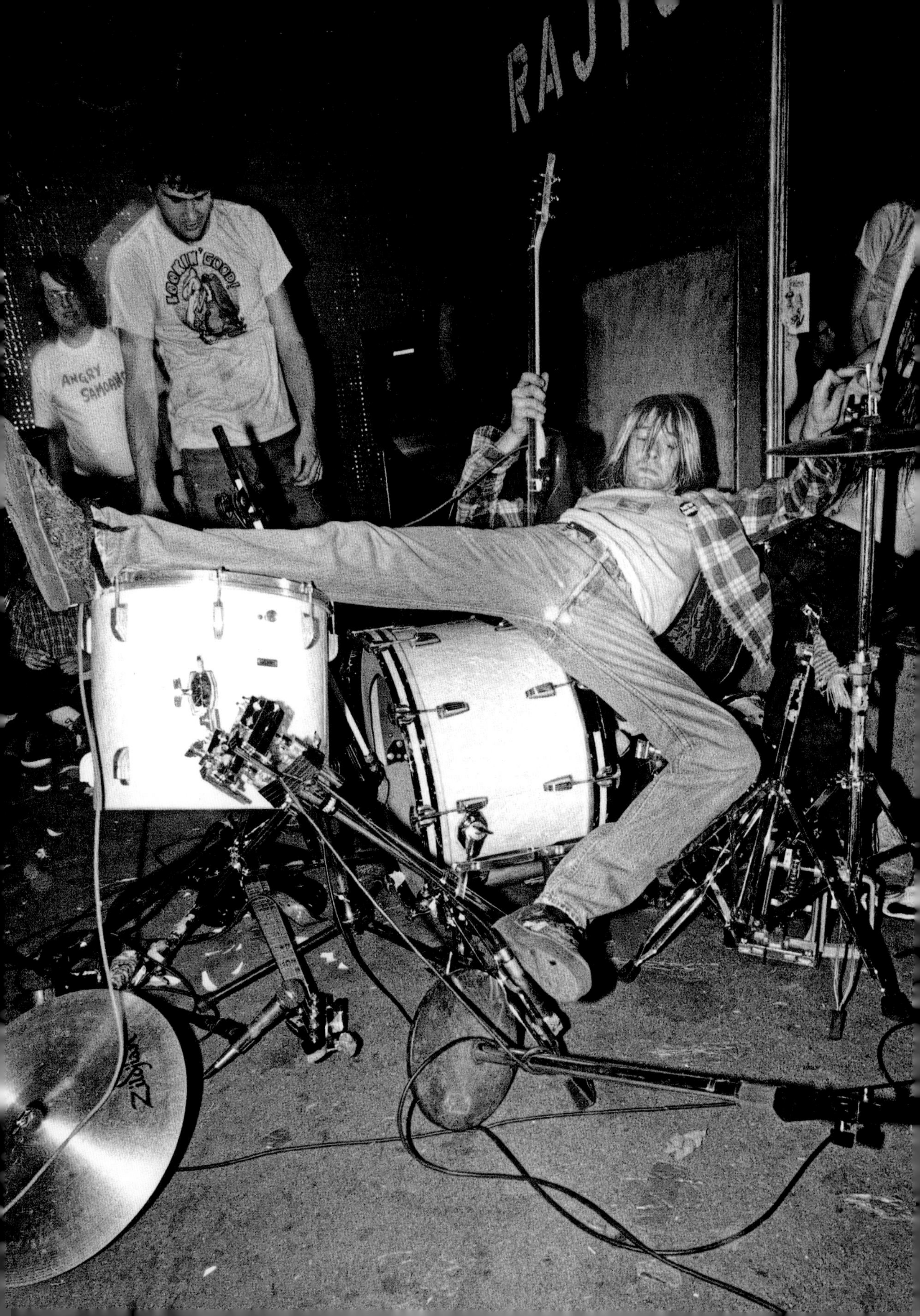
LOOKIN' GOOD!
ANGRY
Zildjian

Crowded House 1985–present

1952+ 1985+

New Zealand's contribution to pop and rock is often overshadowed by that of Australia. But the former, too, has spawned international success stories such as The Chills, OMC, and The Datsuns. None, however, has found fame like Tim Finn's band Split Enz and his brother Neil's Crowded House.

The latter's "Don't Dream It's Over," "Fall at Your Feet," "Into Temptation," and "Weather with You" have become perennial and much-covered classics. Split Enz have also contributed to the family canon, with gems such as "I Hope I Never" and "I Got You." The latter has been covered in concert by Pearl Jam ◀248, who also included, on a 1995 Christmas single for their fan club, a gorgeous version of Split Enz' "History Never Repeats"—recorded live in Auckland, New Zealand, with Neil and Tim Finn.

Crowded House were a huge influence on one of Australia's favorite bands, Powderfinger (named after the Neil Young ◀078 song). "They're amazing songs," enthused singer Bernard Fanning. "[Neil Finn] has this thing where the songs really appeal to you as a person. 'Into Temptation' for example, regardless of what the song's actually about, talks about guilt, which everyone has at some stage. He just sums it up so perfectly in that song."

While Crowded House were on a hiatus, Neil Finn assembled the charity project 7 Worlds Collide. Its 2001 live album features Pearl Jam's Eddie Vedder, Radiohead's 264▶ Phil Selway and Ed O'Brien, The Smiths' 212▶ Johnny Marr, and the multitalented Lisa Germano. All bar Vedder also contributed to a 2009 album, which added Wilco to the starry roster.

June 25, 1952

Brian Timothy Finn is born in Te Awamutu, New Zealand. (His brother Neil will be born in the same town on May 27, 1958.) He and pal Mike Chunn will form Split Ends in 1972.

March 1975

After initial single releases, the renamed Split Enz fly to Australia to kick-start their career. The Australian label Mushroom will issue their debut album in July.

April 1977

Neil Finn is called to London (where Split Enz had based themselves the previous year) to replace founding guitarist Phil Judd. He will make his debut on 1977's *Dizrythmia*.

JANUARY 1980: Top of the charts

Following the success of 1977's *Dizrythmia* and 1979's *Frenzy*, 1980's *True Colours* soared to the top of the Australian and New Zealand charts. Its success was due in no small part to the hit "I Got You," written by Neil. ("I never had problems when Neil wrote songs in Split Enz," said Tim later, "and they turned out to be our best tunes.") The song—a hit in the U.K. and the U.S.A. as well—was a flawless fusion of Split Enz' (left) quirky art rock and Beatles❶-style hooks. "The Beatles were our main influence," observed Tim Finn, "and they were the masters of the three-minute song. So, in a way, we were getting back to our roots." They made another four successful albums, of which two—1981's *Waiata* and 1982's *Time and Tide*—also topped the Australian and New Zealand charts. But in 1984, Tim announced that he was quitting (to join actress Greta Scacchi in London), and the band bid farewell in November.

February 1985

Neil forms The Mullanes, with bassist Nick Seymour and drummer Paul Hester. They relocate to L.A. and live in a crowded house.

May 1, 1987

The renamed Crowded House's self-titled 1986 debut album—a chart-topping, multi-platinum sensation in Australia—earns a gold record in the U.S.A.

July 1988

Temple of Low Men—or, as the band nearly christen it, *Mediocre Follow Up*—meets a muted reception outside Australia and New Zealand. Richard Thompson guests.

January 1990

In Australia, Tim and Neil spend "two glorious weeks locked in a room with a couple of acoustic guitars," writing songs for a mooted Finn Brothers album.

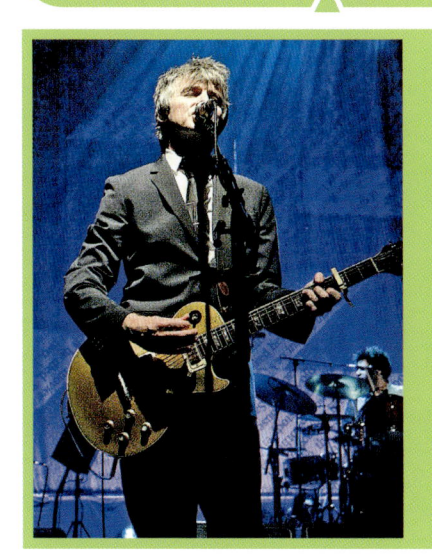

JULY 2, 1991: *Woodface* rebuilds the House

When Crowded House's U.S. label told them to come up with singles for a new album, Neil drew on his work with his brother Tim—who then joined the band. The result was 1991's *Woodface*. Bar the novelty hit "Chocolate Cake," it failed to restore their Stateside fortunes, but the rest of the world fell for hits such as "Weather with You." By the end of 1992, Tim was out, but the band's success continued with 1993's *Together Alone*. However, by 1996, the House had cracked and played a farewell show to 150,000 fans by the Sydney Harbour. Tim and Neil continued with their solo endeavors, which had yielded the joint 1995 album *Finn*. (They would reunite again for 2004's *Everyone Is Here*.) Tim has periodically revived Split Enz since 1992, while Neil and Phil Seymour reunited as Crowded House (left) in 2006 (minus Paul Hester, who killed himself in 2005), adding to their lavish legacy with 2007's *Time on Earth*.

CROWDED HOUSE

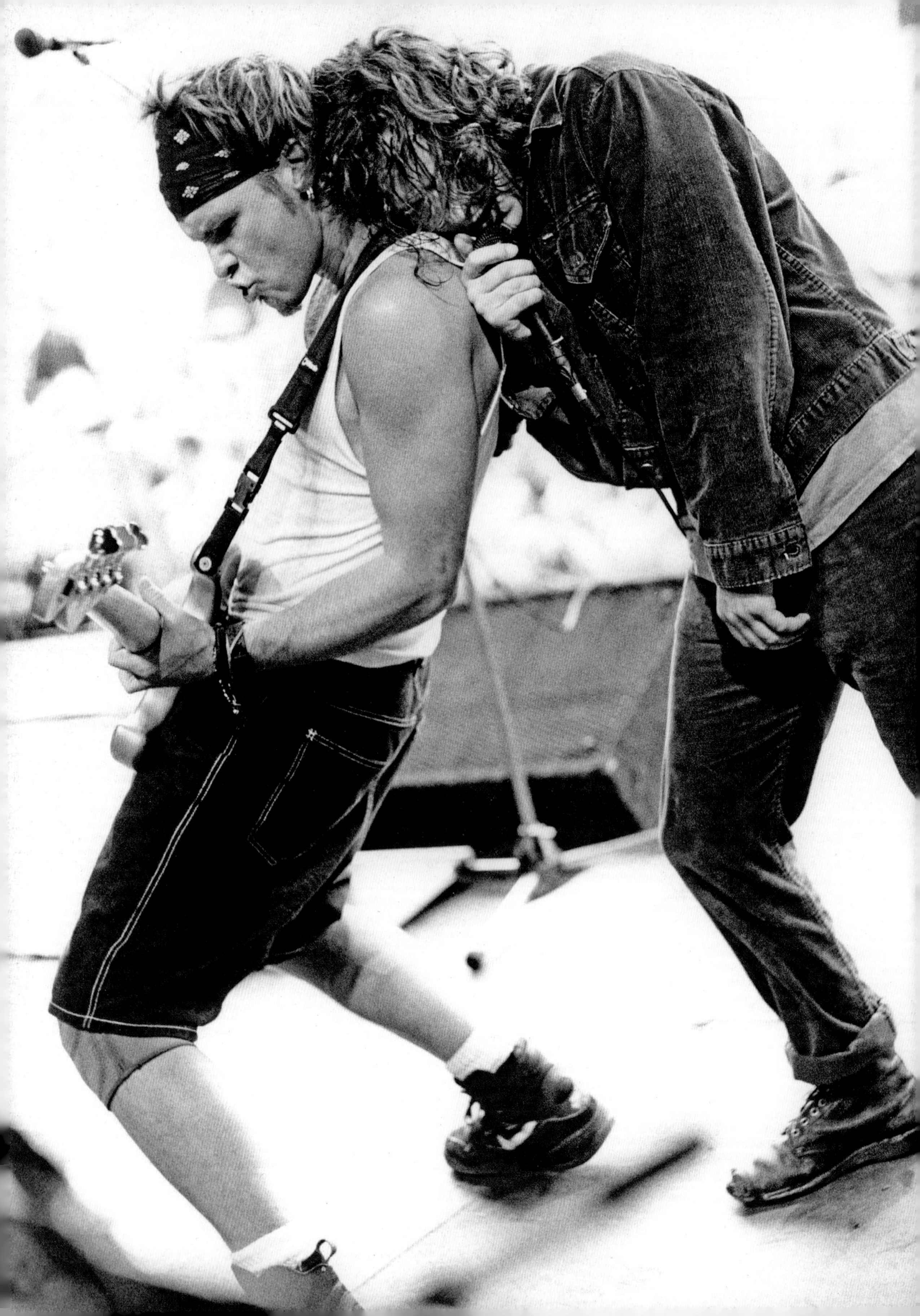

Pearl Jam
1990–present

For a band initially dismissed as pretenders to Nirvana's ◄242 throne, Pearl Jam have remained staggeringly successful. While their grunge-era contemporaries—Soundgarden, Alice in Chains, and Stone Temple Pilots—crashed and burned (and, inevitably, re-formed), Pearl Jam soldiered on. (Every one of their nine studio albums hit the U.S. top five despite their sales suffering a dip.) Pearl Jam's supremacy was established by the end of 1993 (the year before Kurt Cobain's death): their debut *Ten* had outsold Nirvana's *Nevermind* in their native U.S.A. to the tune of one million copies.

> *"They felt real sensitive and real committed . . . They were a band—and that's exciting."*
> —Neil Young

Cobain even resolved to stop being rude about his rivals: "It hurts Eddie [Vedder, singer] and he's a good guy." (To Vedder's face, he said, "You're a respectable human even if your band does suck.")

Pearl Jam had an unorthodox conception. When Andrew Wood, front man with Seattle band Mother Love Bone, fatally overdosed on the verge of fame, the band's bassist Jeff Ament and guitarist Stone Gossard recruited guitarist Mike McCready, and Soundgarden's Chris Cornell and Matt Cameron for the 1992 tribute album *Temple of the Dog*. Gossard, Ament, and McCready then enlisted singer Vedder for a new band, Mookie Blaylock—soon to become Pearl Jam. (They burned through three drummers in four years, before settling on one-time Red Hot Chili Peppers ◄232 sticksman Jack Irons in 1994. His predecessor, Dave Abbruzzese, unsuccessfully auditioned for Guns N' Roses ◄228 in 1997, while Irons was replaced by Matt Cameron in 1998.)

Tours with the Chili Peppers, Neil Young ◄078, and U2 ◄192 put Pearl Jam on the road to riches. In 1992 the hit-laden *Ten* made them champions of their genre. "*London Calling* only sold about 300,000 copies in America," noted Joe Strummer of The Clash ◄170. "Today, Pearl Jam sell nine million."

Success turned Vedder into the unwitting voice of a generation. "No matter what he says," observed Neil Young, "it all gets taken down and quoted back at him." "They remind me a bit of the attitude that early U2 had," said Led Zeppelin's ◄098 Robert Plant. "What they're doing, they're doing because they really mean it. They're not just hangin' on."

The respect that Pearl Jam engendered from their forefathers was reciprocal. Among the covers they have performed are "Can't Help Falling in Love" by Elvis ◄012, "Little Wing" by Hendrix ◄072, "Masters of War" by Bob Dylan ◄062, "You've Got to Hide Your Love Away" by The Beatles ◄044, "Beast of Burden" by The Rolling Stones ◄054, "Everyday" by Buddy Holly ◄020, and "Interstellar Overdrive" by Pink Floyd ◄086. Vedder has inducted the Ramones ◄158 and R.E.M ◄204 into the Rock and Roll Hall of Fame. (Meanwhile, Bruce Springsteen ◄150 hired producer Brendan O'Brien after hearing his albums with Pearl Jam: "They sounded really good.")

"The good ones will survive," observed Jon Bon Jovi in 1996, as grunge bands faltered in the wake of their sudden fame. "Pearl Jam will still be around."

Rearviewmirror (2004) is a fine retrospective that mixes hits ("Last Kiss" and "Given to Fly") with rarities ("I Got Id") and Neil Young ("Man of the Hour" and "Yellow Ledbetter").

Backspacer (2009)—even more tuneful than 2006's *Pearl Jam*—gave them a first U.S. No. 1 since *No Code* (1996). As they prepare for their third decade, the band sound more vibrant than ever.

The inspirational *Murmur* of R.E.M.

Pearl Jam's association with R.E.M. ❶ began long before front man Eddie Vedder (left with R.E.M.'s Michael Stipe) inducted them into the Rock and Roll Hall of Fame in 2007. "I was lucky enough," Vedder recalled, "in the summer of 1984, to get to see R.E.M. play live, in a small place in Chicago . . . It changed how I listened to music . . . After that I started listening to them exclusively . . . I believe I listened to [R.E.M.'s debut album] *Murmur* 1,260 times." When R.E.M. guitarist Peter Buck moved to Seattle, he became a mentor for the city's grunge stars. "The good thing about Pearl Jam," he remarked, "is that they've learned what they don't want to do and they're not doing it. There's a lot of pressure on Eddie, but, you know, he'll deal with it." The acts have since shared the bill at key shows including 1997's Tibetan Freedom Concert in New York, and at a climactic gig on 2004's Vote for Change tour, in Washington, D.C.

Pearl Jam

Connection: 1984

May 5, 1992
Pearl Jam's debut *Ten*—with "Alive," "Even Flow," and "Jeremy"—earns the first of thirteen U.S. platinum awards that it will accrue over the next seventeen years.

November 6, 1993
One month after Nirvana's *In Utero* hit No. 1, *Vs.* tops the U.S. chart, having set a record for first week sales—950,000—that will hold until Garth Brooks breaks it in 1998.

July 10, 1991
In Boston, the band embark on a first tour since adopting the name Pearl Jam (they had been called Mookie Blaylock). They are supporting Buffalo Tom and The Lemonheads.

Influence: 1992

December 10, 1994
Vitalogy enters the U.S. chart at No. 55, based on sales of its first release, on vinyl. Having dropped to 173, it will leap a record-breaking 172 places to No. 1 when the CD is released.

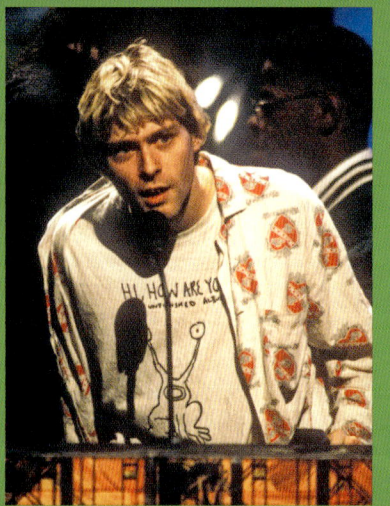

Nirvana—keep your enemies close

"Kurt had a strong sense of achievement," said his former manager. "He kept careful track of how many times Nirvana ❶ videos were played on MTV compared with Pearl Jam." The rivalry eased at a 1992 MTV awards show (left), where Cobain and Eddie Vedder slow-danced to Eric Clapton's ❷ "Tears in Heaven." "I remember going out surfing the next morning," said Vedder in 1994, "and remembering how good that moment felt and thinking, 'Fuck, man, if only we hadn't been so afraid of each other . . .' We were going through so much of the same shit. If only we'd talked, maybe we could have helped each other." (Vedder's response to the pressure was Pearl Jam's raging 1994 album *Vitalogy*.) Even by 2002, Nirvana's specter remained hard to escape: Pearl Jam's *Riot Act* was released within weeks of their rivals' self-titled "best of." "It's tough," Vedder conceded, "to be better than Nirvana's greatest hits."

The leading light of the Ramones

The Ramones'❶ 1976 debut album was, said Pearl Jam's Eddie Vedder, "a beacon for anyone who ever wanted to be in a band . . . the Ramones were our Beatles❷." Two decades after that landmark record, in 1996, Vedder sang the Dave Clark Five's "Anyway You Want It" with the Ramones at their final show, in L.A. (immortalized on 1997's *We're Outta Here!*). Vedder was also a natural choice for the 2003 tribute album *We're a Happy Family*, covering "I Believe in Miracles" and "Daytime Dilemma (Dangers of Love)" with Seattle punk band Zeke. In 2002, Vedder (left, with Johnny Ramone) inducted the band into the Rock and Roll Hall of Fame. "Punk bands now," he noted, "with one record, their first or second, sell ten times the amount that the Ramones did throughout their career with twenty-something records . . . and that's why I go over to Johnny Ramone's house and do yard work three times a week."

❶ 158
❷ 044

Connection 1996

July 7, 1999
Four months after their latest album, *Yield*, turns platinum, Pearl Jam earn a gold award for the fluke hit "Last Kiss," a cover of a 1963 cut by Wayne Cochran & The CC Riders.

March 2001
Five official bootlegs from the tour for the recent *Binaural* album hit the *Billboard* chart. Pearl Jam prove trailblazers: issuing concerts on CD will be commonplace a decade later.

November 2004
After the Vote for Change tour, on which they appeared alongside Bruce Springsteen and R.E.M., the band begin recording the album that will become 2006's *Pearl Jam*.

September 14, 1996
No Code tops the U.S. chart, as it has done in Australia and New Zealand. The album has had a troubled conception—the band are tired and divided —but will soon turn platinum.

Connection 2000

February 8, 2003
Johnny Marr, ex-guitarist with The Smiths, is the opening act in Australia as the band begin their first tour in over two years, in support of their latest album, 2002's *Riot Act*.

October 10, 2009
Backspacer knocks Jay-Z off the U.S. No. 1. It is their first album with Brendan O'Brien since 1998."Bruce has listened to his suggestions," Vedder said. "I think we will, too."

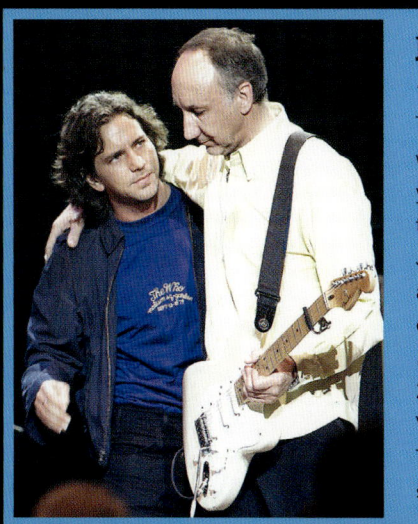

Jamming with The Who

"Bands like Nirvana❶ and Pearl Jam . . ." observed The Who's❷ Pete Townshend (left, with Eddie Vedder), "have, to some extent, ended up winding up their idea of their own youth and their difficulties with being young as a way of validating political ideas, their political frustrations, their anger . . ." The Who's angsty racket touched a nerve with Pearl Jam's Vedder, who sang with Townshend at a 1998 charity show before appearing, on November 27, 2000, with the whole of The Who—check out his gorgeous performance of "I'm One" on the resultant *The Who Live at the Royal Albert Hall*. Vedder returned to the same venue in 2010 to sing in their *Quadrophenia*, and Pearl Jam also graced a 2008 VH1 *Rock Honors* tribute to the band. "It sounded amazing," enthused Townshend. "To think he nearly quit in 1993 and went back to some surfing beach. Lucky he came to speak to Uncle Pete. I told him: submit."

❶ 242
❷ 068

The Prodigy 1990–present

1990+   1998+

While Oasis 260▶ and Blur made "Britpop" a (limited) commercial phenomenon, another British band took the world by storm in the mid-Nineties, with an altogether different sound. That band—The Prodigy—has sold over twenty million records worldwide, more than any other dance act.

Liam Howlett, a devotee of hip-hop and Pink Floyd ◀086, formed the band in 1990. He met Leeroy Thornhill and Led Zeppelin ◀098 nut Keith Flint at an outdoor rave. Soon, MC Maxim Reality was on board, and rave was being brought to the masses. "All we wanted to do when we started off," admitted Howlett, "was play the clubs we were going to as ravers." But when "Charly" hit No. 3 in the U.K. in 1991, a slew of inferior copycat hits led to music critics labeling them "kiddie rave."

After *The Prodigy Experience*, Howlett tried to distance his band from the scene they had spawned by issuing "One Love" under the name Earthbound. His mission was truly accomplished by 1994's *Music for the Jilted Generation*. Fueled by hip-hop and the influence of funk-rock bands such as Rage Against the Machine 254▶, the album established The Prodigy as a dance act for rock fans. *The Fat of the Land* (1997) duly topped charts around the world.

The Prodigy's influence continues to reach far and wide, even ensnaring R&B superstar Rihanna ("I listen to a lot of Prodigy"). As Led Zeppelin's Robert Plant said, "I don't think that they actually decided that a certain era of music was something to hang on to for political and financial and ego gain. They just came blazing out of the corner, and it's brilliant."

1990

Howlett, Thornhill, Flint, and a female pal, Sharky, form The Prodigy, named after a Moog synthesizer. Maxim will join at a first show at the end of the year, and Sharky will leave.

November 21, 1992

"Out of Space"—which samples "I Chase the Devil," a reggae classic produced by Lee "Scratch" Perry—hits the U.K. chart. It will remain a live favorite.

July 16, 1994

...*Jilted Generation* enters the U.K. chart at No. 1. "Voodoo People" samples "Very Ape" by Nirvana. Far from miffed, Dave Grohl will describe the band as "absolutely amazing."

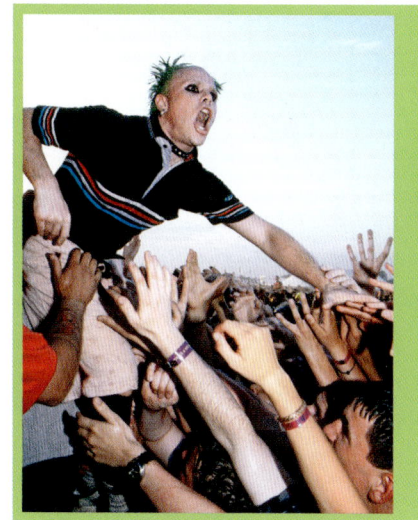

MARCH 18, 1996: A fierce new front man

When the now-iconic "Firestarter" came out, Pet Shop Boy Neil Tennant described it as "not really a song" (he meant it as a compliment); Prodigy's own Liam Howlett agreed, describing it as "more like . . . an energy!" The first Prodigy record to feature Flint (left) on vocals, and their first U.K. No. 1 single, the song ignited controversy for both its lyrics and video, which featured a pierced Flint at his demonic best. Howlett cranked up the rock and hip-hop elements and kept the samples—in this case The Breeders❶ and Art of Noise—and the Prodigy's first worldwide smash was born. Released in the U.S.A. on Madonna's❷ Maverick label, it went gold there. (It was covered by Kiss's❸ Gene Simmons in 2004, with guitar by Dave Navarro of Jane's Addiction❹.) More than a year after the single, *The Fat of the Land* was released to widespread acclaim. It yielded another two controversial smashes: "Breathe" and "Smack My Bitch Up."

❶ 225
❷ 208
❸ 142
❹ 240

August 29, 1998

The Beastie Boys ask that "Smack My Bitch Up" not be played when both bands appear at the U.K.'s Reading Festival. Howlett refuses.

February 22, 1999

Howlett issues the mix album *The Dirtchamber Sessions*, which features the Sex Pistols, Jane's Addiction, KLF, Primal Scream, and lots of hip-hop.

September 4, 2004

Always Outnumbered, Never Outgunned tops the U.K. chart. Oasis' Gallagher brothers guest, while "The Way It Is" is a version of Jackson's "Thriller."

March 1, 2009

Following *Their Law*, a 2005 "best of," *Invaders Must Die* becomes The Prodigy's fifth U.K. No. 1. Dave Grohl drums on two of its songs.

SEPTEMBER 12, 2010: Kings of the festival scene

"There was no one on the dance scene who could create the energy onstage that rock bands did," Liam Howlett (left) said of his band's successful attempt to do exactly that on the festival circuit. A formidable force live, The Prodigy's energy, passion, and spectacular sound—not to mention their impressive visuals—were quite simply made for night-time festival slots. Their move toward a more rock-influenced sound led to a show-stopping appearance at the U.K.'s Glastonbury festival in 1995, while Keith Flint emerged as a Johnny Rotten-esque front man. The Prodigy opened the floodgates for other dance-oriented acts to work their magic at alfresco events. Their Australian acolytes Pendulum are among those to have taken up the challenge. But with a closing set at the U.K. Bestival event in September among their 2010 shows, The Prodigy remain dance's top dogs on the festival circuit.

Rage Against the Machine
1991–present

1991+ 2000+

Although indebted to Public Enemy and Jane's Addiction, Rage Against the Machine took their cocktail of rock, rap, and revolution to commercial heights of which those bands had only dreamed: four multi-platinum albums, including two U.S. No. 1s.

Their personal heritage was as mixed as their music: singer Zack de la Rocha's father is political artist Roberto "Beto" de la Rocha and guitarist Tom Morello is the son of a Kenyan guerilla fighter. Bassist Tim Commerford (a school friend of de la Rocha) and drummer Brad Wilk (who had played in a band called Indian Style with Eddie Vedder, later of Pearl Jam 248, and auditioned for Morello's pre-Rage band Locked Up) completed the lineup.

Despite signing to a subsidiary of the huge Sony, Rage brought articulate protest to their genre. They allied themselves to minority causes and gave up valuable time on the 1993 Lollapalooza 238 tour to mount a silent, nude protest against censorship. "They're my favorite band," noted Liam Howlett of The Prodigy 252, who teamed with Tom Morello on 1997's *Spawn* soundtrack and sampled Rage's "Bulls on Parade" on "Smack My Bitch Up." (Others who have sampled them include Justice and Saul Williams.)

In 2007, the re-formed Rage proved that age had not mellowed them when they called for George W. Bush's administration to be "hung, and tried, and shot." "These guys are over the top," observed right-wing rocker Ted Nugent. "They're lunatic fringe that even your average Democrat liberal doesn't agree with. But, unfortunately, nobody is silencing these guys." Mission accomplished, Rage!

1991

Rage Against the Machine give a first public performance in what their official biography describes as "somebody's living room," in Orange County, California.

1992

Rage issue a twelve-song demo that includes "Bullet in the Head." They also play two Lollapalooza dates and support Suicidal Tendencies and Porno for Pyros.

November 6, 1992

Rage Against the Machine is released, featuring "Killing in the Name" (and, on "Knowing Your Enemy," Maynard James Keenan of Tool and Stephen Perkins of Jane's Addiction).

MAY 4, 1996: *Evil Empire* hits No. 1 on the U.S. chart

❶ 192

❷ 098

By 1996, Rage's debut had gone platinum (and opened the door for nu-metallers such as Korn), and cuts such as "Killing in the Name," "Bullet in the Head," and "Bombtrack" had become anthems for the post-grunge generation. *Evil Empire,* trailed by the jaw-dropping "Bulls on Parade," duly smashed into the U.S. chart at No. 1 (and into top fives around the world)—success repeated by 1999's *The Battle for Los Angeles*. Gaps between their albums were often due to volatile relations within the band. "Me and Tom don't agree," said de la Rocha (left). "We have a different approach to the way our politics are addressed... Ultimately, the contention has served us well." Rage maintained their admirable diversity: they toured with Wu-Tang Clan and U2❶, and Morello contributed to Puff Daddy's reworking of Led Zeppelin's❷ "Kashmir" as 1998's *Godzilla* soundtrack smash "Come with Me."

October 18, 2000

Rage split after de la Rocha issues a statement declaring that the band's "decision-making process has completely failed."

December 5, 2000

Renegades is released, featuring covers of songs by The Stooges, EPMD, Bob Dylan, Cypress Hill, Bruce Springsteen, Afrika Bambaataa, MC5, and others.

September 2001

In the wake of 9/11, Clear Channel compiles a list of songs with "questionable lyrics" that ought not to be aired. It features Rage's entire back catalog.

November 25, 2003

Live at the Grand Olympic Auditorium—with excerpts from Rage's last two shows, in September 2000—is released to minor success.

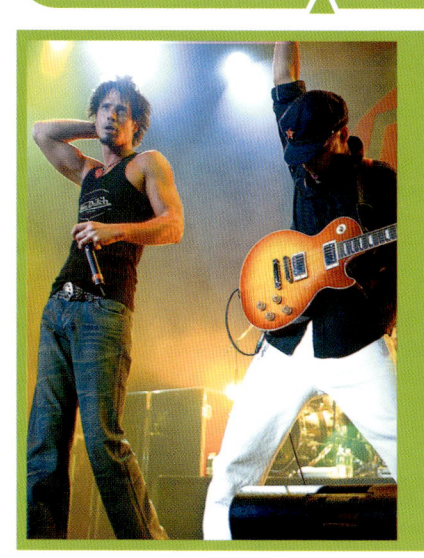

2009: Rage Against *The X Factor*

❶ 226

❷ 025

After Rage's split, Morello, Commerford, Wilk, and Soundgarden singer Chris Cornell (left, with Morello) created Audioslave. The stars were united by Rick Rubin❶, who produced the first two of their three albums. But after six tumultuous years, the band split in 2007. In July of the same year, the reunited Rage returned to the road, kicking off with New York shows accompanied by Public Enemy❷, Cypress Hill, and Wu-Tang Clan. They have since made well-received appearances at various festivals, though there seem to be no plans for a new album. In an entertaining twist, a Facebook group campaigned to make "Killing in the Name" the U.K.'s Christmas No. 1 (over the winner of TV show *The X Factor*, Joe McElderry) in 2009. "It would be kind of funny if a band like Rage Against the Machine got it," noted Paul McCartney. Rage *did* get it, and rewarded their fans with a 2010 tour.

super producer

Dr. Dre
1965–present

Dr. Dre's influence on hip-hop is huge. He helped to launch Snoop Dogg, Eminem, and 50 Cent. Kanye West called Dre's *The Chronic* (1992) "the hip-hop equivalent to Stevie Wonder's *Songs in the Key of Life*. It's the benchmark you measure your album against if you're serious." Fans of his former band N.W.A. range from Rage Against the Machine ◁254—who covered "Fuck tha Police"—to The Prodigy ◁252, who sampled "Express Yourself" on "Wind it Up (Bonus Beats)."

Lauded more for his production than his rapping after he left N.W.A, Dre founded Death Row Records with Suge Knight. A fan of George Clinton, Curtis Mayfield, and Isaac Hayes, Dre reimagined the funk of their era into G-Funk, the laid-back West Coast style that dominated hip-hop for nearly four years.

Dre left Death Row in 1996, amid concerns about Knight's business habits—2Pac 262▷ was being pushed as the major star at the time—and set up his own label, Aftermath Entertainment. One of the label's biggest signings was Eminem, and together they dominated hip-hop in the early Noughties.

The new decade should see the release of Dre's much-mooted final album *Detox*. It reportedly has collaborations with Jay-Z 266▷ (who wrote lyrics for "Still D.R.E.") and Ludacris. The latter admitted, "I always wanted to work with Dr. Dre"—surely a sentiment shared by most hip-hop artists.

"I've looked at pictures that my mom has of me, from when I was four years old, at the turntable . . . reaching up to play the records," Dre told the *Guardian*. "I feel like I was bred to do what I do."

1965+
1991+
1996+

February 18, 1965
André Romelle Young—Dr. Dre—is born in Compton, L.A. His mother later remarries, and one of his stepbrothers, Warren Griffin III, finds success as Warren G.

1984
Dre joins the electro hip-hop act World Class Wreckin' Cru. They also feature Michel'le, his girlfriend and a future solo star. Another member, DJ Yella, will join Dre in N.W.A.

1986
Dre meets Ice Cube, who writes for the Cru's *House Calls*. Dre, Cube, and Yella will be enlisted for N.W.A. by entrepreneur Eazy-E.

❶ 242
❷ 208
❸ 166
❹ 254

AUGUST 8, 1988: *Straight Outta Compton* released

"N.W.A. is the most influential act of the last thirty years," enthused comedian Chris Rock. "Bigger than Nirvana❶, Madonna❷, or the Sex Pistols❸. Nothing has ever been the same since they came . . . It was kind of like the British Invasion for black people." Rock is littered with angry young men, but when N.W.A.—essentially Dre (left), Cube, Yella, Eazy, and MC Ren—unleashed *Straight Outta Compton* (named after the L.A. neighborhood in which they grew up) in 1988, they redefined hip-hop. "Fuck tha Police" caused the biggest stir—the F.B.I. wrote to the record label about its concerns—and continues to be as relevant more than two decades later. The record's influence is far-reaching. Rage Against the Machine❹ cut a version of "Fuck tha Police" in 1996, as did Eazy's protégés Bone Thugs-N-Harmony in 1997, and Sinéad O'Connor described the album as "the best rap record I've ever heard."

HERE WE ARE NOW, ENTERTAIN US

1991

N.W.A. score a U.S. No. 1 with *EFIL4ZAGGIN*, but Cube has quit and Dre (who has established himself as a producer with Michel'le and The DOC) will follow.

April 9, 1992

The film soundtrack title cut "Deep Cover" is Dre's first solo release. It introduces his protégé Snoop Doggy Dogg and is a blueprint for G-Funk.

December 15, 1992

Dre's *The Chronic* is the first album on his Death Row label. It will take off when "Nuthin' but a 'G' Thang" hits, and sell three million in the U.S.A. within a year.

December 11, 1993

Snoop's *Doggystyle*, produced by Dre, enters the U.S. chart at No. 1, with record-breaking sales for a debut artist. It will also be the fastest seller until Eminem, seven years later.

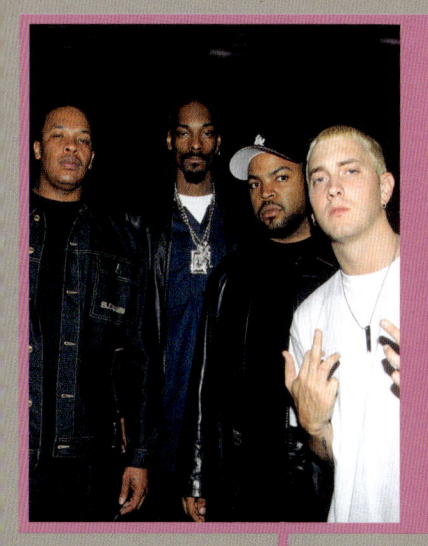

1994: Dr. Dre and Ice Cube reunite

After N.W.A.'s split, Cube had established himself as a superstar, with albums such as 1991's *Death Certificate* (whose "No Vaseline" took his ex-bandmates, including Dre, to task) and 1992's No. 1 *The Predator*. When Dre's G-Funk began to eclipse Cube's music, the latter enlisted Dre for the blood-soaked "Natural Born Killaz," then focused on his movie career—notably with *Friday*, which he wrote and acted in. Its chart-topping soundtrack featured Dre's "Keep Their Heads Ringin'." In 2000, Cube's *War & Peace Vol. 2 (The Peace Disc)* opened with "Hello," featuring both Dre and MC Ren. That year's *Next Friday* soundtrack featured "Chin Check," billed as an N.W.A. reunion. Snoop took the place of Eazy-E, who died from AIDS on March 26, 1995. Most spectacularly, 2000's *Up in Smoke* tour featured Dre, Snoop, Cube, and Eminem (all left), as well as Xzibit and a host of others.

July 13, 1996

"California Love"—2Pac's first single on Death Row, produced by and featuring Dre—hits No. 1 in the U.S.A. It will turn double platinum.

November 26, 1996

The Aftermath is a U.S. top ten album, introducing Dre's new label after he flees Death Row. Its only early success will be with supergroup The Firm.

October 9, 1999

Nine Inch Nails' *The Fragile* tops the U.S. chart. Its cut "Even Deeper" is mixed by Dre, who has otherwise steered clear of crossing into the rock 'n' roll arena.

October 16, 1999

2001—including the superb "Still D.R.E.," featuring Snoop and co-written by Jay-Z—announces Dre's return as a top-billed artist. It quickly sells millions.

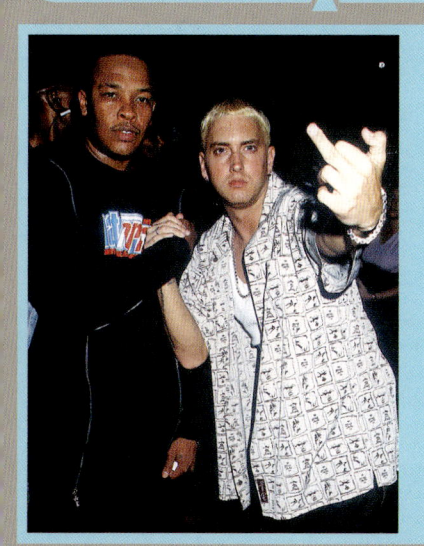

FEBRUARY 21, 2001: Eminem dominates the scene

Almost two years to the day after the release of *The Slim Shady LP*, Dre and his latest protégé Eminem (left) won Best Rap Performance by a Duo or Group for "Forgot About Dre" at the Grammy Awards. Eminem had exploded on to the scene with superior rapping and controversial lyrics in 1999. His debut album had outstanding production, thanks to Dre. (On "Still D.R.E.," the producer had bragged, "Kept my ear to the streets, signed Eminem.") On "Forgot About . . .," Dre rapped, "Who you think brought you the O.G.s, Eazy-Es, Ice Cubes, and The D.O.C.s, the Snoop D-O-double-Gs, and the group that said 'Muthafuck the police'?" Dre has worked on all Eminem's albums and also helped with the latter's own protégé, 50 Cent. "It's almost like a high for me," he admitted. "If I'm out of the studio too long, it feels funny . . . like, 'Damn, this could have been the day I came up with "Billie Jean" . . .'"

DR. DRE 257

Green Day 1989–present

Of the so-called "punk" bands that rose in the early Nineties, none has proved so enduringly successful as Green Day. In no way coy about their influences, they contributed to Iggy Pop's ◀116 *Skull Ring* (2003) and to a Ramones ◀158 tribute. (In fact, Green Day's drummer Tré Cool even named his daughter Ramona.) The band has also covered The Who ◀068 ("A Quick One While He's Away"), Bob Dylan ◀062 ("Like a Rolling Stone"), The Kinks ◀066 ("Tired of Waiting for You"), and John Lennon ("Working Class Hero").

The appreciation has gone in both directions. Elton John ◀126 proclaimed, "I like Green Day," when the band broke big; punk pioneer Patti Smith ◀164 said, "I'm really proud of a lot of the things that the new guard has done;" and Peter Buck of R.E.M. ◀204 marveled, "My son likes Green Day. They were in bands when they were fourteen and put out their own record when the lead singer was seventeen . . . They're heirs to a tradition: you're sixteen, you're a punk, you write punk songs, you make your own record on a small label, you tour." But not everyone has been convinced by the band's punk credentials. "Green Day is really easy listening," judged singer-songwriter Jeff Buckley. "Billy Joel, Green Day—I could see myself listening to that in the same hour."

Maturing songwriting has, without doubt, contributed to the band's longevity, hence 1997's elegiac "Time of Your Life" and 2004's extraordinary *American Idiot.* And their legacy is not purely musical. "The Green Day guys," said Weezer's Brian Bell, "taught us about treating fans nicely."

1972
Billie Joe Armstrong (February 17) and Mike Dirnt (née Pritchard; May 4) are born in California, U.S.A., as is Frank "Tré Cool" Wright III (December 9) in Germany.

1990
Singer-guitarist Armstrong and bassist Dirnt enlist Cool to replace drummer John Kiftmeyer in their band Green Day, formed the previous year.

January 17, 1992
Kerplunk—a second album on the Lookout label, after 1990's *39/Smooth*—builds a buzz about the band. A major label deal will ensue.

AUGUST 17, 1994: Platinum-coated *Dookie*

Thanks to MTV's adoption of "Longview," the first single off the third album (*Dookie*), Green Day became a four-year-old "overnight sensation." A mud fight with the audience at Woodstock II❶ (left) kept them in the public eye as they raced against The Offspring to be the biggest sellers of that year's new punk breed. Five hits pushed *Dookie* to eight million U.S. sales by the time 1995's *Insomniac* appeared. Although that album went double platinum within months, Green Day entered a period in which only a loyal fan base stopped them becoming yesterday's news. "Time of Your Life (Good Riddance)," from 1997's *Nimrod*, gave them a fluke hit (helped by its use in a climactic episode of *Seinfeld*). But 2000's *Warning*—though still a top five hit in the U.S.A.—was the poorest seller of Green Day's major label releases, and they were soon overtaken by Blink-182, another radio-friendly punk band who had risen in their wake.

❶ 114

January 8, 2002
The "best of" *International Superhits* goes gold in the U.S.A. In July, it will be followed by rarities collection *Shenanigans*.

April 17, 2002
Green Day are second on the bill to Blink-182 on the Pop Disaster Tour (also featuring Jimmy Eats World and Saves The Day), which runs to June.

September 30, 2003
Money Money 2020 by The Network is released on Armstrong's Adeline label. Although Green Day deny it, they and several friends *are* The Network.

August 29, 2004
The band headline the U.K.'s Reading Festival to a delirious reception, even for "American Idiot"—still two days from release.

NOVEMBER 10, 2004: Platinum-coated *Idiot*

A roller-coaster decade was washed away when Green Day unleashed not just their best album, but one of modern rock's greats: *American Idiot*. A turbo-charged descendant of The Who's❶ *Quadrophenia*, it went platinum in the U.S.A. within seven weeks of release—a remarkable recovery after 2000's *Warning* had struggled to gold. Thanks to hits such as "Boulevard of Broken Dreams," *American Idiot* topped international charts on its way to an estimated fourteen million sales. A triumphant tour climaxed with shows at the U.K.'s Milton Keynes Bowl, commemorated on 2005's *Bullet in a Bible*. The band united with U2❷ (left) for 2006's "The Saints Are Coming" and made a cameo in 2007's *The Simpsons Movie*. With two more albums—2008's *Stop Drop and Roll!!!* (issued under the pseudonym Foxboro Hot Tubs) and 2009's *21st Century Breakdown*—under their belt, the stadium-filling resurrection continues.

❶ 068
❷ 192

GREEN DAY

Oasis 1991–2009

1991+   2000+

Although Noel Gallagher hero-worshiped John Lennon, he was too media savvy to claim that Oasis were "more popular than Jesus." But that's not to say that such contentious comparisons were not applicable. As Gallagher reminisced in 2007, being bigger than The Beatles ◀044 may have been stretching it, but for a time—in the second half of the 1990s—there were few other bands in the world on whom Oasis could not look down with disdain.

Although the songwriting credits came to be shared out among other members as time passed (especially his bratty brother Liam), it was Noel who was the architect of the sound: a blend of the stomp of Slade, the snotty attitude of the Sex Pistols ◀166, and, naturally, generous helpings of Beatles-esque melodies. T. Rex ◀128 (on "Cigarettes & Alcohol," which appropriates the intro of "Get It On") and The Rolling Stones ◀054 (compare "Lyla" to "Street Fighting Man") were also targets for the musical magpie. Sometimes, the inspiration went far enough for the songs to carry a co-credit—the 1996 B-side "Step Out" was too close to Stevie Wonder's "Uptight (Everything's Alright)" for comfort.

The influences might have been transparent, but that didn't stop them being alchemized into a thrilling adrenaline rush when Oasis were at their best. Of course, Gallagher dismissed notions of the group being mere imitators. "I was a superhero in the Nineties," he declared. "I said so at the time. Paul McCartney, Paul Weller, Pete Townshend, Keith Richards—my first album is better than all their first albums. Even they'd admit that."

260   HERE WE ARE NOW, ENTERTAIN US

August 18, 1991
Liam Gallagher's band The Rain (named after a Beatles B-side) become Oasis for a first show in Manchester. Noel is in the audience and will soon join and take over.

May 31, 1993
The show in Glasgow that does much to persuade Alan McGee of Creation Records to sign the band includes a raucous cover of The Beatles' "I Am the Walrus."

September 10, 1994
Definitely Maybe tops the U.K. chart and becomes one of the fastest-selling British debuts. Oasis' first No. 1 single, "Some Might Say," will follow in 1995.

AUGUST 10, 1996: Making history at Knebworth

Just how big were Oasis? Big enough to shift 250,000 tickets, sell out two shows at the Hertfordshire estate of Knebworth (left), and still leave millions of others disappointed at missing out. The Stones❶, Zeppelin❷, Queen❸, and Pink Floyd❹ had all played there—the rough-and-ready lads from Manchester were now rubbing shoulders with rock royalty. Perhaps they ought to have ended matters, in the words of a live Oasis video issued at the time, there and then. "I always thought we should have bowed out at Knebworth," said guitarist Paul "Bonehead" Arthurs. "Walking out on that stage is a feeling I can't explain: a sea of people." "It's like getting a massive, massive pay rise and buying everything you want," said Noel Gallagher. "What do you do after that? You kind of sink into boredom. Kind of directionless." Nonetheless, every album from 1995's *(What's the Story) Morning Glory?* onward was an international hit.

❶ 054
❷ 098
❸ 144
❹ 086

July 21, 2000
A Wembley Stadium show—later issued as *Familiar to Millions*—includes a cover of Neil Young's "Hey Hey, My My."

July 1, 2002
Former Smith Johnny Marr provides guest guitar on the fifth Oasis album, *Heathen Chemistry*. As usual, it hits the top of the British chart.

January 16, 2004
Drummer Alan White (the 1995 replacement for Tony McCarroll) leaves. He will be replaced by Ringo Starr's son Zak Starkey (who later joins The Who).

August 22, 2005
Noel Gallagher describes "The Importance of Being Idle," the band's eighth U.K. chart-topping single, as "a cross between The Kinks and The La's."

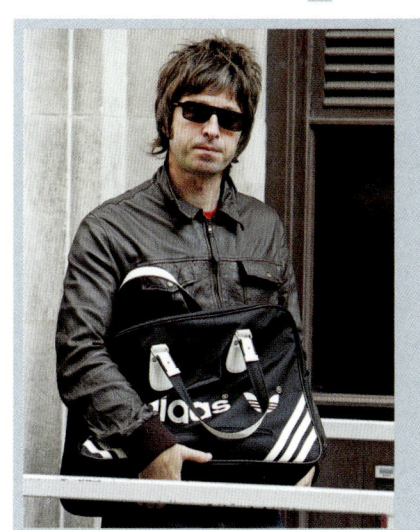

AUGUST 28, 2009: The end

Rock history is full of the black eyes of bruised and battered brotherly relationships—Ray and Dave Davies of The Kinks❶, Don and Phil Everly, The Jesus & Mary Chain's Jim and William Reid, Crowded House's❷ Neil and Tim Finn. And it was always likely to end this way for Noel (left) and Liam Gallagher, too. Their disagreements could be amusing at the start, with one extended and expletive-laden exchange even being released under the title "Wibbling Rivalry" (and just missing the U.K. top fifty). But events took on a darker hue in 2000 when Liam baited his older brother over family issues that concerned his then wife, Meg Mathews, and child; Noel quit that overseas tour. Years of tension reached an inevitable conclusion in 2009: a serious falling-out in France led to Noel leaving the band, as much with "relief" as "sadness." "I simply could not," he said, "go on working with Liam a day longer."

❶ 066
❷ 246

The Notorious B.I.G. & 2Pac
1972–97 & 1971–96

1994+

The Notorious B.I.G. (born Christopher Wallace, May 21, 1972) and 2Pac (born Tupac Shakur, June 16, 1971)—two of the biggest names that hip-hop has ever produced—were murdered within six months of each other, following years of bitter rivalry between them. It was hard to believe that the heavyweights had once been good friends.

Bad blood brewed when B.I.G. soared to fame, seemingly from nowhere, while 2Pac had toiled as a dancer for Digital Underground. "Doesn't Biggie sound like me?" complained Pac in 1994. "Isn't that my style coming out of his mouth?" Things took a nastier turn when 2Pac was shot later that year and accused Biggie of setting him up. When the former signed to L.A.'s Death Row label, he stoked East Coast–West Coast rivalry with Biggie's New York.

Shortly before Biggie's death, he formed hip-hop supergroup The Commission, including Jay-Z 266. A song with the latter, "Brooklyn's Finest," responded to 2Pac's "Hit 'Em Up," in which he claimed to have slept with Biggie's estranged wife, Faith Evans.

"I just wish they'd wipe each other out," cracked Keith Richards. "They have my permission."

Both left impressive statistics. Biggie's *Life After Death*—released, ironically, sixteen days after his death—is certified diamond, for ten million sales in the U.S.A. alone. (One of his verses was posthumously added to Michael Jackson's 122 *Invincible* in 2001.) 2Pac has had five U.S. No. 1 albums (including three posthumous), and a nine million-selling *Greatest Hits*. Pac's posthumous 2004 album *Loyal to the Game* was produced by one of his biggest fans: Eminem.

September 13, 1994

Ready to Die, Biggie's debut, is issued. *Rolling Stone* later say that it "almost single-handedly . . . shifted the focus back to East Coast rap." It will sell four million in the U.S.A.

October 25, 1994

Madonna releases *Bedtime Stories*. 2Pac—who dated the singer—had rapped on its "I'd Rather Be Your Lover," but it was cut from the album.

November 7, 1995

Biggie and 2Pac's "Runnin' (from tha Police)," intended for Pac's *Thug Life* album, is instead issued on the *One Million Strong* compilation.

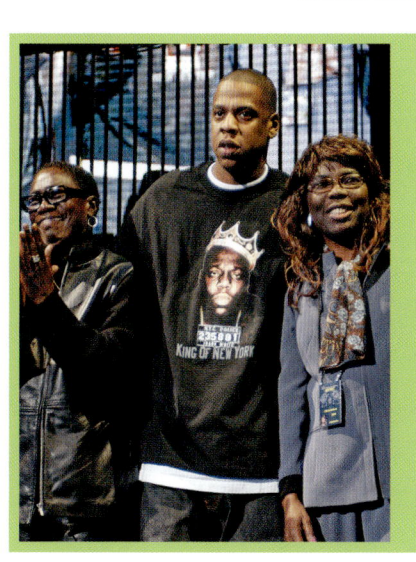

1996 ONWARD: Their legacies live on

Less than six months after 2Pac's death on September 13, 1996 (he'd been shot six days earlier in Las Vegas), the hip-hop world mourned again when Biggie was shot on March 9, 1997—like Pac, in a drive-by, but this time in L.A. But both rappers remain relevant and revered today. As Biggie foretold on his "You're Nobody (Til Somebody Kills You)," his albums continue to sell, and a 2009 biopic, *Notorious*, grossed $40 million in the U.S.A. Similarly, four of 2Pac's five posthumous releases have achieved platinum sales in the U.S.A. alone. (The video for his "I Ain't Mad at Cha," made before his death, depicted him being fatally shot.) Among the tributes to the rapping legends is a sequence in Jay-Z's ❶ movie *Fade to Black*, in which the star (left, with Pac's mother Afeni Shakur and Biggie's mother Voletta Wallace) leads a New York audience in singalongs to hits by both artists.

❶ 266

THE NOTORIOUS B.I.G. & 2PAC

Radiohead 1992–present

1992+   1997+

Restless reinvention can be a quick route to career suicide, but album-by-album morphing hasn't damaged the status of this Oxford quintet as one of rock's biggest—and most fascinating—acts.

American influences were obvious early on. The 1986 Talking Heads album *True Stories* provided the group's name (although the track was called "Radio Head"). Boston standouts the Pixies ◁224 —rather than the Nirvana-led ◁242 Seattle scene— were also an inspiration. Radiohead's breakthrough single "Creep," however, still sounded like a polite version of what was coming out of the East Coast.

Fêted on foreign shores but largely ignored in the U.K., Radiohead broadened their appeal with *The Bends*. Opening for R.E.M. ◁204 on the *Monster* tour in 1995 kept their American profile high, with Michael Stipe saying they were "so good they scare me." Acute anticipation for Radiohead's follow-up, *OK Computer*, was matched by undoubted achievement. The group's Pink Floyd ◁086 fetish produced an update on themes explored in *Dark Side of the Moon*. Roger Waters duly said: "My son Harry gave me *OK Computer*. I really liked it."

Avoiding the mid-career bloat of many of their contemporaries, Radiohead displayed a dwindling interest in formal song structure, replaced by a fascination with artists such as Aphex Twin. Critics predicted disaster, but *Kid A*, *Amnesiac*, *Hail to the Thief*, and *In Rainbows* all hit No. 1 in the U.K. and made the U.S. top three. Multi-platinum artist Dave Matthews spoke for many when he said: "I wonder if it's even possible for them to be bad on record."

September 21, 1992

"Creep" is adopted by college radio in the U.S.A. It will later be co-credited to the writers of The Hollies' hit "The Air that I Breathe" (one of whom is the father of one of The Strokes).

March 13, 1995

Radiohead's second album, *The Bends*, is released to widespread acclaim. Yorke says of the title track: "That was our Bowie pastiche."

May 15, 1995

The video for "Fake Plastic Trees," from *The Bends*, is directed by Jake Scott (son of movie director Ridley), who also helmed the "Everybody Hurts" promo for R.E.M.

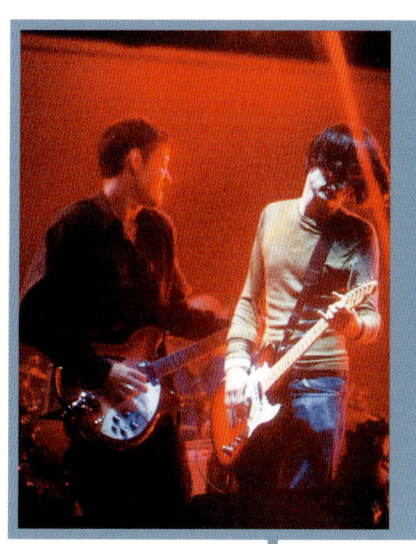

JUNE 28, 1997: A memorable Glastonbury

Glastonbury festival founder Michael Eavis called Radiohead's June 1997 performance (left, guitarists Ed O'Brien and Jonny Greenwood): "The most inspiring festival gig in thirty years." Similar plaudits came thick and fast, including a feature in *Q* magazine that rated it the best concert of all time, with The Beatles❶, Nirvana❷, U2❸, Sex Pistols❹, and The Stone Roses all eating the band's dust. About the only people *not* having a great time on that Saturday in Somerset were Radiohead themselves. "Everything broke on stage," said O'Brien. "It turned into the worst concert and the worst night of our lives." No one else agreed. "It changed the way I looked at music," said Tom Smith of the Editors. "Britpop was exciting, but I saw something in Radiohead that made me think a little more, touched me deeper." Another Glastonbury headliner by them in 2003 proved to be just as touching and memorable.

❶ 044
❷ 242
❸ 192
❹ 166

September 8, 1997

Thom Yorke teams up with American alt-rockers Sparklehorse to record a version of "Wish You Were Here" by Pink Floyd.

May 21, 1998

Yorke provides the vocals for three Roxy Music songs on the soundtrack of the movie *Velvet Goldmine*. They also feature Suede guitarist Bernard Butler.

December 10, 1998

The band plays an Amnesty International show in Paris. Peter Gabriel, also on the bill, will sing "Street Spirit (Fade Out)" on his covers set *Scratch My Back* (2010).

August 6, 2001

Ed O'Brien says their single "Knives Out" is a tribute to The Smiths: "I only went to Manchester [University] . . . because of The Smiths."

OCTOBER 10, 2007: A revolution—*In Rainbows*

All of 2000's *Kid A* had appeared online well before its official release, but Radiohead didn't follow the litigious route favored by Metallica❶. And, for 2007's *In Rainbows*, an innovative method was found to deliver the music to the marketplace: the tracks were downloadable in digital format, but fans could decide how much to pay. "It was a thrill," said singer Thom Yorke. The approach was endorsed by many. "This was how we used to operate," said Paul McCartney. "I remember John [Lennon], for instance, writing 'Instant Karma' and demanding it was released the following week." Muse❷'s Dominic Howard could see the benefits: "A band like that doing it on their own shakes up the record companies and helps them realize that they are gradually becoming more and more useless." Subsequent releases have been similarly progressive, with Radiohead showing no signs of leaving a league of their own.

❶ 218
❷ 270

RADIOHEAD 265

Jay-Z 1969–present

1969+ 2003+

When Jay-Z topped the bill at the Glastonbury festival in the U.K. in 2008, he was one of the most controversial choices of headliner in the event's history. "I'm sorry, but Jay-Z?" complained Noel Gallagher of Oasis ◂260▸. "No chance. Glastonbury has a tradition of guitar music . . . I'm not having hip-hop at Glastonbury. It's wrong." Jay-Z's response? He opened his set with a tongue-in-cheek take on the 1996 Oasis hit "Wonderwall."

Before the festival, Chris Martin offered support to his friend: "Coldplay ◂276▸ *not* playing and Jay-Z playing is exactly what needs to happen . . . he's the best rapper in the world." Two years later, The White Stripes' ◂272▸ Jack White said of working with Jay-Z, "He's brilliant . . . he's the best thing going in hip-hop and has been for years."

Born and raised in Brooklyn, New York, Jay-Z went to the same school as The Notorious B.I.G. ◂262▸ and Busta Rhymes. A feud with fellow rapper Nas and spats with 2Pac ◂262▸, plus a colorful background as a street hustler, made his eventual move to the mainstream all the more interesting.

A sound businessman, he took over as president of Def Jam ◂222▸ in 2004, twenty years after Rick Rubin ◂226▸ had established the label.

Jay-Z's status was proved by a 2003 "retirement" show. The Roots, Missy Elliott, Beyoncé, R. Kelly, and Mary J. Blige guested, as did Biggie Smalls' and 2Pac's mothers. (The excellent movie of the event, *Fade to Black*, was produced by Pink Floyd's ◂086▸ producer Bob Ezrin.) "I'm the new Sinatra," he brags on 2009's "Empire State of Mind"—no doubt.

266 HERE WE ARE NOW, ENTERTAIN US

December 4, 1969

Shawn Corey Carter (a.k.a. Jay-Z, a reference to a subway line) is born in Brooklyn, New York. He will celebrate his birthdate on *The Black Album*'s "December 4th."

June 25, 1996

Jay-Z issues his debut album, *Reasonable Doubt*. It boasts duets with The Notorious B.I.G. and Mary J. Blige, and a chorus based on a sample of a Nas song.

March 24, 1999

"Hard Knock Life"—the (near) title track of what will be Jay-Z's best-selling album—goes gold in the U.S.A. Sampling a song from *Annie*, it is also his first big hit outside the U.S.A.

SEPTEMBER 11, 2001: Making his own blueprint

❶ 262
❷ 262
❸ 174

Having claimed Biggie Smalls'❶ throne as king of the New York hip-hop scene after the latter's demise, Jay-Z continued toward stardom with the release of *The Blueprint* in 2001. This accelerated his four-year feud with Nas, caused by "Takeover." (The track badmouthed Jay-Z's fellow New York rapper, after Nas declined to appear in a video with his rival and took exception to Jay-Z ridiculing Prodigy of Mobb Depp.) After the feud grew more vicious and personal, the pair reconciled in October 2005 at Jay-Z's I Declare War show in New York (left), at which Nas was a surprise guest. Jay-Z followed *The Blueprint* with *The Blueprint²: The Gift & the Curse* in November 2002. It had a more poppy feel and featured Jay-Z's future wife, Beyoncé, on "03: Bonnie & Clyde" (which sampled "Me and My Girlfriend" by 2Pac❷ and "If I Was Your Girlfriend" by Prince❸). It also marked the start of Jay-Z's move to being an international star.

November 25, 2003

Just days after the release of *The Black Album* (whose producers include Eminem), Jay-Z stages a "retirement" show in New York.

January 3, 2005

Jay-Z becomes president of Def Jam. Before he steps down in 2007, he will oversee the rise of Rihanna, on whose smash hit "Umbrella" he will appear.

February 13, 2005

The Rick Rubin-produced "99 Problems" wins Best Rap Solo Performance at the Grammys. In 2009, Jay-Z will perform it at Obama's presidential inauguration.

December 14, 2006

Kingdom Come, mixed by Dr. Dre, goes double platinum in under a month. It includes "Beach Chair," a duet with Coldplay's Chris Martin.

JANUARY 23, 2010: Moving to the mainstream

❶ 192
❷ 276

By the time Jay-Z released the charity single "Stranded (Haiti Mon Amour)" with Rihanna, and U2's❶ Bono and Edge in 2010, he was a global superstar. His willingness to experiment led to *Collision Course*, an album of mash-ups with Linkin Park in 2004. The track "Numb/Encore" won Best Rap/Sung Collaboration at the Grammys; Linkin Park and he performed it with Paul McCartney (left)—incorporating "Yesterday"— at the awards that year. Jay-Z's friendship with Chris Martin led to him appearing on a remix of Coldplay's❷ "Lost!" and at two shows with the band at London's Wembley Stadium in 2009. His slot at Glastonbury in 2008 was the first time a hip-hop artist headlined the main stage. And, thirteen years into his hit-making career (a lifetime by hip-hop standards), the stunning "Empire State of Mind," featuring Alicia Keys, became his first U.S. No. 1 (with him as the lead artist), in late 2009.

JAY-Z   267

Daft Punk 1993–present

2001+

A negative review in the now-defunct British music weekly *Melody Maker* gave two Parisian musicians the perfect name for their new band. The music of their former incarnation, Darlin', was dismissed as "a bunch of daft punk." *Et voilà!*

Daft Punk's Thomas Bangalter and Guy-Manuel de Homem-Christo originally bonded over a love of Elton John ◀126, The Rolling Stones ◀054, The Beach Boys ◀050, and Iggy and The Stooges ◀116. While their music is usually described as a hybrid of house, acid house, electro, rave, and techno, rock can be heard pulsating through much of it, too.

"Da Funk"—from their debut *Homework* (1995) —first got them noticed, especially when DJs The Chemical Brothers started playing it in their sets, having spotted its dancefloor-filling potential.

The duo shocked hardcore fans by going more disco and synth-pop: first with Bangalter's 1998 smash "Music Sounds Better with You" by his side-project Stardust, then on Daft Punk's sample-heavy second album, 2001's *Discovery*. But the hit "One More Time" swept away the naysayers' complaints.

Notable for their futuristic appearance, Daft Punk started out wearing masks, before evolving to full robot regalia. Like The Prodigy ◀252 and Orbital before them, their astounding visuals and euphoric tunes all add up to a spectacular live proposition. (Their performance at Lollapalooza ◀238 in 2007 was hailed by *Pitchfork* as a "much-needed reminder of the still-potent power of communicative pop.")

They remain perhaps the coolest act in modern music; fêted by Madonna ◀208, adored by fans.

March 12, 2001

The second album, *Discovery*, has its European release. A massive success, it provides the soundtrack to their film *Interstella 5555: The 5tory of the 5ecret 5tar 5ystem*.

June 14, 2005

"Technologic," from *Human After All*, is released. A year later, Busta Rhymes samples it for his "Touch It," and Missy Elliott will sing it on a remix.

April 29, 2006

Daft Punk perform in the U.S.A. for the first time since 1997, at the Coachella Festival. They will play at Lollapalooza in 2007.

FEBRUARY 10, 2008: R&B meets electro

Hip-hop heavyweight Kanye West sampled Daft Punk's 2001 song "Harder, Better, Faster, Stronger" on his "Stronger" in 2007. "Our song had a good sound," enthused de Homem-Christo, "but when [the DJ] put Kanye's record on, the sound was really fat. It sounds really big." "Stronger" went on to win Best Rap Solo Performance at the fiftieth Grammy Awards in 2008. Daft Punk made a surprise appearance at the ceremony (left), with their trademark pyramid stage set, teaming up with West for a version of the track created especially for the show. This also marked the duo's first-ever television appearance in their fourteen years together. The audio-visual extravaganza continued in 2009 and 2010, when Daft Punk remixed their material for the game *DJ Hero*, signed up to provide the soundtrack for the movie *Tron: Legacy*, and appeared in a *Star Wars*-themed commercial for Adidas.

DAFT PUNK

Muse 1997–present

1998+   2006+

If ever a band has shaped a sound screaming to bust into stadium-sized venues, it is Muse—clear successor to the rock throne once occupied by Queen ◀144. Front man and songwriter Matt Bellamy has an innate flair for creating music full of grandiose entrances and dramatic exits; as part of The Tornados, his father George had played rhythm guitar on the monster 1962 hit "Telstar." That song had been about an orbiting satellite, but Bellamy, Jr. has taken Muse much further into the galaxy, especially on 2006's *Black Holes & Revelations*.

Unlike bands such as Radiohead ◀264, who reintroduced progressive rock by stealth, there has been nothing of the Trojan horse about Muse. The science-fiction themes of many of their songs hark back to prog progenitors Yes, Genesis, and Pink Floyd ◀086. But, as a sign of the breadth of their influences, a cover of Nina Simone's "Feeling Good" featured on 2001's *Origin of Symmetry*.

Queen played two nights at Wembley Stadium, London, in July 1986; the Muse trio—from Devon, England—did the same almost twenty-one years later. "I think I was pretty much as terrified as I've ever been for a gig," said bassist Chris Wolstenholme.

In the face of what *NME* described as a "cataclysmic clash of . . . Rachmaninoff and Rage Against the Machine," no territory has stood a chance of resisting Muse's charms—not least the U.S.A., where 2009's *The Resistance* went top three. "Very good boys and extremely talented," remarked Queen guitarist Brian May, "and, like us, they have their tongue in cheek a lot of the time."

December 24, 1998

The band signs to Maverick, Madonna's U.S. record label. Serj Tankien of art-metallers System of a Down makes an attempt to sign the band to *his* label, but is unsuccessful.

October 4, 1999

Muse issue their debut album, *Showbiz*. Producer John Leckie's résumé includes The Fall, The Stone Roses, Radiohead, New Order, and Magazine.

August 26, 2002

Coldplay's Chris Martin says of "Clocks," issued this day: "It was inspired by Muse." The band had supported Muse and will also draw on their "Megalomania" for "Fix You."

JUNE 27, 2004: Glastonbury triumph (and tragedy)

Muse were not a universally popular choice for the closing Sunday night set at the U.K.'s 2004 Glastonbury festival (although for the band, who had been coming to the festival since they were teenagers, it was a dream come true). They had released only three albums at the time (not counting 2002's live/rarities collection, *Hullabaloo Soundtrack*), with 2003's *Absolution* being the most recent. "That gig was a defining point in the life of this band," said bassist Wolstenholme. "We went in as underdogs and a lot of people were saying, 'Why are Muse headlining this festival? They're not a big band.' I think a lot of people wanted us to fail and we didn't. We went out there and had the best gig of our lives." But in the midst of triumph, tragedy struck. Bill Howard, father of drummer Dominic, collapsed and died backstage shortly after their set. "It was almost not believable," said front man Bellamy (left).

May 13, 2006

"Supermassive Black Hole" receives its first live airing. Says Bellamy of the song: "We've added a bit of Prince and Kanye West."

July 11, 2006

"Knights of Cydonia," issued on *Black Holes & Revelations*, nods to "Telstar." "The guitar sound . . . ," admits Bellamy, "that was deliberate."

September 25, 2008

The band are awarded honorary doctorates by the University of Plymouth, in their native Devon, U.K. "I'm pretty sure we're not worthy," says Bellamy.

March 25, 2009

Muse support U2 on the latter's 360° tour, allowing concert-goers to witness a face-off between two of the world's best live acts.

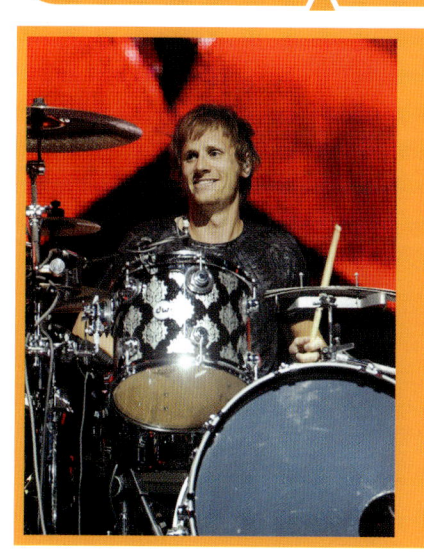

❶ 144

SEPTEMBER 14, 2009: All hail the new Queens

The influence of Queen❶ on Muse has hardly been a state secret but it reached new levels on 2009's *The Resistance*, a No. 1 album around the world. In particular, much of "United States of Eurasia (+Collateral Damage)" is pure Freddie and the gang. "When we did that in the studio, we laughed a lot because it was so uplifting," said drummer Dominic Howard (left). "It's a real chest-out, hand-in-the-air moment in the song." Queen guitarist Brian May was flattered by the imitation: "I think it's great stuff. I like the way they let their madness show through. Always a good thing in an artist." Jerry Ewing, editor of *Classic Rock* magazine, said Muse may even have achieved what many thought impossible and actually outdone Queen for over-the-top effrontery. "They make records that Queen would blush at," he said. And, like their beloved forebears, Muse have also become one of the world's most spectacular live acts.

MUSE 271

The White Stripes 1997–present

1997+ 2003+

Jack White owes much to Iggy Pop ◀116 and The Stooges. As a youth, he discovered their *Fun House*—described by White as "the best rock 'n' roll record ever made"—in a dumpster behind his Detroit home. It changed his life. Years later, a song from that album plays in the background of a scene featuring Jack and Meg White—the charismatic and enigmatic duo who are The White Stripes—in the movie *Coffee and Cigarettes* (which, coincidentally, also features Iggy Pop). "I'm in debt to The Stooges for life," Jack told *Mojo* in 2007, but they are not this formidable songwriter's only influence.

The diverse influences and styles in The White Stripes' music range from rockabilly (they've played a live version of Johnny Cash's ◀018 "Get Rhythm") to swamp-blues, garage rock, metal, country (they regularly cover Dolly Parton's "Jolene"), and show tunes. Their intense sound ("amazingly raw," said Kevin Shields of My Bloody Valentine) is anchored by Meg's rudimentary (self-taught) percussion.

Jack starred alongside Led Zeppelin's ◀098 Jimmy Page and U2's ◀192 The Edge in the 2009 documentary *It Might Get Loud*. His place among legends had already been cemented when he appeared onstage with The Rolling Stones ◀054 (commemorated in Martin Scorsese's 2008 movie, *Shine a Light*). And, of a key influence, he's said, "I've got three fathers—my biological dad, God, and Bob Dylan ◀062." (He called Dylan for advice when producing an album by Wanda Jackson.)

Moby sums it up: "I love White Stripes. They're a very interesting force in contemporary music."

July 24, 1997

Jack (born July 9, 1975, in Detroit, Michigan) and Meg (December 10, 1974, in Detroit) form The White Stripes. Their self-titled debut album will be issued in 1999.

March 24, 2000

The couple (who claimed to be siblings) divorce, having married in 1996 (when Jack —born John Anthony Gillis —took Meg's surname).

August 18, 2001

The duo's breakthrough *White Blood Cells* (later *Rolling Stone*'s nineteenth best album of the decade) hits the chart in the U.K., where they and The Strokes are hyped hugely.

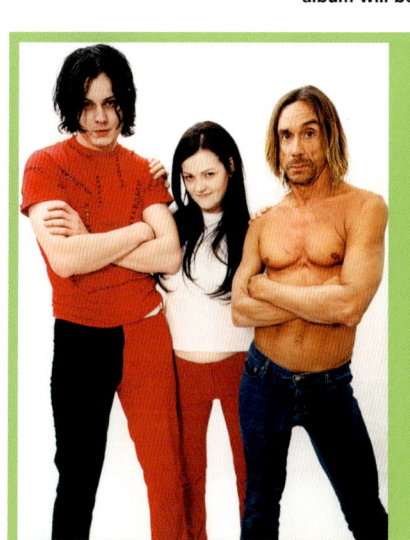

AUGUST 29, 2002: Lego video makes them stars

When Jack White asked Lego for pieces to be packaged with the "Fell in Love with a Girl" single, he was told sternly that they market only to under twelves. Fast forward to August 2002, when the song's Lego-animated video won three MTV awards and Lego came a-knocking on Jack's door. Typically, he stuck to his principles and sent them packing. In the clip, the duo jumped and strummed their way through a building block world. It looked simple but took fifteen animators six weeks to make. "There's something charming and naive about their use of black, red, and white imagery," said director Michel Gondry, referring to their strict sartorial rules. "I made a parallel between that and the basic-ness of the color of Lego blocks." The newly made stars even befriended Jack's hero, Iggy Pop❶ (left). "They have real accomplishments, that group," said their fellow Detroit dweller. "I love Jack, I see him all the time."

❶ 116

September 18, 2003

Rolling Stone ranks Jack at No. 17 in the 100 Greatest Guitarists of All Time, ahead of Pete Townshend and Frank Zappa.

February 8, 2004

The Stripes' major label debut *Elephant* wins a best album Grammy. It has topped the U.K. chart and spawned their anthem "Seven Nation Army."

June 2005

Jack marries model Karen Elson, weeks after meeting her on the video of "Blue Orchid" from *Get Behind Me Satan*. (Meg will marry Patti Smith's son in 2009.)

May 2007

Icky Thump's title track gives the duo a first U.S. top forty hit. It will be their best-selling single at home, going gold in 2008.

SEPTEMBER 11, 2007: Enforced hiatus

Meg's acute anxiety issues onstage caused the cancellation of tour dates in 2007 and a lengthy hiatus. "She is a very shy girl, a very quiet and shy person," explained the fiercely protective Jack. "Meg is the best part of this band. It never would have worked with anybody else, because it would have been too complicated . . . It was my doorway to playing the blues." In the meantime, Jack's irrepressible energy and passion for music found multiple outlets. Not content with founding indie supergroups The Raconteurs and The Dead Weather, he set up the independent Third Man Records and produced his wife's debut album. He also produced an album for Loretta Lynn and created the theme for the 2008 James Bond movie *Quantum of Solace* with Alicia Keys (left). The Stripes released *Under Great White Northern Lights*— their first live album, accompanied by a documentary—in March 2010.

THE WHITE STRIPES

Gorillaz 1998–present

1998+   2005+

While not the most original of concepts—The Archies had done it in the late Sixties—a virtual band, comprised of four cartoon members, seems a very twenty-first-century idea. Gorillaz—2D, Murdoc, Noodle, and Russel—were formed in 1998 as a reaction against manufactured bands. It was the brainchild of Damon Albarn, singer with Britpop legends Blur, and comic book artist Jamie Hewlett, the creator of *Tank Girl*. "We were moaning," said Hewlett, "about the fact that when we grew up it was The Clash ◂170, the Pistols ◂166, the Specials ◂178, and why were there no bands like that?"

The band's self-titled debut album was released in 2001 and sold more than seven million copies, earning them an entry in the Guinness Book of World Records as the Most Successful Virtual Band. Later that year, they released "911," a single with D12 (bar Eminem) and Specials singer Terry Hall about the devastating attacks on the World Trade Center.

Four years later, "Feel Good Inc."—featuring De La Soul—achieved critical and commercial success, peaking at No. 14 in the U.S.A. and being nominated for Record of the Year at the 2006 Grammys. The track featured on *Demon Days* (2005), which also included Shaun Ryder (Happy Mondays), Neneh Cherry, and Blondie's ◂172 Debbie Harry, and was produced by Danger Mouse of Gnarls Barkley.

"Stylo" (featuring Bobby Womack and Mos Def), the first single from 2010's *Plastic Beach*, has been described as the "*Saturday Night Fever* soundtrack on MDMA." It is disco updated for the Noughties, and another genre added to the Gorillaz' bow.

HERE WE ARE NOW, ENTERTAIN US

1998

Albarn and his then flatmate, Hewlett (whose house parties have attracted Kate Moss and Radiohead), form Gorillaz after a drunken debate about the contemporary music scene.

March 17, 2001

The band's first single "Clint Eastwood"—named for the Eastwood movie *The Good, the Bad and the Ugly*—hits the U.K. chart at No. 4.

February 20, 2002

Gorillaz (who asked for their nomination for the previous year's Mercury Music Prize to be withdrawn) are nominated for six Brit awards, but go home empty handed.

MAY 5, 2003: Back to the Blur job

Blur's seventh album, *Think Tank*, was released in the U.K. in May 2003. Coming four years after their previous release, *13*, it had more in common with Gorillaz than with Britpop, with hip-hop, dub, jazz, and African beats augmenting the band's customary guitar-based sound. The critics loved it. More than four years later, Albarn was named by Q magazine as one of its "21 Artists who Changed Music," thanks to his innovative, genre-defying work as a member of Blur, Gorillaz, and The Good, The Bad & The Queen. Guitarist Graham Coxon (left, with Albarn)—to many, Blur's most talented member—quit during the making of *Think Tank* (part produced by Norman "Fatboy Slim" Cook) but Albarn's talent, and willingness to experiment, meant that Blur's brilliance was undiminished.

August 5, 2005

Demon Days goes platinum in the U.S.A. (it will double that total). Albarn, says *Spin* magazine, "has great taste in other people's music."

February 8, 2006

At the Grammys, Gorillaz perform with Madonna, using hologram technology. They perform mash-ups of "Feel Good Inc." and "Hung Up."

February 9, 2008

Bananaz, a documentary about the band, premieres at the Berlin International Film Festival. It features De La Soul, Cuban star Ibrahim Ferrer, and Dennis Hopper.

January 26, 2010

"Stylo" is digitally released. Soul legend Bobby Womack had appeared on it at the behest of his granddaughter —a big fan of Gorillaz.

MARCH 9, 2010: A star-packed album

❶ 092

❷ 170

Plastic Beach, released in March 2010 to top three positions around the globe (including No. 1 in Australia), is Gorillaz' most star-studded album—Lou Reed❶, Snoop Dogg, Mark E. Smith of The Fall, and The Clash's❷ Paul Simonon and Mick Jones all feature. Albarn and Simonon had previously worked together on 2007's *The Good, The Bad & The Queen*, with Simon Tong (The Verve's former guitarist, who had deputized for Graham Coxon in Blur) and Tony Allen (Fela Kuti's former drummer and co-founder of the Afrobeat movement). In 2009, Albarn had participated in a rapturously received Blur reunion at the U.K.'s Glastonbury festival, but the new year found him headlining California's Coachella festival with the band that seem best to capture his wandering spirit.

GORILLAZ 275

Coldplay 1997–present

1996+ 2005+

Bono of U2 ◀192 said, in 2005, "Chris [Martin] is a songwriter in the high British line of [The Beatles'] ◀044 Paul McCartney, [The Kinks'] ◀066 Ray Davies, and [Oasis'] ◀260 Noel Gallagher." High praise indeed. But when it comes to the comparisons of Coldplay to U2, Martin says it's like "comparing a high jumper with an astronaut."

As with their contemporaries Muse ◀270, Coldplay were influenced by Radiohead ◀264 and Jeff Buckley, especially on their first two albums, *Parachutes* (2000) and *A Rush of Blood to the Head* (2002). *X&Y* (2005) showed that they were willing to experiment, with "Talk" based on Kraftwerk's ◀148 "Computer Love," while the Eno ◀138-produced *Viva la Vida . . .* (2008) tipped its hat to influences ranging from My Bloody Valentine to Tinariwen.

The band's lack of rock 'n' roll excess led to some criticism—ex-Creation Records boss Alan McGee famously described them as "bedwetters' music."

But there were plenty of fans in high places. Noel Gallagher said: "I listen to 'Violet Hill' and it's like The Beatles. I just think Chris Martin is a great songwriter." (He added that his brother Liam "thinks their stuff sounds like Annie Lennox.") The Killers' 280▶ Brandon Flowers named them as "one of the bands that we always admired." And Kasabian singer Tom Meighan observed of their staggering U.S. success, "What they've done for British music over here is amazing. I love that band."

Chris Martin has also worked with Jay-Z ◀266, and the band's songs have been covered by artists as diverse as Aimee Mann and Avril Lavigne.

HERE WE ARE NOW, ENTERTAIN US

September 1996

Singer Chris Martin meets guitarist Jonny Buckland at university in London. They initially form a group called Pectoralz and will be joined by bassist Guy Berryman.

February 22, 1998

Minus keyboard player Tim Rice-Oxley (later to found Keane), who Martin tried fruitlessly to enlist, the band play a first show as "The Coldplay," in London.

June 26, 2000

"Yellow"—which drummer Will Champion says sounded like a Neil Young song to start with—is released. Its top five U.K. success will pave the way for *Parachutes* to hit No. 1.

AUGUST 26, 2002: Success rushes in

The release of 2002's *A Rush of Blood to the Head* sealed Coldplay's status as global superstars. It went top five around the world, hitting No. 1 in both the U.K. and Australia. Martin stated that its title track is an homage to Johnny Cash❶, whom he considered one of "the greatest . . . men with just guitars." The phenomenally successful album has sold more than eleven million copies worldwide and contains a multitude of hits, including "In My Place," "The Scientist" (written after Martin had been listening to George Harrison's "All Things Must Pass") and "Clocks" (inspired by "Megalomania" by Muse❷). Both the first and last of these won Grammys, with Martin dedicating his win for "Clocks" to Cash. In 2002, Coldplay headlined the main stage of the U.K.'s Glastonbury festival (left)—just two years after they had performed at the same event, in an inconspicuous mid-afternoon slot, on the second stage.

❶ 018
❷ 270

June 2005

X&Y tops charts worldwide (it will be the year's biggest seller). Its "Speed of Sound" is influenced by "Running Up That Hill" by Kate Bush.

July 2, 2005

Performing at Live 8, Coldplay include a verse of "Rockin' All Over the World," the first song played at the original event in 1985, by Status Quo.

December 14, 2005

The live favorite "Fix You" becomes their fifth gold single in the U.S.A. Berryman admits that it was partly inspired by Jimmy Cliff's "Many Rivers to Cross."

June 11, 2008

Viva la Vida or Death and All His Friends (again the biggest seller of its year) is released. Its title refers to Mexican artist, Frida Kahlo.

SEPTEMBER 18, 2009: Another live triumph

When Coldplay announced that Jay-Z❶ (left) and Girls Aloud were to support them at two Wembley Stadium dates in London in September 2009, there were a few raised eyebrows. But Martin had always been open about his love of pop. A source told British newspaper *The Sun* that "Coldplay are huge pop fans. They love Take That . . . Girls Aloud are the ideal support group . . . Chris Martin is a fan and had them on his wishlist from the start of tour plans." Similarly, his friendship and admiration for Jay-Z started in 2006. They worked together on the Jay-Z track "Beach Chair" and performed it together when Jay-Z played the Royal Albert Hall in September 2006. Then, during the 2009 Wembley dates, the rapper joined them onstage for "Lost!" Coldplay have also recorded a duet with pop diva Kylie Minogue❷—"Luna"—which was meant to be included on *Viva la Vida*.

❶ 266
❷ 203

COLDPLAY 277

Kings of Leon 2000–present

2003+

One of the least plausible recipes for musical success in recent years has featured lashings of Lynyrd Skynyrd, mixed with a soupçon of The Strokes. But from these and other tangled roots, (Followill) brothers Caleb, Nathan, and Jared, and their cousin Matthew, have become one of the world's best-loved bands. "I can sit in the back seat of a car," mused Noel Gallagher of Oasis ◀260, "pontificating about how great the Kings of Leon [are]." (Nathan responded: "'Wonderwall' and all that stuff, that was when I was a junior and senior in High School. So it was huge. So I did my fair share of making out or crying to a couple of those songs.")

The Kings, remarked Eddie Vedder of Pearl Jam ◀248, "hit a reflex in me. They opened for U2 ◀192 and we hung out, and the next night we played 'Slow Night, So Long' [from *Aha Shake Heartbreak*]. I bashed some tambourines—it was exciting."

The band have also supported Bob Dylan ◀062, whom Caleb had tried to emulate on *Youth & Young Manhood*. "He actually came in our dressing room," recalled the singer of their last show with Dylan, "and told us he was depressed because we were getting off the tour." The Pretenders' Chrissie Hynde hailed Kings of Leon as the first band in a decade to pique her interest, and they have even attracted admirers in Radiohead ◀264. "We had no idea how big fans of ours they were," admitted Nathan.

"I'm happy for those guys," enthused Dave Grohl of the Foo Fighters. "When I hear live drums and real guitars and people singing on the radio, it makes me feel that there's still hope for this world."

August 19, 2003

The Kings' debut, *Youth & Young Manhood*, is released. "We're from the South and we hadn't exactly escaped it at that point," Caleb will say.

February 22, 2005

Aha Shake Heartbreak is released. "It's really stripped down . . ." enthused Brit rocker Paul Weller, "but the result is really tough and muscular."

April 8, 2007

Because of the Times tops the U.K. chart, a feat it will replicate in New Zealand and Ireland. At home it hits No. 25, as did *Aha Shake* . . .

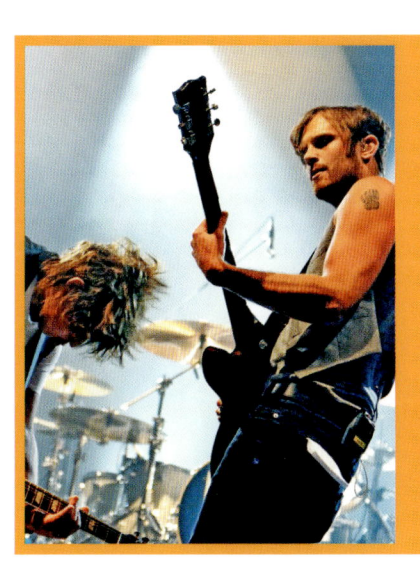

MARCH 13, 2009: Kings finally strike gold at home

"Ed [Vedder, Pearl Jam❶] actually called it immediately," said Kings of Leon front man Caleb Followill. "He was one of the first people to hear *Only By the Night*, and he said, 'You're about to ride a big wave.' I don't even think he liked the record. But he knew immediately that we were about to go through something big." After years of adulation everywhere bar their U.S. homeland, the band became stars even there with their fourth album (home of the U.K. No. 1 "Sex on Fire"), which went gold six months after its release. This success was partly down to the band's adoption of a more mainstream sound, notably on the smash "Use Somebody." "A lot of the people that we tour with, we end up sounding like," admitted Jared, tongue-in-cheek, to *Spin*. "And when we see them next, they'll tell us that they feel like they're ripping us off . . . U2's❷ new stuff? Bob Dylan's❸ new stuff? Blatant rip-off!"

❶ 248
❷ 192
❸ 062

KINGS OF LEON   279

The Killers 2001–present

2001+   2004+

It was through a 2001 small ad in the back of a Las Vegas newspaper that The Killers were formed. Guitarist Dave Keuning listed Queen ◀144, Oasis ◀260, The Cure, U2 ◀192, and The Beatles ◀044 as influences, attracting flamboyant lead singer, Brandon Flowers. Bassist Mark Stoermer and drummer Ronnie Vannucci completed the lineup.

The Killers' name was inspired by a fictional band in the video for "Crystal" by New Order (with whom they went on to perform live). A love of 1980s synth-pop and iconic British bands influenced their first album, *Hot Fuss* (2004), which was a critically lauded smash. Although critics were keen to point out the myriad Eighties influences, such as Duran Duran ◀200, Flowers remarked, "I like David Bowie ◀134 just as much."

The Killers changed direction with their second album, *Sam's Town* (2006)—front man Flowers had discovered a love of Bruce Springsteen ◀150 and the E Street Band around 2004, which he described as "very profound, no different to when I discovered The Smiths ◀212." The album received a mixed reaction from fans and critics, although it yielded the hit and live favorite "When You Were Young."

A collection of rarities and B-sides, *Sawdust* (2007), followed. It included "Tranquilize," with Lou Reed of The Velvet Underground ◀090, and a cover of "Romeo and Juliet" by Dire Straits.

2008's *Day & Age* took the band back to their pop roots. Its sound was partly inspired by Elton John ◀126, with whom they collaborated on 2008's Christmas single, "Joseph, Better You than Me."

2001

Brandon Flowers is dumped by synth-pop band Blush Response, after refusing to move from Las Vegas to Los Angeles. An Oasis show will push him in a rockier direction.

September 29, 2002

Independent label Lizard King signs The Killers on the strength of five songs after being passed their demo by Warner Bros.

October 22, 2003

A performance at New York's annual CMJ Music Marathon will be swiftly followed by a worldwide deal with Island. (My Morning Jacket will also prosper after playing there.)

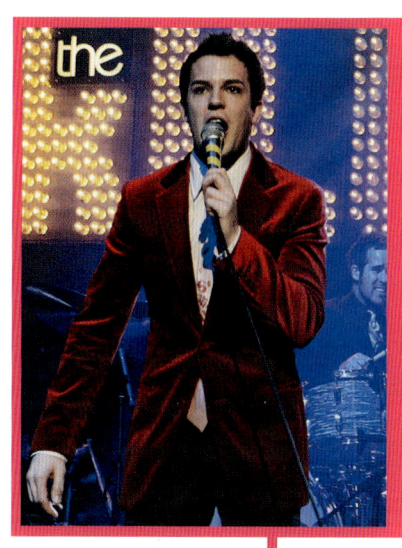

JUNE 15, 2004: "Hot Fuss" released in the U.S.A.

With its glitzy neon cover—seemingly inspired by the band's hometown of Las Vegas—and an Elvis❶-style logo, would The Killers' debut album live up to its artwork? In a word, yes. Nominated for best rock album at the 2005 Grammy Awards, it has—more than five years on from its release—sold over seven million copies. "All These Things That I've Done" became a live singalong favorite of "Hey Jude" proportions— it was the only track the band performed on the British leg of Live 8❷ in July 2005. Robbie Williams, Coldplay❸, and U2❹ all incorporated the line, "I got soul, but I'm not a soldier" into songs they performed that day. As huge fans of U2, this was high praise. Jay-Z❺ also declared himself a fan, particularly of "Mr. Brightside" (which quotes David Bowie's❻ "Queen Bitch"). "My favorite part of the song," the rapper enthused, "is when they repeat, 'It was only a kiss! It was only a kiss!'"

❶ 012
❷ 214
❸ 276
❹ 192
❺ 266
❻ 134

December 2, 2004

The Killers appear on the popular American teen TV show *The OC*, and will see their popularity soar in their home country.

2005

After a fine set in 2004, the band are asked to headline the U.K.'s Glastonbury festival when Kylie Minogue pulls out. Not yet ready, they decline.

November 8, 2006

Despite a mixed reception, *Sam's Town*—named after Las Vegas' Sam's Town Hotel and Gambling Hall—goes platinum in the U.S.A. within a month of release.

November 30, 2008

Day & Age is the band's third U.K. No. 1 album. Producer Stuart Price had helmed *Confessions on a Dance Floor* by Madonna.

FEBRUARY 18, 2009: A killer collaboration

Following on from a show-stopping performance at the 2009 Brit Awards in the U.K., which saw Brandon Flowers singing "It's a Sin" with one of his favorite bands, the Pet Shop Boys, as well as Lady Gaga❶, The Killers were joint headliners with Coldplay❷ at a War Child charity show, also in February, in London. A mutual love-in between the bands led Flowers to tell the crowd, "It's great to be partnered with Coldplay. I remember when I first saw the video for 'Yellow,' they were a real inspiration. It made me think we had a real chance, so we're honored to be here with them." The concert ended with two encores, the second of which saw The Killers and Coldplay doing a rousing rendition of "All These Things That I've Done," with U2's❸ Bono and Take That's Gary Barlow joining the two front men (left). This track's popularity with such famous fans helped seal its status as a modern classic.

❶ 241
❷ 276
❸ 192

THE KILLERS   281

Index

Entries in **bold** refer to artists, labels, producers, clubs, and festivals with two or four-page features. Entries in semibold refer to panel features.

? & The Mysterians 142
2D 274
2Pac 126, 256, 257, **262–3**, 266, 267
4 To Go 80
50 Cent 256

A

Abba 83, 101, 210
Abbey Road studio 87
Abbruzzese, Dave 249
ABC 198
AC/DC 58, 59, 61, 83, **182–3**, 218, 220, 222, 226
Adam & The Ants 103
Adams, Bryan 80, 104, 180, 193, 215
Adams, Ryan 91, 126
Adler, Steven 228, 231
Aerosmith 16, 43, 54, **61**, 76, 94, 101, 113, 140, 143, **154–7**, 182, 228, 231, 232
Aftermath Entertainment 256
Agnostic Front 161
Aguilera, Christine 53, 57, 210
AIRA Awards 203
Akon and Colbie Caillat 30
Alan Parsons Project, The 88
Alanoshi Festival 105
Albarn, Damon 67, 274, 275
Albini, Steve 207, 244
Ales, Barney 37
Alexander, Dave 117
Allison, Mose 68
Almond, Marc 198
Altamont festival 80
Ament, Jeff 119, 249
American Flyer 43
American Recordings 222
Amesbury, Bill 142
Amnesty International 152, 193
Amos, Tori 82, 91, 92, **105**, 106, 150, 196, 205, 242
Anderson, Jon 41, 198
Anderson, Laurie 105, 138
Angel & The Snake 173
Angel 143
Animal Collective 50
Animals, The 73, 74
Anthony, Michael 156
Anthrax 130, 167, 223
Appel, Mike 151
Appice, Carmine 109
Appice, Vinnie 109, 110
Apple label 48
Arcade Fire 137
Ardent Records 53
Arista Records 67
Arnold Corns 136
Art of Noise 199, 253
Arthurs, Paul 261
Artwoods, The 54
Asheton, Ron 117, 119
Asheton, Scott 117
Asylum Records 64
Atlantic 52, **82–3**, 84, 100, 101

Atomic Rooster 83
ATV Music 125
Aucoin, Bill 142
Audioslave 227
Avory, Mick 55, 67
Axton, Estelle 52
Ayers, Kevin 48

B

B-52's, The 117
Bachelors, The 38
Back Street Crawler 61
Bad Brains 161
Bad Company 100, 131, 147
Bad Religion 141
Bad Seeds 202, 203
Badfinger 140
Badu, Erykah 30
Baez, Joan 64
Baker, Ginger 41, 75, 169
Baldry, Long John 126
Ballard, Florence 32
Ballard, Glen 51
Bananarama 179
Band Aid 199
Band of Gypsys 37, 75
Band, The 64, 89, 126, 140
Bangles, The 223
Banks, Pete 41
Barrett, Syd 48, 86, 87, 88, 89, 137
Bators, Stiv 163
Bauhaus 58, 128, 134
Bay City Rollers 162
Beach Boys, The 21, 23, 28, 81, 86, **50–1**, 126, 140, 268
Beastie Boys 126, 170, 183, 193, 209, **222**, 226, 253
Beatles, The 12, 14, 15, 20, 23, 28, 29, 30, 32, 33, 38, 39, 40, 41, 42, 43, **44–7**, 48, 49, 50, 51, 54, 58, 66, 74, 75, 76, 79, 81, 87, 88, 98, 100, 101, 110, 122, 124, 127, 130, 140, 148, 158, 168, 171, 172, 192, 198, 209, 218, 231, 242, 243, 244, 251, 260, 261, 276, 280
Be-Bop Deluxe 48
Beck, Jeff 18, 42, **43**, 57, 59, 60, 73, 87, 89, 99, 155
Bee Gees 82, 134
Beeryman 277
Belew, Bill 15
Bell, Maggie 70
Bell, William 52, 53
Bellamy, Matt 192, 270
Bennett, Veronica "Ronnie" 28, 29
Berry, Chuck 12, 23, **40**, 60, 152, 182
Berry, Bill 205, 206
Berrymen, Guy 276
Best, Pete 38, 39, 44
Bevan, Bev 109
Beyoncé 266
Beyond, The 48
Big Bopper, The 21
Big Star 53
Binder, Steve 23
Birdsong, Cindy 32
Birthday Party, The 202
Björk 105, 210
Black Crowes, The 52, 94, 143, 155

Black Sabbath 38, **41**, 49, 59, 94, **108–11**, 183, 244
Black, Bill 13
Black, Frank 51
Blackmore, Ritchie 49, 73
Blackwell, Chris 130, 131
Blauel, Renate 127
Blige, Mary J., 126, 157, 192, 223, 266, 267
Blind Faith 20
Blondie 21, 117, 158, 160, **162**, 164, **172–3**, 274
Blues Incorporated 55
Bluesology 126
Blur 66, 67, 86, 274, **275**
Blush Response 281
Bob & Earl 57, 130
Bob Marley and the Wailers 130
Bock, Peter 94
Bogart, Neil 142, 143
Bolan, Marc 86, **128–9**, 134, 142, 172, 207, 212, 213, 231
Bolder, Trevor 136
Bon Jovi 107, 130, 150, **157**
Bonham, John 98, 99, 111
Bono 12, 57, 62, 65, 71, 129, 139, 148, 150, 152, 170, 174, **192–5**, 200, 206, 208, **216**, 267, 281
Bono, Sonny 28
Booker T. & The MG's 52, 53
Boomtown Rats 180, 214
Boppin' Elf 142
Bordin, Mike 109, 111
Bowie, David 32, 44, 47, 48, 51, 52, 57, 58, 59, 60, 67, 71, 79, 89, 91, **93**, 117, 118, 119, 126, 128, 129, **134–7**, 138, 139, 141, 144, 149, 150, 172, 173, 178, 197, 198, 201, 212, 213, 215, **217**, 224, 230, 244, 280, 281
Boyer, Elisa 27
Boyz II Men 30
Boyzone 194
Bozzio, Terry 76
Bradbury, John 179
Bramlett, Bekka 96
Breeders, The 155, **225**, 253
Brenton, Jackie 16
Brewer, Don 140
Bristol, Johnny 32
Brit Awards 71, 125, 210, 275, 281
Brooks, Garth 101, 250
Brown, James 14, **22–5**, 36, 44, 109, 125, 155, 175, 222, 233
Brown, Ruth 82
Browne, Jackson 93
Bruce, Jack 41, 75
Bruford, Bill 41
Brunning, Bob 95
Buck, Peter 159, 192, 205, 206
Buckingham, Lindsey 94, 95, 96
Buckland, Johnny 277
Buckley, Jeff 77, 107, 165, 212
Buckley, Tim 77
Buddy & Bob 21
Buffalo Springfield 79, 80
Buggles, The 198
Burckhard, Aaron 243
Burdon, Eric 74

Burke, Alexandra 107
Burke, Clem 162, 173
Burnette, Billy 95
Burton, Clifford 219
Busey, Gary 21
Bush, Kate 49, 105, 126, 134, 139, 174, 277
Busta Rhymes 266, 269
Butler, Geezer 109, 110, 111
Buzzcocks 168, 170
Byrds, The 53, 64, 74, 80, 206
Byrne, David 139, 162

C

Caballe, Monserrat 147
Cale, John 91, **92**, 93, 107, 117, 138, 139, 160, 164, 168
California Raisins, The 37
Cameo 143
Cameron, Matt 249
Campbell, Glen 29, 51
Cantrell, Jerry 94
Capitol Records 48, 49, 51
Captain Beefheart 77, 88
Cardew, Cornelius 138
Carey, Mariah 130, 131, 207, 222
Carin, John 216
Carmen 60
Cars, The 180
Carter, June 18, 19
Casablanca Records 142–3
Cash, Johnny 16, 17, **18–19**, 44, 57, 62, 64, 104, 150, 172, 192, 193, 196, 202, 203, 218, 223, 227, 232, 272, 277
Cat Power 244
Cave, Nick 18, 79, 91, 106, **202–3**, 218, 227, 238
Cavern Club 44
CBGB 160–3, 164, 173
CBS label 124, 156, 170
Chaka Khan 104, 105, 131, 174
Chambers, Martin 231
Champion, Will 277
Chandler, Chas 73, 74, 75
Channing, Chad 243
Chapman, Mark David 47, 140, 173
Chapman, Tracy 152
Charles, Ray 26, 39, 82
Charlie Watts Quintet 57
Cheap Trick 143
Chemical Brothers, The 115, 148, 268
Cher 28, 143, 298
Chess label 16
Chic 83, 200, 209
Child 151
Child, Desmond 157
Chills, The 246
Chimes, Terry 109, 170
Chocolate City label 143
Chuck Wagon Gang 16
Chunn, Mike 247
City Boy 180
Clapton, Eric 41, 47, 56, 57, 59, 60, 71, 74, **75**, 85, 87, 89, 130, 127, 171
Clarke, Allan 151
Clarke, Stanley 43
Clarke, Vince 197

282   INDEX

Clash, The 14, 71, 96, 109, 152, 159, 169, **170–1**, 179, 192, 203, 249, 274, 275
Classics, The 80
Clayton, Adam 131, 192, 193
Clayton, Merry 80
Cliff, Jimmy 277
Clinton, George 24, 25, **143**, 175, 232, 233, 238, 256
Coachella Festival 269, 275
Cobain, Kurt 15, 68, 75, 78, 107, 111, 144, 155, 156, 165, 167, 171, 207, 224, 234, 241, 242–5, 249, 250
Cochran, Eddie 40
Cocker, Jarvis 125
Cocker, Joe 59, 113, 126, 205
Cohen, Leonard 28, 62, **106–7**, 202, 244
Coldplay 44, 48, 138, 192, 224, 266, 267, 271, **276–7**, 281
Cole, Richard 70
Collen, Phil 180
Collins, Judy 64, 103
Collins, Phelps 25
Collins, Phil 36, 46, 60, 214
Collins, William "Bootsy" 25, 109
Columbia Records 18, 48, 62, 64, 82, 83, 84, 152, 222
Commerford, Tim 254
Commission, The 262
Concert for Bangladesh 64
Conley, Arthur 53
Contours, The 32
Cook, Bryan 206
Cook, Dale (see Cooke, Sam)
Cook, Paul 167, 169
Cooke, Sam 26–7, 37, 53, 62, 73, 84
Cooper, Alice 51, 71, 76, 77, 83, 127, 140, 141, **156**, 228
Copeland, Stewart 162
Corgan, Billy 89, 109, 155, 187, 205, 241
Cornell, Chris 36, 159, 240, 249, 255
Costello, Elvis 105, 152, 179
Country Joe & The Fish 112
Coventry Automatics, The 179
Coverdale, David 49, 53, 101, 198
Cowboy Junkies, The 92
Cox, Billy 73, 75
Coxon, Graham 275
Cream 41, 59, 75, 82
Creation Records 261
Creatore, Luigi 27
Creedence Clearwater Revival 37
Crenshaw, Marshall 21
Crespo, Jimmy 156
Crickets, The 20, 21, 44
Croce, Jim 231
Crosby, Bing 103
Crosby, David 80
Crosby, Stills & Nash 79, 81
Crosby, Stills, Nash & Young 80, 103, 113
Crover, Dale 243
Crow, Sheryl 176
Crowded House 246–7, 261
Crystals, The 28
Cuccurullo, Warren 76, 201
Cult, The 227

Cuomo, Rivers 21
Cure, The 137, 168, 185, **186**, 196, 212, 280
Curtis, Ian 117, 186, 187
Curtis, King 20

D
D'Angelo 31
D12 274
Daft Punk 148, **268–9**
Dakar, Rhoda 179
Daltrey, Roger 68, 69, 70, 71
Dammers, Jerry 178
Damned, The 128, 159, **168**, 169, 170
Danger Mouse 44
Danzig, Glenn 18
Darlin' 268
Datsuns, The 246
Dave Clark Five, The 67, 158
Davie Jones 134
Davies, Dave 67, 261
Davies, Ray 66, 67, 261
Davis, Miles 174
Davy Jones & The Lower Third 59
Dawson, Colin 69
De La Rocha, Zack 164, 165, 254, 255
De La Soul 274, 275
Deacon, John 144, 147
Dead Boys 163, 231
Dead Weather, The 273
Deal, Kim 225
Dean, Elton 126
Death Row Records 256
Decca Records 55, 56, 58, 82
Dee Dee (Douglas Calvin) 158, 159, 160, 162
Dee Felice Trio 24
Dee, Kiki 127
Dee-Lite 25
Deep Purple 48, **49**, 59, 67, 73, 76, 91, 109
Def Jam 222–3, 226, 227, 266, 267
Def Leppard 129, 134, 152, 180, **181**
Deftones 200
Delaney & Bonnie 96
Delfonics, The 176
Denny, Sandy 126, 131
Depeche Mode 18, 91, 106, 134, 148, **196–7**, 203, 227
Depp, Johnny 119, 203
Destiny's Child 203
Destri, Jimmy 173
Detours, The 69
Devo 139
Devonshire Studios 111
Di'Anno, Paul 191
Dickinson, Bruce 191, 231
Dictators, The 161
Diddley, Bo 38, 39, 171
Dido 138
Digital Underground 262
DiLeo, Frank 124
DiMucci, Dion 21, 29
Dinder, Klaus 149
Dio, Ronnie James 109, 110
Dion, Celine 42, 156, 210, 244
Dire Straits 59

Dixie Chicks 226
Dixon, Willie 95
Dolenz, Micky 73
Dollar 198, 199
Donato, David 109
Doors, The 73, 75, 93, 118
Douglas, Jack 156
Downes, Geoff 198
Dr. Dre 98, 143, **256–7**, 267
Dr. Zoom & the Sonic Boom 151
Drake, Nick 92, 130
Dream Theater 126
Dreja, Chris 99
Dresden Dolls, The 134
Dufay, Rick 156
Duffy, Billy 212
Duffy, Stephen 201
Duran Duran 48, 78, 91, **200–1**, 215, 280
Durst, Fred 115
Dylan, Bob 12, 13, 18, 19, 27, 46, 52, 57, 61, **62–5**, 74, 77, 79, 81, 84, 103, 104, 105, 107, 112, 118, 125, 134, 136, 176, 192, 202, 203, 208, **217**, 233, 242, 249, 255, 272
Dylan, Jakob Luke 64

E
E Street Band 152
Eagles 79, 88, 100, 104, 126, **132–3**, 172, 227, 228
Earth 41, 110
Earth, Wind & Fire 42, 43
Earthbound 252
Easton, Elliot 141
Easybeats, The 136, 182
Eazy-E 257
Ed Banger & The Nosebleeds 212
Eddy, Duane 28, 79
Edge, The 139, 158, 165, 192, 193, 194, 267
Eels 174
Electric Circus 160
Electric Flag 75
Elektra label 118
Elliott, Cass 71
ELO 109
Elton John 42, 47, 50, 59, 70, 71, 105, 106, **126–7**, 129, 132, 231, 234, 242, 268, 280
Emerson, Lake & Palmer 83, 130
EMI 38, 42, 44, **48–9**, 87, 89, 144, 192, 201, 233
EMI Electrola GmbH 49
Eminem 127, 155, 256, **257**, 267
Emperors of Soul 33
En Vogue 85
Eno, Brian 91, 92, 117, 122, **138–9**, 193, 276
Entwistle, John 68, 69, 70, 71, 99, 112
Epstein, Brian 46
Erasure 197
Eric B. and Rakim 25
Ertegun, Ahmet 8, 101
Esquires, The 80
Etheridge, Melissa 131
Eurythmics 85, 179, 212
Evans, Dave 183

Everly Brothers, The 39, 230, 260
Exploding Plastic Inevitable 91

F
Faces, The 56, 159
Fairport Convention 13, 130
Faith No More 109, 111
Faithfull, Marianne 60, 131, 220
Fall Out Boy 130
Fall, The 110, 168, 275
Famous Flames, The 23
Fanny 141
Farner, Mark 140
Farrell, Perry 240
Feedback 192
Felder, Don 133
Ferry, Bryan 138, 216
Festival of Unrecorded Rock Talent 161
Fingers, Johnny 214
Finn, Tim 246, 247
Finn, Micky 128
Finn, Neil 246, 247
Flack, Roberta 83
Flaming Lips, The 88
Flea 89, 161, 232, 233, 234
Fleetwood Mac 50, 56, 59, **94–7**, 132, 155, 232, 234
Fletcher, Andy 197
Flint, Keith 252, 253
Flowers, Brandon 150, 187, 200, 212, 276, 280, 281
Floyd, Eddie 52, 53
Fogerty, John 57
Fontana label 130
Foo Fighters 98, 137, 144, 152, 174, 244, 278
Foreigner 180, 181
Forrest, Jimmy 23
Foster, Dave 243
Four Seasons, The 51
Four Tops 30, 31, 142
Fowley, Ken 28
Francis, Black 218
Frank Black and The Breeders 225
Frankie Goes to Hollywood 150, 198, **199**
Franklin, Aretha 23, 26, 53, 56, 65, 82, **84–5**, 126
Franklin, Carolyn 84
Franklin, Melvin 80
Frantz, Chris 162
Franz Ferdinand 172
Fred Byler & The Tunetts 52
Free 59, 61, 94, 130
Free and Bad Company 147
Frey, Glenn 104, 132
Fripp, Robert 138
Frusciante, John 187, 196, 233, 234
Fun Boy Three 179
Funkadelic 143

G
Gabriel, Peter 103, 152, 193
Gahan, Dave 196, 197
Gallagher, Liam 260
Gallagher, Noel 212, 213, 260, 266, 278
Galluci, Don 118

INDEX 283

Garbage 168, 173
Gaye, Marvin 26, 30, 31, 32, 33, **36–7**
Geffen Records 230
Geldof, Bob 89, 180, 214, 216, 217
General Public 171
Genesis 36, 59, **61**, 83, 270
Gentry, Bobbie 48
George, Lowell 92
Germano, Lisa 246
Gerry & The Pacemakers 38
Gers, Janick 191
Gilbert, Gillian 186
Gillan, Ian 49, 109, 110
Gillen, Ray 109
Gilmour, David 49, 70, 71, 75, 87, 88, 89, 127, 137, 199, 200, 210, 214, 215, **216**
Girls Aloud 200, **277**
Glass, Philip 107
Glastonbury festival 253, 266, **271**, 275, 277, 281
Godley & Creme 199
Golding, Lynval 178
Gordon, Kim 164
Gordy, Berry 30, 31, 32, 33
Gore, Martin 91, 106, 197, 203
Gorillaz 44, 48, **274–5**
Gossard, Stone 249
Graduates, The 38
Graffin, Greg 141
Grafton, Anthony 138
Graham, Larry 174
Grammy Awards 19, 32, 33, 65, 84, 124, 127, 152, 176, 180, 210, 244, 257, 269, 273, 274, 277, 280
Grand Funk Railroad 140
Grant, Peter 100
Grateful Dead 65, 112
Green Day 67, 68, 113, 119, 159, 194, 227, 239, 241, **258–9**
Green River 109
Green, Peter 56, 94, 95, 96, 155, 232
Greenwood, Colin 207
Grinderman 202, 203
Groening, Matt 76
Grohl, Dave 98, 111, 144, 152, 218, 224, 243, 244, 253
Grundy, Bill 168
Guns N' Roses 43, 61, 62, 117, 118, 122, 125, 126, 129, 134, **163**, 200, 218, 220, **228–31**, 234, 242
Guthrie, Arlo 64
Guthrie, Woody 64
Gypsy Sun and Rainbows 75

H

Halfnelson 140
Haggard, Merle 19
Halford, Bob 109
Hall & Oates 141
Hall, Terry 178, 179, 274
Hamilton, Tom 155
Hammett, Kirk 57, 74, 219, 231, 241
Hammond, John 62, 84
Hancock, Herbie 103, 105
Happy Mondays 92
Hardin, Eddie 39
Harper, Rob 170

Harris, Emmylou 105
Harris, R. H. 26, 27
Harris, Steve 191
Harrison, George 28, 38, 46, 47, 49, 64, 65, 87, 107, 126, 140, 209
Harrison, Nigel 173
Harry, Debbie 105, 117, 158, 159, 160, 164, 172, 173, 274
Hartley, Keef 61
Harvest Records 48
Harvey, Mick 202
Havens, Richie 112
Hawkwind 74, 169
Hayes, Isaac 52, **53**, 256
Haywood, Lance 33
Headon, Topper 170, 171
Heads 139
Heart 103
Hectics, The 144
Hell, Richard 160
Helm, Levon 126
Hendrix, Jimi 37, 41, 44, 46, 53, 58, 59, 61, 62, 68, **72–5**, 109, 112, 113, **114**, 115, 130, 155, 180, 202, 249
Henley, Don 103, 106, 132
Henson, Jim 105
Herd, The 55
Hester, Paul 247
Hetfield, James 19, 219, 220, 241
Hewlett, Jamie 274, 275
High Flying Birds, The 80
High Numbers, The 69
His Little Green Men 17
HMV 48
Hocus 180
Hoffman, Abbie 112
Hohman, Andreas 149
Hold Steady, The 150
Hole 241, 244
Holland, Brian 32
Holland-Dozier-Holland 29, 32
Hollies, The 80, 151
Holloway, Brenda 33
Holly, Buddy 20–1, 44, 55, 73, 249
Homme, Josh 98, 244
Hook, Peter 185, 186
Hooker, John Lee 58
Horn, Trevor 198–9
Houston, Whitney 84
Howard, Dominic 271
Howard, Pete 171
Howe, Steve 198, 199
Howlett, Liam 178, 252, 253
Huey Lewis & The News 181
Hughes, Glenn 109
Human League 94
Humpy Bong 144
Hutchence, Michael 200, 202, 203
Hütter, Ralf 149
Hynde, Chrissie 67, 119, 159, 203, 278
Hype 136
Hype, The 192

I

Ian, Janis 143
Ice Cube 143, **257**
Idol, Billy 70, 71, 103

Iggy Pop 30, 54, 67, **116–19**, 134, 137, 138, 149, 168, 169, 173, 182, 207, 218, 225, 228, 231, 244, 268, 272, 273, 285
Indian Style 254
Infante, Frank 173
INXS 77, 82, 200, 202, 203, **216**
Iommi, Tony 109, 110, 111, 244
Iron Maiden 48, 59, **190–1**, 219, 232
Irons, Jack 233, 249
Isaak, Chris 77
Isbell, Jeffrey 228
Island Def Jam 130, **222**
Island Records 130–1
Island Universal 130
Isle of Wight festival 75
Isley Brothers, The 73, 74, 142

J

J. Geils Band, The 83
J.B.'s, The 25
Jackson 5, The 30, **33**, 122, 124
Jackson, Jackie 33, 122
Jackson, Janet 103, **104**, 122, 186
Jackson, Jermain 122
Jackson, Marlon 33, 122
Jackson, Michael 23, 25, 33, 44, 51, 88, **122–5**, 132, 174, 199, 208, 209, 218, 228, 231, 242, 262
Jackson, Randy 33, 124
Jackson, Tito 33, 122
Jacksons, The 124
Jades, The 80
Jagger, Mick 12, 23, 30, 32, 44, 46, 55, 56, 58, 62, 70, 71, 82, 94, 101, 137, 155, 178, 215, 217, 227
Jam, The 59, 67, 168
James, Maynard 255
James, Rick "Super Freak" 30, 79, 80, 138, 175
Jane's Addiction 91, 92, 234, 238, **240**, 241, 253, 254, 255
Jay-Z 44, **223**, 227, 251, 256, 262, 263, **266–7**, 276, 281
Jefferson Airplane 112, 168
Jennings, Waylon 19, 20, 21
Jesus and Mary Chain, The 91, 261
Jethro Tull 59, 190, 130, 220
Jimi Hendrix Experience 41, 68, **72**, 73, 74
Jimmy James and the Blue Flames 73
Joel, Billy 124, 127
Joey (Jeff Hyman) 158, 159
John Lennon/Plastic Ono Band 46
John Mayall's Bluesbreakers 56, 95
John's Children 128
Johnny & the Moondogs 44
Johnny (John Cummings) 158, 159
Johnson, Brian 83, 182
Johnson, Marv 31
Johnson, Robert 95
Johnston, Bruce 28, 50, 51
Jolson, Al 84
Jones, Brian 55, 56, 57
Jones, Daryl 57
Jones, Grace 131, **199**, 201
Jones, John Paul 83, 98, 99, 110, 244
Jones, Kenney 56, 70, 71
Jones, Mick 170, 181, 189, 203

Jones, Quincy 124, 175, 187
Jones, Steve 118, 167, 200
Jones, Tom 198
Joplin, Janice 75
Joy Division 91, 117, 134, 168, **184–7**, 197, 213
Joyce, Mike 212
Judas Priest 95, 109, 190, 191
Junior's Eyes 41

K

Kaiser Chiefs 37
Kansas 146
Kasabian 276
Kaye, Lennie 165
Kaye, Tony 41
k.d. Lang 105
Keane 277
Keisker, Marion 16
Keuning, Dave 280
Keys, Alicia 65, 137, 174
Kid Rock 126
Killers, The 67, 92, 136, 150, **187**, 200, 212, 214, 239, 276, **280–1**
King Bees, The 134
King Crimson 83, 130, 198
King Records 23
King, Albert 53
King, B. B. 193
King, Ben E. 28
King, Carole 100
Kings of Leon 239, **278–9**
Kingsmen, The 118
Kinks, The 55, **66–7**, 109, 136, 159, 261
Kirwan, Danny 95
Kiss 29, 56, 59, 64, 77, 109, 112, 130, **142**, 191, 230, 253
Knack, The 111
Knebworth festival 47, 88, 101, 261
Knight, Gladys 33, 37, 122
Knight, Jean 51
Knight, Suge 256
Knopfler, Mark 65, 77
Korn 115, 161
Korner, Alexis 55
Kossoff, Paul 61, 94
Kraftwerk 48, **148–9**, 158, 185, 276
Kramer, Joey 155, 156
Krauss, Alison 101
Kravitz, Lenny 57, 174
Kristal, Hilly 160, 162
Kuti, Fela 139

L

Lady Gaga 241, 281
Lang, Michael 114
Lange, Mutt 180–1
Lauper, Cyndi 103, 105, 174
Le Bon, Simon 200
Lead Singers' Club 200
Leadon 132
Leaves, The 74
Led Zeppelin 14, 25, 57, 59, 61, 67, 68, 70, 77, 81, 82, 83, 94, 95, **98–101**, 103, 110, 144, 146, 147, 155, 156, 157, 180, 182, 201, 217, 218, 222, 242, 244, 249, 252, 261, 272

Lee, David 74
Lee, Geddy 104
Lee, Tommy 220
Leeds, Alan 23
Lemmy 74, 110
Lennon, John (later Ono Lennon) 12, 13, 26, 28, 29, 38, 43, 44, 46, 47, 49, 56, 62, 76, 107, 109, 126, 127, 136, 140, 159, 170, 260
Lennox, Annie 85, 172
Levene, Keith 169
Lewis, Jerry Lee 17, 39, **40**, 119
Libertines, The 171
Liebezeit, Jaki 139
Limp Bizkit 113, **115**
Little Feat 92
Little Junior Parker 16
Little Richard 12, 17, 23, 26, 39, **40**, 73, 74, 124
Live Aid 65, 71, 89, 101, 127, 180, 193, 201, 209, **214–17**
Live8 194, **214–17**, 281
Lizard King label 281
Lloyd, Richard 139
Locked Up 254
Lofgren, Nils 81
Lollapalooza **238–41**, 254, 255, 268
Lord, Jon 67
Louie Bellson Orchestra 24
Love, Courtney 94, 185, **241**, 244
Love, Darlene 15
Love, Mike 50
Lovering, David 225
Lovin' Spoonful, The 28, 113, 206
Lulu 75, 134
Lydon, John 167, 168, 169, 233
Lynne, Jeff 47, 65
Lynyrd Skynyrd 80, **81**, 278

M
M.I.A. 170
Maal, Baaba 138
Mac 94, 96
MacColl, Kirsty 67
MacGowan, Shane 203
MacLise, Angus 91
Madness 178
Madonna 12, 21, 30, 44, 117, **119**, 122, 127, 174, 175, 201, **208–11**, 214, 215, 217, 222, 225, 263, 268, 271, 275, 281
Mamas and the Papas, The 51, 71
Manic Street Preachers 170
Mann, Aimee 51
Manson, Marilyn 25, 111, 159, 164, 173, 190, 196, 232
Manson, Shirley 168
Marillion 59
Marley, Bob 130, 175
Marquee, The 41, 55, **58–61**, 69, 100, 144, 186
Marr, Johnny 212, 213, 246, 251, 261
Martha & the Vandellas 32, 36
Martin, Chris 48, 192, 224, 266, 267, 271, **276–7**
Martin, George 42–3, 47
Martin, Giles 47
Martin, Jim 111
Martin, Tony 109

Marvelettes, The 32, 36
Mason, Dave 96
Mason, Nicholas 87, 88, 89
Mason, Nick 60
Massive Attack 169, 210
Matlock, Glen 167, 168, 169
Maverick label 253, 271
Max's Kansas City 160
Maxwell Demon 138
May, Brian 144, 147, 231, 244, 270
Mayfield, Curtis 85, 194, 256
Mayor McCheese 150
MC Maxim Reality 252
MC5 117, 255
McCarroll, Tony 261
McCartney, Paul 12, 21, 28, 29, 38, **43**, 44, 46, 47, 48, 49, 51, 69, 71, 81, 87, 122, 124, 125, 158, 198, 215, 244, 255, 260, 267
McCready, Mike 249
McEwan, Joe 26
McGee, Alan 167, 261, 276
McGhee, Stick 82
McGuinn, Roger 64, 206
McGuinness, Paul 117, 139, 194
McKagan, Duff 118, 201
McKagan, Michael 228
McLachlan, Sarah 105, 239
McLaren, Malcolm 167, 198, 199
McLean, Don 21
McVie, Christine 95, 96
McVie, John 95, 96
Meat Loaf 140, **141**, 180
Meco 143
Meighan, Tom 276
Meisner 132
Melody Maker 69, 100, 161
Merchant, Natalie 103
Mercury, Freddie 144, 214, 216, 220, 244
Merseybeat 44
Metallica 18, 57, 59, 67, 74, 81, 92, 111, 113, **115**, **218**, 203, **218–21**, 227, 231, 232, 239, 241, 242
MGMT 138
Michael, George 24, 85, 126, 147
Midler, Bette 83, 217
Miles, Buddy 37, 75
Miller, Steve 88
Millie 131
Million Dollar Quartet, The 17
Mills, Mike 205, 206
Minogue, Kylie 175, **203**, 277, 281
Miracles, The 31, 32, 33, 36, 70
Missing Persons 201
Missy Elliott 266, 269
Mitchell, Chuck 104
Mitchell, Joni 64, 79, 80, 89, **102–5**, 113, 132, 138, 175, 208
Mitchell, Mitch 41, 73
Moby 187, 200, 272
Mojo 25, 42, 53, 182, 272
Mojos, The 136
Monkees, The 46, 73, 76, 134, 169
Monroe, Bill 16
Monsters of Rock Festival 61, 230
Monterey Pop Festival 53, 73, 74, 114
Moody Blues, The 68

Mookie Blaylock 249, 250
Moon, Keith 68, 69, 70, 71, 99, 141
Moore, Gary 94
Moore, Sam 52, 53
Moore, Scotty 13
Morello, Tom 115, 240, 254
Morgan Studios 110
Morissette, Alanis 51
Morris, Kenny 168
Morris, Stephen 186
Morrison, Jim 75
Morrison, Sterling 91, 93
Morrissey, Stephen 48, 164, 205, 212, 232
Mother Love Bone 249
Mothers of Invention 77
Mötley Crüe 94, 155, 157, 167, 220, 230
Motörhead 74, 110, 159, 167, 244
Motown 16, 29, **30–3**, 36, 37, 80, 122, 124, 142, 208, 215
Mott The Hoople 136
Move, The 74
MTV Music Awards 81, 209, 273
Mudoc 274
Mullanes, The 247
Mullen, Larry 192, 193
Murray, Dave 191
Muscle Shoals Sound studio 65
Muse 192, 212, 239, **270–1**, 276, 277
Mushroom label 247
Mustaine, Dave 219
Muthers, The 77
My Bloody Valentine 272
Mynah Birds 80

N
N.W.A. 37
Nash, Graham 80, 104
Nathan, Syd 23
Navarro, Dave 115, 234, 253
Nazz 140
Neil, Vince 230
Nelly 157
Nelson, Sandy 28
Nelson, Willie 19, 48, 103, 194
New Barbarians, The 101
New Order 186, 187, 213, 280
New Yardbirds, The 59, 60, **99**, 110
New York Dolls 126, 140, **141**, 160, 167, 212
Newman, Randy 79
Newsted, Jason 219
Nice, The 74, 83
Nickelback 126
Nicks, Stevie 82, 94, 95, 96, 132, 173, 175, 203
Nico 91, 92, **93**
Nielson, Rick 143
Nilsson, Harry 71
Nine Inch Nails (NIN) 19, 113, 115, 117, 137, 196, 244, 257
Nirvana 15, 68, 75, 78, 91, 98, 107, 109, **111**, 124, 134, 137, 200, 207, 218, 224, 227, 228, 234, 238, 239, **242–5**, 249, 250, 256
Nitzsche, Jack 28
NME 67, 161, 187, 198, 270
No Doubt 178

Noodle 274
Notorious B.I.G., The 262–3, 266, 267
Novoselic, Krist 243
Nugent, Ted 254
Numan, Gary 174

O
O'Brien, Brendan 152, 249
O'Brien, Ed 246
O'Connor, Sinéad 89, 174, 176
Oakley, Phil 93
Oasis 39, 44, 138, 167, 212, 252, **260–1**, 266, 276, 278, 280, 281, 276
Odetta 64
Offspring, The 159
Oldfield, Mike 198
OMC 246
Ono, Yoko 46, 203
Orbit, William 210
Orbital 268
Organisation 149
Osborne, Joan 176
Osbourne, Ozzy 41, 94, 109, 110, 111, 219, 239

P
Page, Jimmy 15, 47, 57, 59, 60, 61, 67, 68, 70, 94, 98, 99, 100, 101, 155, 272
Paice, Ian 91
Palmer, Bruce 80
Palmer, Robert 67, 130, 131, 200
Panter, Horace 178
Pantera 109
Parker, Alan 89
Parker, Charlie 57
Parker, Robert 13
Parliament 25, 142, **143**
Parlophone label 42, 48
Patti Smith Group 165
Peaches 117, 119
Pearl Jam 62, 68, 81, 119, 159, **163**, 207, 224, 233, 234, 238, 242, 243, 246, **248–51**, 254, 278, 279
Pectoralz 277
Pendleton, Harold 58
Peretti, Hugo 27
Perkins, Carl 17, 43
Perkins, Stephen 238, 255
Perry, Joe 42, 94, 101, 143, 155, 156, 182, 231
Pet Shop Boys 108, 192, 196, 205, 253, 281
Peter, Paul & Mary 62
Petty, Norman 20
Petty, Tom 18, 65, 96, 103, 161, 227, 230, 244
Phil Spector International label 29
Philles label 28, 29
Phillips, Anthony 61
Phillips, Chynna 51
Phillips, Dewey 13
Phillips, John 51
Phillips, Sam 13, 16, 17, 18
Phillips, Simon 71
Phish 88
Phoenix 94

Pickett, Wilson 165
Pickwick Records 91
Pierson, Kate 117
Pink Floyd 41, 47, 48, 49, 50, 58, 59, 60, 70, 71, 74, 75, 77, **86–9**, 96, 103, 126, 128, 137, 139, 146, 167, 168, 174, 180, 192, 199, 200, 201, 214, 216, 232, 234, 244, 249, 261, 266, 270
Pitney, Gene 28, 29, 203
Pixies 51, 79, 106, 137, 155, 210, **224–5**, 228, 238, 239, 242
Plant, Robert 15, 25, 47, 82, 98, 99, 100, 101, 103, 110, 155, 156, 205, 217, 249, 252
Pogues, The 203
Pointer Sisters 151
Polar Studios 83
Police, The 59, 92, **163**, 193
Polka Tulk Blues Band, The 41
Polygram 142
Porno for Pyros 255
Porter, David 52, 53
Powell, Cozy 109
Power Station, The 129
Prater, Dave 52
Presley, Elvis 12–15, 16, 17, 18, 21, 23, 27, 40, 44, 52, 54, 62, 64, 76, 82, 96, 98, 101, 127, 134, 136, 150, 167, 202, 212, 218, 249, 281
Presley, Lisa Marie 14, 125
Preston, Billy 26, 40
Pretenders, The 67, 159, 198, 203, 231, 278
Pretty Things, The 55, 100, 136
Primal Scream 203, 253
Primes, The 32
Primitives, The 91
Prince 23, 73, 91, 103, **104**, 105, **174–7**, 193, 208, 209, 267
Priority label 37
Procul Harem 99, 129
Prodigy, The 178, 179, 199, 239, 243, **252–3**, 256, 268
Psychedelic Stooges, The 118
Public Enemy 12, 24, **25**, 170, 176, 190, 222, 223, 227, 254, 255
Public Image Ltd. 76, 139, **169**, 233
Puff Daddy 255
Pulp 125

Q

Q-Tip 103
Quaife, Pete 67
Quarrymen, The 44
Queen 48, 137, **144–7**, 176, 193, 214, **216**, 220, 241, 242, 244, 261, 270, **271**, 280

R

R.E.M. 86, 91, 94, 106, 159, 165, 192, **204–7**, 242, 243, 244, 249, **250**, 251
Rabin, Trevor 199
Raconteurs, The 273
Radiation, Roddy 179
Radiohead 44, 48, 86, 138, 169, 232, 239, 207, 224, 246, **264–5**, 270, 276, 278

Rage Against the Machine 62, 113, **115**, 150, 152, 164, 165, 170, 227, 234, 238, 240, 252, **254–5**, 256, 270
Rain, The 261
Rainbow 49, 109
Raitt, Bonnie 79, 151, 176
Rambo 150
Ramone, Joey 29, 162, 182, 218, 228
Ramone, Johnny 251
Ramones 28, 29, 62, 139, **158–9**, 163, 218, 228, 239, 249, 251
Rare Earth 33
Ravens, The 67
RCA label 13, 134
Reading Festival 244, 253
Red Hot Chili Peppers 79, 89, 109, 113, **115**, 126, 143, 159, 187, 196, 227, **232–5**, 238, 240, 242, 249
Redding, Noel 41, 73
Redding, Otis 26, 52, **53**, 83
Reddy, Helen 143
Reed, Lou 37, 53, 71, 91, **92**, 93, 193, 200, 201, 275, 280
Regents, The 21
Reid, Keith 129
Reid, Terry 99
Reznor, Trent 137
Rhoads, Randy 110
Rhodes, Nick 201
Rice-Oxley, Tim 277
Richard, Cliff 48, 191
Richards, Keith 12, 20, 23, 26, 40, 54, 55, 56, 58, 83, 85, 94, 101,117, 127, 131, 169, 182, 242, 260, 262
Richie, Lionel 30, 32, 125
Righteous Brothers, The 28, 29
Rihanna 267
Riley, Billy 17
Riley, Terry 92
Ripples & Waves Plus Michael 122
Roberg, Tex 38
Robinson, Chris 155
Robinson, Smokey 26, 27, 30, **31**, 32, 33, 37, 70
Rock and Roll Hall of Fame 21, 57, 67, 81, 85, 89, 93, 101, 111, 119, 132, 152, 159, 164, 165, 173, 183, 194, 208, 231, 244, 249
Rock in Rio festival 231
Rocking Kings, The 73
Rodgers, Nile 209
Rodgers, Paul 147
Rogers, Claudette 31
Rolling Stone 23, 26, 40, 65, 83, 104, 122, 127, 161, 187, 222, 227, 241, 242, 263, 273
Rolling Stones, The 12, 21, 23, 29, 30, 33, 36, 40, 49, 52, 53, **54–7**, 58, 60, 62, 65, 67, 80, **82**, 86, 126, 136, 137, 144, 168, 170, 192, 214, 228, 242, 249, 260, 261, 268, 272
Rollins, Henry 240
Ronettes, The 28, 29, 50
Ronson, Mark 212
Ronson, Mick 136
Ronstadt, Linda 51, 81, 132, 150
Roots 266
Rory Storm & The Hurricanes 39

Rose, Axl 118, 126, 134, 144, 157, 167, 193, **228**, 230, **231**
Ross, Diana 30, 32, 33, 37, 122, 143
Ross, Ronnie 136
Rossington, Gary 81
Roth, David Lee 51, 156, 230
Rother, Michael 149
Rotten & Co. 170
Rotten, Johnny 70, 79, 118, 169, 171
Rourke, Andy 212, 213
Roxy Music 130, **138**
Rubber Band 25
Rubin, Rick 18, 23, 25, 157, 183, 222, 223, **226–7**, 233, 255, 266, 267
Rudd, Phil 183
Runaways, The 28
Rundgren, Todd 50, **140–1**, 165
Run-DMC 157, 222, 226, 232
Rush, Tom 103, 104
Russel 274
Russell, Leon 29, 64
Ryan, Barry 168

S

Saint-Marie, Buffy 103
Sakamoto, Ryuichi 169
Sales, Hunt 140
Sales, Tony 140
Sam & Dave 52, **53**
Sandom, Doug 69
Santana 94, 112, **114**
Santana, Carlos 73
Santiago, Joey 225
Satellite Records 52
Satriani, Joe 57, 232
Schneider, Florian 149
Schult, Emil 149
Scorpions ,The 48, 89
Scorsese, Martin 57, 81, 124, 272
Scott, Bon 83, 182, **183**
Scratch Orchestra 138
Screaming Trees 111
Seal 198
Searchers, The 39
Sebastian, John 113, 206
Seeger, Pete 64
Seger, Bob 132, 165
Selecter the 178
Selway, Phil 246
Sepultura 109
Severin, Steve 168
Sex Pistols 48, 49, 58, 59, 70, 71, 79, 86, 117, **118**, 128, 132, 159, **166–9**, 170, 171, 186, 200, 201, 231, 253, 256, 260, 274
Seymour, Nick 247
Shakira 226
Shangri-Las, The 172
Shaw, Sandie 164
Sheridan, Tony 38
Shields, Kevin 165, 272
Shockle, Hank 190
Siberry, Jane 103
Silverstone, Alicia 157
Simmons, Gene 77, 142, 143, 253
Simon & Garfunkel 59, 223
Simonon, Paul 170, 275
Simons, Ed 148
Simple Minds 164

Simpsons, The 71, 76, 156, 183, 234, 238
Singer, Eric 109
Siouxsie & The Banshees 92, 128, 167, **168**, 238
Sixx, Nikki 155
Slade 74, 260
Slash 61, **118**, 122, 125, 155, 157, 190, 218, 230
Slayer 222, 226
Sledge, Percy 82
Sleepwalkers 28
Slits, The 168, 171
Slovak, Hillel 233
Sly & The Family Stone 24, 41, 100, 112, **114**, 174, 233
Small Faces 70, 168
Small, Biggie 262, **263**, 267
Smash label 40
Smashing Pumpkins, The 89, 109, 137, 155, 172, 185, 187, 196, 205, 238, **241**
Smile 144
Smith, Adrian 186
Smith, Chad 144, 232
Smith, Fred 173
Smith, Mark E., 110
Smith, Patti 54, 62, 92, 93, 140, 151, **164–5**, 174, 192, 205, 242, 273
Smith, Robert 137, 168, 185, **186**, 196, 212
Smiths, The 48, 159, 161, 164, 168, 205, **212–13**, 232, 246, 251, 261, 280
Snoop Dog 256, 257, 275
Social Distortion 161
Soft Cell 129
Soft Machine, The 48, 88, 126
Sonic Youth 91, 103, 164, 238, 241
Sonny & Cher 60, 82
Soul Stirrers 26, 27
Soundgarden 18, 36, 111, 159, 239, 240, 243, 249, 255
Souther, J. D. 104
Spacemen 3 91
Sparks 131, 140
Spears, Britney 157, 210
Special A.K.A., The 179
Specials, The 178–9, 274
Spector, Phil 15, **28–9**, 50, 82, 107, 150, 158, 196
Spectrum, Schwann 82
Spencer Davis Group 39
Spencer, Jeremy 95
Spice Girls 126
Spinal Tap 57, 76, 234
Split Enz 244, 247
Springfield, Dusty 100
Springsteen, Bruce 18, 19, 26, 62, 67, 81, 125, **150–3**, 156, 158, 165, 170, 174, 192, 193, 199, 231, 240, 244, 249, 251, 255, 280
Squire, Chris 41
Squires, The 80
Staffell, Tim 144
Stanley, Paul 142, 230
Staple Singers 52
Star-Club 38–41, 44
Starclub 39

Stardusters, The 80
Starkey, Zak 71, 261
Starlite Wranglers 13
Starr, Edwin 33
Starr, Ringo 39, 43, 44, 46, 47, 64, 71, 87, 129, 261
Status Quo 277
Stax 52–3, 82
Steel Mill 151
Steel Pulse 130
Steel Town label 122
Stefani, Gwen 176, 178, 208
Stein, Chris 160, 173
Steinman, Jim 141, 180
Stephens, Barbara 52
Stevens, Cat 130
Stevens, Sufjan 105
Stewart, Dave 179
Stewart, Ian 55, 57
Stewart, Jim 52, 53
Stewart, Nick 131
Stewart, Rod 26, 56, 70, 126, 127, 198, 200
Stilettos, The 160, 173
Stills, Stephen 79, 80, 126
Sting 18, 70, 105, 152, 193, 215
Stipe, Michael 165, 205, 207
Stoermer, Mark 280
Stone Age 98, 244
Stone Roses, The 231
Stone Temple Pilots 82
Stooges, The 92, 117, 118, 119, 159, 160, 167, 202, 242, 255, 272
Street Band 81
Strokes, The 278
Strong, Barrett 30, 33
Strummer, Joe 14, 152, 170, 171, 249
Stubblefield, Clyde 24
Styx 146
Subway Sect 171
Sue label 130
Suicidal Tendencies 255
Summer, Donna 142, **143**, 210, 234
Summers, Andy 163
Sumner, Bernard 213
Sun Records 16–17, 18, 40
Supertramp 59
Supremes, The 30, **32**, 33
Sutcliffe, Stuart 38, 44
Sweet, The 168
Swingin' Blue Jeans 39

T
T. Rex 48, 128, 129, 260
Talking Heads 138, **139**, **162**, 173
Talmy, Shel 66
Tamla Record Company 30, 31, 32, 37
Taupin, Bernie 126
Taylor, Andy 200
Taylor, James 81, 105
Taylor, John 201
Taylor, Johnnie 27
Taylor, Mick 56
Taylor, R. Dean 33, 55
Taylor, Roger 144, 147, 201
Teddy Bears, The 28
Teen Kings 17
Temptations, The 26, 30, 31, 32, **33**, 80

Tennant, Neil 196, 205, 253
Terrell, Jean 32
Terrell, Tammi 33, 36
Them 136
Them Crooked Vultures 98, 244
Thin Lizzie 94
Third Man Records 273
Thomas, Chris 167
Thomas, Rufus 16, 52, 157
Thompson Twins, The 209
Thompson, Charles 225
Thompson, Richard 103, 105, 174, 247
Thornhill, Leeroy 252, 253
Thornton, Big Mama 16
Thunders, Johnny 161, 163
Timberlake, Justin 107, 210, 226
Tin Machine 140
Tom Petty & The Heartbreakers 161
Tommy (Tamás Erdélyi) 158, 159
Tony Flow and the Miraculous Masters of Mayhem 233
Took, Steve Peregrine 128
Tool 255
Toots & the Maytals 130
Tosh, Peter 130
Townsend, Pete 54, 57, 60, 66, 67, 68, 70, 71, 73, 87, 89, 112, 129, 130, 137, 192, 251, 260
Traffic 96, 130
Traveling Wilburys, The 47, **65**
Troggs, The 60, 74, 206
Trouser Press 29
Trujillo, Robert 219
Tubes, The 140
Tucker, Maureen 91, 93
Turner, Ike and Tina 29, 51
Turner, Tina 71, 85, 126, 174, 217
Twain, Shania 180
Tyler, Steven 36, 54, 61, 101, 113, 140, 155, 156, 157, 161, 231
Tyrannosaurus Rex 128, **129**

U
U2 12, 14, 18, 44, 57, 62, 71, 91, 92, 93, 106, 117, 130, **131**, 134, 139, 148, 150, 152, 158, 159, 164, 165, 170, 172, 173, 174, 178, 187, **192–5**, 200, 205, 206, 214, 215, 216, 229, 231, 242, 249, 255, 267, 276, 272, 281
UFO 42
UFO Club 87
Ulrich, Lars 190, 220, 241
Ultravox! 42, 139, 214
Universal group 30
Ure, Midge 214
Utopia 140

V
Vai, Steve 57, 67, 76, 169
Valens, Ritchie 21
Valentine, Gary 172
Van Halen 156
Van Halen, Alex 143, 156
Van Halen, Eddie 32, 51, 67, 74, 124, 143,156
Van Morrison 26, 89
Van Zandt, Steve 151, 152, 158
Van Zant, Ronnie 81

Vandross, Luther 85
Vannucci, Ronnie 289
VAST 162
Vaughan, Stevie Ray 57
Vedder, Eddie 71, 81, 119, 159, 207, 246, 249, 250, 251, 254, 278, 279
Vega, Alan 117
Velvet Revolver 167
Velvet Underground, The 37, 43, 51, **90–3**, 107, 117, 134, 136, 160, 164, 200, 202, 206, 280
Velvetones, The 73
Verlaine, Tom 169
Vicious, Sid 86, 118, 132, 146, 167, 168, **169**, 230
Vig, Butch 111, 243
Village People, The 142
Vincent, Gene 39, **40**
Virgin records 48, 49
Visconti, Tony 128, 129, 137, 138
Vito, Rick 96
Voidoids 160

W
Wainwright, Rufus 106, 107
Waits, Tom 18, 119, 150, 159, 173
Wakeman, Rick 83, 136, 198
Walker, Dave 109
Wall of Sound 28, 107
Wallflowers, The 64
Walsh, Joe 100, 132, 133
War 74
Ward, Bill 109, 111, 173
Warner Bros. records 175, 176, 205, 207, 281
Warsaw 139
Was, Don 118
Water, Roger 216
Waters, George 87, 88, 89
Waters, Muddy 58
Waters, Roger 60, 62, 215, 232
Watts, Charlie 36, 54, 58
Watts, Tom 131
Weezer 21, 224
Weissleder, Manfred 38, 39
Welch, Bob 95
Weller, Paul 84, 168, 260, 279
Wells, Greg 80
Wells, Mary 32
Wendy & Lisa 103
West, Kanye 210, 223, 239, 256, **269**
Weston, Bob 95
Wexler, Jerry 84, 85
Weymouth, Tina 162
White Stripes, The 30, 57, 62, 117, 203, 266, **272–3**
White, Alan 39, 261
White, Jack 57, 266, 272, 273
White, Meg 272
White, Ronnie 32
White, Snowy 96
Whitesnake 49, 53, 76, 101, 109, 198
Whitfield, Norman 33
Whitford, Brad 155, 156
Who, The 14, 31, 54, 56, 57, 59, 60, 66, **68–71**, 87, 99, 112, 126, 128, 129, 130, 134, 136, 144, 168, 179, 192, 214, **251**

Wilde, Kim 71
Wilder, Alan 197
Wilk, Brad 254
Williams, Alyson 24
Williams, Hank 202
Williamson, James 117
Wilson Phillips 51
Wilson, Anthony 185
Wilson, Brian 28, 50, 51, 81, 86, 126
Wilson, Carnie 51
Wilson, Jackie 14, 17, 30
Wilson, Mary 32, 209
Wilson, Wendy 51
Winehouse, Amy 131, 178
Wings 43, 46, 244
Winter, Johnny 75
Winwood, Steve 70, 130, 131
Wire 48
Wobble, Jah 138, 139, 169
Wolf, Howlin' 73
Wolstenholme, Chris 270
Womack, Bobby 26, 27, 84, 274, 275
Wonder, Stevie 30, **32**, 33, 36, 43, 85, 105, 124, 233
Wood, Andrew 249
Wood, Art 55
Woodmansey, Woody 136
Woods, Ronnie 55, 56, 57
Woodstock 70, 73, 75, 80, 100, **112–15**, 234
Wray, Link 17
Wreckage 144
Wright, Nick 216
Wright, Richard 87, 89
Wright, Simon 183
Wyman, Bill 55, 57

X
XTC 141

Y
Yardbirds, The 58, 59, **60**, 61, 75, 99, 136, 155
Yazoo 197
Yes 41, 59, 82, 83, 136, **198**, 199, 270
Yo La Tengo 91
York, Peter, 39
Yorke, Thom 169, 207, 232
Young, Angus 182, 183
Young, Malcolm 182, 183, 183
Young, Neil 51, 52, 57, 62, 65, **78–81**, 101, 103, 104, 134, 136, 137, 205, 242, 244, 247, 249
Young, Roy 38
Yule, Doug 91, 93

Z
Zaire 74 25
Zapp 25
Zappa, Frank 49, **76–7**, 109, 140, 200, 201, 233
Zevon, Warren 206
Zombie, Rob 159

INDEX 287

Picture Credits

Every effort has been made to trace all copyright owners but if any have been inadvertently overlooked, the publishers would be pleased to make the necessary arrangements at the first opportunity. (Key: t = top; b = bottom; tl = top left; tr = top right; bl = bottom left; br = bottom right)

2 Mick Rock/Retna Pictures **12** Hulton Archive/Getty Images **13t** Charles Trainor/Time & Life Pictures/Getty Images **13b** Sipa Press/Rex Features **14t** MGM/The Kobal Collection **14b** Michael Ochs Archives/Getty Images **15t** Michael Ochs Archives/Getty Images **15b** Ebet Roberts/Getty Images **16** Michael Ochs Archives/Getty Images **17t** Michael Ochs Archives/Getty Images **17b** Hulton Archive/Getty Images **18** Sony BMG Music Entertainment/Getty Images **19b** Twentieth Century Fox/Photofest/Retna **20** CBS Photo Archive/Retna **21t** Rex Features **21b** Richard Cummins/Corbis **22** David Corio/Michael Ochs Archives/Getty Images **24t** Everett Collection/Rex Feature **24b** Robin Little/Getty Images **25t** Echoes/Getty Images **25b** Steve Double/Retna **26** Michael Ochs Archives/Getty Images **27b** Bettmann/Corbis **28** Michael Ochs Archives/Corbis **29t** Ray Avery/Getty Images **29b** Michael Ochs Archives/Getty Images **30–31** Dezo Hoffmann/Rex Features **31b** Michael Ochs Archives/Getty Images **32t** Dezo Hoffmann/Rex Features **32b** LAMedia Collection/Sunshine/Retna **33t** David Redfern/Getty Images **33b** Michael Ochs Archives/Getty Images **36** Evening Standard/Getty Images **37t** GAB Archives/Getty Images **37b** Ron Galella/WireImage/Getty Images **38–39** K & K Ulf Kruger OHG/Getty Images **40tl** Siegfried Loch – K & K/Getty Images **40tr** Colin Escott/Michael Ochs Archives/Getty Images **40bl** K & K Ulf Kruger OHG/Getty Images **40br** Dieter Radtke – K & K/Getty Images **41tl** Jan Persson/Getty Images **41tr** K & K Ulf Kruger OHG/Getty Images **41bl** Gilles Petard/Getty Images **41br** Ellen Poppinga/K&K/Getty Images **42** David Graves/Rex Features **44** Keystone/Hulton Archive/Getty Images **45** Fiona Adams/Getty Images **46t** John Loengard/Time Life Pictures/Getty Images **46b** Michael Ochs Archives/Getty Images **47t** AFP/Getty Images **47b** Tommy Hanley/Getty Images **48** Gems/Getty Images **49t** Tony Mottram/Retna **49b** Peter Still/Getty Images **50** NBCUPhotobank/Rex Features **51t** Michael Ochs Archives/Getty Images **51b** Aaron Rapoport/Retna **52** SIPA Press/Rex Features **53t** Michael Ochs Archives/Getty Images **53b** Hulton Archive/Getty Images **54–55** John Hoppy Hopkinks/Getty Images **55b** David Farrell/Getty Images **56t** Reg Burkett/Express/Getty Images **56b** Andrew Putler/Getty Images **57t** Jan Olofsson/Getty Images **57b** DMI/Time & Life Pictures/Getty Images **58–59** Paul Slattery/Retna **60tl** Paul Popper/Popperfoto/Getty Images **60tr** Chris Morphet/Getty Images **60bl** Jack Kay/Express/Getty Images **60br** Michael Putland/Getty Images **61tl** Chris Walter/WireImage/Getty Images **61tr** Michael Putland / Retna **61bl** Tony Mottram/Retna **61br** Tony Mottram/Retna **62** Photofest/Retna **63** King Collection/Retna **64t** Bill Ray/Time & Life Pictures/Getty Images **64b** Neal Preston/Corbis **65t** Neal Preston/Corbis **65b** Weinstein/Everett/Rex Features **66** GAB Archive/Getty Images **67t** Bentley Archive/Popperfoto **67b** Theo Wargo/WireImage/Getty Images **68–69** Michael Ochs Archives/Getty Images **69b** Paul Ryan/Michael Ochs Archives/Getty Images **70t** Charlie Gillett Collection/Getty Images **70b** Adrian Boot/Retna **71t** John Selby/Rex Features **71b** 20th Century Fox Televison/Gracie Films/The Kobal Collection **72** Bruce Fleming/Getty Images **74t** Chris Ware/Keystone Features/Getty Images **74b** Jan Olofsson/Getty Images **75t** Jan Persson/Getty Images **75b** Herb Schmitz/Retna **76** Tolca/Sunshine/Retna **77b** Michael Ochs Archives/Getty Images **78** Peter Doherty/Retna **80t** Michael Ochs Archives/Getty Images **80b** Gijsbert Hanekroot/Sunshine/Retna **81t** Neal Preston/Retna **81b** Jeff Kravitz/FilmMagic/Getty Images **82** Michael Putland/Retna **83t** Peter Mazel/Sunshine/Retna **83b** Michael Putland/Retna **84** Express Newspapers/Getty Images **85t** David Redfern/Getty Images **85b** Gems/Getty Images **86** Adrian Boot/Getty Images **87t** Dister/Dalle/Retna **87b** Michael Ochs Archives/Getty Images **88t** Mick Gold/Getty Images **88b** Ian Dickson/Getty Images **89t** Rob Verhorst/Getty Images **89b** John D McHugh/AFP/Getty Images **90** Adam Ritchie/Getty Images **92t** Mick Gold/Getty Images **92b** Theo Wargo/WireImage/Getty Images **93t** Mick Rock/Getty Images **93b** Adam Ritchie/Getty Images **94** Barry Schultz/Sunshine/Retna **95t** Michael Putland/Retna **95b** Sunshine/Retna **96t** Peter Still/Getty Images **96b** Norman Bailey/Ampix/Headpress/Retna **97** Sunshine/Retna **98–99** Chris Walter/Photofeatures/Retna **99b** Jorgen Angel/Getty Images **100t** Chris Walter/WireImage/Getty Images **100b** Graham Wiltshire/Hulton Archive/Getty Images **101t** Jeffrey Mayer/WireImage/Getty Images **101b** Ross Halfin/Getty Images **102** Michael Ochs Archives/Getty Images **104t** Frank Micelotta/Getty Images **104b** Rocky Widner/Retna **105t** Michel Linssen/Getty Images **105b** Mosenfelder/Getty Images **106** Roz Kelly/Michael Ochs Archives/Getty Images **107t** P. Ullman/Roger Viollet/Getty Images **107b** Rob Watkins/Retna **108** Chris Walter/WireImage/Getty Images **110t** Peter Tarnoff/Retna **110b** Chris Walter/WireImage/Getty Images **111t** Kevin Mazur/WireImage/Getty Images **111b** Stephen Lovekin/WireImage/Getty Images **112–113** John Dominis/Time & Life Pictures/Getty Images **114tl** Tucker Ransom/Hulton Archive/Getty Images **114tr** Tunick/Retna **114bl** Tunick/Retna **114br** Holland/Sunshine/Retna **115tl** Ebet Roberts/Getty Images **115tr** Neal Preston/Retna **115bl** Robb D. Cohen/Retna **115br** Robert Spencer/Retna **116** Mick Rock/Retna **118t** Ian Tilton/Retna **118b** Tom Hill/WireImage/Getty Images **119t** Eric Robert, Stephane Cardinale, & Thierry Orban/Sygma/Corbis **119b** Kevin Mazur/WireImage/Getty Images **122** Michael Ochs Archives/Getty Images **123** Fabrice Demessence/Dalle/Retna **124t** Brian Stein/Retna **124b** Lynn Goldsmith/Corbis **125t** Kevin Mazur/WireImage/Getty Images **125b** The Kobal Collection/Columbia Pictures **127t** Ian Dickson/Getty Images **127b** Dave Hogan/Getty Images **128** Evening Standard/Getty Images **129t** Martyn Goodacre/Retna **129b** Maurice Hibberd/Evening Standard/Getty Images **130** Fikisha Cumbo/Retna **131t** Paul Slattery/Retna **131b** Eric Benetti/Retna **132** Gijsbert Hanekroot/Sunshine/Retna **133t** Michael Putland/Retna **133b** George Chin/Retna **134** David Bebbington/Retna **135** Mick Rock/Retna **136t** Mick Rock/Retna **136b** Cinema 5/Photofest/Retna **137t** Taka/Dalle/Retna **137b** Jeff Davy/Retna **138** Brian Cooke/Getty Images **139t** Ebet Roberts/Getty Images **139b** Kevin Mazur Archive 1/WireImage/Getty Images **140** Lynn Goldsmith/Corbis **142** Chris Walter/WireImage/Getty Images **143t** Sunshine/Retna **143b** Michael Putland **144** Michael Putland/Retna **145** Mick Rock/Retna **146t** Fin Costello/Getty Images **146b** Barry Schultz/Sunshine/Retna **147t** Tony Mottram/Retna **147b** Howard Denner/Retna **148** Peter Pakvis/Getty Images **149t** Ebet Roberts/Getty Images **149b** Dave Hogan/Getty Images **150** Clayton Call/Getty Images **151t** Peter Mazel/Sunshine/Retna **151b** Michael Putland/Retna **152t** Neal Preston/Retna **152b** Drew Farrell/Retna **153** Ebet Roberts/Getty Images **154** Neal Preston/Corbis **156t** Tolca/Sunshine/Retna **156b** Michael Putland/Retna **157t** Chris Vooren/Sunshine/Retna **157b** Ron Galella/WireImage/Getty Images **158** Kees Tabak/Sunshine/Retna **159t** Kees Tabak/Sunshine/Retna **159b** David Klein/Getty Images **160–161** Ebet Roberts/Getty Images **162tl** Richard E. Aaron/Getty Images **162tr** Ebet Roberts/Getty Images **162bl** Roberta Bayley/Getty Images **162br** Stephanie Chernikowski/Getty Images **163tl** Roberta Bayley/Getty Images **163tr** Ebet Roberts/Getty Images **163bl** Ira Rosenson/Retna **163br** Tony Mottram/Retna **164** Peter Mazel/Sunshine/Retna **165t** Rynski/Dalle/Retna **165b** Paul Natkin/WireImage/Getty Images **166** Kees Tabak/Sunshine/Retna **168t** Kees Tabak/Retna **168b** Erik Auerbach/Retna **169t** Adrian Boot/Retna **169b** Faux/Dalle/Retna **170** Michael Putland/Retna **171t** Neal Preston/Corbis **171b** Paul Slattery/Retna **172** Mick Rock/Retna **173t** Mick Rock/Retna **173b** Howard Denner/Retna **174** Ross Marino/Sygma/Corbis **175t** Kees Tabak/Sunshine/ Retna **175b** Compix/Sunshine/Retna **176t** Robert Spencer/Retna **176b** Gary Hershorn/Reuters/Corbis **177** LAMedia Collection/Sunshine/Retna **178** Adrian Boot/Retna **179t** Michael Grecco/Getty Images **179b** Samir Hussein/Getty Images **180** Corbis **181t** Marty Temme/WireImage/Getty Images **181b** Paul Natkin/WireImage/Getty Images **182** Peter Mazel/Sunshine/Retna **183t** Michael Ochs Archives/Getty Images **183b** Ashley Maile/Retna **184** Martin O'Neill/Retna **186t** Martyn Goodacre/Retna **186b** Steve Double/Retna **187t** Martyn Goodacre/Retna **187b** Mick Rock/Retna **190** Tony Mottram/Retna **191t** Ebet Roberts/Getty Images **191b** Mick Hutson/Getty Images **191t** Paul Slattery/Retna **193t** Adrian Boot/Retna **193b** George Rose/Getty Images **194t** Mick Hutson/Getty Images **194b** Kevin Mazur/WireImage/Getty Images **195** Rob Verhorst/Getty Images **196** Adrian Boot/Retna **197t** Adrian Boot/Retna **197b** Ashley Maile **198** Michael Putland **199t** Retna 5/Retna **199b** Adrian Boot/Retna **200** Paul Edmonds/Retna **201t** GAB Archive/Getty Images **201b** Robb D. Cohen/Retna **202** Emma Svensson/Retna **203t** Bob King/Getty Images **203b** Danny Clifford/Getty Images **204** Stuart Nicholls/Retna **206t** Bill Davila/Retna **206b** Paul Natkin/WireImage/Getty Images **207t** Martyn Goodacre/Retna **207b** Robb D. Cohen/Retna **208** Michael McDonnell/Hulton Archive/Getty Images **209t** Simon Holmes/Retna **209b** Ron Galella/WireImage/Getty Images **210t** Frank Micelotta/Getty Images **210b** Rhav Segev/Retna **211** Chris Polk/FilmMagic/Getty Images **212** Paul Slattery/Retna **213t** Kevin Cummins/Getty Images **213b** William E Sharp/Retna **214–215** Popperfoto/Getty Images **216tl** Fin Costello/Getty Images **216tr** Phil Dent/Getty Images **216bl** Hulton Archive/Getty Images **216br** Popperfoto/Getty Images **217tl** Georges DeKeerle/Getty Images **217tr** Larry Busacca/Retna **217bl** Ebet Roberts/Getty Images **217br** Ken Regan/Camera 5/Retna **218** Miguel Gutierrez/AFP/Getty Images **219t** Pete Cronin/Getty Images **219b** Mick Hutson/Getty Images **220t** Mick Hutson/Getty Images **220b** Morena Brengola/Getty Images **221** Ashley Maile/Retna **222** Ebet Roberts/Getty Images **223t** Ian Dickson/Getty Images **223b** Raymond Boyd/Michael Ochs Archives/Getty Images **224** Youri Lenquette/Dalle/Retna **225t** Ebet Roberts/Getty Images **225b** Martyn Goodacre/Retna **226** Kevin Mazur/WireImage/Getty Images **227t** Charles J. Peterson/Time Life Pictures/Getty Images **227b** Kevin Mazur/WireImage/Getty Images **228** Jeffrey Mayer/WireImage/Getty Images **229** Kevin Mazur/WireImage/Getty Images **230t** Neal Preston/Retna **230b** Paul Natkin/WireImage/Getty Images **231t** Michael Putland/Retna **231b** Martin Philbey/Retna **232** Gary Malerba/Corbis **233t** Ebet Roberts/Getty Images **233b** Ian Dickson/Getty Images **234t** Tim Mosenfelder/Getty Images **234b** Kevin Winter/WireImage/Getty Images **235** Ken Regan/Getty Images **238–239** Roger Kisby/Getty Images **240tl** John Shearer/WireImage/Getty Images **240tr** Ebet Roberts/Getty Images **240bl** Steve Eichner/WireImage/ Getty Images **240br** John Shearer/WireImage/Getty Images **241tl** Tim Mosenfelder/Getty Images **241tr** Ed Danninger/Retna **241bl** Steve Eichner/WireImage/Getty Images **241br** Jason Squires/WireImage/Getty Images **242** Charles Peterson/Retna **243t** JJ Gonson/Getty Images **243b** Marty Temme/WireImage/Getty Images **244t** Jay Blakesberg/Retna **244b** MJ Kim/MPL Communications Ltd/Getty Images **245** Charles Peterson/Retna **246** Patrick Ford/Getty Images **247t** Lisa Haun/Michael Ochs Archives/Getty Images **247b** Kristian Dowling/Getty Images **248** Lance Mercer/Retna **250t** Kevin Mazur/WireImage/Getty Images **250b** Kevin Mazur/WireImage/Getty Images **251t** Kevin Mazur/WireImage/Getty Images **251b** Dave Hogan/MP/Getty Images **252** Chris Davison/Retna **253t** Mick Hutson/Getty Images **253b** Nick Stevens/Retna **254** Lindsay Brice/Michael Ochs Archives/Getty Images **255t** Tim Mosenfelder/Getty Images **255b** Theo Wargo/WireImage/Getty Images **256** Neal Preston/Corbis **257t** Kevin Mazur/WireImage/Getty Images **257b** Bill Davila/Retna **258** John Shearer Archive/WireImage/Getty Images **259t** Neal Preston/Retna **259b** Chris Graythen/Getty Images **260** Paul Slattery/Retna **261t** Mick Hutson/Getty Images **261b** Jon Beretta/Carl Sims/Rex Features **262–263** Al Pereira/Michael Ochs Archives/Getty Images **263b** Kevin Mazur/WireImage/Getty Images **264** Steve Double/Retna **265t** Peter Still/Getty Images **265b** Isifa/Getty Images **266** Antonio Pagano/Retna **267t** Scott Gries/Getty Images **267b** Kevin Mazur/WireImage/Getty Images **268–269** Bob King/Getty Images **269b** Kevin Mazur/WireImage/Getty Images **270** Jeff Kravitz/FilmMagic/Getty Images **271t** James McCauley/Rex Features **271b** Tim Mosenfelder/Getty Images **272** Stephen Lovekin/WireImage/Getty Images **273t** Mick Hutson/Getty Images **273b** MGM/Everett/Rex Features **274** Dave Hogan/Getty Images **275t** Jim Dyson/Getty Images **276** Neil Lupin/Getty Images **277t** Tim Rooke/Rex Features **277b** Landov/Retna **278–279** Chris Gordon/Getty Images **279b** Fabrice Demessence/Dalle/Retna **280** Rob Watkins/Retna **281t** Jo Hale/Getty Images **281b** Andrew Willsher/Getty Images

The author would like to thank Olivia McLearon for her writing and sub-editing; Chris Bryans, Gerry Kiernan, and Mark Bennett for their invaluable assistance; Rob Dimery and the team at Quintessence for all their help and support; and, last but not least, my wife Herita for her patience and good humor. The publishers would like to thank Anthony McAndrew at Retna for providing so many fantastic images.